Object-Oriented System Development

Object-Oriented System Development

Dennis de Champeaux
Douglas Lea
Penelope Faure

Addison-Wesley Publishing Company

Reading, Massachusetts   Menlo Park, California   New York
Don Mills, Ontario   Wokingham, England   Amsterdam   Bonn
Sydney   Singapore   Tokyo   Madrid   San Juan
Paris   Seoul   Milan   Mexico City   Taipei

The publisher offers discounts on this book when ordered in quantity for special sales. For more information, please contact:

Corporate & Professional Publishing Group
Addison-Wesley Publishing Company
One Jacob Way
Reading, Massachusetts 01867

Library of Congress Cataloging-in-Publication Data

De Champeaux, Dennis.
   Object-oriented system development/Dennis De Champeaux, Douglas
Lea, and Penelope Faure.
     p.   cm.
  Includes bibliographical references and index.
  ISBN 0-201-56355-X
  1. Object-oriented programming (Computer science). 2. Computer
software—Development. I. Lea, Douglas. II. Faure, Penelope.
  III. Title.
QA76.64.D43   1993
005.1'2—dc20

93-9331
CIP

ISBN 0-201-56355-X

Text printed on recycled and acid-free paper.

2 3 4 5 6 7 8 9 CRW 97969594
Second Printing, February 1994

Contents

Preface

Object-oriented (OO) programming has a growing number of converts. Many people believe that object orientation will put a dent in the software crisis. There is a glimmer of hope that OO software development will become more like engineering. Objects, whatever they are now, may become for software what nuts, bolts and beams are for construction design, what *2-by-4*s and *2-by-6*s are for home construction, and what chips are for computer hardware construction.

However, before making this quantum leap, object-oriented methods still have to prove themselves with respect to more established software development paradigms. True, for small tasks the war is over. Object-oriented programs are more compact than classic structured programs. It is easier to whip them together using powerful class libraries. Inheritance allows "differential programming", the modification in a descendant class of what is wrong with a parent class, while inheriting all of its good stuff. User interfaces, which are often sizable fractions of small systems, can be put together easily from object-oriented libraries.

Delivering large object-oriented software systems routinely and cost effectively is still a significant challenge. To quote Ed Yourdon: "A system composed of 100,000 lines of C++ is not to be sneezed at, but we don't have that much trouble developing 100,000 lines of COBOL today. The real test of OOP will come when systems of 1 to 10 million lines of code are developed."[1]

The development of large systems is qualitatively different from that of small systems. For instance, a multinational banking conglomerate may want a system supporting around-the-clock access to the major stock markets in the world. They may additionally want to integrate accounts for all worldwide customers, providing fault-tolerant distributed transaction services. The banking conglomerate cannot realize this system by relying exclusively on a bundle of smart programmers. Instead,

---

[1] To be fair and accurate, systems of 100,000 lines of C++ and those of 1,000,000 lines of COBOL are often of the same order of magnitude in complexity.

as enshrined by the structured paradigm, analysis and design must precede pure implementation activities. OO methods are known by experience to scale up to such large systems. For example, Hazeltine [106] reports a project with "about 1000 classes, 10 methods per class, involving an average of 40 persons over 2 years."

This book is intended to help the reader better understand the role of analysis and design in the object-oriented software development process. Experiments to use structured analysis and design as precursors to an object-oriented implementation have failed. The descriptions produced by the structured methods partition reality along the wrong dimensions. Classes are not recognized and inheritance as an abstraction mechanism is not exploited. However, we are fortunate that a multitude of object-oriented analysis and design methods have emerged and are still under development. Core OO notions have found their home place in the analysis phase. Abstraction and specialization via inheritance, originally advertised as key ingredients of OO programming, have been abstracted into key ingredients of OO analysis (OOA). Analysis-level property inheritance maps smoothly on the behavior inheritance of the programming realm.

A common selling point of the OO paradigm is that it is more "natural" to traverse from analysis to implementation. For example, as described in [77], developers at Hewlett-Packard who were well versed in the structured paradigm reported that the "conceptual distances" between the phases of their project were smaller using OO methods. Classes identified in the analysis phase carried over into the implementation. They observed as well that the defect density in their C++ code was only 50% of that of their C code.

However, more precise characterizations of why this might be so and how best to exploit it are still underdeveloped. The black art mystique of OO methods is a major inhibitor to the widespread acceptance of the OO paradigm. Hence we have devoted ample attention to the process aspects of development methods.

Will this book be the last word on this topic? We hope not. The object-oriented paradigm is still developing. At the same time, new challenges arise. Class libraries will have to be managed. Libraries for classic computer science concepts can be traversed using our shared, common knowledge. But access to application specific domain libraries seems to be tougher. Deciding that a particular entry is adequate for a particular task without having to "look inside" the entry is a challenge. Will the man-page style of annotations be sufficient? Our experience with man-pages makes us doubt that it will be.

Further horizons in OO are still too poorly understood to be exploited in the construction of reliable systems. For example, some day methods may exist for routinely developing "open systems" of "smart" active objects inspired by the pioneering work of Hewitt.[2] While active object models do indeed form much of the foundation of this book, their furthest-reaching aspects currently remain the focus of research and experimental study.

The object oriented paradigm, and this book, may impact different software professionals in different ways:

Analysts. OO analysis is a fairly new enterprise. There is an abundance of unexplored territory to exploit. On the other hand there are few gurus to rely on when the going gets tough. The OO paradigm *is* tough going when one has been inundated with the structured way of thinking. While structured analysis is supposed to be implementation technique independent, it turns out to have a built-in bias toward classical implementation languages. Its core abstraction mechanism is derived from the procedure/function construct. Letting structured abstractions play second violin to object and inheritance takes some effort.

Designers. OO design is as novel as OO analysis. By virtue of object orientation, more activities in the design phase and links to both analysis and implementation can be distinguished than has been previously possible. Our treatment focuses on the continuity of analysis and design, thus presenting many descriptive issues that are normally considered as "OO design" activities in the context of OOA. On the other side, it pushes many decisions that are usually made in the implementation phase into design.

Implementors. OO implementation should become easier when the task of satisfying functional requirements has been moved into the design phase. Implementation decisions can then concentrate on exploiting the features of a chosen configuration and language needed to realize all the remaining requirements.

---

[2]Some quotes from this manifesto paper [110]: "This paper proposes a modular ACTOR architecture and definitional method for AI that is conceptually based on a single kind of object: actors... The formalism makes no presuppositions about the representation of primitive data structures and control structures. Such structures can be programmed, micro-coded or hard-wired in a uniform modular fashion. In fact it is impossible to determine whether a given object is 'really' represented as a list, a vector, a hash table, a function or a process. Our formalism shows how all of the modes of behavior can be defined in terms of *one* kind of behavior: *sending messages to actors*." We briefly discuss open systems of actors in Chapter 22.

Software engineers. OO software development is becoming a viable alternative to structured development. The application domains of both appear virtually the same. While the structured version has the advantage of currently being better supported by CASE tools, the object-oriented version will most likely become even better supported.

Project managers. Experience with OO methods may be obtained using a throwaway, toy example to go through all the phases. The promise of large scale reuse should justify the transition costs. Software development planning is notoriously hard. This text addresses this topic by formulating a generic development scenario. However, foolproof criteria for measuring progress are as yet unavailable.

Tool builders. The OO community needs integrated tools. In addition to object orientation, team effort, version control, process management, local policies, metrics, all need support.

Methodologists. We cite open issues and unsolved problems throughout the text, usually while discussing further readings.

Students and teachers. While the object-oriented paradigm is rapidly overtaking industrial software development efforts, few courses address fundamental OO software engineering concepts untied to particular commercial methods. We have successfully used material in this book as a basis for one-semester graduate and undergraduate courses, one-week courses, and short tutorials[3].

---

[3] A team-based development project is almost mandatory for effective learning in semester courses, but raises logistics problems common to any software engineering course. Projects should neither be so big that they cannot be at least partially implemented by a team of about three students within the confines of a semester, nor be so small that they evade all systems-level development issues. Successful projects have included a version of ftp with an InterViews[142] based interface, and a simple event display system for Mach processes. To implement projects, students who do not know an OO programming language will need to learn one long before the end of the course. One way to address this is to teach the basics of OOP in a particular language and other implementation pragmatics early on, independently of and in parallel with the topics covered in this book. For example, in a course meeting two or three times per week, one class per week could be devoted to programming and pragmatics. As the semester continues, this class could focus on project status reports and related discussions. This organization remains effective despite the fact that the contents of the different classes are often out of synch. By simplifying or eliminating project options corresponding to the contents of Chapters 22 through 26, final implementation may begin while still discussing how these issues apply to larger efforts.

Others. The reader may think at this point that this book is relevant only for large system development. We don't think so. Even in a one-hour single-person programming task, activities applying to a large system can be recognized. The difference is that these activities all happen inside the head of the person. There is no written record of all the decisions made. The person may not even be aware of some of the decisions. We hope that everyone will obtain a better understanding of the overall development process from this book.

This text does not aim at defining yet another OO "method". Instead, we aim to give a minimum set of notions and to show how to use these notions when progressing from a set of requirements to an implementation. We reluctantly adopt our own minimal (graphical) analysis and (textual) design notations to illustrate basic concepts. Our analysis notation (**OAN**) and design language (**ODL**) are "lightweight" presentation vehicles chosen to be readily translatable into any OO analysis, design, and programming languages and notations you wish to use. (Notational summaries may be found in the Appendix.)

Most of what we have written in this book is not true. It is also not false. This is because we are in the *prescriptive* business. Software development is a special kind of process. We describe in this book a (loosely defined) algorithm for producing a system. Algorithms are not true or false. They are appropriate for a task or not. Thus this book should contain a correctness proof that demonstrates that the application of its methods invariably yields a desired system. However, due to space limitations, we have omitted this proof.

More seriously, we have tried to decrease the fuzziness that is inherent in prescriptive text by giving precise *textual* descriptions of the key notions in the respective methods. We have tried to be precise as well, in describing how analysis output carries over into design and how the design output gets massaged into an implementation. Thus we obtain checks and balances by integrating the methods across the development phases. This, of course, provides only a partial check on the correctness of the methods. Their application will be their touchstone.

We are opinionated regarding formal techniques. We want to offer software developers "formality a la carte". Developers may want to avoid rigorous "mathematical" precision as one extreme, or may want to provide correctness proofs of a target system against the requirements as another extreme. We leave this decision to the developer. As a consequence for us, we avoid introducing notions for which the semantics are not crystal clear. As a result, the developer can be as formal as desired. Since we were at times unable to come up with concise semantics, we have omitted some modeling and design notions that are offered in other accounts.

While we have tried to provide a solid foundation for the core concepts, we are convinced as well that a true formalist can still point out uncountably many ambiguities. On the other side, we simply do not understand most of the material in this book sufficiently well to trivialize it into recipes.

Although one can read this book while bypassing the exercises, we do recommend them. Some exercises ask you to operationalize the concepts in this book. Others are quick "thought questions", sometimes even silly sounding ones, that may lead you into territory that we have not explored.

Acknowledgments

Together, we thank our editors Alan Apt and John Wait, and reviewers Jim Coplien, Lew Creary, Desmond D'Souza, Felix Frayman, Watts Humphrey, Ralph Johnson, and Hermann Kaindl.

DdC thanks Alan Apt for being a persistent initiator to this enterprise. He has an amazing ability to exploit your vanity and lure you in an activity that is quite hazardous to plain family life. On the way he gives encouragement, blissfully ignoring the perilous situation in which the writer has maneuvered him/herself. Donna Ho provided an initial sanity check. Patricia Collins expressed very precisely her concerns about domain analysis.

DL thanks others providing comments and advice about initial versions, including Umesh Bellur, Gary Craig, Rameen Mohammadi, Rajendra Raj, Kevin Shank, Sumana Srinavasan, and Al Villarica. And, of course, Kathy, Keith, and Colin.

We remain perfectly happy to take blame for all remaining omissions, stupidities, inaccuracies, paradoxes, falsehoods, fuzziness, and other good qualities. We welcome constructive as well as destructive critiques. Electronic mail may be sent to oosd@g.oswego.edu.

Chapter 1

Overview

1.1 Scope

The development of a software system is usually just a part of finding a solution to a larger problem. The larger problem may entail the development of an overall system involving software, hardware, procedures, and organizations.

In this book, we concentrate on the software side. We do not address associated issues such as constructing the proper hardware platform and reorganizing institutional procedures that use the software to improve overall operations. We further limit ourselves to the "middle" phases of OO system development. We discuss the initial collection of system requirements and scheduling of efforts only to the extent to which they impact analysis. Similarly, we discuss situation-dependent implementation matters such as programming in particular languages, porting to different systems, and performing release management only with respect to general design issues. Also, while we devote considerable attention to the process of OO development, we do not often address the *management* of this or any software development process. We urge readers to consult Humphrey [117], among other sources, for such guidance.

We cannot however, ignore the *context* of a software system. The context of any system is simply that part of the "world" with which it directly interacts. In order to describe the behavior of a target system, we have to describe relevant parts of the immediate context forming the boundary of the system. Consequently, one may argue that the apparatus that we present in this book could be used for modeling nonsoftware aspects as well. We do not deny potential wider applicability, but we have no claims in that direction.

1.1.1   Running Example

Many examples in this text describe parts of the following system of automated teller machines (ATMs):

We assume that the American Bank (AB) has partly decentralized account management. Every branch office has equipment to maintain the accounts of its clients. All equipment is networked together. Each ATM is associated and connected with the equipment of a particular branch office. Clients can have checking, savings and line of credit accounts, all conveniently interconnected. Clients can obtain cash out of any of their accounts. A client with a personal identification number (PIN) can use an ATM to transfer funds among attached accounts. Daemons can be set up that monitor balance levels and trigger automatic fund transfers when specifiable conditions are met and/or that initiate transfers periodically. Automatic periodic transfers to third party accounts can be set up as well.

We will expand on these requirements as necessary. For presentation reasons, we often revise descriptions from chapter to chapter. Our examples represent only small fragments of any actual system.

1.2   Objects

Objects have complex historical roots. On the declarative side, they somewhat resemble *frames*, introduced in artificial intelligence (AI) by Marvin Minsky [161] around 1975. Frames were proposed in the context of knowledge representation to represent knowledge units that are larger than the constants, terms, and expressions offered by logic. A frame represents a concept in multiple ways. There is a descriptive as well as a behavioral component. A frame of a restaurant would have as a descriptive component its prototypical features – being a business, having a location, employing waiters, and maintaining seating arrangements. The behavioral component would have scripts. For example, a customer script outlines stereotypical events that involve visiting a restaurant.

Objects and frames share the property that they bring descriptive and behavioral features closely together. This shared feature, phrased from the programming angle, means that the storage structures and the procedural components that operate on them are tightly coupled. The responsibilities of frames go beyond those of objects. Frames are supposed to support complex cognitive operations including reasoning, planning, natural language understanding and generation. In contrast, objects for software development are most often used for realizing better understood operations.

On the programming side, the **Simula** [66] programming language is another, even older, historical root of objects. Unsurprisingly, **Simula** was aimed at supporting simulation activities. Procedures could be attached to a type (a class in **Simula**'s terminology) to represent the behavior of an instance. **Simula** supported parallelism, in the approximation of coroutines, allowing for many interacting entities in a simulation.

Simula objects share the close coupling of data and procedures. The concurrency in **Simula** was lost in **Smalltalk**, **Eiffel**, **Objective-C**, **C++**, and other popular OO programming languages. However, parallelism has reentered the OO paradigm via OO analysis methods and distributed designs. Modeling reality with "active" objects requires giving them a large degree of autonomy.

The notion of whether objects have a parallel connotation or not is currently a major difference between OO analysis and OO programming. Since we expect OO programming languages to evolve to support the implementation of distributed, parallel systems, we expect this difference to decrease. The parallel OO paradigm is well positioned to meet these upcoming demands.

1.2.1 Definitions

Like "system", "software", "analysis", and "design", the term "object" evades simplistic definition. A typical dictionary definition reads:

> *object*: a visible or tangible thing of relative stable form; a thing that may be apprehended intellectually; a thing to which thought or action is directed [186].

Samplings from the OO literature include:

> An object has identity, state and behavior (Booch [39]).

> An object is a unit of structural and behavioral modularity that has properties (Buhr [44]).

Our own working definition will be refined throughout this book. We define an object as a conceptual entity that:

- is identifiable;
- has features that span a local state space;
- has operations that can change the status of the system locally, while also inducing operations in peer objects.

1.3   Development Paradigms

The structured analysis (SA) paradigm [234] is rooted in third generation programming languages including Algol, Fortran, and COBOL. The procedure and function constructs in these languages provide for a powerful abstraction mechanism. Complex behavior can be composed out of or decomposed into simpler units. The block structure of Algol-like languages provides syntactic support for arbitrary many layers. Applied to the development of systems, this abstraction mechanism gives prominence to behavioral characterization. Behavior is repeatedly decomposed into subcomponents until plausibly implementable behavioral units are obtained.

The abandonment of sequential control flow by SA was a major breakthrough. Procedure invocations have been generalized into descriptions of interacting processes. The "glue" between the processes are data flows, the generalization of data that is passed around in procedure invocations. Processes represent the inherent parallelism of reality. At the same time, the use of processes produces a mapping problem. One has to transform a high level, intrinsically parallel description into an implementation that is usually sequential. As we will see, the OO paradigm faces the same mapping problem.

The starting point for process modeling resides in the required behavior of the desired system. This makes SA a predominantly top-down method. High level process descriptions are consequently target system specific, and thus unlikely to be reusable for even similar systems. As a result, a description (and a subsequent design and implementation) is obtained that is by and large custom fit for the task at hand.

OO software development addresses the disadvantage of custom fitting a solution to a problem. At all levels of the development process, solution components can be formulated that generalize beyond the local needs and as such become candidates for reuse (provided we are able to manage these components).

Other aspects of OO development are available to control the complexity of a large system. An object maintains its own state. A history-dependent function or procedure can be realized much more cleanly and more independently of its run-time environment than in procedural languages. In addition, inheritance provides for an abstraction mechanism that permits factoring out redundancies.

1.3.1   Applicability

Are the applicability ranges of the object-oriented paradigm and the structured paradigm different? If so, how are they related? Is one contained in the other?

Can we describe their ranges?

As yet there is not enough evidence to claim that the applicability ranges are different, although OO may have an edge for distributed systems. Structured analysis thrives on process decomposition and data flows. Can we identify a task domain where process decomposition is not the right thing to do, but where objects can be easily recognized? Conversely, can we identify a task where we do not recognize objects, but where process decomposition is natural? Both cases seem unlikely.

Processes and objects go hand in hand when we see them as emphasizing the dynamic versus the static view of an underlying "behaving" substratum. The two paradigms differ in the sequence in which attention is given to the dynamic and static dimensions. Dynamics are emphasized in the structured paradigm and statics are emphasized in the OO paradigm. As a corollary, top-down decomposition is a strength for the SA approach, while the grouping of declarative commonalities via inheritance is a strength for the OO approach.

1.3.2 Mixing Paradigms

The software development community has a large investment in structured analysis and structured design (SD). The question has been raised repeatedly whether one can mix and match components from the structured development process with components of the OO development process. For instance, whether the combination of SA + SD + OOP or SA + OOD + OOP is a viable route.

Experts at two recent panels[1] denied the viability of these combinations (but see Ward [224] for a dissenting opinion). A key problem resides in the data dictionaries produced by structured analysis. One cannot derive generic objects from them. Inheritance cannot be retrofitted. Also, the behavior of any given object is listed "all over the place" in data flow diagrams.

Consequently and unfortunately, we cannot blindly leverage SA and SD methods and tools. However, OO analysis methods exist that do (partially) rely on SA to describe object behavior; see [76] for a comparative study.

---

[1] *OOPSLA/ECOOP* '90 and *OOPSLA* '91

1.3.3   Development Methods

Within a given paradigm, one may follow a particular *method*[2]. A method consists of:

1. A notation with associated semantics.
2. A procedure/pseudo-algorithm/recipe for applying the notation.
3. A criterion for measuring progress and deciding to terminate.

This book does not introduce yet another new method for OO development. We instead attempt to integrate methods representative of the OO paradigm. Our OO analysis notation is just borrowed from multiple sources. Still we have given it a name, OAN (Our Analysis Notation), for easy referencing. In part II, we introduce ODL (Our Design Language), a language with similarly mixed origins. Summaries of each are presented in the Appendix. When necessary to distinguish our views from those of others, we will refer to these simply as "our method" (OM).

1.4   Development Phases

No author in the area of software development has resisted denouncing the waterfall model. Everyone agrees that insights obtained downstream may change decisions made upstream and thus violate a simple sequential development algorithm. The notion of a development process in which one can backtrack at each point to any previous point has led to the fountain metaphor (with, we assume, the requirements at the bottom and the target system at the top).

Whether the development process has few feedback loops (the waterfall model) or many (the fountain model) depends on several factors. The clarity of the initial requirements is an obvious factor. The less we know initially about the desired target system, the more we have to learn along the way and the more we will change our minds, leading to backtracking.

Another factor might be the integration level of tools that support the development process. A highly integrated development environment encourages "wild" explorations, leading to more backtracking. On the other hand without tool support,

---

[2]We use the word *method*, not *methodology*. The primary meaning of methodology is "the study of methods" which is the business of philosophers. The secondary meaning of methodology is method. Since that is a shorter word we refrain from joining the methodology crowd. (Similarly, we prefer using technique over technology.)

we may be forced to think more deeply at each stage before moving on because back-tracking may become too costly. The development style of team members may be a factor as well.

It has been said that the object-oriented paradigm is changing the classic distinctions between analysis, design and implementation. In particular, it is suggested that the differences between these phases is decreasing, that the phases blur into each other. People claim that the OO paradigm turns every programmer into a designer, and every designer into an analyst. We are willing to go only part way with this view. There is empirical evidence from projects in which objects identified in the requirements phase carried all the way through into the implementation (see [77]). We will see as well that notions and notations used in analysis and design are similar, lending more support for this thesis.

On the other hand, intrinsic differences among phases cannot be forgotten. Analysis aims at clarifying what the task is all about and does not go into any problem solving activity. In contrast, design and implementation take the task specification as a given and then work out the details of the solution. The analyst talks to the customer and subsequently (modulo fountain iterations) delivers the result to the designer. The designer "talks", via the implementor, with hardware that will ultimately execute the design. In a similar vein we do not want to blur the difference between design and implementation. Contemporary OO programming languages have limitations and idiosyncrasies that do not make them optimal thinking media for many design tasks.

It is, in our opinion, misleading to suggest that phase differences disappear in the OO paradigm. Objects in the analysis realm differ significantly from objects in the implementation phase. An analysis object is independent and autonomous. However, an object in an OO programming language usually shares a single thread of control with many or all other objects. Hence, the design phase plays a crucial role in bridging these different computational object models.

1.4.1 Prototyping

Prototyping[3] and exploratory programming are common parts of OO analysis, design and implementation activities. Prototyping can play a role when aspects of a target system cannot be described due to lack of insight. Often enough, people can easily decide what they do *not* want, but they cannot describe beyond some vague

---

[3]We avoid the trendy phrase *rapid* prototyping since no one has yet advocated slow prototyping.

indications what is to be produced.

Graphical user interfaces are an example. What makes a particular layout on a screen acceptable? Must a system keep control during human interaction by offering menu choices or should control be relinquished so that a user can provide unstructured input?

These kinds of question are sometimes hard or impossible to answer. Prototyping experimental layouts can help. The situation resembles that of an architect making a few sketches so that a customer can formulate preferences.

As long as the unknown part of the requirements is only a fragment of a system, OO analysis cooperates with prototyping. Exploratory programming is called for when most of the requirements are not well understood. Research projects fall into this category. Programming in artificial intelligence is an example. Problem solving by analogy is particularly murky behavior. Exploratory programming can be a vehicle for validating theories and/or for obtaining better conjectures.

We feel that *purely* exploratory programming applies to an essentially different set of tasks than the more tractable (although possibly very large) tasks to which the methods described in this book apply. Formulated negatively, the methods in this book may not apply when the development task is too simple or when the task is too hard.

Elucidating functionality is just one of the motivations for prototyping. We have so far used "prototyping" primarily in the sense of "throwaway prototyping" – aimed at gathering insights – in contrast to "evolutionary prototyping" – aimed at implementing a system in stages. A prototyping activity may have both aims but they need not coincide (see [70]). In Part II, we describe a framework for design prototyping that is explicitly evolutionary in nature. Similarly, performance constraints may require empirical evaluation via implementation-level prototyping.

1.4.2   Development Tools

Acceptance of the fountain metaphor as the process model for software development has profound ramifications. Beyond toy tasks, tool support and integration of different tools is essential in enabling backtracking. Of course these tools also need to support versioning, allow for traceability, and cater to team development. These are quite stringent requirements, which are currently not yet satisfied. Various groups are working on the standards to achieve tool control and data integration [188]. Manipulating objects in all phases of the development process should make it easier to construct an integrated development environment. We consider these issues in more detail in Chapter 12 and 15.

1.5 Summary

Software systems are often components of general systems. This book discusses only object-oriented approaches to developing software systems. The roots of the OO paradigm include AI frames and programming languages including Simula.

The structured paradigm focuses on decomposing behaviors. The OO paradigm focuses on objects, classes, and inheritance. The two paradigms do not mix well. While the OO paradigm tightly integrates the development phases of analysis, design and implementation, intrinsic differences between these phases should not be blurred. OO methods are compatible with prototyping efforts, especially those constructed in order to elucidate otherwise unknown requirement fragments.

1.6 Further Reading

Standard non-OO texts include Ward and Mellor's *Structured Development for Real-Time Systems* [223] and Jackson's *Systems Development* [119]. OO texts that cover the full life cycle include Booch's *Object Oriented Design with Applications* [39] and Rumbaugh et al's *Object Oriented Modeling and Design* [192].

Yearly proceedings are available from the principal OO conferences, *OOPSLA* (held in the Western hemisphere) and *ECOOP* (Europe). Both originally focused on programming and programming languages but have more recently broadened their attention to the full life cycle.

1.7 Exercises

1. Analysis aims at giving an unambiguous description of *what* a target system is supposed to do. Enumerate the differences, if any, of an analysis method for characterizing software systems versus an analysis method for characterizing hospital systems, or any other nonsoftware system with which you are familiar.

2. Consider whether the following list of items could be objects with respect to the definition given in Section 1.2: an elevator, an apple, a social security number, a thought, the color green, yourself, a needle, an emotion, Sat Jun 1 21:35:52 1991,

the Moon, this book, the Statue of Liberty, high tide, the taste of artichoke, 3.141..., (continue this list according to its pattern, if there is one).

3. In general, prototyping may be seen as "disciplined" hacking that explores a narrow well defined problem. Would the throwaway connotation of a produced artifact in this characterization change as the result of an overall OO approach?

Part I

Analysis

Chapter 2

Introduction to Analysis

2.1 Purpose

The analysis phase of object-oriented software development is an activity with:

Input: A fuzzy, minimal, possibly inconsistent target specification, user policy and project charter.

Output: Understanding, a complete, consistent description of essential characteristics and behavior.

Techniques: Study, brainstorming, interviewing, documenting.

Key notion for the descriptions: Object.

The final item in this list distinguishes object-oriented analysis from other approaches, such as Structured Analysis [234] and Jackson's method [119].

2.1.1 Importance

Constructing a complex artifact is an error-prone process. The intangibility of the intermediate results in the development of a software product amplifies sensitivity to early errors. For example, Davis [70] reports the results of studies done in the early 1970's at GTE, TRW and IBM regarding the costs to repair errors made in the different phases of the life cycle. As seen in the following summary table, there is about a factor of 30 between the costs of fixing an error during the requirement phase and fixing that error in the acceptance test, and a factor of 100 with respect to the maintenance phase. Given the fact that maintenance can be a sizable fraction of software costs, getting the requirements correct should yield a substantial payoff.

Development Phase	Relative Cost of Repair
Requirements	0.1 – 0.2
Design	0.5
Coding	1
Unit test	2
Acceptance test	5
Maintenance	20

Further savings are indeed possible. Rather than being aimed at a particular target system, an analysis may attempt to understand a domain that is common to a family of systems to be developed. A *domain analysis* factors out what is otherwise repeated for each system in the family. Domain analysis lays the foundation for reuse across systems.

2.1.2   Input

There are several common input scenarios, generally corresponding to the amount of "homework" done by the customer:

- At one extreme, we can have as input a "nice idea". In this case, the requirements are most likely highly incomplete. The characterization of the ATM system in Chapter 1 is an example. The notion of a bank card (or any other technique) to be used by a customer for authentication is not even mentioned. In this case, elaboration on the requirements is a main goal. Intensive interaction between analyst and client will be the norm.

- In the ideal case, a document may present a "totally" thought-through set of requirements. However, "totally" seldom means that the specification is really complete. "Obvious" aspects are left out or are circumscribed by reference to other existing systems. One purpose of the analysis is to make sure that there are indeed no surprises hiding in the omissions. Moreover, a translation into (semi) formal notations is bound to yield new insights in the requirements of the target system.

- In another scenario, the requirements are not yet complete. Certain trade-offs may have been left open on purpose. This may be the case when the requirements are part of a public offering for which parties can bid. For instance, we can imagine that our ATM example is a fragment of the requirements formulated by a bank consortium. Since the different members of the consortium may have different regulations, certain areas may have been underdefined and left to be detailed in a later phase. A main aim of the analysis will be the precise demarcation of these "white areas on the map".

- A requirements document may propose construction of a *line of products* rather than one system in particular. This represents a request for an OO *domain analysis*. Domain analysis specifies features common to a range of systems rather than, or in addition to, any one product. The resulting domain characterization can then be used as a basis for multiple target models. Domain analysis is discussed in more detail in Chapter 13. Until then, we will concentrate most heavily on the analysis of single target systems. However, we also note that by nature, OO analysis techniques often generate model components with applicability stretching well beyond the needs of the target system under consideration. Even if only implicit, some form and extent of domain analysis is intrinsic to any OO analysis.

Across such scenarios we may classify inputs as follows:

Functionality: Descriptions that outline behavior in terms of the expectations and needs of clients of a system. ("Client" is used here in a broad sense. A client can be another system.)

Resource: Descriptions that outline resource consumptions for the development of a system (or for a domain analysis) and/or descriptions that outline the resources that an intended system can consume.

Performance: Descriptions that constrain acceptable response-time characteristics.

Miscellaneous: Auxiliary constraints such as the necessity for a new system to interface with existing systems, the dictum that a particular programming language is to be used, etc.

Not all these categories are present in all inputs. It is the task of the analyst to alert the customer when there are omissions.

As observed by Rumbaugh et al [192], the input of a fuzzy target specification is liable to change due to the very nature of the analysis activity. Increased understanding of the task at hand may lead to deviations of the initial problem characterization. Feedback from the analyst to the initiating customer is crucial. Feedback failure leads to the following consideration [192]: If an analyst does exactly what the customer asked for, but the result does not meet the customer's real need, the analyst will be blamed anyway.

2.1.3   Output

The output of an analysis for a single target system is, in a sense, the same as the input, and may be classified into the same categories. The main task of the analysis activity is to elaborate, to detail, and to fill in "obvious" omissions. Resource and miscellaneous requirements often pass right through, although these categories may be expanded as the result of new insights obtained during analysis.

The output of the analysis activity should be channeled in two directions. The client who provided the initial target specification is one recipient. The client should be convinced that the disambiguated specification describes the intended system faithfully and in sufficient detail. The analysis output might thus serve as the basis for a contractual agreement between the customer and a third party (the second recipient) that will design and implement the described system. Of course, especially for small projects, the client, user, analyst, designer, and implementor parties may overlap, and may even all be the same people.

An analyst must deal with the delicate question of the feasibility of the client's requirements. For example, a transportation system with the requirement that it provide interstellar travel times of the order of seconds is quite unambiguous, but its realization violates our common knowledge. Transposed into the realm of software systems, we should insist that desired behavior be plausibly implementable.

Unrealistic resource and/or performance constraints are clear reasons for nonrealizability. Less obvious reasons often hide in behavioral characterizations. Complex operations such as Understand, Deduce, Solve, Decide, Induce, Generalize, Induct, Abduct and Infer are not as yet recommended in a system description unless these notions correspond to well-defined concepts in a certain technical community.

Even if analysts accept in good faith the feasibility of the stated requirements, they certainly do not have the last word in this matter. Designers and implementors may come up with arguments that demonstrate infeasibility. System tests may show nonsatisfaction of requirements. When repeated fixes in the implementation and/or design do not solve the problem, backtracking becomes necessary in order to renegotiate the requirements. When the feasibility of requirements is suspect, prototyping of a relevant "vertical slice" is recommended. A mini-analysis and mini-design for such a prototype can prevent rampant throwaway prototyping.

2.2 Models

Most attention in the analysis phase is given to an elaboration of functional requirements. This is performed via the construction of *models* describing objects, classes, relations, interactions, etc.

2.2.1 Declarative Modeling

We quote from Alan Davis [70]:

> A *Software Requirements Specification* is a document containing a complete description of *what* the software will do without describing *how* it will do it.

Subsequently, he argues that this what/how distinction is less obvious than it seems. He suggests that in analogy to the saying "One person's floor is another person's ceiling" we have "One person's how is another person's what". He gives examples of multiple what/how layers that connect all the way from user needs to the code.

We will follow a few steps of his reasoning using the single requirement from our ATM example that clients can obtain cash from any of their accounts.

1. Investigating the desired functionality from the user's perspective may be seen as a definition of *what* the system will do.

   The ability of clients to obtain cash is an example of functionality specified by the user.

2. "The next step might be to define all possible systems ... that could satisfy these needs. This step clearly defines *how* these needs might be satisfied. ..."

   The requirements already exclude a human intermediary. Thus, we can consider different techniques for human-machine interaction, for example screen and keyboard interaction, touch screen interaction, audio and voice recognition. We can also consider different authentication techniques such as PIN, iris analysis, handline analysis. These considerations address the *how* dimension.

3. "On the other hand, we can define the set of all systems that could possibly satisfy user needs as a statement of *what* we want our system to do without describing *how* the particular system . . . will behave."

The suggestion to construct this set of all systems (and apply behavior abstraction?) strikes us as artificial for the present discussion, although an enumeration of techniques may be important to facilitate a physical design decision.

4. "The next step might be to define the exact behavior of the actual software system to be built . . . This step . . . defines *how* the system behaves . . ."

This is debatable and depends on the intended meaning of "exact behavior". If this refers to the mechanism of the intended system then we subscribe to the quotation. However, it could also encompass the removal of ambiguity by elaborating on the description of the customer-ATM interaction. If so, we still reside in *what* country. For example, we may want to exemplify that customer authentication precedes all transactions, that account selection is to be done for those customers who own multiple accounts, etc.

5. "On the other hand, we can define the external behavior of the actual product . . . as a statement of *what* the system will do without defining *how* it works internally."

We may indeed be more specific by elaborating an interaction sequence with: "A client can obtain cash from an ATM by doing the following things: Obtaining proper access to the ATM, selecting one of his or her accounts when more than one owned, selecting the cash dispense option, indicating the desired amount, and obtaining the delivered cash." We can go further in our example by detailing what it means to obtain proper access to an ATM, by stipulating that a bank card has to be inserted, and that a PIN has to be entered after the system has asked for it.

6. "The next step might be to define the constituent architectural components of the software system. This step . . . defines *how* the system works internally . . ."

Davis continues by arguing that one can define what these components do without describing how they work internally.

In spite of such attempts to blur *how* versus *what*, we feel that these labels still provide a good initial demarcation of the analysis versus the design phase.

On the other hand, analysis methods (and not only OO analysis methods) do have a *how* flavor. This is a general consequence of any modeling technique. Making a model of an intended system is a constructive affair. A model of the dynamic dimension of the intended system describes *how* that system behaves. However, analysts venture into how-country only to capture the intended externally observable behavior, while ignoring the mechanisms that realize this behavior.

The object-oriented paradigm puts another twist on this discussion. OO analysis models are grounded in object models that often retain their general form from analysis (via design) into an implementation. As a result, there is an illusion that *what* and *how* get blurred (or even should be blurred). We disagree with this fuzzification. It is favorable indeed that the transitions between analysis, design, and implementation are easier (as discussed in Chapter 15), but we do want to keep separate the different orientations inherent in analysis, design, and implementation activities.

We should also note that the use of models of any form is debatable. A model often contains spurious elements that are not strictly demanded to represent the requirements. The coherence and concreteness of a model and its resulting (mental) manipulability is, however, a distinct advantage.

2.2.2 Objects in Analysis

OO analysis models center on objects. The definition of objects given in Chapter 1 is refined here for the analysis phase. The bird's eye view definition is that an object is a conceptual entity that:

- is identifiable;
- has features that span a local state space;
- has operations that can change the status of the system locally, while also inducing operations in peer objects.

Since we are staying away from solution construction in the analysis phase, the objects allowed in this stage are constrained. The output of the analysis should make sense to the customer of the system development activity. Thus we should insist that the objects correspond with customers' notions, and add:

- an object refers to a thing which is identifiable by the users of the target system – either a tangible thing or a mental construct.

Another ramification of avoiding solution construction pertains to the object's operator descriptions. We will stay away from procedural characterizations in favor of declarative ones.

Active Objects

Some OO analysis methods have made the distinction between *active* and *passive* objects. For instance Colbert [58] defines an object as active if it "displays independent motive power", while a passive object "acts only under the motivation of an active object".

We do not ascribe to these distinctions, at least at the analysis level. Our definition of objects makes them *all* active, as far as we can tell. This active versus passive distinction seems to be more relevant for the design phase (cf., Bailin [20]).

This notion of objects being active is motivated by the need to faithfully represent the autonomy of the entities in the "world", the domain of interest. For example, people, cars, accounts, banks, transactions, etc., are all behaving in a parallel, semi-independent fashion. By providing OO analysts with objects that have at least one thread of control, they have the means to stay close to a natural representation of the world. This should facilitate explanations of the analysis output to a customer. However, a price must be paid for this. Objects in the programming realm deviate from this computational model. They may share a single thread of control in a module. Consequently, bridging this gap is a major responsibility of the design phase.

2.2.3   Four-Component View

A representation of a system is based on a core vocabulary. The foundation of this vocabulary includes both static and dynamic dimensions. Each of these dimensions complements the other. Something becomes significant as a result of how it behaves in interaction with other things, while it is distinguished from those other things by more or less static features. This distinction between static and dynamic dimensions is one of the axes that we use to distinguish the models used in analysis.

Our other main distinction refers to whether a model concentrates on a single object or whether interobject connections are addressed. The composition of these two axes give us the following matrix:

	inside object	between objects
static	attribute	relationship
	constraint	acquaintanceship
dynamic	state net and/or	interaction and/or
	interface	causal connection

Detailed treatments of the cells in this matrix are presented in the following chapters.

The static row includes a disguised version of entity-relationship (ER) modeling. ER modeling was initially developed for database design. Entities correspond to objects, and relations occur between objects.[1] Entities are described using attributes. Constraints capture limitations among attribute value combinations. Acquaintanceships represent the static connections among interacting objects.

The dynamic row indicates that some form of state machinery is employed to describe the behavior of a prototypical element of a class. Multiple versions of causal connections capture the "social" behavior of objects.

Inheritance impacts all four cells by specifying relationships among *classes*. Inheritance allows the construction of compact descriptions by factoring out commonalities.

2.2.4 Other Model Components

The four models form a core. Additional models are commonly added to give summary views and/or to highlight a particular perspective. The core models are usually represented in graphic notations. Summary models are subgraphs that suppress certain kinds of detail.

For instance, a summary model in the static realm may remove all attributes and relationship interconnections in a class graph to highlight inheritance structures. Alternatively, we may want to show everything associated with a certain class C, for example, its attributes, relationships in which C plays a role, and inheritance links in which C plays a role.

An example in the dynamic realm is a class interaction graph where the significance of a link between two classes signifies that an instance of one class can connect in some way or another with an instance of another class. Different interaction mechanisms can give rise to various interaction summary graphs. Another model component

---

[1]The terms "relation" and "relationship" are generally interchangeable. "Relationship" emphasizes the notion as a noun phrase.

can capture prototypical interaction sequences between a target system and its context. Jacobson [120] has labeled this component *use cases*. They are discussed in Chapters 10 and 12.

All of these different viewpoints culminate in the construction of a model of the intended system as discussed in Chapter 10.

2.3   Process

Several factors prevent analysis from being performed according to a fixed regime. The input to the analysis phase varies not only in completeness but also in precision. Backtracking to earlier phases is required to the extent of the incompleteness and the fuzziness of the input. Problem size, team size, corporate culture, etc., will influence the analysis process as well.

After factoring out these sources of variation, we may still wonder whether there is an underlying "algorithm" for the analysis process. Investigation of current OO analysis methods reveals that:

- The creators of a method usually express only a weak preferences for the sequence in which models are developed.

- There is as yet no consensus about the process.

- There appear to be two clusters of approaches: (1) Early characterization of the static dimension by developing a vocabulary in terms of classes, relations, etc. (2) Early characterization of the behavioral dimension, the system-context interactions.

We have similarly adopted a weak bias. Our presentation belongs to the cluster of methods that focuses on the static dimension first and, after having established the static models, gives attention to the dynamic aspects. However, this position is mutable if and when necessary. For instance in developing large systems, we need top-down functional decompositions to get a grip on manageable subsystems. Such a decomposition requires a preliminary investigation of the dynamic realm. Chapter 9 (Ensembles) discusses these issues in more detail. A prescribed sequence for analysis is given via an example in Chapter 10 (Constructing a System Model). A formalization of this "algorithm" is given in Chapter 12 (The Analysis Process).

2.4   Summary

Analysis provides a description of *what* a system will do. Recasting requirements in the (semi) formalism of analysis notations may reveal incompleteness, ambiguities, and contradictions. Consistent and complete analysis models enable early detection and repair of errors in the requirements before they become too costly to revise.

Inputs to analysis may be diverse, but are categorizable along the dimensions of functionality, resource constraints, performance constraints and auxiliary constraints.

Four different core models are used to describe the functional aspects of a target system. These core models correspond with the elements in a matrix with axes static versus dynamic, and inside an object versus in between objects.

Analysis is intrinsically non-algorithmic. In an initial iteration we prefer to address first the static dimension and subsequently the behavioral dimension. However, large systems need decompositions that rely on early attention to functional, behavioral aspects.

2.5   Further Reading

We witness an explosion of analysis methods. A recent comparative study [76] describes ten methods. A publication half a year later [130] lists seventeen methods. Major sources include Shlaer and Mellor [200, 203], Booch [39], Rumbaugh et al [192], Wirfs-Brock et al [230], and Jacobson et al [121].

2.6   Exercises

1. Discuss whether analysis, in the sense discussed in this chapter, should be performed for the following tasks:

   (a) The construction of a new **Fortran** compiler for a new machine with a new instruction repertoire.
   (b) The planning for your next vacation.
   (c) The repair of faulty software.
   (d) The acquisition of your next car.
   (e) The remodeling of your kitchen.
   (f) The decision to get married.
   (g) The reimplementation of an airline reservation system to exploit five supercomputers.

(h) A comparative study of OO analysis methods.

2. Analysis is a popular notion. Mathematics, philosophy, psychiatry, and chemistry all have a claim on this concept. Is there any commonality between these notions and the notion of analysis developed in this chapter?

3. Do you expect the following items to be addressed during OO analysis?

(a) Maintainability.
(b) Quality.
(c) The development costs of the target system.
(d) The execution costs of the target system.
(e) The programming language(s) to be used.
(f) The reusability of existing system components.
(g) The architecture of the implementation.
(h) The relevance of existing frameworks.

Chapter 3

Object Statics

3.1   Instances

In previous chapters, we have shown definitions of objects, but we do not expect that the reader has a "gut level" understanding of what they are beyond the things that are usually encountered in everyday life. We surmise that everyone starts out this way. Thus, an object can be your boyfriend, NYC, the Ferrari in the showroom which is beyond your means, the Taj Mahal, etc. At the same time, objects can be non-tangible things (provided that someone wants to see it that way) such as a bank transaction, a newspaper story, a phone call, a rental car contract, a utility bill, an airline reservation, a bank account, etc.

Our graphical notation for a singular object is simply a dot. For example an instance of the class *Account*:

- *account_12345*

The heading of this section is "instances", not just "objects". We use the notion of an instance when we want to emphasize that an object is a "member" of a class. In Chapter 2, we were already using the notion of instance in the context of "... an instance of one class ..." In most methods, each object is perceived as being a member of a certain *class*.

3.2   Classes

Sometimes we need to talk about a particular instance in our system model. For example, a bank may maintain some key "system" accounts. We may want to describe a few special employees, e.g., the executive officers. Usually, however, collections of objects, so-called classes[1] are described.

A class stands for a family of objects that have something in common. A class is not to be equated with a set of objects, although at any moment we can consider the set of instances that belong to the class. A class may be seen as what all these sets have in common. In technical terminology, a class stands for the *intension* of a particular characterization of entities, while the set of objects that conform to such a characterization in a certain period is known as the *extension* (see Carnap [49]).

Notationally, a rectangle surrounds the name of a class. For example, the class *Account* is depicted as:

Account

An object is an instance of at least one and at most one class. Certain methods allow an object to change, during its lifetime, the class of which it is an instance. This freedom increases the expressive power of the analysis method. But since most OO software development methods and languages do not support this feature, and since the effects of change may be described by other means, we refrain from this practice.

Individual objects are primarily characterized by an indication of which class they belong. For example:

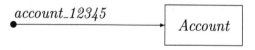

The arrow between the instance and its class is called the ISA relationship. This is not the same as the class inheritance relationship discussed in Chapter 7.

This instance characterization is insufficient. At this stage, we do not have available the means, beyond naming, to distinguish multiple instances of the class *Account*.

---

[1]The notions of "type" and "class" are sometimes distinguished in the implementation realm. A type is the abstract characterization of a particular "family" of objects, while a class is then the actual realization in a particular programming language of that type. We will uniformly use the term "class". Later in Part II we refer to directly implementable versions as "concrete".

In general, we avoid using names to describe individual objects, because usually objects do not have natural names. Just consider the examples given earlier – a bank transaction, a newspaper story, a phone call, a rental car contract, a utility bill, and an airline reservation. Instead, descriptions are used that somehow denote unique entities. Attributes of objects will do the descriptive job.

3.3   Attributes

Real-life entities are often described with words that indicate stable features. Most physical objects have features such as shape, weight, color, and type of material. People have features including date of birth, parents, name, and eye color. A feature may be seen as a binary relation between a class and a certain domain. Eye color for example, may be seen as a binary relation between the class of *Eyes* and an enumerated domain {*brown, blue, yellow, green, red*}. A domain can be a class as well, for example, in the case of the features *parents, spouse, accountOwnedBy*, etc.

The applicability of certain features (i.e., the features themselves, not just their values) may change over time. For example, frogs and butterflies go through some drastic changes in their lifetime. We avoid this kind of flexibility. Thus, a class is characterized by its set of defining features, or *attributes*. This collection of features does not change. (We later present tricks for getting around this limitation.)

The notion of a (binary) relation crept into the previous discussion. The reader may wonder how we can discuss them here since we have relegated them to another model in our four-component view. We make a distinction between attribute (binary) relationships that represent intrinsic, definitional properties of an object versus relationships that describe contingent, incidental connections between objects. Because we, as analysts, are in control, we can *prescribe* for an object what is definitional and what is incidental. For example, in a particular system we may agree that for the class *Person* a *social-security-number* is a defining attribute while a *parent* feature is seen as an incidental relationship. In another system, the reverse choices could be made.

We illustrate the notation for attributes with a class *Account* that has:
- attribute *accountNumber* of value domain *AccountNumber* and
- attribute *currency* of value domain *Currency*.

A graphical notation for these attribute names and attribute values is:

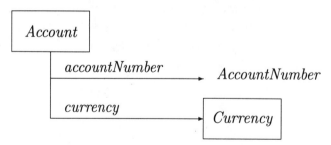

This representation indicates that *AccountNumber* is a "data value" domain and that *Currency* is a class. It is debatable whether we should make such a distinction between values and objects. For instance, one can take the stance that integers, strings, and 32-bit reals are all objects as well. Although we will be very picky about the resulting distinctions in Part II, either way is fine with us. We use the convention that unboxed value domains do not represent classes. Consequently, if we change our mind and represent the *currency* attribute as a data value, we would unbox it.

3.3.1 Attributes of Instances

Attributes can be employed to describe an instance of a class by indicating how it "scores" with respect to the attributes. In the following example, we depict a particular instance of the class *Account:*

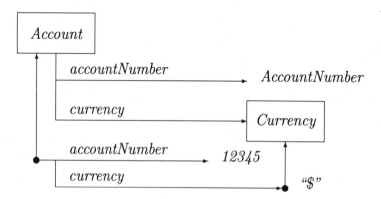

Note that attribute names have been repeated in the instance. An alternative approach would use graphic notation to link up the attributes of the instance with the attributes in the class, as in:

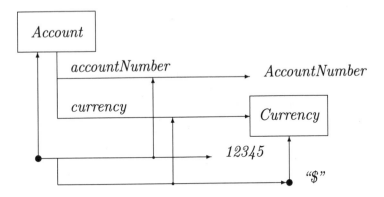

3.4 Attribute Features

We have attached attributes to objects. The next step is to give, in a sense, attributes to attributes. We will call them *features* to avoid too much confusion.

Two features of attributes have been encountered already, the attribute's relation name, which is sometimes called the *role* name, and the value domain. Here we expand the features that can be associated with an attribute. We should stress that using these features is optional and can be ignored in first rounds or even all together.

3.4.1 Defaults

Sometimes it is useful to indicate a default initial value for an attribute. A generous bank may, for example, give a surprised new customer an account with an initial balance of $10. Since sheep are usually white, their color attribute can be given this default value.

A revised *Account* class includes a notation for indicating a default value of an attribute:

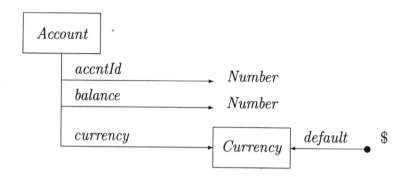

3.4.2 Probability

We may want to associate with an attribute our knowledge about the distribution of
the values in the value domain. (A default value need not correspond with the value
that has the highest probability.) As an example, consider the class *Human* with
the attribute *age*. The probability distribution corresponds here with a demographic
profile. A designer may want to exploit this information.

We avoid introducing special notation. One option is to list *(value, probability)*
pairs. For numerical domains, a probability distribution function may be specified.
Any other mathematical notation may be invoked as needed.

3.4.3 Multiplicity

A *multiplicity* feature associates more than one value to an attribute. We use the
notation *[N:M]*, where $0 \leq N \leq M$. *N* indicates the minimum number of values and
M indicates the maximum number. A few conventions simplify the notation:
  · We usually abbreviate *[N:N]* as *[N]* to represent a multiplicity of exactly *N*.
  · We usually omit a multiplicity indicator when the multiplicity is *[1]*.
For example, the class *Hand* might contain the attribute *finger* with a value domain
of class *Finger* and a multiplicity constraint of [0:6]. This requires an explanation
indeed. A hand remains a hand even when all the fingers have been amputated.
That explains the minimum 0. The 6 has been chosen because Anne Boleyn had a
hand with six fingers.

This multiplicity notation is sometimes not expressive enough. Consider a family
of vehicles where the number of wheels per vehicle is 3, 4, 6 or 10. In general, a

multiplicity indicator can be any arbitrarily complex description of a set of natural numbers. Given this state of affairs, we omit additional notation beyond observing that predicate calculus provides formal precision and unbounded expressiveness.

Optional Attributes. Using a zero lower bound in the multiplicity feature of an attribute indicates that possession of the attribute is "optional". This allows instances that effectively do *not* have that attribute. This is a way around the limitation of freezing a collection of attributes for a class.

For example, a bank has branches, each having departments. We assume that departments consist of a department head and subdepartments. This creates a recursive structure that bottoms out by making subdepartments optional. Thus, a nonmanagerial employee is a department head that does not supervise subdepartments. For illustration, we restrict the branching ratio of departments to six:

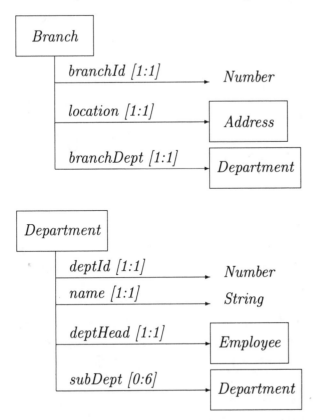

Multiplicity default and probability.   Multiplicity indications may be dressed up with more knowledge if this information is beneficial for a design and/or implementation. For example, a reasonable default multiplicity for the number of wheels of a car is four. A probability distribution for the multiplicity feature denoting the number of children per parent might be obtained through an empirical sampling.

3.4.4   Qualifiers

The range of an attribute value can be restricted in any of several senses. We *always* fix an attribute to a particular domain. The values of an attribute of an object must remain within the indicated domain throughout the lifetime of the object. The domain for an attribute listed in a class may be narrowed down to only one possible value. For example, the class *Albino* has for its *color* attribute the value *white*. Intermediate domain restrictions that do not limit attributes to only one value may be expressed via constraints (see Section 3.5).

Several other senses of restriction are common enough to group under broad categories, allowing simpler qualification:

- We may require that an attribute value for each instance of the class to be *fixed* (immutable) when the object is created and initialized. This value may differ across different instances, but it may not vary across time for any instance. *Fixed* attributes differentiate instances from peer objects that are members of the same class.

- We may require that the value of an attribute be *common* to all instances of a class, even without knowing what that value should be. The common value may also change across time. For example, all instances of class *Account* might need to record transactions using a *common LogFile*. The exact file may change over time.

- The category of *unique* attributes is the extreme opposite of *common*. A *unique* attribute is one whose value differs for each instance of a class. For example, the value of attribute *accntId* should be unique to each instance of class *Account*.

Qualifiers including *fixed*, *common*, and *unique* may be annotated in any convenient fashion. For example, the following class *Client* has a social security number attribute that is both unique for each instance and remains fixed over its lifetime:

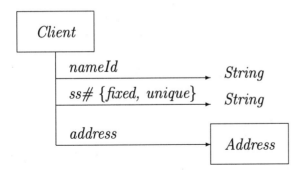

3.5 Constraints

Constraints may be used to rule out certain attribute value combinations for all instances of a class. Consider a *Department* that has the attributes *head* and *treasurer*, both having *Employee* as their value domain. We may want to indicate that these positions cannot be filled by the same person. These kinds of constraints may be expressed in any convenient notation. For example:

$$head \neq treasurer.$$

For clarity, attributes in such expressions may be qualified with *self*. We assume that every class supports by default an attribute *self* which refers for each object to itself:

$$self.head \neq self.treasurer.$$

Constraints can refer to other attribute features. Consider, for example, a *Polygon* with attributes *angle* and *side*. We certainly want to express that the multiplicity features of these attributes are the same.

A constraint can reach beyond the boundary of an object. Assume a class *Person* with the attribute *spouse* having the *[0:1]* value domain *Person* and the attribute *sex* with the value domain *[male, female]*. We may want to express the following constraints (among others):

- The spouse of a spouse is the original person:
$$self = self.spouse.spouse.$$

- The sex of a person and the person's spouse are different:
$$self.sex \neq self.spouse.sex$$

Many constraints involving multiple objects are more easily and naturally expressed via relations. We discuss relational constraints in Chapter 4.

3.5.1   Derived Attributes

A special case of a constraint is an expression that describes an attribute functionally, in terms of one or more other attributes.

For example, consider a class *Person* with the attributes *dateOfBirth*, *dateOfMarriage* and *ageAtMarriage*. The *ageAtMarriage* attribute may be defined as a function of the other two.

Codependencies are possible as well. A *Triangle* class with attributes *sideLength*, *angle*, *bisector*, *surfaceArea*, etc., will have constraints on each attribute that refer to the others. For a different kind of example, consider the class *Account* with a multivalued attribute *balance* and a multivalued attribute *transaction*. We have the following codependencies:

$$balance(n + 1) = balance(n) + transaction(n),$$
$$transaction(n) = balance(n + 1) - balance(n).$$

3.6   Identifying Objects and Classes

In this section, we describe some preliminary issues in the identification of objects, or rather, their classes. We cannot claim that a procedure exists that can be followed blindfolded. In fact, after developing further modeling apparatus, we devote much of Chapter 12 to the further investigation of these identification, vocabulary, and process issues.

We focus here on elements of small and medium problems. The OO paradigm induces a bottom-up way of modeling, designing, and subsequently implementing a system. The atomicity of objects induced by encapsulation is the key cause. But analyzing a large system in a bottom-up fashion is out of the question. A leveling technique is needed in order to tackle a large system in top-down mode, and is required anyway to preserve the hierarchies that are "naturally" present in large man-made systems. In this book, we use *ensembles* as a special kind of object that allows decomposition. The treatment of ensembles is deferred to Chapter 9.

3.6.1   Developing Vocabulary

As a first approximation one can scrutinize the requirements document, if there is one, and consider the nouns, or better yet, the noun phrases in the document. As an example we have put in *italics* the noun phrases of the running ATM example of Chapter 1:

We assume that *the American Bank (AB)* has partly decentralized account management. *Every branch office* has *equipment* to maintain *the accounts of its clients*. *All equipment* is networked together. *Each ATM* is associated and connected with *the equipment of a particular branch office*. *Clients* can have *checking, savings and line of credit accounts*, all conveniently interconnected. *Clients* can obtain *cash* out of any of their *accounts*. *A client* with *a personal identification number (PIN)* can use *an ATM* to transfer *funds* among *attached accounts*. *Daemons* can be set up that monitor *balance levels* and trigger *automatic fund transfers* when *specifiable conditions* are met and/or that initiate transfers periodically. *Automatic periodic transfers to third party accounts* can be set up as well.

We have to pick the winners from the collection of noun phrases:
- the individual object *the American Bank*;
- the classes *branch office, account, client, equipment*;

while avoiding the losers *balance level* and *specifiable condition*.

3.6.2 Classes and Attributes

There is a great amount of freedom in refining vocabulary. Iteration over the set of candidate classes helps weed it out. The first round identifies classes only by their names. Subsequent rounds refine and distinguish among class characterizations via attributes. (We postpone using inheritance to exploit commonalities among classes until Chapter 7.)

When two classes have identical attribute descriptions, they may be synonyms. But having identical attribute names is not sufficient for two classes to be equal. For example, the difference between the classes *Triangle* and *RightTriangle* resides in the latter having a constraint expressing that one of the angles is 90°. Thus, attributes plus optional constraints compose class definitions.

Classes versus Roles

Deciding when a notion is a class and when it is an attribute's role name can be puzzling. In [41], the following example is given with respect to *father*:

(1) Ron is a new father.
(2) Ron is the father of Rebecca.

In (1) father appears to be a class, while in (2) father acts like a role name of a (multivalued) attribute. This example is typical. When a sentence with a questionable concept can be extended (as in "father *of* ... "), it is normally a relational attribute with a suppressed attribute value (see Chapter 4).

3.6.3   Unique Versus Multiple Instances

Novice OO analysts sometimes wonder whether OO methods are applicable because their application classes have only a single instance. A notorious example is the car cruise control system with unique instances *Speed Indicator, Desired Speed, Brake Pedal,* and *Carburetor* (see Chapter 5).

Having classes with predominantly only one instance should not be a reason to abandon an OO approach. Objects are encapsulated entities that improve conceptual, design, and implementation sanity. In addition, reuse of classes across application boundaries is more promising than non-OO concepts, design fragments, or code.

For example, our "requirements document" contains the AB bank as a unique entity:

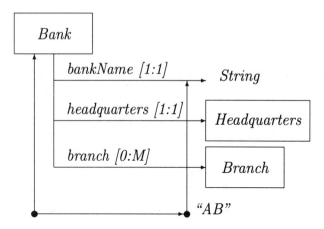

Also, the AB bank most likely needs a unique entity that tells all interested parties in AB what the day's interest rate is. This suggests the introduction of a unique instance of a class with attributes including *savingsAccountInterest, lineOfCreditInterest,* etc.

3.6.4   Persistent Versus Transient Objects

Objects need not exist very long in a system to still be full-fledged instances of full-fledged classes. For example, an analyst is free to construe *events* in the application domain as objects. Thus we can make the pragmatic distinction between objects that denote (semi) persistent entities in an application domain versus objects that denote transient entities. Being able to capture the proper details should be a guide for an analyst in choosing between persistent and transient objects.

For example, our requirements description refers to *transfers* between two accounts (e.g., to transfer funds from a savings account to a checking account). A *Transfer* class describes the static dimension of such transient objects:

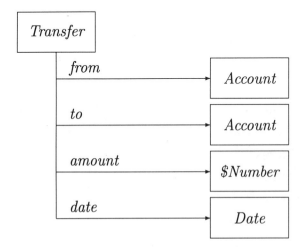

3.6.5 Statics and Dynamics

Static considerations may be insufficient to differentiate classes. We can still have variations based on behavioral differences. For example, one kind of calculator may support only addition and subtraction, while another one with the same attribute structure (at an appropriate abstraction level) also supports multiplication and division. However, we are emphasizing for now class identification, and especially characterization, via the static features of the objects that constitute a class.

This may sound counterintuitive. Some entities are easier to describe via their dynamic (potential) dimension. For instance, a pilot is a person that can *fly* a plane. Even so, remember that the static and dynamic dimensions of an entity are complementary notions that can add and build onto the other. Change is perceived against a background of constancy. Dually, constancy is merely the inability to perceive a slow rate of change. In addition, our treatment of the static dimension of objects before addressing the dynamic dimension should not be seen as an imperative for the OO analysis *process*.

For example, an automated teller machine can be understood as a device that can support a range of financial transactions. (The term *machine* in its name already emphasizes the dynamic aspect.) However, it may still be described in terms of its static features. The following first impression for class *ATM* (to be revised extensively in coming chapters) lists attributes indicating functional components of an ATM machine:

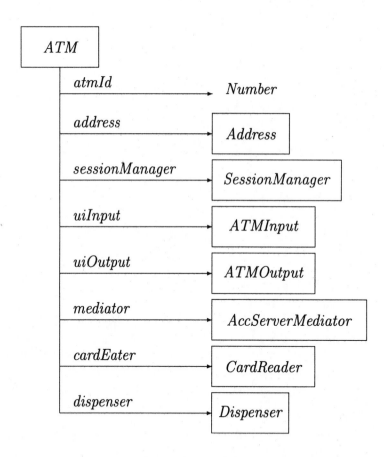

For a different kind of example, the following *TransferDaemon* class represents the static dimension of procedures that are run periodically to transfer an amount provided a condition is met. For instance, such a procedure may automatically transfer money to a savings account when a checking account has too much money.

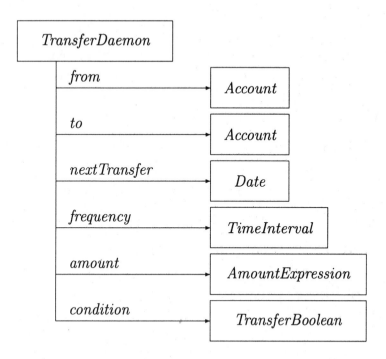

The *TransferDaemon* class will be revisited in Chapter 10 after we have developed behavior modeling. For now, we sketch out characterizations of the attributes that help to control dynamics:

TimeInterval describes how often a transfer will be attempted. Possible values can range from minutes (or perhaps even shorter) to months (or even longer).

AmountExpression is any expression describing the amount to be transferred. This might just be a fixed sum. Alternatively, we can envision that the AB bank allows for amounts that are functions of certain parameters. For example, to maintain a certain balance in the *from* account, it might take the form:
(the balance of the from account) – (a fixed sum).

TransferBoolean describes a truth-valued function to be used to block the transfer when certain conditions are not met. For example, a value calculated by the function outlined in the previous attribute should not be too small, or one may want to constrain the maximum amount on the target account.

3.7   Summary

This chapter describes a (graphical) language to capture the static dimension of objects. Attributes and attribute features are introduced. Attributes are seen as special binary relations help *define* a prototypical instance of a class. This is in contrast to relations that reflect contingent connections between objects as induced by a particular target application. Attribute features and constraints further describe and restrict attributes and their combinations. Generic classes capture parametric commonalities across families of classes.

We have illustrated the notions in this chapter with several examples from the ATM domain. Most are first approximations, built upon in subsequent chapters. For now, classes referred to but not expanded are left as exercises to the reader.

3.8   Further Reading

Attributes are a keystone for our treatment. They play similar roles in most published OOA methods. But at least two methods ignore them or even avoid them. Booch [39] downplays the importance of defining objects and classes through static aspects. He characterizes objects by state, behavior and identity, in that order. Attributes are also avoided by Embley et al [89]. They see an object as a node in a network of connections (relationships). As a consequence they feel that the distinction between a relationship and an attribute is to be postponed to the design phase.

3.9   Exercises

1. Identify objects, introduce their classes, give attributes, their features and constraints as suggested by the following text:

   Mr. White is married. He teaches OO Software Engineering classes on Fridays. He is a part-time member of the faculty at the CS Department of the All-Smart Institute. His 23-year-old son John was enrolled in the OOA class that Mr. White taught in the previous semester. John does not like broccoli. Mrs. White uses a ten-speed for transportation to and from the campus (she teaches Philosophy at the same institute). Class size is limited at the institute to 14 students. The faculty at the institute, when seen as parents, have at most two children. The sister of John has a boyfriend that is two years younger than she is and plays two different instruments.

2. A "meta" constraint on a class may express how many instances it can have in a particular target system. As a special case, a constraint may express for a class that it has only *one* instance. Would such a construct obviate the notion of an instance? Consider the notions of the president of a company, New Year, the first day of the year, Washington, the capital of the United States, and the headquarters of a bank.

3. Describe a set of classes that represent entities in your kitchen.

Chapter 4

Object Relationships

In this chapter, we provide further apparatus for capturing the static dimension of a system or domain of interest. In the previous chapter, we looked at objects in isolation. Here we consider static regularities among objects. We discuss relations in the tradition of entity-relationship (ER) modeling. An example is the *Ownership* relation that connects objects in the class *Client* and objects in the class *Account*.

4.1   Relationships

A relationship may be seen as a named family of typed tuples. They are typed in the sense that the nth element in a tuple is an instance from a specific domain or class. The *signature* of a relationship is just a listing of these types. For example, the signature of the *Ownership* relationship is (*Client, Account*) since it has a family of 2-tuples where the first domain is the class of *Clients* and the second domain is the class of *Accounts*.

Following the tradition of the data modeling community and other OOA methods, a diamond is used to depict a relationship in our graphical notation. A diamond is connected via edges to the domains of the tuple elements. Obviously, we will always have at least two edges. For example, to indicate that class *Client* and class *Account* are connected by the relationship *Own*:

In the same way that we may want to refer to particular instances of classes in a particular target system, we may want to express that certain instances actually belong to a relationship. For example, we may want to express that a particular client owns a particular account. An instance of a relation is represented with a diamond containing a filled circle:

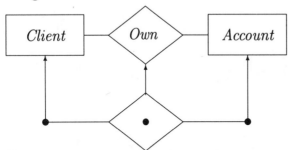

Graphical notation can sometimes cause an ambiguity when a relationship connects identical domains. For example, the *Supervise* relationship between two *Person*s is described in textual representations by ordering the arguments, as in:

  Supervise(Person, Person).

We can agree that the first argument represents the supervisor and the second argument the "supervisee" (person that is being supervised). To avoid ambiguity in diagrams we can add role names, as in (letting *Spv* stand for *Supervise*):

The *arity*, or number of elements in the signature is another way of classifying relationships. Binary relations (such as *Own* and *Supervise*) have tuples of length two. Ternary relations have tuples of length three. Examples include:

InBetween, a relationship among three *Location*s. For example, Chicago is in between San Francisco and New York.

TravelTimeBetween, a relationship among two *Location*s and a *TimeInterval*. For example, the travel time between New York and San Francisco is six hours.

ParentsOf, a relationship among three *Person*s. For example, John and Mary are the parents of Susanna.

ResideInSince, a relationship among a *Person*, a *Location*, and a *Date*. For example, John resides in Stockholm since December.

BorrowedFrom, a relationship among two *Person*s and a *Thing*. For example, John borrowed a lawn mower from Mary. ("*Thing*" here is perhaps too broad. Can someone borrow the Sun?)

We can have relations with tuple lengths larger than three as well. Graphically, more than two edges are obviously required for relationships with arity greater than two. For example, we may construe *Transfer* as a relation among a pair of accounts, an amount, and a date (letting *Trans* stand for *Transfer(fromAccount, toAccount, amount, date)*):

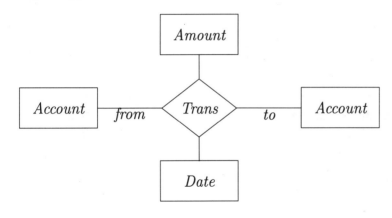

4.1.1 Features

In Chapter 3, we attached features to attributes in order to capture more semantics. Similarly, features can be attached to the tuple domains of a relationship.

Cardinality

Consider a domain in which an *account* cannot have more than one owner. This means that a particular instance of *Account* can occur not more than once in an *Own* tuple. *Cardinalities* (the relational versions of multiplicities) may be used to indicate such properties. Here, we can add the cardinality notation *[0:1]* to the diagram:

Alternatively, we could express that each client can own one to multiple accounts and each account can have one to multiple owners:

As another example, we may want to express that a peculiar group of *Client*s have at least three but at most five accounts with:

The date that a client becomes a customer may be described as a relationship. Each client must have exactly one start date. A client may have started on the same date as another client. Letting *CsSn* stand for *CustomerSince(Client, Date)*:

Qualifiers

Relationships may be classified according to their technical properties. See any discrete mathematics text (e.g., [151]) for fuller descriptions of properties including:

Reflexive: For all x, $R(x, x)$ holds; i.e., every element is necessarily related to itself. For example, the relationship *SameAgeAs*.

Symmetric: For all x and y, $R(x, y)$ implies $R(y, x)$; i.e., the relationship is "bidirectional". For example, the relationship *SiblingOf*.

Transitive: For all x, y, z, if $R(x, y)$ and $R(y, z)$ hold, then $R(x, z)$ holds. For example, the relationship *AncestorOf*.

4.1.2 Constraints

In the same way that constraints provide supplementary information about simple attributes, additional constraints may express restrictions on the allowed instances of a relation. For example, we can rephrase the fact that instances of class *Person* have the attribute *spouse* as a binary relationship *Spouse* between *Person* and *Person* (assuming the *spouse* attribute has been eliminated from class *Person*):

The *[0:1]* cardinality captures a monogamy restriction.

As before, we may want the ability to express that the sex of the partners is different. (This would also imply that a person cannot be his or her own spouse.) In addition, we may want to express age restrictions on the *Person* tuple elements. We omit notation conventions for expressing these constraints; see Chapter 3 for suggestions.

4.1.3 Parametric Relation Instances

The instances of one relation, or more commonly, the attributes of a class may be constrained to be instances of another relation. For example, consider a simplified *Family* class containing (only) one *parent* and (only) one *child* attribute, along with a binary relationship *Custody* capturing the fact that one person has custody over another person.

We would like to express the constraint that in each *Family*, the parent must have custody over the child. This requires that the parent and child must also be instances of the *Custody* relationship. However, simple relation instances cannot be used to state this. They indicate the existence of particular instances of a relation. We need here a way to say that *any* persons in the *parent* and *child* roles must also be instances of the *Custody* relationship. This leads to the concept of a *parametric relation instance* (see [40]). "Parametric" in this context refers to the fact that the exact identity of the relation instance is a variable (parameter), different for each instance of class *Family*.

We indicate parametric relation instances (PRIs) with an open dot. For example, the following diagram says that the *parent* and *child* in a *Family* must be members of a *Custody* relationship. The relational constraint applies to all instances of the class:

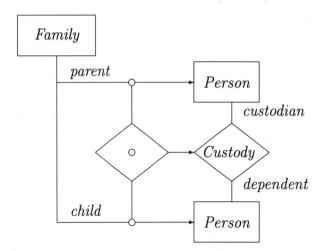

[Note that the *Person* boxes in this diagram are used in two different ways, as attribute domains and as relation domains. For further economy at the expense of readability, we could have drawn only one *Person* box, used in four ways.]

The parametric relation instance places constraints on the instances of *Family* that one may construct. If we wanted a class in which the parent is not always the custodian, we might for example introduce another attribute, *nonCustodyChild* with the same value domain *Person*.

4.2   Collections

Collections represent groups of objects. They may be employed when describing those objects that fall under a common relationship or need to be manipulated in a common fashion.

4.2.1   Sets

Sets are the most well-known and useful kinds of collections. We have introduced sets indirectly in the scope of regular classes. Any multivalued attribute has a set for its domain. Sets may also be employed explicitly as primitive notions (cf., [89]). We restrict ourselves to typed sets where all elements of the set belong to an indicated class (including subclasses of that class – see Chapter 7).

A set is to be distinguished from a class. A set must be defined in an extensional way, by construction, optionally in combination with a filtering characterization. Thus we *exclude* here intensionally defined subclasses, such as:

Accounts with a balance over $1000,

but we *include*:

Accounts in our database with a balance over $1000.

Other examples include a branch with an attribute representing a set of its local accounts (if this association is not represented as a relationship) and similarly for the local clients of a branch.

Once we have sets, we can open the floodgates and adjoin to our representational apparatus the notations that are available in set theory. These include:

∩ for intersection,

∪ for summation,

\ for subtraction,

⊂ for the subset relationship,

⊃ for the superset relationship.

We denote sets by expressing their domains as "arguments". For example, a set of branches is denoted as *SET(Branch)*. Observe that we now have two ways to describe multivalued attributes; sets and multiplicity features. The following two depictions may be treated as equivalent:

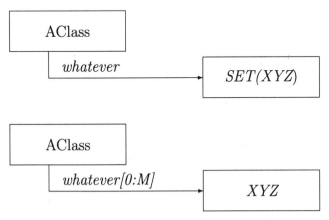

Multiplicity and set notations may be combined, for example, when we introduce multivalued attributes where each individual value is a set. In the following example the class *School* treats its faculty as an undifferentiated set of employees and treats the student body as a family of sets of students:

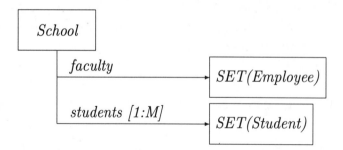

When a multivalued attribute would have more specific multiplicity bounds, as in
[3:7], the corresponding set notation may be annotated accordingly in any agreed on
manner.

4.2.2   Other Collections

If necessary, the analyst is invited to employ other collection notations and the usual
operations associated with them:

Sequences. For example, the class *String* may be described as *SEQ(Char)*. Other
examples include the ATM attribute *logOfSessions*, which has as value domain
SEQ(Session).

Arrays. For example, the class *2D-4-5-grid* may be described as *ARRAY[3:4](Point)*.
The days of a year can be represented as an array, for instance, to record a
savings account interest rate for that time period: *ARRAY[365](Day)*.

Bags. For example, the collection of accounts involved in receiving funds in a certain
time period may be described as a *BAG(Account)*. Since an account may receive
funds more than once we can have repetitions.

4.2.3   Generic Classes

Additional collections and related constructs may be defined as *generic* classes. These
classes capture the commonalities of a broad range of other classes. Inheritance
(see Chapter 7) is an excellent mechanism to exploit abstract classes and create
more specific versions. Generic classes instead use the style of procedure or function
variables to express genericity.

Our notations for sets and other collections are special cases of that for generic classes. By convention we use upper case names for generic classes. For example, the following generic class *QUEUE* has instances with elements of type *X*.

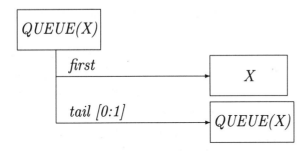

When the class *Job* happens to be around, we can introduce the class *QUEUE(Job)*.

4.3   Identifying Relationships

4.3.1   Relationships versus Classes

Analysts often have some freedom in whether to use classes versus relationships to represent static features of a domain. The notion of *Transfer* is an example. It was represented as a *class* in Chapter 3 but as a relationship in this chapter.

The main consideration is that classes and relationships describe different kinds of instances. As defined in Chapter 2, objects (class instances) have identity, features, and operators that may change state across time and communicate with other objects. Instances of relationships do not necessarily share these properties. A relation instance need not be ascribed an independent identity. It may be fully characterized merely by listing the elements of the tuple. Relation instances need not have any intrinsic properties outside of those of the tuple. And they cannot change state or communicate with other objects at all.

Analysts may choose the approach that appears most appropriate to the task at hand. When aspects of a purported relation appear class-like, or vice-versa, descriptions may change accordingly.

Intensional Versus Extensional Definition

The ways in which classes and relationships are defined also differ. Classes list the central defining characteristics of identifiable objects in a domain. As noted in Chapter 3, classes provide *intensional* descriptions of objects by listing their defining properties rather than their members.

Like sets, relationships are normally described in a partially *extensional* fashion. Most relationships describe tuples corresponding to the state of affairs in the "world" and are determined by circumstances. Thus, they have been obtained by some form of observation. The *Ownership* relation is an example. In this case, the family of tuples is simply a set, and in practice is a "small" finite set. For all practical purposes, relational modeling deals only with extensionally defined relations in which the family of tuples is small and can conceivably be handled by storage media that will satisfy resource requirements constraints.

While a useful guide, this distinction does not *intrinsically* separate classes from relationships. Intensionally defined relationships may provide a definition (e.g., a predicate) that characterizes which tuples belong to the relation and which do not. Grandparenthood defined as being the parent of a parent is an example. Another example from the realm of math is the successor relationship relating every natural number N with its successor $N + 1$. Here, the family of tuples is still a set, although not small and in fact of infinite size. Relationships where the family of tuples is not a set any longer are possible as well.

4.3.2 Relationships versus Attributes

In Chapter 3, we mentioned that an attribute may be seen as a special binary relationship between the central object and an entity in the value domain. As a result of the similarity between attributes and binary relationships, an analyst must take care not to prematurely absorb binary relationships into a class definition.

The main conceptual issue is whether a feature is definitionally intrinsic to an object. One question to ask is whether every instance of a class is *necessarily* related to a member of the other domain. In the former case it is normally a genuine attribute; in the latter case it is better represented as a relationship. On the other hand, one should be pragmatic as well. For example, in spite of the existence of *Gliders*, it makes sense to see *Engine* as a *[0:M]* (multivalued) attribute of *Airplane*. Consequently, *Gliders* may be described as effectively lacking the attribute *Engine* by giving them the multiplicity feature *[0]*.

A related question is whether one object is conceptually "in control" of the values assumed in the other domain. This generally corresponds to whether an object may contain transitions (see Chapter 5) that directly change the value. If so, it is appropriate to list it as an attribute. For example, in Chapter 3 we listed the "relationship" between an *Account* and the *Number* representing the current balance as an attribute. Account objects are in control of their own balances, may alter them within transactions, etc.

As another example, in Chapter 6 we will introduce *acquaintance* relations describing the partners in object interactions. In order to describe the behavior of an object in its full generality, independent of the role it may play in a particular target system, we may need to describe a handle to another, as yet unknown, object with which it needs to interact. Binary acquaintance relations serve this need. However, when one object must be able to determine its partner(s), this information may be listed in attribute form.

Functions

Functional relationships (or just "functions") represent the meeting point of these considerations. A tuple component of a relation depends functionally on the other components if its value is uniquely determined by the other components. The cardinalities *[0:1]* and *[1:1]* for any of the domains indicate a functional dependency. The cardinality *[0:1]* reflects a *partial* function that need not "hit" every element in the domain.

For example, the following diagram indicates that every person has precisely one mother, and every mother has at least one child. Letting *Mo* stand for the *MotherOf* relation:

Functions are among the most common kinds of relationships. In functional relationships, at least one direction of the relation associates a single element of one domain to those in the other. It is convenient and often reasonable to treat them as attributes in functional direction if this appears central to the definition of the class. In this sense (as exploited in design – see Chapter 16) all attributes are functions. For example, to indicate that each person must have a mother:

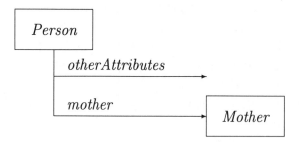

Similarly, consider the *MaintainedBy(Account, Branch)* relation saying that an account must be maintained by one branch, and a branch maintains at least one, possibly more accounts. This could be described as a functional relationship (letting *MnBy* stand for *MaintainedBy*):

Alternatively, the *Account* class could have an attribute *maintainer* with domain *Branch*. The "other" direction in a functional relationship may also be described as an attribute when this contributes to the definitional characterization of a class. However, in this case, the attribute normally has a *SET* domain. For example, each *Branch* could have an attribute *maintainedAccts* with domain *SET(Account)*.

More generally, any binary relationship may be described with a *pair* of possibly set-valued functional attributes (one per domain) when it is meaningful to do so. However, the "equal partnership" implicit in the idea of describing pairs of functional attributes is better captured as a relationship proper.

The extreme case of a functional relationship is a *one-to-one* function, where the cardinalities of both domains are *[1:1]*. In this case, each element of one domain is "matched' with a unique element of the other. (If one of the domains has cardinality *[0:1]*, this instead represents a partial one-to-one function). For example, the "relationship" between an *Account* and its *accountNumber* is one-to-one, as would be a relationship between *Departments* and *Managers* saying that each department has a unique manager and each manager manages a single department. These relationships are most naturally captured as attributes. When doing so, attribute multiplicity notation may be extended as *[1:1]-[1:1]*, or abbreviated as *unique* to indicate this property.

We summarize these classifications by showing how some standard function categories are described as attributes:

One-to-One: A function is one-to-one if each distinct argument maps to a distinct result. This corresponds to *unique*.

Pure: A function is pure if multiple applications with the same argument always give the same result. This corresponds to per-object *fixed*.

Singular: A function is singular (or fully many-to-one) if it always gives the same answer, regardless of argument. This corresponds to per-class *common* (i.e., constraining all instances to possess the same value).

Partial: A function is total if it is defined for each possible argument. Otherwise it is partial. Partial functions are denoted with *[0:1]* multiplicities.

Multivalued: A multivalued (or one-to-many) function corresponds to either *[1:N]* multiplicities or *SET* or other collection domains.

4.4   Summary

Relationship modeling captures generally static connections between objects. Relationships may be distinguished across dimensions including arity, domains, and cardinality. Relationship notation may be embellished with additional features and constraints. Collections, especially sets, may be used to describe groups of objects bearing a common relationship or role.

4.5   Further Reading

Relationships have been treated extensively in relational database theories and generic entity-relationship modeling; see for instance Ullman [221] and Maier [150].

Relationships are widely employed in OOA methods. As discussed in Chapter 3, attributes are avoided in Embley et al [89]. Instead they emphasize the importance of relationships. They also describe set membership as a relationship between two classes where one provides the "raw material" instances and the other represents the sets constructed from them. Wirfs-Brock et al [230], describe several special relationships including *PartOf*, *DependsUpon*, *HasKnowledgeOf*, *IsAnalogousTo*, and *isKindOf*. Relationships are not employed directly in the OMT method of Rumbaugh et al [192]. They use the similar concept of *associations* instead.

4.6   Exercises

1. Formulate a relation that has tuples of length four, five, . . . Try to avoid relations that are constructed by adjoining time and/or space qualifiers as in: John travels *from A to B on Sunday*.

2. Can the following information be represented as relationships?

   (a) The balance of an account ten days ago.
   (b) Accounts associated with the zip code(s) of their owners.
   (c) Employees located in Toronto.
   (d) The grandparents of the children living in Springfield.
   (e) The weather report of 2001 January 1.
   (f) The molecular structure of H_2O.
   (g) The contents of a library.
   (h) The public transportation schedule in LA (assuming they have one).
   (i) The recipes in a cookbook.
   (j) The patterns of traffic lights at an intersection.
   (k) The contents of an encyclopedia.
   (l) The grammar of FORTRAN.

3. Give examples of generic classes having one, two, . . . arguments.

4. Discuss whether the following families of objects can be represented as a set and/or as a class.

   (a) The states of the US.
   (b) The members of your family.
   (c) The atoms in the universe.
   (d) The inhabitants of Berlin.
   (e) The colors of the rainbow.
   (f) The natural numbers.
   (g) The days of the week.

5. Redo exercise 1 from the previous chapter but this time exploit relationships as well. Compare your solutions.

   Identify objects, introduce their classes, give attributes, their features and constraints as suggested by the following text:

   Mr. White is married. He teaches OO Software Engineering classes on Fridays. He is a part-time member of the faculty at the CS Department of the All-Smart Institute. His 23-year-old son John was enrolled in the OOA class that

Mr. White taught in the previous semester. John does not like broccoli. Mrs. White uses a ten-speed for transportation to and from the campus (she teaches Philosophy at the same institute). Class size is limited at the institute to 14 students. The faculty at the institute, when seen as parents, have at most two children. The sister of John has a boyfriend that is two years younger than she is and plays two different instruments.

Chapter 5

Object Dynamics

In this and the next chapter, we concentrate on the characterization of behavior. The dynamics of individual objects are discussed in this chapter. The next chapter focuses on "social" interactive behavior between objects. We begin with some preliminary considerations about what it is we are trying to describe.

5.1 Describing Behavior

Behavior description is a notoriously difficult problem. Physics borrows from mathematics the notion of differential equations to describe changing entities, fluids, gases, etc. This trick is unavailable to us. The behavior of the entities in our domains of interest practically never satisfy differential equations. Even a simple device like a piston engine is beyond the formalisms of differential equations.

Algorithmic description languages are also not available at the level of analysis. The strengths of these languages lie in detailing *how* a particular desired behavior can be realized. That is not what we want in analysis. We need only the ability to provide a precise description of *what* constitutes a desired system's behavior. For instance in the case of a prototypical system we would want to describe context interaction sequences.

Phrased compactly, *procedural* behavior descriptions should be traded in favor of *declarative* descriptions.

We face the little problem that purely declarative description languages are as yet still mired in theoretical problems. It is in fact one of the core problems in artificial intelligence and knowledge representation.

5.1.1   Background

The Frame Problem (identified at the end of the 1960s [155]) stands for, at least, the following questions:

- What are the necessary and sufficient preconditions for applying an operator?

  In order to start a car, one needs to turn the ignition key. Thus an obvious precondition is that the car key be available. Does the start-the-car operator also have to mention that the car has an ignition lock? That the battery is not dead? That there is fuel in the tank? That the spark plugs in the engine have not been removed?

- What are the effects or postconditions of an operator?

  An antenna pops out when a car is started. Is that a part of the postcondition of starting a car? Usually as a result of the exposed antenna a horrible commercial is heard. Is that also a part of the postcondition? There are no set rules for limiting postconditions.

- What is a state description language that allows efficient representation of sequences of states?

  An operator changes the "world". One cannot simply add new assertions that describe the new aspects to a previous world description. For example, when we have the assertion that a door is open, and we perform an operation, close-the-door, we cannot simply add that the door is now closed. The knowledge that open and close exclude each other would generate a contradiction. Time or situation indexing of assertions does not work in practice because a successor state does not have access to assertions in previous states whose truth value obviously has not changed. For example, if a door is opened while it is raining, we would know in the subsequent state that the door is open, but we would have lost the rainy weather condition. Other approaches run into similar snags.

In spite of vigorous research [42], not much progress has been made to solve these issues in a generic fashion.

5.1.2   Characterizing Transitions

The task of analysis is usually somewhat easier than that of AI. Most applications do not require support for planning or plan execution of robots. It is sufficient that

OOA notations disambiguate human-to-human communication. At the same time, notations must not be sloppy. We want to have a smooth, easy transfer into design notations, which in principle need the rigor of machine executability.

The fact that we usually deal with closed, artificial worlds provides further simplifications. We are able to delineate once and for all what our concepts are within the scope of a system or a set of systems. In real life most concepts have the crispness of vapor.

Since a powerful, purely declarative description language is not available, most analysis methods use representations that are at least somewhat procedural. Structured methods use data flow diagrams (DFDs). A node in a DFD stands for a process, and can be recursively decomposed in the same manner as functions can be decomposed into ultimately elementary, obvious operations.

OOA methods mainly use augmented transition network diagrams to express the behavior of objects. Transition networks are quite declarative, especially when states, transition guards, and transition actions are defined in a rigorous way.

Transition networks are "state machine diagrams" augmented in several ways:

- The "firing" of a transition can be dependent on the state of an object, reception of an event, and any other auxiliary guards.

- Operations of unbounded complexity may be described for each transition. For example (as discussed in Chapter 6), they may include bidirectional synchronized interaction with other objects.

- Before entering a destination state, a transition may create an event that may in turn be received by one or more other objects.

The ability to describe complex operations on state transitions can easily be misused. For example, an analyst can create a transition network with one state and a single transition that connects this state with itself and which concentrates all functionality of the object into this transition. It is unlikely that this yields a conceptually clear representation of an object's behavior.

5.1.3 Parallelism

For the sake of discussion, we say that two activities are in parallel when they proceed at the same time. Some real-life entities possess parallel features. A person seen as an entity harbors an amazing amount of parallelism, if not at the mental level then at least at the physiological one. Cars perform many activities at the same time the engine runs: Each wheel turns, the gears in the transmission turn, the wipers are on, the generator feeds the battery, lights are switched on and off, etc. The engine itself contains lots of parallelism.

In spite of these considerations, we prefer to stick to the limitation of having only a single thread of control per object. We consider a transition to be atomic, although we allow switches between different transition networks if an object has more than one.

How do we reconcile this restricted computational object model against arguments for parallelism?

- We already have an abundance of parallelism. *Every* object has its own thread of control, and executes concurrently with other objects. We see it as a challenge to exploit this kind of parallelism to explain and describe apparent parallelism inside entities.

- Parallel transitions inside an object make the mapping of analysis outputs into design even harder. In some low-level designs, a single thread of control is shared by all objects. Even in distributed systems, there will be many fewer computers than objects. Mapping analysis objects with each having a single thread of control into low design objects is already quite a challenge. We prefer to avoid the additional complexity of dealing with objects that have internal parallelism. The assumed atomicity and independence of transitions at the analysis level allow corresponding design and implementation activities to proceed in a more familiar and tractable fashion.

- Allowing parallelism inside an object is a potential source for the introduction of "magic", ill-defined behavior, which is need of analysis for clarification. Since we are doing analysis, we will avoid the magic in the first place.

We will consider apparent parallelism as an invitation to explicitly identify *multiple* objects operating concurrently. Some entities do harbor multiple "machines" that act in parallel. Our strategy will be to treat such an entity as an encapsulator for constituent machines, each of which are themselves objects. We have labeled these encapsulators *ensembles* and we have devoted Chapter 9 to their treatment. An ensemble is an object having a single thread of control, while at the same time connoting an entity with internal parallelism.

5.1.4 Characterizing States

Our final preliminary issue is to nail down what counts as a *state*.

Two different interpretations of states are seen in OO analysis methods (e.g., [89, 192]), *passive* and *active*. (This is a completely separate distinction than that between passive and active *objects* discussed in Chapter 2.)

What are their differences? A major difference is that passive states can be defined precisely, while active states are as yet quite fuzzy notions.

A passive state of an object can be defined in terms of the attributes of the object. An object is in such a state if, from the perspective of the object, nothing changes except time. Doors being open or closed are examples of such states of affairs. The openness of the door can be defined by referring to an attribute of the door, say, *frAngle*, the angle of the door with respect to its frame. And similarly for its closedness. These definitions can be used to show that these states exclude each other, as is required for different states. By any reasonable definition of state, one cannot be in two states at the same time.

In contrast, an active state refers to a situation in which an object is involved in an ongoing process. The English language has a particular syntactic form for these situations, verb+ing. Thus we can have a door that is *opening* or *closing*. We can have a person that is in the active state of *typing*, *turning a key*, *writing a check*, etc. In [89] these states are typified as "interruptible activities".

The use of active states (in addition to passive ones) has the apparent advantage of increasing the expressive power of the formalism. The problem, however, is that proponents have not indicated what entering an active state means. Are these processes themselves objects? If so, is another object constructed and set in motion? If not, does this mean that a fresh process is started? Or does it mean that a suspended process is resumed? Similar problems surround leaving an active state. Does this mean that a process or object dies? Or does it mean it is suspended? Similarly, the notion of "interruptible" is quite powerful yet underdefined.

As a result of such questions, we will avoid active states. However, we discuss in Section 5.2.4 how to emulate active with passive states. It is also possible to give an object self-knowledge so that it can report that it is engaged in an verb+ing activity. Such an active condition can be referred to by other objects if necessary.

5.2 Transition Networks

A transition network is an abstraction of a process. It exploits our categorizations of behavior as sequences of identifiable and classifiable changes, the transitions. A state is the abstraction that connects what "happens" between the end of a transition and the beginning of a follow-up transition. A state also allows the introduction of branching. More than one transition can lead out of a state. Guards associated with transitions will determine which, if any, subsequent transition will be chosen when a state is entered.

A transition network always has a finite, usually small, number of states. A transition is a binary directed connection between pairs of states.

5.2.1 State

A state "bridges" transitions, provides a choice point for alternative continuation transitions, and is a resting place when no follow-up transition qualifies.

This is a technical characterization of states. The analyst's perspective of a state of an object should emphasize that a state makes sense for a customer. It should be a part of the "natural", "public" lifecycle of an object. For example, *open*ness and *closed*ness of a *Door* are most likely indeed states that are relevant from a customer's viewpoint. Similarly, a checking account can be in either an *ok* state or in an *overdrawn* state. As another example, an ATM can be in the states *available* and *unavailable*.

Our graphical notation for a state is a circle, for example, state *closed:*

Identification and naming of the relevant states of an object can be firmed up by defining the states in terms of attributes:

Door: We assume that the class *Door* has an attribute *frAngle* with value domain *Degrees* in the range [0, 180]:

> **closed** $0 = frAngle$
> **ajar** $0 < frAngle < 45$
> **open** $45 \leq frAngle \leq 180$

Checking account: We assume that *CheckingAccount* has an attribute *balance* with value domain *number*:

ok $0 \leq balance$
overdrawn $balance < 0$

ATM: The availability of an ATM may be described by introducing attribute *available?* with values $\{y, n\}$ (yes/no) as its value domain, and associated states:

available $available? = y$
unavailable $available? = n$

This is an example of an object that has "self-awareness" of where it resides in the collection of its possible states. The definition of these two states will become more satisfactory when we elaborate (and modify) the class *ATM* later in this chapter.

We have been semi-formal in defining states. States need not always be elaborated this deeply. It may be preferable to first get a preliminary insight about the set of states, described only with informative names. On the other hand, insisting on precise definitions in terms of attributes provides a mutual check on the static and the dynamic model. In addition, it provides a preliminary view of the characterization of operators associated with transitions.

Initial State

A transition network needs a special state, which is the initial state that describes the state of affairs for a newly created object. The description of this state can be facilitated when default values have been formulated for attributes. An initial state has the syntactic feature that it has at most one inbound transition that can initialize the object. Graphically, we represent an initial state with an arrow leading in from "nowhere":

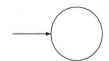

Exit State

A transition network may have an exit state. Entering this state means that the object ceases to exist. A single outbound transition can be associated with such a state to express a testament operation. Graphically:

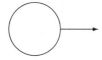

Checking State Definitions

When states are precisely described, they can be checked against one another to ensure that they denote mutually exclusive states of affairs. Consider the states S_1 and S_2 each defined respectively by the property P_1 and P_2. The states should exclude each other, since an object can be only in one state at a time. This means that:

> P_1 implies $not(P_2)$, and
> P_2 implies $not(P_1)$.

For example, in our *CheckingAccount* example:

> $S1 = ok$, $P1 = (0 \leq balance)$,
> $S2 = overdrawn$, $P2 = (balance < 0)$.

Showing that P_1 implies $not(P_2)$ boils down to:

> $(0 \leq balance)$ implies $not(balance < 0)$.

Since we can rewrite $not(balance < 0)$ into $(0 \leq balance)$, we are done. Similarly, showing that P_2 implies $not(P_1)$ amounts to:

> $(balance < 0)$ implies $not(0 \leq balance)$.

Again we rewrite the right hand side: $not(0 \leq balance)$ into $(balance < 0)$ and we are done. Consequently, our states are well defined in the sense that they satisfy the mutual exclusion feature.

Of course, satisfaction of mutual exclusion does not mean that the state definitions themselves are relevant from a modeling perspective. It only demonstrates that when each state captures a relevant state of affairs for an object then these states may coexist in a transition network.

5.2.2 Transitions

A transition models an object that leaves an originating state and goes into a target state (which may be the same as the originating state). A transition is *atomic*. An object cannot be interrupted after it has left a state and has not yet reached the target state; not even during a suspension caused by an action during the transition. Thus, we avoid (possibly indirect) recursive transitions.

Transitions have standard graphical representations as directed links between circles representing states; see, for example [152, 89]. Added to the link is a box to represent respectively a guard, an action, and an optional event. A canonical example of two states connected by a transition is:

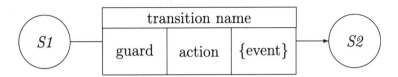

When we need a more global view of a transition network, we may suppress the details of the transitions:

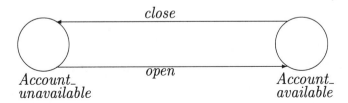

The guard, action, and event components of a transition will be discussed in turn.

Guard

A guard is a condition (boolean-valued function) that must be satisfied in order for the transition to occur. For example, a transition that effects a withdrawal on an account may have as guard the condition that the balance have sufficient funds. A guard for a transition that achieves an open door may be the condition that the door is not locked.

A guard in a transition network associated with an object may refer directly to any attribute of the object. Attributes of other objects may be referred to as well. This requires having a handle on those external objects, for instance, via a relationship or an attribute that has an external object as value. References may be repeatedly tracked through several different objects. As an example, consider a guard that checks whether the sum total of balances of attached accounts has a certain property. This would require finding an attribute or relation that describes the accounts and then accessing their balances.

A guard can optionally refer to an event. Because input events are intrinsically associated with object interaction, we defer details to Chapter 6.

Checking guards.   A state can have more than one outbound transition associated with it. Different guards should ensure that at most one condition at the time can be satisfied. For example, if a door is ajar, one can either close it or open it (or leave it as is), but one cannot achieve two changes at the same time.

Just as states in a transition network must be mutually exclusive, we have an exclusion property for the guards associated with transitions emanating out of a particular state (assuming that there is more than one transition). More specifically, when there are two guards G_1 and G_2, we should show:

G_1 implies $not(G_2)$, and
G_2 implies $not(G_1)$.

For example, consider a state *PreDebit* in the state space of *Account* out of which two transitions emerge respectively with the guards:

$debit \leq balance$, a regular debit, and
$debit > balance$, an overdrawn debit.

These guards obviously exclude each other.

Action

An action description is the second component of a transition. This action must be a terminating activity. It may affect the attributes of *self*. Similar to the guard, an action can refer to any attribute, locally or remotely. As we will see in the next chapter, an action may also entail bidirectional interactions with external objects.

The form of description may vary. We can have:
- informal action verbs such as "sort" and "debit";
- more elaborate informal descriptions;
- structured English descriptions;
- formal preconditions and postconditions; and
- even data flow diagrams.

Offhand we cannot prescribe the complexity of an action within a transition. That is the choice of the analyst. However, these actions must be plausibly implementable without requiring an analysis after "all of the analysts have gone home".

Formal preconditions and postconditions are certainly the scariest looking options in this list. However, when states and guards have been described precisely, it is likely that almost all of the work has been done already. The initial state together with the guard constitutes the precondition. The target state expresses most of the postcondition. (The situation does get a bit more complex under object interaction; see Chapter 6.)

Actions corresponding to our examples include the following.

Door: The definition of states *closed*, *ajar* and *open* allows (among others) a transition that originates in *closed* and terminates in *open*. The action on this transition is described by a postcondition that says that the *frAngle* attribute must obtain a value between 45 and 180 degrees. (This "action" corresponds only to a simulation. In a robotic context an effectuator would have to perform the real action to achieve the intended effect.)

Checking Account: We described earlier the states *ok* and *overdrawn*. This allows, for example, a transition that goes from the *ok* state into the *overdrawn* state. This reflects a withdrawal that surpasses the balance. A likely action for this transition is described by the postcondition:

$$balance' = balance - w,$$

where w is the amount withdrawn. The unprimed occurrence of *balance* in this assertion (not assignment!) stands for the value or extension of the balance attribute before the operation, the primed occurrence stands for the value or extension after the operation.

Event

Actions affect the state of affairs of the object in which the state transition occurs. The reader may have wondered how a door obtains its new frame-angle attribute value. Similarly, a checking account will not internally create withdrawal (and deposit) amounts. Interaction between objects is necessary. We defer further elaboration to Chapter 6.

5.2.3 Exceptions

By analogy to the notion of defensive programming, an analyst may build in defenses against anomalous situations. Events, which serve as the gateways for data flowing into an object, are an obvious source for anomalies. A guard may not be smart enough to recognize illegal data that are subsequently passed on to an action. An analyst may want to indicate what is to be done when an action error occurs.

We use the following notation for dealing with exceptions:

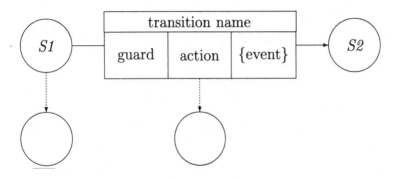

This diagram shows two exception links. The one emanating from state *S1* can be used for dealing with a timing constraint that prohibits staying in state *S1* for too long (see Section 11.2). The other exception link deals with exceptions that arise in the transition. The action part may, for instance, rely on communication with another party. This interaction may produce unexpected results, yield a time-out, etc. Exceptions are never associated with guards or event generation.

5.2.4 Active State Emulation

As promised, we provide an emulation of active states. The key idea is to exploit the fact that an active state is interruptible "at all times". Quotes have been used to emphasize that a process is in fact interruptible only at discrete moments. In between these moments, a process is "deaf". Thus an interruptible process can be represented as a loop with a transition that leads back into the state where it originates and that does a little bit of activity on the way:

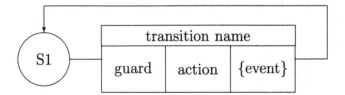

Although we have argued against active states in transition networks, it is sometimes necessary to refer to an object that is actively looping. This can be obtained by giving an object an attribute that expresses whether or not it is engaged in a particular cyclic transition.

For example, we may want to have a display lamp be *off* or *on* depending on whether an engine is *off* or is *running*. This would be established by giving *Engine* the attribute *running*. A *displayLamp* may consult this attribute provided it has a handle on the corresponding *engine* object.

5.3   Examples

5.3.1   ATM

We illustrate the main concepts and notations with our ATM machine example. The following ATM transition network diagram includes an additional notation. The two boxes with double vertical boundaries represent abstracted subnetworks with the same start state and target state as the double-sided box. In both occurrences of the double-sided boxes the start and target states just happen to be the same.

We leave these subtransitions unelaborated for now (but see Chapter 10). An example of a Maintenance (*Mntnc*) subtransition network would be one where the bill-dispenser is replenished. An example of a Menu Action is a subtransition network that dispenses cash.

The transition network is quite naive. For example, we have omitted alertness constraints. A time-out transition is certainly warranted for the state that expects the customer to provide a PIN number. All the ugly details of reading in the digits of a PIN are ignored as well. The transition from *Finished* (*Fnshd*) to *Idle* is too coarse, and should refer to at least two transitions, the machine ejecting the card and the customer taking the card out of the machine. (We will address these and other refinements in later chapters.)

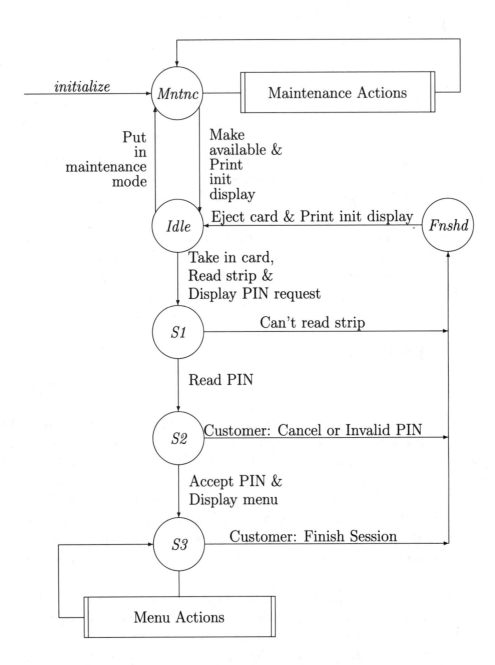

This transition network is still quite high level. We have characterized the states and the transition only by names. To be more precise, we sketch a fragment of the *ATM* class definition.

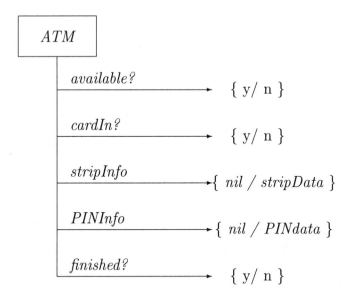

This characterization looks different than the one given in Section 3.6. The attributes specified here can be *added* to the one given in Section 3.6. The new attribute definitions permit rigorous definitions for the states in our transition diagram. The following table describes the states uniquely on the basis of attribute value combinations.

	Mn	Id	S1	S2	S3	Fi
available?	n	y	y	y	y	y
cardIn?	n	n	y	y	y	y
stripInfo	nil	nil	nil	ok	ok	nil
PINInfo	nil	nil	nil	nil	ok	nil
finished?	n	n	n	n	n	y

For example, the *Maintenance* state has the *available?* attribute set to n(o), while all other states have this attribute set to y(es). As another example, the states *S2* and *S3* differ with respect to the *PINInfo* attribute. In *S2*, we have either that the customer has pressed the cancel button (not represented here) or we have an as yet unverified PIN number. In *S3*, we have obtained a verified and accepted PIN number.

The following example transition comes into action when the card's strip info cannot be decoded. Observe that the *finished?* attribute is set in order to conform to the properties of the *Finished* state.

	Can't read strip		
	guard	action	{event}
	$not(OK(stripInfo))$	*finished?'* = Yes	

S1 ─────── [Can't read strip table] ─────▶ *Fnshd*

Another transition leads from *S1* to *S2* when the card's strip can be decoded successfully. Observe again that we set *stripInfo'* in order to conform to the characterization of *S2*. The action GetPIN refers to an interaction with another object and is beyond the current discussion; we will revisit it in the next chapter. Also note that the guards of the two transitions emanating from *S1* exclude each other, and that they cover all possibilities; thus an object will never get stuck in *S1*.

	Read PIN		
	guard	action	{event}
	$OK(stripInfo)$	*stripInfo'* = ok *PINInfo'* = GetPIN	

S1 ─────── [Read PIN table] ─────▶ *S2*

5.3.2 Car Cruise Control

We present a fragment of the ubiquitous car cruise control (CCC) machinery. A CCC has several components that can be modeled as objects: An object that keeps track of a desired speed, an object that interfaces with the carburetor, sensor objects, objects that interface with control panel buttons, sliders, etc. We will deal here with a "brain" object of class *CCC* that keeps track of the different states in which the CCC system can be. We quote from a real manual:

> When engaged, this device takes over the accelerator operation at speeds above 30 mph ... The controls ... consist of a speed SET button and a control slide.
>
> **To Activate:** When the vehicle has reached the desired speed, push the SET button to move the control slide to the ON position. This will establish memory and activate the system. Remove your foot from the accelerator.

Pushing the control slide from the OFF to ON while the vehicle is in motion establishes memory at the speed, but does not activate the system. The slide may be left in the ON position when the vehicle is parked.

To Deactivate: A soft tap on the brake pedal or normal brake ... while slowing the vehicle will deactivate speed auto control without erasing the memory. Pushing the control slide to the OFF position, or turning off the ignition, erases the speed memory.

To Resume Speed: Push the control to the RESUME position and the vehicle will return to the previously memorized speed...

To Vary the Speed Setting: You can reset the control to any desired speed by accelerating or slowing to that speed and pressing the SET button...

The transition network for the prototypical object *ccc* in *CCC* has three states. The states may be defined in terms of properties of the attributes in *CCC*. Because *ccc* is the brain of the CCC system, we give it knowledge about the state of the CCC system. We give it an attribute *state* with value domain the set { *off, sim, on* }, where *sim* stands for *speedInMemory*. Since all of the transitions depend on external events, with respect to *ccc*, we sketch only an abstracted network. Details of the transitions, except their names, are suppressed:

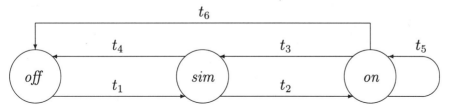

t_1 occurs when the vehicle's speed is at least 30mph and the control slide goes from the OFF to the ON position.

t_2 occurs when the SET button has been depressed or the control slide is pushed into the RESUME position.

t_3 occurs when the brake pedal is depressed.

t_4 occurs when either the control slide goes from the ON to the OFF state or the ignition is turned off.

t_5 occurs when the SET button is depressed. Observe that t_5 leads to the same state as where it comes from.

t_6 is like t_4 but originates in the *on* state.

5.4   Reducing Complexity

Transition networks have the questionable reputation that their size can get out of hand for realistic applications. We discuss three strategies, state abstraction, subnet abstraction, and independent transition networks. A fourth, inheritance, is discussed in Chapter 7. These may be employed to fight exponential explosions.

5.4.1   State Abstraction

We encountered six transitions in the transition network of *ccc*. The transitions t_4 and t_6 are nearly the same. The only difference is that they originate in different states, respectively *speedInMemory* and *on*. It is always a good idea to find ways to factor out commonalities. In this case, we may introduce a "superset" state *simOrOn*, with interpretation that the *ccc* object is in either of the states *speedInMemory* or *on*. Subsequently, we remove the transitions t_4 and t_6 and introduce instead a transition t_{4_6} that leads from *simOrOn* to *off*.

Harel [104, 105] has introduced a graphical notation, stateCharts, for this state abstraction convention. In this notation, the *CCC* transition network becomes:

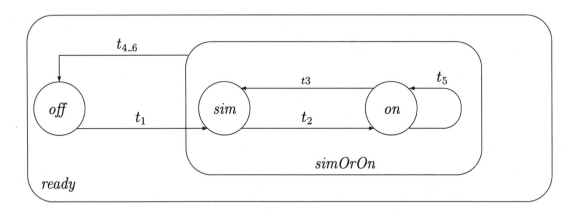

The transition t_{4_6} leads out of *sim* and out of *on*. A transition in the other direction (e.g., t_1) cannot point to *simOrOn* because this would yield an ambiguity.

The outermost state, *ready*, represents an extreme form of state abstraction. An object of class *CCC* is in the abstract state *ready* whenever it is quiescent (i.e., not engaged in a transition). It is possible and useful to define transitions leading from *ready* to *ready*. For example, there are surely many interactive transitions that perform the actual cruise control. Some of them may operate differently when the object is in states *off*, *sim*, or *on*. Others may operate in exactly the same way regardless of state, and so may be defined at this topmost level. By convention, a transition connecting an abstract state to itself is interpreted as leading back to the precise state from which it originated.

5.4.2 Subnetwork Abstraction

Sometimes we may connect two states, S_1 and S_2, with a high-level transition. Such a transition is high level in the sense that it represents a transition subnetwork that has a single entry, corresponding with S_1, and in which all paths leads to exits that can be identified with S_2. We use a "double-bar" notation for abstracted subnetworks, as was illustrated earlier for the Maintenance actions in the ATM example:

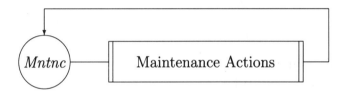

Abstraction may be performed prospectively (before expanding the individual transitions) when it is known that all transitions must link the indicated states. In this case, abstracted subnetworks serve only as placeholders for further analysis.

Retrospective abstraction of a subnetwork after all transitions have been specified is a useful simplification device. The subnetwork that has been taken out may also be used as a source of inspiration for the design of other transitions.

5.4.3 Independent Transition Networks

A class may possess several separable sets of transitions. This often arises when the transitions operate on disjoint sets of attributes. This situation in turn often arises when a class has multiple disjoint superclasses (see Chapter 7).

The complete transition network can be conceptualized as one large transition network that is made up of the Cartesian product of the individual, contributing networks. A straightforward graphical representation of such a Cartesian product grows rapidly out of hand due to exponential growth of the required number of states and transitions. Harel [104, 105] has introduced a graphical convention for these product spaces. Two (or more) transition networks are simply enclosed in an abstracted set where the transition networks are separated by dashed lines.

For example, the following Cartesian product transition network might describe a refrigerator, with one network representing whether the motor is running or not and the other network representing whether the door is open or closed:

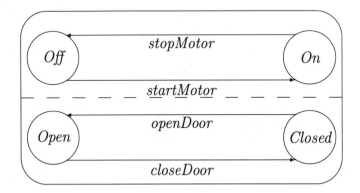

The diagram abbreviates the Cartesian product of the two independent sets of states and transitions that would otherwise need to be represented explicitly as:

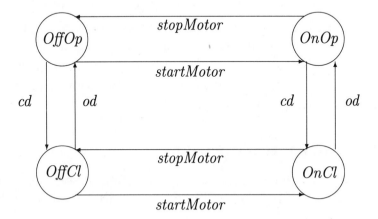

Here, *cd* and *od* abbreviate *closeDoor* and *openDoor*. The state *OffOp* represents the motor being off and the door being open. The others are defined similarly.

The use of independent "parallel' transition networks adds conciseness and understandability to models, but may be applied only when different parts of a transition network are truly disjoint. As a safeguard, the states, guards, and actions within the transitions in one independent network should not refer to attributes used in the definition of the other networks.

5.5 Summary

The behavior of objects may be modeled using transition networks. There are no restrictions on the complexity of an action associated with a transition. It is the responsibility of the analyst to avoid "magical" actions that require an analysis by themselves. For this and other reasons, we argued against assuming parallelism inside objects (but see Chapter 9).

The states of our transition networks are static. We avoid so-called "active" states. We advertised defining states rigorously via properties of attribute value configurations. This opens the door for more discipline by being able to show that different states, as suggested by their names, are different indeed. Transitions may be described in a similarly rigorous fashion. In particular, the exclusion of guards associated with different transitions emanating out of a state may be demonstrated.

State abstraction, subnet abstraction and multiple transition networks may be employed to reduce complexity of transition networks.

5.6 Further Reading

Most OO analysis methods use transition networks in some form or another to describe the behavior of objects. The variant used by Shlaer and Mellor [200, 203] associates actions with states instead of with transitions as we have done (and most others do). Their actions are executed when a state is entered. They advocate using data flow diagrams to detail the description of an action.

Embley et al [89] are among those arguing for parallelism inside objects:

> Besides interobject concurrency, objects in OSA may exhibit intraobject concurrency. Intraobject concurrency allows an individual object to exhibit concurrent states or actions. A person, for example, may be talking on the phone while taking notes. A copy machine can copy and staple at the same time.

A different approach to object behavior is advocated by Wirfs-Brock et al [230]. Their CRC method avoids modeling of prototypical objects independent of the role(s) played in a target system. Instead, behavior is formulated in terms of client-server contracts, responsibilities and collaborations.

5.7   Exercises

1. Show the mutual exclusion property for the states *closed, ajar* and *open* defined for a *Door* in this chapter.

2. Assume that an *Account* has a state S with two emanating transitions *Withdraw* and *Deposit*, both leading back to S. Formulate guards for these transitions and show that they satisfy mutual exclusion.

3. The car cruise control machinery actually supports more functionality:

   > When the system is activated, tapping the SET button will increase the speed settings by small increments.
   >
   > Holding the SET button depressed allows vehicle to coast to a lower setting.

   Can this functionality be expressed by an extension of the transition network given in this chapter? If so, what are these extensions? If not, what has to be done instead?

4. Select another component of the CCC system and develop a static and dynamic model for it.

5. Give a static and dynamic model of:

   (a) A tube of toothpaste.
   (b) A VCR.
   (c) A car's 5-speed stick shift.
   (d) A racing bike's 10-speed gear system.
   (e) A chess game.
   (f) A LISP EVAL function.
   (g) A soccer or football match.

Chapter 6

Object Interaction

Object interaction patterns may be placed in two broad categories, differing with respect to the roles played by the participants:

- An event producer object and one or more event consumer objects.

  Producer-consumer interaction involves only unidirectional ("one-way") communication. Examples include a user selecting a menu item, a buyer sending a purchase order to a supplier, and a report generator sending a report to a printer. An event may have multiple consumers. For example, a stock quotation service may broadcast stock prices to all "interested" parties.

- A client object and a server object.

  Client-server interaction involves bidirectional synchronized communication. A client requests that an operation be performed by a server, and waits for a reply. Both the request and the reply may contain other transmitted data. This pattern is seen in common "service" procedure or function invocations.

Bidirectional patterns are quite popular in OOA, in part because they readily map onto the object interaction mechanisms available in most OO programming languages. This fact leads to a terminology mismatch. One might suspect that the "message passing" supported by OO programming languages would correspond to one-way asynchronous interaction. This is *not* the case. Instead, in languages such as Smalltalk, C++, etc., a "message" is a synchronized bidirectional procedure (or function) invocation. To avoid such connotations, we often use the term "event" rather than "message" to encompass either of these interaction styles and their variants.

6.1   Transitions

We will look in more detail at transition descriptions discussed in the previous chapter, this time concentrating on the interactive aspects of the guard, action, and event components of our transition diagrams. Transition notation concentrates on the behavioral properties of a single object. It describes what an object expects from the context without specifying any particular context, and how an object contributes to the context. It does this without any assumption about the context beyond the existence of event providers and event consumers.

For interactive transitions, we split the box holding the guard to separate a regular boolean condition and the dependency on an event. We leave the action box as is. The box for an optional event can be utilized to describe values that are available to the members of the audience:

transition name		
guard	action	{event}
condition	pre- and postconditions and/or pseudocode and/or · · ·	{v_{out}}
{event(v_{in})}		

S1 → [table] → S2

6.1.1   Guard

A guard may contain a condition referring to any or all of:

- Attributes of *self*
- Attributes of other objects.
- A named event.
- Data associated with the event.

In the design phase, references to objects other than *self* within guards will necessitate construction of "read-only" attribute access operations and related processing that have no impact at the current level of description (see Chapter 16). In analysis, we freely list all required guard conditions without worrying about the underlying mechanics.

Firing a transition requires that the condition *and* the event, if specified, are satisfied. If the event does not entail data transfer, it is a pure trigger, an "invitation" for the recipient to engage in a state transition. A declarative description of such a trigger can rely on an invariant indicating that certain state combinations of objects are to be maintained. For example, whether an engine is in the *off* or *on* state may be reflected by a particular indicator light. Consequently, a state change of the engine must correspond with a state change of the indicator light.

An input event may contain other data (v_{in}) sent as "arguments". A guard that depends on an external event may contain a *signature* description regarding the types of expected data, as well as any other constraints. This data becomes available, of course, within the transition network of the recipient. The properties and types of data produced by the originator of an event should satisfy expectations expressed by a guard of a recipient.

As an example, consider a transition that performs a mutation of the balance of an account. The guard expects an input event that carries the amount *mut* to be added or subtracted. This transition may insist, for example that a negative amount does not leave the balance negative. Thus, this knowledge can be added to the event guard box:

$$balance + mut \geq 0.$$

6.1.2 Action

An action is a terminating activity that can affect local attributes. Action components may be broken into two categories:

· changes in attribute values, and
· embedded client-server interactions that help the object obtain the listed state transition.

For example, an *Account* withdrawal transition may result in the adjustment of its *balance* attribute:

$$balance' = balance - mut.$$

The transition may also require interaction with another object to determine the kind of currency to be delivered to the customer. We have no special notation for bidirectional interaction with a server out of the action box. However, class interaction diagrams can provide more graphical detail about bidirectional interactions.

6.1.3   Event

The creation of an event is optional in a transition. When it is present, it has a name and a description of values (v_{out}) be passed on to the audience of the event. The intended interpretation is that these events are issued *after* the listed transition actions have been completed. The *reply* event in client-server interaction falls in this category. For example, an *Account* withdrawal transition may send the new *balance'* value as a reply value. Other events may be included as well. For example, the withdrawal transition may generate an event picked up by a transaction logging service.

Details about the audience for the event may or may not be available. If a class has a narrow purpose, it may be obvious which objects make up the audience, what their transitions are and what values are to be sent over. For example, an ignition lock of a car should pass a turn-key event to the start engine. Alternatively, we may know nothing about the audience. For example, the recipient of a mouse event is any object to which the mouse is at that time attached. To play it safe and have maximum flexibility, we minimize commitments about the audience. We will later introduce a notation that captures communication partner information. Since the audience may consist of multiple recipients, we cover not only point-to-point messaging, but also broadcasting. This facilitates "to whom it is concerned" interaction descriptions.

6.2   Sending and Receiving Events

The following table provides a pragmatic classification of transitions with respect to input and output events. Most of the entries are self-explanatory. The last row describes a transition that waits for an event, optionally receives data, performs an operation, and generates an event, again optionally passing data along to the audience of the second event.

guard depends on event	transition creates event	type of transition
no	no	internal transition
yes	no	input port
no	yes	output port
yes	yes	transducer

Service Transitions

A special form of transducer transition is common enough to single out for special treatment. We use a special notation for *service transitions*, those that process "services" provided by one object to others. This notation represents the special features of service transitions:

1. The initial state is the same as the successor state. Usually, we may label this as topmost state, *"ready"*.

2. By convention, a service transition is invoked via its transition name. We use *service* as a stand-in for this name in the guard box. It may also carry data describing the nature of the service request. The guard depends only on this event, ensuring that the service is "always" available.

3. The output *reply* event is directed toward the originator of the input event. It may carry data representing the results of the service.

4. This state – transition combination is a complete transition network (possibly in parallel with other transition networks).

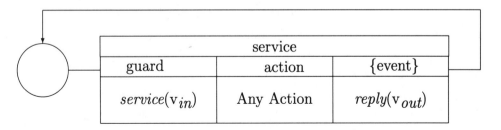

Observe the superficial structural similarity of a service transition and the emulated active states diagram given in Section 5.2.4. The difference is that the guard in an emulated active state refers to the attributes of the object, while a service transition refers to an outside invoking event.

6.2.1 Readiness

A transition "fires up" when an event specified in its guard occurs and other conditions in the guard are satisfied. This raises the issue of what will happen when an event is generated, but a recipient cannot honor the corresponding transition because either it is in a state in which no corresponding guards are satisfied or it is busy in another transition.

Transitions may define the consequences of an object receiving each kind of event when it is not in a state that ordinarily handles it. For completeness, models should specify the effects of accepting each receivable event in each possible state. Alternative transitions include the following.

Inaction.   The event is "intentionally" ignored by the recipient. A transition leading back to the originating state consumes the event without any other actions or consequences. An example is a button mounted on a floor to be used for registering an elevator direction (up or down). This button is associated with a state space having two states:

- · no request was received, the button lamp is *off*,
- · a request was received, the button lamp is *on*.

Pushing the button while the lamp is *on* generates an event that is ignored.

Queuing.   The event is queued by the recipient. A transition leading back to the originating state contains an action placing the event on a queue. An example is an elevator accepting floor button events specifying the floors to which it should arrive. These events may be queued and then serviced in some order.

Queueing implicitly assumes the existence of a state with an associated queue that contains those "remembered" events that cannot be honored right away. The intended semantics is that when such a state is entered, its queue is investigated to verify whether a transition can be "fired up". We leave the issue open how the queue is to be ordered and insist only that some commitment be made.

Exception.   The event causes an error condition. A transition contains an action leading to an error state in the recipient, an error indicator event directed to the sender, and/or events directed to one or more other error handlers.

6.2.2   Communication

Inaction, queuing, and exceptions do not address cases in which an event is issued to a recipient that is busy within another transition. Interpretations must reflect underlying assumptions about the nature of object communication. Several are available. While they may reflect vastly different assumptions, each may be employed to similar effect. Details do not impact the general form of analysis models.

Asynchronous communication. We assume asynchronous communication by default. A sender may always issue an event, regardless of the status of the recipient(s). Producer-consumer interaction involves one-way *send-and-forget* events, including those directed to multiple recipients. Client-server interaction still requires synchronized waiting by clients. Asynchronous communication frameworks may be further categorized by their assumptions about the underlying media:

Unbuffered: Any event that is not accepted in a timely manner is lost.

Buffered: The media holds events until receivers are able to accept them.

Additional refinements are possible. The media may "spontaneously" lose events with some known probability, buffers may have known properties and limitations, etc.

In asynchronous systems, senders need not, and generally cannot distinguish situations in which events have not yet been received from those in which they have been received but then internally queued. Similarly, senders cannot distinguish event loss or recipient failure from other postponements.

Synchronous communication. Analysts may alternatively adopt synchronous communication assumptions. Here, when a sender attempts to issue an event to a busy recipient, it is *blocked* waiting for the recipient to finish the current transition. Applied to producer-consumer interaction, this corresponds to synchronous "rendezvous" interaction in which the producer waits for the consumer to be ready to accept the event, but does not wait for a reply. This may in turn lead to a normal transition by the recipient or any of the above alternatives. Applied to client-server interaction, synchronous communication corresponds to one part of the process in which the client waits for the server to issue a reply.

In this framework, asynchronous communication may be modeled via synchronous communication in which every sender-recipient pair is connected by one or more objects serving as communication buffers. Conversely, rendezvous interaction may be described in asynchronous frameworks via bidirectional communication idioms in which the recipient notifies the sender on receipt.

Preemption. Synchronous frameworks may include preemption requirements as well. One may require that an event issued while a recipient is in the midst of another transition conceptually cause that transition to be "terminated". Interruptible transitions may be modeled as variants of the emulated active states described in

Chapter 5. Preemptive events may be acted upon immediately, queued, ignored, or handled via exceptions.

Preemption significantly complicates models, so must be used with care. Modeling preemption requires that analysts break conceptually meaningful transitions into their finest granularity components, thus specifying all possible "listening points" during which objects may accept preemptive events.

6.2.3   Interaction Protocols

One-way interaction may be construed as "deeper" than bidirectional interaction. A bidirectional interaction protocol may be decomposed into two one-way interactions. Other protocols, including the following, may be constructed as well. (We postpone more precise descriptions of the underlying mechanics to Part II, Chapters 20-22.)

Acknowledgments.   A receiver of an asynchronous one-way message may send back an acknowledgment of receipt to the sender. This sometimes assists timing analysis. Without acknowledgment, the originator has "no idea" how much time it takes for the recipient to receive and act upon a message. With an acknowledgment of reception, the originating object obtains insight in the triggering time (an upper bound) but its waiting time is unbounded in the absence of other knowledge.

Callbacks.   Rather than issuing acknowledgments, event consumers may generate any kind of event that will be picked up by the original producer, including a "reply" of any sort. These interaction schemes are usually termed *callbacks*, since a receiver "calls back" the sender by issuing an appropriate event. Refinements of this explicit request-reply pattern form the "syntactic sugar" needed to express synchronized bidirectional interaction in terms of one-way interaction.

Forwarding.   One object may serve as an event mediator for several others, accepting and forwarding requests on their behalf. Examples include task delegations[1] in which a "manager" object breaks up tasks into pieces (each perhaps requiring special capabilities) and distributes these subtasks to "worker" objects. In bidirectional ver-

---

[1]We use the term "delegation" in an intentionally looser sense than sometimes seen in the OO literature. We use it to refer to interactions with objects that somehow help the host perform a particular service or responsibility. We discuss other variants in Chapter 22.

sions, the mediator may also forward back a reply from a worker to the client. These patterns are described in more detail in Chapter 9.

Multicast. A producer may issue an event received by each member of a certain *SET* or other collection. Bidirectional forms include those in which the sender collects replies from any, some, or all recipients.

Time-outs. Any object engaged in a synchronized interaction may include time-outs that cause it to stop waiting for a reply, acknowledgment, or other event. Time-outs may be specified using the concepts and notations of Section 5.2.3.

Self-interaction. A producer object may generate an event for which it just so happens to later serve as the consumer. This is only as useful and common as mailing oneself a letter.

We avoid client-server self-interaction. An object cannot simultaneously wait for and perform a service or transition, since this would entail being in two states at once. In contrast, many programming languages support (possibly indirect) recursive self invocations by "suspending" one operation in order to perform another, ultimately "unwinding" back. Remember though, that analysis objects are autonomous computational entities. At a declarative level, recursive transitions raise the same questions discussed with respect to active states in Chapter 5. Any usage invites clarification. For example, if one wishes to describe objects supporting some form of suspension, the corresponding transition machinery must be described. Since recursive invocation plays essentially no role in modeling and problem characterization, we will not do so. However, in Chapter 19 we describe design-level recursion of "local" computations that implement analysis-level *actions*.

6.3 Interaction Notations

Transition network notations describe the behavior of a prototypical element of a class independently of the role that the instances of the class will play in a particular target system. In this section, we describe notations that indicate the dynamics among partners in an interaction.

6.3.1   Interaction Diagrams

Interaction diagrams are directed graphs with classes as nodes and interaction connections as vertices. The classes belong to a particular application (or a generic framework). A connection from the class *A* to the class *B* means that instances of class *A* may communicate in the indicated fashion with instances of class *B*.

We have two different kinds of connections. Synchronized bidirectional arcs connect a client class and a server class:

Asynchronous one-way arcs connect an event producer class and event consumer class:

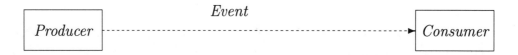

Other line styles and conventions could be introduced to abbreviate variant interaction protocols including those described in the previous section.

An interaction diagram may also include a "stepping stone" marker that glues together different views of an interaction. These may be used to resolve event name mismatches between producers and consumers, as well as to accommodate multiple producers and/or consumers. For example:

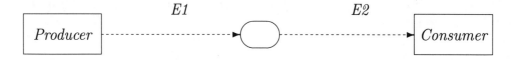

Stepping-stone ovals may be eliminated by resolving event name mismatches within the associated classes and specifically directing events to particular recipients. However, it is preferable to instead interpret them as design-level requirements, obligating designers to install mechanisms that instantiate the indicated connections. This provides flexibility in how designs may support object interaction without requiring analysts to commit to particular mechanisms.

6.3.2 Acquaintance Relations

Interaction diagrams describe the nature of interaction among instances of different classes, but they do not indicate the precise identities of the partners of any given interaction. This knowledge is generally not available when a class is defined. There are two reasons for this. First, an interaction partner may be different for each instance of the class. The class cannot "hard-wire" the knowledge. Second, we normally want to define a class in a generic fashion so that it can be used in multiple, open-ended contexts.

Thus, when a class is defined we *should* not know what the communication partners are for the instances. Instead, we should specify only the "contract" for bidirectional interactions, or the "obligations" and the "expectations" for one-way interactions. Any communication partner satisfying these constraints will do.

This position is argued forcefully by Sullivan and Notkin [213]:

> In dynamic modeling ... object-oriented analysis generally fails to externalize representations of behavioral relationships, instead casting them in terms of direct communications among the related classes. This produces exactly the intertwining of definitions that externalizing architectural relationships was intended to avoid. ...
>
> We show that implicit invocation is the dual of explicit method invocation and that adding an implicit invocation mechanism makes it possible to externalize behavioral relationships.

A generic solution for introducing partnership information is to establish an *acquaintance* relationship that relates clients, servers, and services for bidirectional interaction and producers, consumers, and transitions for one-way interaction. For example, an acquaintance relation may describe those objects involved in withdrawals:

Generally, every interaction diagram may be associated with an acquaintance relation describing those partners from each of the classes that communicate in the indicated manner. Conversely, a single acquaintance relation may cover several kinds of interaction among the listed participants.

Acquaintance relations may be annotated and used in the same way as any other relation. For example, cardinalities may be added to indicate that each sender may interact with multiple recipients. Parametric instances of the relation may be employed to describe interaction constraints among attributes of a class.

Listing partnerships via acquaintance relations normally provides sufficient information for designers to arrange that the appropriate interactions occur (see Chapters 16 and 18). Alternatively, when appropriate and desirable, these matters may be spelled out within analysis models.

For example, interaction partners may possess attributes referring to the appropriate acquaintance relationship. A client-server partnership can determine the partner of such an attribute. An event generator can similarly determine the audience for the event. Updating this relationship in the action part of a transition can reflect either changing the server in a client-server partnership or the modification of the audience for an event generator.

There are many simpler special cases. For example, this information may be recorded as attributes inside clients (or event generators) only. The identities of new partners may be transmitted as event input and output data. Also we may know all about a particular object's servers and/or audience at the time it is created. If so, we may introduce *fixed* attributes at class definition time, to be set upon initialization.

6.3.3   Interfaces and Signatures

Design and implementation level object-oriented notations collect the names and data associated with events, forming *interfaces* describing the input and output capabilities of the instances of each class. *Signatures* listing the names of all receivable events and the domains of associated arguments and results facilitate a form of partial verification. Signature verification for an interaction consists in showing that the client indeed sends the right kinds of arguments and can handle the reply. This may be performed without having to look inside a design or implementation.

Signature verification alone is *not* sufficient to demonstrate correctness. For example, integer addition has the same signature as integer multiplication, but when an addition is demanded by a client a multiplication offered by a server would be incorrect. More complete interface characterizations require that client and server expectations be matched via semantic descriptions, as shown in the examples in Section 6.4.

Of course our examples are quite small. In practice, full-blown theorem proving may be required to verify the correctness of interactions. Still, while many people believe that formal techniques cannot be applied in practice because current deductive machinery is not powerful enough, we believe instead that a key problem is the unavailability of solidified annotation languages and the unavailability of sizable collections of knowledge formulated in such annotation languages to analysts, designers and implementors.

The story becomes more complicated when asynchronous one-way interaction is considered. Signature characterizations are again insufficient. But adding semantic characterizations, as for the synchronized case, is still not enough. We have to ascertain, among other things, that a recipient obtains the correct one in a series of events generated by an event producer; see [73, 90, 15].

Interface descriptions play a more central role in the design phase than in analysis. We postpone the introduction of interfaces and signature-based methods to Part II of this book. However, if desired, interface descriptions may be constructed as summary models in analysis. The design notation presented in Part II includes constructs useful in signature verification and related efforts.

6.4   Examples

We revisit the refrigerator example briefly introduced in Chapter 5. The top half of the network belongs to the engine of the refrigerator. The bottom half describes whether the door is open or closed:

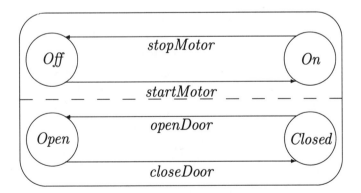

We will add the requirement that the motor will go in the *off* state as a side effect of the *openDoor* transition, provided the motor is in the *on* state. We will expand the relevant transitions of the door and the motor. Since both of them are generic, we are not able to express the requested causal connection. That is not surprising after all. Why would a door know anything about motors? Why would we "hard-wire" a dependence of a motor's behavior on changes in a door?

The *openDoor* transition for the door may be described by elaborating its guards, actions, and events. Because a door can always be opened when it is closed, the condition for the transition is just *TRUE*. However, someone has to open the door. The transition requires an external event, *OpenDoor*, that does not carry any other associated data. There are no required actions associated with the transition, but the event *DoorOpens* must be generated before entering the *Open* state. Again, this event carries no data.

Closed ───

Open Door		
guard	action	{event}
TRUE		*DoorOpens*
OpenDoor		

──→ Open

We proceed with the similar transition for the motor. The relevant part of this transition is the guard in which we see the dependency on an event *haltMotor*:

On ───

Stop Motor		
guard	action	{event}
TRUE		
haltMotor		

──→ Off

The motor may simply ignore a *haltMotor* event when it is already off:

Off ───

Ignore Halt Request		
guard	action	{event}
TRUE		
haltMotor		

──→ Off

Observe that the names of the events generated by the door and expected by the motor do not match up. We may "glue" them together using interaction diagrams.

We can hook up the event generated when the door opens with the event expected by the motor to stop when it is running. For illustration, we also extend the example with a temperature sensor that generates an event *TmpLow* when the temperature drops below a certain threshold. Thus we have effectively modeled a disjunction of events that can cause the motor to halt:

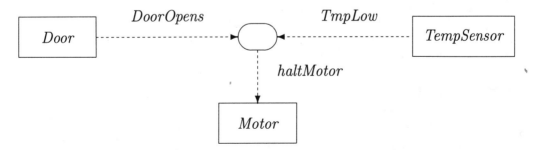

6.4.1 ATM

We revisit a fragment of the ATM transition network from Chapter 5:

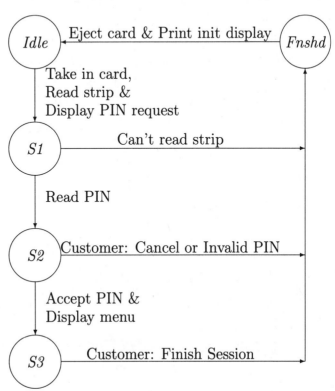

In Section 5.3.1 we described the transition:

Read PIN			
guard	action	{event}	
OK(stripInfo)	*stripInfo'*=ok *PINInfo'*=GetPIN		

S1 — [table] → *S2*

Reconsider how the ATM object may obtain the PIN data. The original *Read PIN* transition induces the "magical" function GetPIN to obtain the PIN data. We will be more realistic here. Our ATM object is the overall controller for the physical ATM. We assume that we have similar control objects for physical subsystems such as the CRT output, the keyboard, the card reader, the bill dispenser, etc.

Let *atmInput* be the intermediary object between the physical keyboard subsystem and our ATM control object. A synchronous interaction to obtain the PIN data can be achieved by replacing GetPIN by GetPIN(*atmInput*). We assume then that the *atmInput* has a service transition called GetPIN which in its action part produces either the expected PIN number collected from the keyboard (in some agreed representation) or the information that the Cancel button was activated.

Alternatively, we can establish an asynchronous connection. We assume then that the *atmInput* object has a transition Provide-user-input, which sends its data via an event Keyb-in that carries the data obtained from the keyboard (ignoring time-outs):

Provide-user-input			
guard	action	{event}	
User-data	*Out'* = *(PIN-data* *or Cancel)*	*Keyb-in(Out')*	

Subsequently, this event can be picked up by the *ATM* via the transition:

Read PIN			
guard	action	{event}	
OK(stripInfo) *KB(PINInfo')*	*stripInfo'* = ok		

S1 — [table] → *S2*

In order for this work, we still have to "glue together" the event producers view with the event consumers view in an interaction diagram:

We can increase our confidence that two communication partners have been plugged together correctly by describing from both ends what is produced and what is expected. As a first approximation (ignoring event sequencing) we get for the event producer:

4-digit-number(Out') or Out' = "cancel"

and for the event consumer:

4-digit-number(PINInfo') or PINInfo' = "cancel".

Thus, we have a good match indeed.

Client-Server Interactions

We continue with an example connecting two classes in a client-server relationship. We assume that an ATM class has a transition named *PINCheck*. This transition has in its action box an invocation of an Authenticator server. A card code and user-provided PIN are sent to the Authenticator possessing a service transition named *CheckPin*. This server will reply with *yes* or *no* depending on whether the correct PIN has been provided.

<table>
<tr><td>ATM</td><td>PINCheck(cardId, userPin) = out
◇- ◄
CheckPin(idOfCard, PIN) = reply</td><td>Authenticator</td></tr>
</table>

This diagram gives us confidence that the requested service formulated by the client transition corresponds with the functionality offered by the server transition.

This confidence may be strengthened by specifying the domains of the exchanged data. For example, the two input arguments could be passed along as strings of digits of a certain length. The output could be a boolean value in any agreed on notation.

We can be even more precise when both interaction parties more fully specify what they expect and what they can offer. We may then verify that these descriptions match up. For example, the client could expect that the reply value, which it refers to as *out*, satisfies:

$$out \; = \; Encrypt(cardId, \; userPin),$$

where *Encrypt* stands for a particular one-way algorithm. Similarly, the server may offer to return:

$$reply \; = \; Encrypt(idOfCard, \; PIN).$$

This would settle the matter; expectations and obligations do indeed match. Observe that for this to succeed both parties have to agree on a common annotation vocabulary.

6.5   Summary

In one-way interactions, a producer generates events that are picked up by one or more event consumers. In synchronized bidirectional interaction, the client waits for the server to reply to a request. There are additionally three strategies for dealing with the situation in which a recipient of an event cannot handle it right away, ignoring the event, queuing it, or raising an exception. Many variant communication and interaction protocols exist.

Interaction diagrams are useful in the construction of a target model. Strict encapsulation means that we do not have to conform to incidental naming conventions of services and/or events. Thus we employ "glue" conventions to bridge mismatches between clients and consumers and between event producers and event consumers.

Knowledge of the actual partners in any interaction need not, and normally should not be known when a class is created. Acquaintance relations may be used to describe these partners. Verification of interaction specifications may be performed by analyzing the expectations and offerings of each participant.

While we have employed a purely declarative framework, we have by now defined the semantics of an abstract object computational model that may be exploited in design. The following figure summarizes some highlights of a "typical" object using a partly *ad hoc* notation.

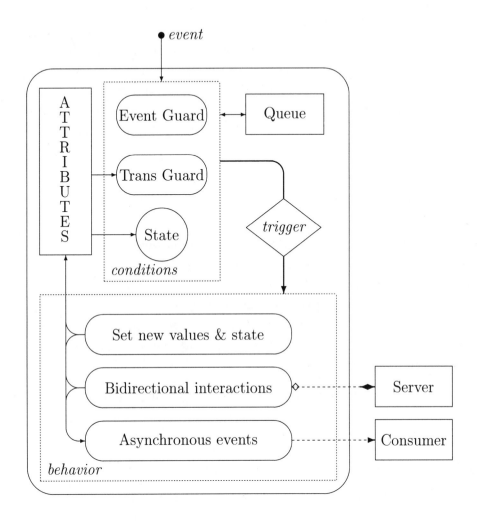

6.6 Further Reading

Alternative views on behavior specification may be obtained by abstracting away from the OO perspective. Davis [70] surveys techniques for representing behavioral requirements. These include finite state machines; StateCharts [104, 105]; Petri nets; decision tables and trees; PDL (Programming Design Language), also known as structured English and pseudocode; REVS (Requirements Engineering Validation System) [71, 23, 8], an approach for "stimulus rich" applications; RLP (Requirements Language Processor)[68, 69], an approach emphasizing the use of typical dialogs or stimulus-response sequences; SDL (Specification and Design Language) [191], a graphical language supporting the primitives state, stimulus, response, task, and decision; and PAISley (Process-oriented, Applicative, and Interpretable Specification Language) [236, 237], an executable language for describing embedded systems.

At the very least, we may conclude that the quest for a proper behavior specification is not a recent enterprise. The main twist that OO provides is the decomposition of a system description in weakly dependent entities that interact according to compatible protocols.

6.7 Exercises

1. Classify the following as asynchronous, synchronous, both, or neither:
   (a) Interactions between the cogwheels in a gearbox.
   (b) Interactions between people in a conversation.
   (c) Interaction between a typist and the keyboard.
   (d) Interactions between a citizen and the state regarding tax payments.
   (e) The flows of liquids in a system of reservoirs, sinks, pressure regulators, valves, junctions, pumps, etc.

2. Model the interaction protocols of a business telephone system you know, perhaps including:
   (a) Dialing.
   (b) Call forwarding.
   (c) Voice mail.
   (d) Automatic callbacks.
   (e) Holding.
   (f) Conference calls.

3. Consider an elevator. (a) Model the interactions between buttons on floors, buttons in the elevator, the elevator controller, etc. (b) Add multiple elevators.

4. Reconsider the refrigerator with a motor, a temperature sensor, and a door. The motor turns on and off primarily as prescribed by the temperature sensor. However the motor also halts when the door is opened and restarts when the door is closed, provided that it is supposed to run according to the temperature sensor. Describe the classes of all relevant entities, and give the transition networks. Try introducing a motor controller object.

5. Consider a situation in which a tap is used to fill a bucket. Can you describe this setting with objects? In particular, can you model the changing water level in the bucket? If not, why not? If so, sketch the object interactions.

Chapter 7

Class Relationships

Inheritance is a core concept of the object-oriented paradigm, emerging in two basic contexts, abstraction and reuse.

Abstraction

First, one may recognize that two constructs A and B have something in common. To avoid having to deal twice with this shared aspect, one may create a construct C that captures the commonality, remove this commonality from A and B and restore it in A and B by letting them inherit from C. Consider *Apples*, *Pears*, and *Oranges*. It may pay off to introduce the notion of *Fruit* and factor out in *Fruit* the commonalities of apples, pears, and oranges. Similarly, it may pay off to introduce the class *Account* to capture the commonalities in *CheckingAccount*, *SavingsAccount*, *BusinessAccount*, etc. Hierarchical abstraction of common features contributes to the overall human understanding of the objects and classes comprising a system.

Reuse and Specialization

A second reason for using inheritance can arise during model construction. During the construction of, say, class D, one may recognize that a desired feature of D has been developed already and is available in, say, class E. Instead of reconstructing this feature, one establishes a directed inheritance link between D and E. The more specialized class D reuses all features of E. In the programming realm, this is sometimes known as "programming by differences".

7.1   Property Inheritance

The notions subject to inheritance in an analysis, a design, and an implementation are respectively properties, computation, and code. Since classes are not described through code in the analysis phase, we have a more abstract notion of inheritance than seen in OO programming, *property inheritance*. Properties consist of declarative class features and associated constraints. (We consider only *explicit* features and constraints ruling out features, values, etc.) Property inheritance is in fact the foundation for inheritance at the design and implementation level (see Chapter 16).

Property inheritance is a relation between a *subclass* and a *superclass*. Class Q is a subclass of superclass P when every attribute, constraint, and transition network of P is also an attribute, constraint and transition network of Q and wherever P participates in a relationship Q does as well. Additionally, the subclass Q is "stronger" than P. Instances of Q have all the definitional properties defined in class P, but are also constrained by at least one additional definitional feature. Thus, the family of instances of Q is a subfamily of the instances of P. In more detail:

Attributes: If all instances of P possess attribute a, then so do all instances of Q. All features and constraints applying to a in P also apply to a in Q.

Relationships: If there is a relationship between P and a class R, then there is a relationship between Q and R as well. If this relationship is functional and all of P is in the domain of the relationship, then for every instance q in Q there is an associated instance r in R.

Transitions: If the behavior of P is described by a transition network with state S and transition T, then Q has state S and transition T as well.

Interactions: If instances of P may interact with, accept event input data describing, and/or generate output event data describing instances of a class R, then so may instances of Q.

All classes may be considered to be subclasses of a common base. We consider class *Any* to describe any object. It thus serves as the root of any inheritance hierarchy. The class defines no attributes or transitions. *Any* is an example of a class that is not directly (deterministically) instantiable. No object is a member only of class *Any*, but instead of one of its subclasses (or *their* subclasses, or ...). Non-instantiable classes are common results of superclass abstraction.

7.2 Subclasses

One can simply declare that a class is a subclass of another, for example that class *CheckingAccount* is a subclass of the class *Account*. It is, of course, much more defensible to provide a reasoned justification of why the class is a subclass of the other. In general, inheritance is justifiable when the subclass description imposes additional features and/or constraints without invalidating any properties described in the superclass.

We will give a set of more precise justifications, along with examples. In this section we focus on the definition of a subclass Q with a single superclass P. We will later broaden this to include multiple inheritance. This list of justifications is not exhaustive. Computational justifications will be introduced in Part II (especially Chapter 16).

It is certainly possible to define subclasses justified by more than one application of these cases. It is another matter whether bundling multiple cases into one inheritance relationship is a wise conceptualization. A good rule of thumb is to proceed step-by-step, while at the same time limiting construction to subclasses that have a "natural" interpretation.

Additional Attribute

Q adds an attribute to those that it has obtained from P. As an example, a *Room* has the subclass *Bathroom* with the attribute *bath* of domain *Bathtub*:

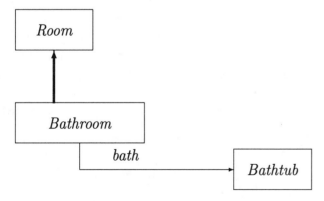

As illustrated here, our graphical notation of the superclass-subclass inheritance relation is an arc directed to the superclass.

For another example, consider a bank to be a family of branches where the headquarters is considered to be a special branch. This suggests defining the class *Head-*

quarters as a subclass of *Branch*. We can distinguish these two classes by giving *Headquarters* an additional attribute *president* with domain *Employee*:

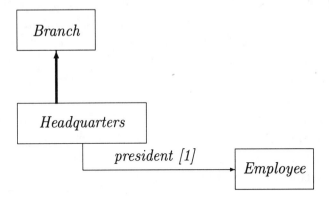

A variation on this justification is for Q to require that additional elements be contained in a *SET* or other collection attribute defined for P, assuming that P does not possess any constraints (e.g., collection size bounds) that preclude this.

Additional Transition

A subclass Q inherits everything in parent class P, including its transition network. In the simplest case, the transition network for Q is the same as the transition network for P. This provides transitions "for free" in the subclass. However, it is possible that the transition network of Q contains additions to P's transition network.

A subclass may contain additional attributes that in turn generate new states and transitions. For example, a savings account may have an attribute that describes the interest rate. As a result, the behavioral description may have an additional transition that accounts for interest debits. Other examples include:

- Let P be a particular kind of editor. Q does the same and supports in addition an undo operation.
- Let P be a particular kind of car. Q has exactly the same features, however it has the additional behavior that it can be operated in four-wheel drive.

Additional Constraint

Subclass Q may differ from P because Q carries an additional constraint on the attributes of P. For example, let P be the class of *Customers*, and Q the class of

GoldenCustomers (*GC*) with the feature that they have been customers for at least ten years.

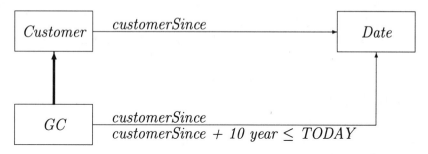

Narrowed Multiplicity

A special case of additional constraint is a narrowed multiplicity feature. For example, let P be the class of *Airplanes* with the multivalued attribute *engine* having multiplicity feature *[0:M]* stating that a plane has zero or more engines. Now let Q be the class of gliders where we narrow down the multiplicity feature of *engine* to *[0]*:

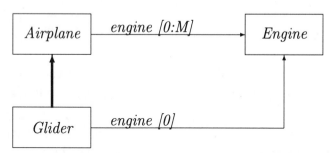

As another example, consider the class of bikes that can have as instances unicycles, bicycles, and tricycles:

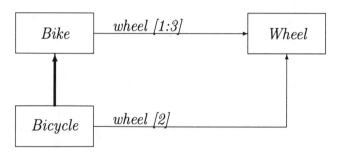

Narrowed Domain

Assume that P has an attribute with the class PR as a value domain. Subclass Q differs from P because it has for this attribute the value domain QR instead of the value domain PR, where QR is a subclass of PR. Thus, we see that the subclass notion has a recursive component.

As an example, let P be the class *Person* having the attribute *countryOfBirth* where the value domain PR is equal to *Country*. Let Q be the class *European*. We choose *EuropeanCountry* as the corresponding value domain QR. Indeed, with this choice QR is a subclass of PR and thus Q is a subclass of P:

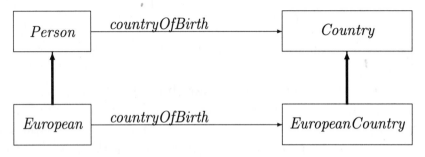

Fixed Domain

Subclass attributes may be narrowed down to fixed values. To extend the previous case, instead of being restricted to a subclass of PR, Q's attribute may be fixed to a certain value of PR, say, qr.

Elaborating the previous example, *Canadian* becomes a subclass of *Person* by fixing the value domain of *countryOfBirth* to the instance *Canada* of the class *Country*.

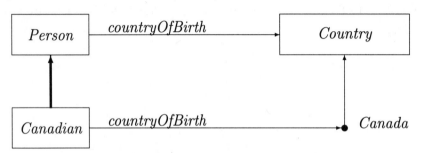

Similarly, we can obtain the subclass *Albino* out of *Mammal* by fixing a color attribute in *Mammal* to *white*:

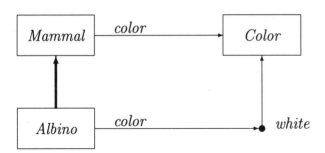

Refined Transition

The definition of property inheritance states that any property true of all instances of superclass P must be true of all instances of subclass Q. The same remarks thus hold for each transition individually. As with static properties, refined transitions may impose *additional* constraints as long as they do not conflict with those of their bases. In particular:

1. The guard in Q's version of a transition must be true whenever that in P's version is true. A guard describing input event data (arguments) in Q's version must be no more restrictive than that in P's version. Subclass versions may even accept less constrained data than the base. (This is sometimes termed *argument contravariance.*)

2. Q's version may include additional actions, for example, to set attributes listed in Q but not P. It may also include different actions that have equivalent effect with respect to the state and attribute settings defined for P, as long as they do not invalidate properties that hold for P. For example, an action that results in an attribute being set to *true* in P's version cannot be redefined to set it to *false* in Q's version.

3. Q's version may list additional output events. For example, a checking account deposit transition may generate a *makeReceipt* event in addition to updating the balance. Also, output event data (results) in Q's version must obey P's constraints. Subclass versions may even *strengthen* guarantees about reply values. (This is sometimes termed *result covariance.*)

Most considerations governing guard, action, and event refinement impact subclassing mechanics with respect to the interfaces and signatures employed at the design level (Chapter 21) where different subclasses describe different ways of representing and computing properties.

7.3   Multiple Inheritance

A subclass may have two or more superclasses, inheriting all properties and constraints from each. For example, we may introduce an account that combines the features of a checking account and a savings account, a so-called *BahamaAccount*:

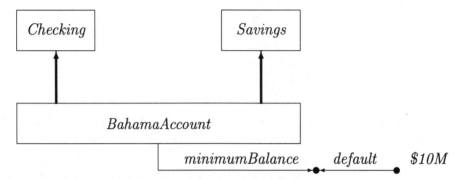

Careless use of multiple inheritance can result in the introduction of frivolous subclasses that do not describe any possible instance. For example, one may define a meaningless subclass that inherits from, say, both *Account* and *Mammal*. Such constructions may be avoided by demanding that every defined class be illustrated with at least one prototypical instance.

7.3.1   Attribute Ambiguity

In multiple inheritance, equal attributes from multiple sources are projected into a single occurrence. This is one reason that different concepts and roles should not be associated with the same name in OO models. For example, consider the class of employees who are also clients:

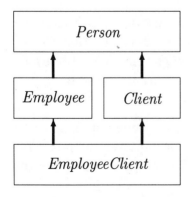

Multiple inheritance may lead to ambiguity when a subclass inherits a feature that has two or more different interpretations in the different superclasses. For example, suppose that both the class *Employee* and the class *Client* introduce an attribute *address*. Assume that the value domain for *address* in *Employee* is, say, *LongAddress* (supporting an extended zip code), while the value domain for *address* in *Client* is *ShortAddress*. What is the domain for *address* in *EmployeeClient*?

It is the responsibility of the analyst (and/or a support tool) to avoid or repair these ambiguities. Here, one solution is to redefine the class *Client* by making it a subclass of the class *ClientNA*, which is like the original *Client* class but does *not* have the *address* attribute. The *ShortAddress* attribute may then be added to *Client*. Class *EmployeeClient* avoids the address ambiguity by inheriting from both *Employee* and *ClientNA*. Letting *LA* stand for *LongAddress* and *SA* for *ShortAddress*, we obtain:

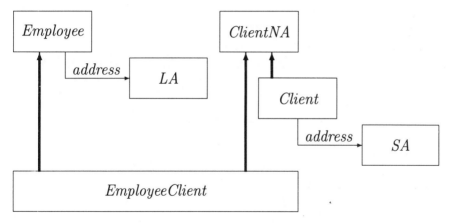

Alternatively, the ancestor class *Person* could be subdivided in an analogous fashion. For example, subclass *PersonWithLongAddress* could be made the common superclass of *EmployeeLA* and *ClientLA*. Pushing the distinction up one level has the advantage of addressing similar ambiguities that may arise in any additional *Person* subclasses that are introduced. An even better strategy is to use only one form of *Address*, if this is possible.

7.4 Sibling Relationships

The relationship among the n sibling subclasses $Q_1, Q_2, \ldots Q_n$ of superclass P may be stronger than indicated by the mere fact that they are all subclasses of the same superclass. We discuss three special cases, exclusion, covering, and partitioning.

7.4.1 Exclusion

We may know that sibling subclasses are definitionally disjoint, thus exclude each other. Among other constraints, this implies that if we have an instance of Q_1 then we know that this instance does not satisfy the definitional characteristics of Q_2, $\ldots Q_n$.

For example, clients may be divided into two definitionally exclusive categories:

P = the class of clients

Q_1 = those clients that are also employees

Q_2 = those clients that are not employees.

For another example, assume that different account subclasses have been characterized in terms of attributes and/or constraints such that they are, in principle, mutually exclusive:

$Account = BankAccount + ClientAccount$

$ClientAccount = Personal + Joint + Business$

A "+" is conventionally used in textual listings of disjoint classes. We also denote this graphically as follows:

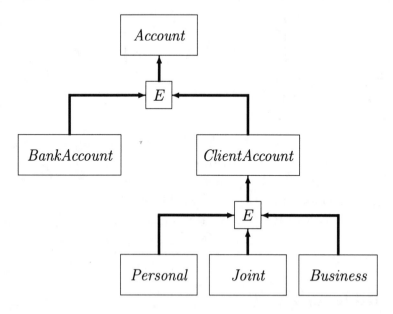

The subclasses in a family of subclasses Q_1, Q_2, $\ldots$, Q_n of P bearing an exclusion property are connected in an indirect way to the superclass P. Their family membership is expressed by connecting them first to an intermediate box which is in turn is attached to the superclass. This notation is also used for covering and partitioning. To discriminate among them, we put an *E*, *C*, or *P* in the little intermediate box.

7.4.2 Covering

A set of subclasses Q_1, Q_2, ..., Q_n of P may be defined such that any instance of P *must* belong to at least one of the listed subclasses. As in the previous case, this property applies to any actual collection of instances of P.

An ill-defined example is a classification of humans into children, adults and elderly. This yields overlap because the boundary between children and adults is fuzzily defined and a particular person can be considered to belong to more than one class.

As a precise example, consider a classification of bank clients in three overlapping categories, where the ambiguity of a client qualifying for more than one category is to be resolved at the discretion of a branch manager:

P = the class of clients
Q_1 = regular clients with balances less than \$1M
Q_2 = golden clients with balances over \$0.8M but less than \$1B
Q_3 = platinum clients with balances over \$0.8B.

7.4.3 Partitioning

When a set of subclasses Q_1, Q_2, ..., Q_n of P satisfy the exclusion property *and* the covering property, we have a *partitioning* of P.

We have encountered a partitioning already in the example:

P = the class of clients
Q_1 = those clients that are also employees
Q_2 = those clients that are not employees.

Every client is either an employee or not, thus we have the covering property. We agreed already on the exclusion property.

As another example, consider the classification of people according to which region of the world in which they reside: Africa, America, Antarctica, Asia, Australia, Europe, Oceania. These categories cover the world and exclude each other. A sometimes-useful technique for transforming an exclusion into a partitioning is to define an "other" class that describes all features not possessed in the exclusive classes otherwise defined. This "other" class may later be expanded into subclasses. For example, people of the world could be partitioned simply as:

Citizen = American + NonAmerican

Later, if necessary, the *NonAmerican* class could itself be partitioned:

    NonAmerican = European + African + . . .

In turn, each of these may be subject to further refinement, for example:

    European = British + Continental.

Partitioning sibling classes often makes them easier to reason about. All possible instance classifications are accounted for. Partitioning properties (when they can be ascertained) also have ramifications for design and subsequent implementation. For example, they sometimes simplify the construction of conditional expressions. When we know about or have estimates of the relative sizes of a partitioning, we should register these insights as well.

If some instances may belong to the superclass only, and not of any particular subclass, then these measures do *not* partition all instances into exactly one of the subclasses. For example, people whose citizenship may change can be described only as *Citizen*, not one of its subclasses. When variability on such a dimension is the norm, the entire subclass structure is usually best employed to describe partitioned *attributes* of instances of other classes, not as the main classification hierarchy.

7.4.4   Multiple Relationships

A class may bear more than one family of exclusions, coverings and/or partitionings. These sets are *independent* (or *orthogonal*) when the intersection of any tuple of subclasses taken from the different characterizations is nonempty. As an example, consider the following sets of properties describing *Humans*:

    Nationality = American + NonAmerican

    Gender = Female + Male

    Height = Short (< 1.6m) + *Medium + Tall* (> 1.8m).

All crossings are permitted. For example, the intersection of Americans, females, and people of height less than 1.6m leads to a meaningful class.

Assuming that each of these have been described as subclass structures, there are two variant techniques for using them to derive new subclasses, attribute narrowing and *mixin*[1] inheritance. In the first, properties are listed as attributes of a base class, and narrowed in subclasses. The superclass may list unconstrained domains, and the subclass constrained ones:

---

[1]The term "mixin" has grown to be used so commonly in a particular technical sense to have lost its hyphen. This also true of a few other terms, including "callback".

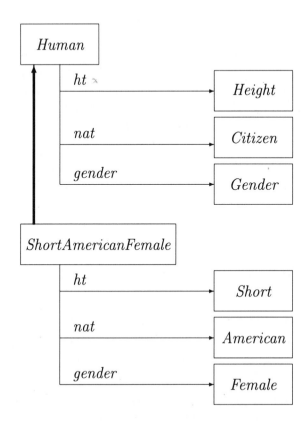

Using mixin inheritance, classes representing completely independent properties are "mixed together" via multiple inheritance in the target class. The superclasses used in mixin inheritance are often totally useless, and even unnatural by themselves, but readily combine with others to form meaningful classes. For example:

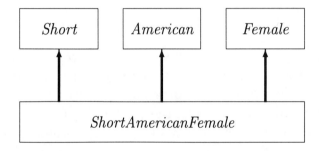

Independence

The previous example illustrated two different strategies for relating partitioned attribute structures through inheritance. While similar, these are *not* always equivalent in effect. For example, consider a *MailingLabel* class with a set of attributes containing no explicit codependency constraints:

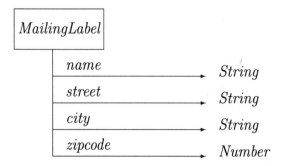

While unstated, there *are* some implicit constraints among the attributes, especially the fact that together they describe an actual postal address. However, these constraints are not even specifiable without recourse to a model of the entire postal system, and thus, probably, of the entire planet.

There are many ways in which these properties could have been factored into classes. One extreme is to create a class for each attribute and then to use multiple inheritance to bind them together:

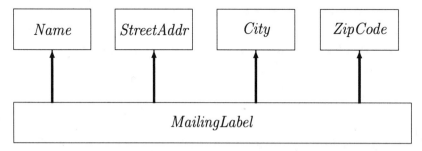

This class structure suggests that the different aspects of a *MailingLabel* may be viewed "in isolation". But this is not necessarily true, especially if each of the mixed-in classes contains a transition that changes the value of the single attribute it maintains. Changing, say, the *city* surely requires changes in the *zipcode*. When properties are truly orthogonal, multiple inheritance is a good way of describing property combinations. But the implicit constraints that the parts together form a legal address indicate otherwise here (and in nearly all similar situations). Most often, interdependencies are much more explicit than in this example, thus arguing immediately against multiple inheritance.

Here, an intermediate factoring is more attractive. By isolating the address properties in an *Address* class, we can still structurally reflect the cohesion of the address attributes. The *MailingLabel* class then connects the address to a name. By doing this, we will have created an *Address* class that seems generally useful beyond what is needed for mailing label purposes.

Construction of an *Address* class is, of course, a pretty obvious maneuver. But once we have broken out *Address*, we can think about extending and refactoring this new class. For example, it seems like a bad idea to use a zip code attribute, since this only applies to addresses in the United States. It seems safe to say that all addresses, world wide, need street and city properties (or surrogates such as post office boxes, which are OK since these are just uninterpreted string attributes). But different countries have different postal codes and/or other information required on mailing labels. This could be captured through standard subclassing mechanics.

Adding Attributes

As illustrated in the previous example, inheritance may be used to help elicit and flesh out tacit dependencies among attributes. Attempts to factor classes into hierarchies may also reveal *attributes* that were not originally listed in classes, but only implicitly assumed.

For example, an *Employee* class might be defined as a subclass of *Person*, with additional attributes such as *salary*. But there may be other properties that distinguish employees from people in general that nobody bothered to list. Assuming that this class is used in our banking application, an obvious one is the predicate *worksForAB*, which is true for employees but not others, and similarly for *isEmployed*, *mayParkInEmployeeLot*, and perhaps many others.

It is sometimes difficult to avoid implicit distinctions during initial class definition. There may be innumerable ways in which objects of conceptually defined subclasses differ from those of their superclasses. These are only made explicit when analysts notice their importance in a given model or hierarchy. Leaving them implicit can be a source of error. Of course, the best solution is to add appropriate attributes. For example:

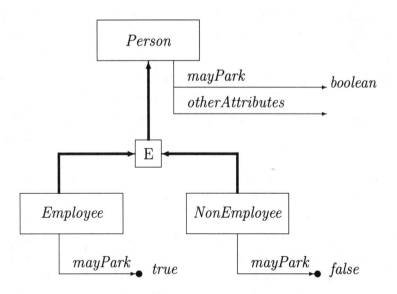

Alternative Notations

A simple and useful device for organizing attempts to factor and partition classes forms the heart of the **Demeter** tool system [141]. Classes and properties may be viewed in a notation similar to that used for describing formal grammars. In the **Demeter** notation, any class may have only properties (written using "=") or may be a superclass of any of a number of alternative subclasses (written as ": ... | ... ").

For example, suppose we started dissecting our *MailingLabel* class as:

    MailingLabel = Name Address
    Address: USAddress | CanadianAddress
    USAddress = Street City ZipCode
    CanadianAddress = Street City CanadianPostalCode

After looking at things in this way, we might decide to transform it into:

    MailingLabel = Name Address
    Address = Street City PostalCode
    PostalCode: ZipCode | CanadianPostalCode

The **Demeter** system itself incorporates a number of other constructs and notations. Various partitioning criteria and transformation algorithms may be applied to such representations. For example, it is a good idea to push attributes as far upwards in a hierarchy as they can go without breaking any interdependency constraints. Even without tools, this grammatical technique can be a valuable aid.

7.5 Set Operations

In Chapter 4 we described *sets* as extensionally defined analogs of classes. Analogs of set operations may be applied to existing classes to derive new candidate classes:

Intersection. For example, those persons who are clients as well as employees may be described as *Client ∩ Employee*.

Summation. For example, household furniture may be described as ∪(*Table, Chair, Couch, Bed*).

Subtraction. For example, persons who are clients but not employees may be described as *Client \ Employee*.

Class intersection (∩) has been encountered before. It corresponds to multiple inheritance. Class summation (∪) is similar to abstraction into common superclasses, and subtraction (\) is similar to specialization via partitioning.

However, the subclass relations described earlier are based on *properties* of instances while these set operations focus on the families of instances themselves. While they may be used directly, set expressions are often better viewed as invitations to recast the resulting classes in terms of properties and then apply the resulting mechanics.

Moreover, these operations must be applied carefully to avoid the definition of meaningless classes. For instance, the class *RectangularAccount* is obtained by intersecting Rectangle and Account. Similarly, *EvenNumber* and *NonEvenNumber* surely yield an empty intersection because they form a partitioning of numbers. *Raven* and *Albino* are also not recommended for intersection. Subtracting *Adult* from *Human* is fine. The reverse subtraction is troublesome.

7.6 Inheritance of Relations

Inheritance may also be used to abstract and refine relations. Justifications for how a relation *S* can become a specialization of a relation *R* are similar to those for classes. The most common forms follow.

Additional Constraint

Relation S differs from R because the domains of S are subject to an additional constraint. For example, consider the relation between ATMs and branches with respect to where the ATMs are located. Some (perhaps most) of the ATMs reside at the same location of a particular branch. Others are in malls, airports, etc. The relationship *ATMAssociatedWithBranch* (*As*) is uncommitted about the location of an ATM. The refined relation *ATMAttachedToBranch* (*At*) holds only for attached ATMs:

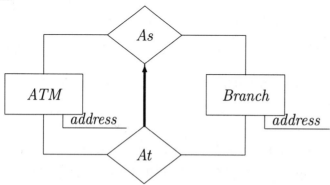

$$ATM.address = Branch.address$$

Narrowed Domain

A relation may be specialized by narrowing down one or more of its domains. For example, consider the subrelation of *fraudulent* account ownership. Letting *Crim* stand for *CriminalClient*, *LAcc* for *LaundryAccount*, and *FrOwn* for *FraudulentOwn*:

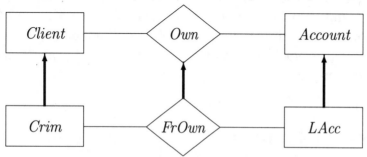

Similarly, a *Transfer* relationship between accounts may be specialized to an *InterestTransfer* between *BankAccount* and *Savings*. Letting *Trans* stand for *Transfer*, *BA* for *BankAccount*, and *ITrans* for *InterestTransfer*:

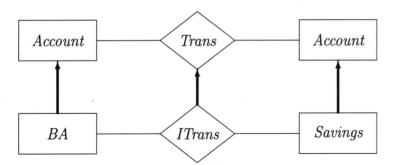

A narrowed domain may also result from multiple inheritance. For example, If we have been convinced that we can safely create *EmployeeClient*, we can use this class to refine an *Own* relationship into an *Own** subrelationship, as in:

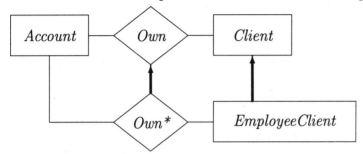

A more classic example of domain narrowing is the ternary relation $R(i, j, k)$ among the integers i, j, and k corresponding to addition:

$$i + j = k$$

and the ternary relation $S(e, f, g)$ among the *even* integers e, f, and g also with:

$$e + f = g.$$

Fixed Domain

Fixing a domain of S to a specific value in the corresponding domain of R effectively means that the arity of the relation S is less than the arity of R. For example, consider again the ternary relationship $R(i, j, k)$ among the integers i, j, and k corresponding to:

$$i + j = k,$$

A refined relation $S(i, k)$ can describe successors by fixing $j = 1$:

$$i + 1 = k.$$

This may be viewed as a projection of the ternary relation R to the special binary relation S:

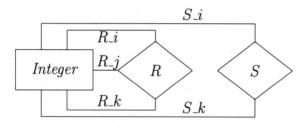

7.7   Summary

Redundancies among classes can be factored out using (multiple) inheritance. Inheritance lays the foundation for abstraction as well as for a powerful version of reuse. Inheritance may also induce relationships among sibling classes, including exclusion, covering, and partitioning. Another approach to deriving classes focuses on set operations. A second use of inheritance refines relationships in order to achieve similar abstraction and redundancy reductions.

7.8   Further Reading

Representative approaches to OO inheritance and subclassing are described in the books edited by Lenzerini et al [139] and Shriver and Wegner [205]. A somewhat more formal framework for enumerating subclass justifications may be found in [134]. Opdyke [171] discusses other pragmatic issues in the factoring of classes.

We have been careful in this chapter to stay away from code inheritance in order to deal first with property inheritance, the foundation of what some others call subtyping. Some analysis methods are less conservative. As an example, we quote from Wirfs-Brock et al [230]:

> *Inheritance* is the ability of one class to define the behavior and data structure of its instances as a superset of the definition of another class or classes. . . . Inheritance also allows us to reuse code; the wheel need not be reinvented every time.

7.9 Exercises

1. We have advocated introducing subclasses through the mechanism of applying only one of the subclassing mechanisms at a time. Multiple inheritance will in general deviate from this advice. Is the advice wrong? Should multiple inheritance be avoided?

2. To obtain justification for relationship inheritance, we looked into the justification of class inheritance. Check the list of class justifiers and try to construct additional justifiers for relationship inheritance. Consider, for example, multiple inheritance for relations.

3. Consider a domain with which you are familiar, for example, a university environment, a kitchen, a hardware store, etc. Describe fragments of such a domain exploiting (multiple) inheritance.

4. Section 7.2 gave justifications for subclassness. Are there other justifications rooted in the static realm? If you cannot find others, can you prove that the given list is exhaustive?

5. Does it make sense to make *Human* a subclass of *Mammal* and *Male* and *Female* subclasses of *Human*? If not, what would be an alternative?

6. Give an example of classes related by inheritance, possibly involving multiple inheritance, where there are at least four levels of parent – child classes.

7. As discussed in [192], inheritance may be used to capture regularities of *events*. Exemplify this by creating classes and subclasses describing *MouseEvents*.

8. Consider whether one could construct classes using operators that represent:
   (a) Swedish electrical engineers residing in Melbourne.
   (b) Swedish electrical engineers not residing in Melbourne.
   (c) Grandparents with only male grandchildren.
   (d) Morning flights out of Kennedy Airport to LA or Paris.
   (e) Federal laws that have not been enforced since 1900.

Chapter 8

Instances

In previous chapters, we have modeled general properties of instances via their classes. In this chapter, we discuss methods for describing those objects that actually exist in a given target system.

8.1   Subclasses and Instances

Previous chapters have introduced core notions and notations for describing software systems. Most of these notions aim at introducing general "vocabulary" that can be used not only for describing a particular system, but also related systems. This is one reason why basic OOA techniques may be used for an object-oriented *domain analysis*. As discussed in Chapters 2 and 13, domain analysis is an activity that identifies generic, core concepts, frameworks, architectures, etc., that are likely to be relevant for the analysis of multiple future systems in the target domain. Nearly all OOA activities ordinarily produce at least some models that are more general than necessary for the system at hand. Indeed, this is a distinct advantage of the OO approach.

However, construction of any *particular* system often requires that instances of more specialized classes be put together into a system configuration. For example, most of our illustrative *Account*, *ATM*, *Client*, etc., classes have been fairly generic. They have not always included features that may be peculiar to the instances that populate *American Bank*.

The need to specialize immediately raises the question: How much class-based specialization is enough? For example, must the *Account* class be specialized to

ABAccount, or can each account object in the American Bank system be described simply as an instance of class *Account?*

When one class *adds* attributes (perhaps with corresponding states and transitions) to those of another, then subclassing is always called for unless the added attribute may be meaningfully considered as optional (*[0:1]*) in the superclass. In other cases, it is sometimes a matter of raw judgment whether a class should be divided into subclasses describing groups of instances or whether those instances should be described as variants of the same class. Initial models usually provide at least preliminary commitments about the depth and granularity of subclassing for a particular domain. Target system-specific refinements are not always bound by such commitments. Sometimes it is sensible to use deeper or even shallower hierarchies.[1]

For example, in our *MailingLabel* classes (Chapter 7), we might have been content to declare that all *MailingLabels* contain an uninterpreted *string* value representing postal codes. In that case, U.S., Canadian, French, etc., codes could all be accommodated without having to declare subclasses. In the other direction, we could have created one subclass per *City*, and grouped instances even more finely. Ultimately, we could have isolated every individual mailing label object in its own unique class.

While there can be no recipes for making decisions about when to use subclasses and when to use instances, some guidelines exist. Generally, *over*classification is easier to deal with than *under*classification. The extreme tactic of defining one class *Object* with all possible attributes listed as optional and all possible input events ignored does not get you very far in object-oriented development. On the other hand, the extreme case of defining one class per entity *can* be tolerated if all reasonable superclasses have also been defined. Others need only use those properties in which they are interested, by referencing the appropriate superclass. *Prototype*-based OO systems (e.g., the OO language SELF [222]) implicitly take a form of this extreme position by not even supporting a *class* construct. There are only individuals, along with mechanisms for creating new individuals with properties similar to those of existing ones. Class-based frameworks allow simpler descriptions of commonalities among objects. However, even here, the notion that each object has a unique identity might be interpreted in part as a way of making up for the coarse granularity of most class descriptions. Unless all objects of a class share all properties and are immutable, when the specific values of a set of attributes are required, one must describe, say,

---

[1]Similar concerns apply in the design phase, where concretely instantiable classes are defined as subclasses of analysis-level classes. Different subclasses and/or instances are constructed to reflect different ways of representing and computing static and dynamic properties. See Chapter 16.

"instance *XYZ_423*", rather than "any instance of class *XYZ*".

We illustrate other considerations with the ubiquitous example of whether to create class *Square* as a subclass of *Rectangle*.

Constraints. Subclassing is by far the best way to subdivide sets of instances that carry additional invariant constraints. For example, it may be insufficiently precise to construct square objects only as instances of class *Rectangle*. Declaring a `Square` class allows simpler expression and exploitation of the definitional requirement that squares are rectangles with sides that are always equal.

Client interactions. When different subsets of instances interact with different kinds of clients or support significantly different client applications, these clients become easier to model if the instances are differentiated through subclassing. For example, if squares are drawn by special-purpose square rendering objects, then distinguishing them as different subclasses simplifies description of the different interactions. This is an application of the justification rule in Chapter 7 for subclassing on the basis of narrowed relations. If the *SquareRenderer* is a subclass of *Renderer*, then the acquaintance relation between *Square* and *SquareRenderer* specializes that between *Rectangle* and *Renderer*.

Mutability and state abstraction. If instances of *Rectangle* may change their dimensions (and thus sometimes are square and sometimes not) then squareness constraints are not invariant, and the definition of a *Square* subclass might do more harm than good. Indeed, if the *Rectangle* class contains transitions that change one dimension without changing the other, a *Square* class should not inherit them, and cannot be defined as a subclass. State abstraction is a more useful alternative. It would be more fitting to define and employ an *isSquare* state in the *Rectangle* class to discriminate rectangles that happen to have equal sides. This state may even be defined via a *class* serving as the domain of an appropriate attribute.

Nonsubclassed groupings. One reasonable compromise for squares would be to define both *Square* and *Rectangles* as classes, but not to make *Square* a subclass of *Rectangle* or vice versa. They may however share some other ancestor that does not list mutative transitions. Rectangles that just happen to be square for a while would not belong to class *Square*. The resulting subclass structure is not always as simple or aesthetically pleasing, but can make for good pragmatics. This is entirely analogous to programming language distinctions between `reals`, that sometimes assume integral values, versus `integers`, that always do. Even though there are some deeper relations between them, they are treated as distinct unrelated types for the sake of practicality.

8.2   Metaclasses

In the same way that a class has instances, we may consider regular *classes* to be instances of a *metaclass* named *Meta*. This allows all properties of regular classes to be described in a common manner. Metaclasses provide a purely declarative basis for analysis level descriptions of object management. We can summarize descriptions of classes presented in previous chapters by defining class *Meta*, that includes as *attributes* those features we have ascribed to regular classes. One possible version is as follows:

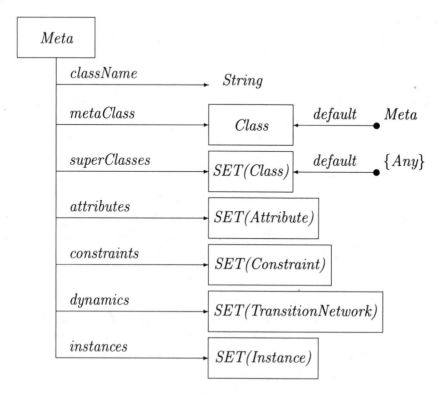

8.2.1 Object Construction and Deletion

By giving *Meta* the attribute *instances* we specify that every regular class can keep track of its instances. Describing the mechanism for creating and deleting instances is now a matter of establishing service transitions:

New		
guard	action	{event}
new	$I = fresh\text{-}instance$ $instances' =$ $instances \cup \{I\}$	$reply(I)$

The *fresh-instance I* must be initialized in accord with all constraints and defaults. There may be several variant *New* services that include requests to override defaults. A similar transition describes the deletion of an instance:

Delete		
guard	action	{event}
$delete(I)$	$instances' =$ $instances \setminus \{I\}$	$reply$

8.3 Parametric Instances

While we may use metaclasses to describe the construction of instances in a target system, we would also like to be able to refer to the instances more abstractly, without necessarily having to say anything about how or when they are created. To enable this, we introduce the notion of a *parametric* instance (PI).

Like a regular instance, a PI denotes a unique instance of a certain class which is fixed over the lifetime of a system. However, unlike a normal instance, there is no commitment about the exact identity of the instance. PIs are similar to roles (attributes) in ordinary classes in that they describe *any* instance that may occupy such a role. They differ only in that PIs describe "top-level" roles that are not necessarily listed within other classes in a system.

For example, in our banking domain, we may want to focus on the subsystem of a branch – not a particular branch, but a generic branch. We would like the ability to refer within this system to the branch itself. We may not want to freeze the branch to a particular instance, because we want to have a description that applies to any branch. Thus, we choose to represent the branch as a PI.

We use open circles to denote parametric instances. For example, our branch PI:

Usually, the most notable features of a parametric instance lie in its relationships to other PIs. These may be expressed using parametric relation instances (PRIs), first encountered in Chapter 4. For example, to indicate that a certain unique employee manages a certain unique branch:

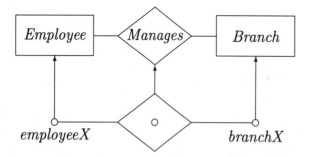

In addition, we may introduce a "utility" bank account that is associated with the branch via the relationship *BranchBankAccount* (abbreviated as *BrBnkA*). We show as well that the branch manager is the "owner" of the branch account in the sense that he or she is *Authorized* to deal with this account:

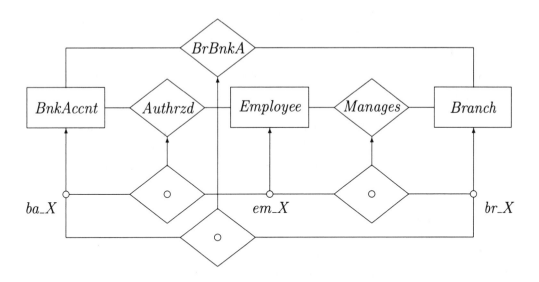

An alternative to using multiple PIs is to construct a class *System* that includes as attributes all stable instances in the system. A single PI of class *System* may then be used to represent the system. The attributes of *System* may be constrained using parametric relation instances in exactly the same way as is done for PIs.

8.4 Summary

Instances must be specified to populate a particular system. Description of target-system-specific instances is sometimes facilitated by subclassing. Metaclasses provide a declarative framework for describing class features and object construction and deletion. Networks of parametric instances joined by parametric relation instances express features and constraints of the instances in a target system. These allow for the construction of generic models where we need instances, but do not as yet want to commit to what these instances are.

8.5 Further Reading

There are few existing alternatives to the constructs described in this chapter. An exception is Embley et al [89] who introduce (in addition to instances) the notion of a class that has only a single instance. This facilitates the representation of top level notions such as "the president of the company", "the personnel department", "headquarters", without having to be specific about a unique president, personnel department or headquarters.

The reader interested in meta-stuff is encouraged to study [128]. A quote from its introduction:

> Metaobject protocols are interfaces to the language that give users the ability to incrementally modify the language's behavior and implementation, as well as the ability to write programs within the language.

8.6   Exercises

1. Consider making a model of an elementary school. What classes, specialized classes, and parametric instance(s) would you introduce?

2. Extend the transition network of *Meta* to describe

    (a) The introduction and removal of user class attributes.
    (b) The introduction and removal of user classes.

Chapter 9

Ensembles

The bottom-up flavor of the object-oriented paradigm sometimes causes the analysis of large systems to be problematic. While inheritance provides *property* abstraction and decomposition mechanisms not available in other methods, it does not provide *task* decomposition mechanisms equivalent to those found in structured analysis (SA). Every process in an SA data flow diagram (DFD) can be "naturally" decomposed into a sub-DFD in which the subprocesses together achieve the required top level data transformations. In this chapter, we describe constructs offering these decomposition advantages while at the same time preserving the inheritance and behavior modeling advantages of OO.

Decomposition serves several related needs in software development. Large problems must be subdivided so they may be addressed by multiple analysts. Independence among the pieces of decomposed problems leads to more tractable modeling and reasoning. Also, the practical design and implementation of systems is possible only when these different pieces can be constructed independently of others. We can appreciate the need for decomposition when we look at some of the entities occurring in some large systems:

A large corporation: a division, a department, an employee, a project, a production unit, a product, an order, a floor in a building, a location code, etc.

An airline system: a flight, an airplane, a flight attendant, a client, a flight schedule, a special meal order, a service schedule, a luggage door, a payment scale, etc.

A bank: an interest rate, a branch office, a teller machine, a corporate account, a loan officer, the overseas department, a monthly statement, etc.

One cannot deny objecthood to any of these notions. However, their juxtaposition imparts an uneasy feeling. The notions and methods described in previous chapters do not provide the requisite means for decomposing problems into relatively independent pieces. To resolve this situation, we introduce different abstraction levels via special objects, *ensembles*, whose properties facilitate task decomposition and a top-down analysis mode.

9.1   Ensembles

Ensembles share with other objects the modeling apparatus outlined in previous chapters. An ensemble has attributes, has an associated state-transition machine, and has the ability to interact with other objects.

An ensemble differs from the kinds of objects described in Chapter 3 in that it stands for a cluster or bundle of less abstract entities that are each either objects or lower level subensembles. These *constituents* are described as *internal* to the ensemble, thus "hidden" from other objects. Constituents interact only among each other or within the encompassing ensemble. In other words, the ensemble acts as a gateway or manager between its constituents and the rest of the system and its context.

While the dynamics of an ordinary object may be conceptualized as a sequential machine, an ensemble connotes an entity with internal parallelism. For example, in the bank domain, we can see an account as an object when only one transaction at a time is permitted. On the other hand, a loan department with several loan officers would be an ensemble because its constituents, the loan officers, may be operating in parallel.

An ensemble hides details of its constituent objects and subensembles that are irrelevant outside the ensemble, somewhat analogous to an object in OO programming that hides its internal implementation details. We have previously ignored these aspects of OO *encapsulation* to focus on the declarative structure of objects and classes. As illustrated below, many objects that we have previously modeled using unencapsulated classes are more appropriately described as ensembles.

9.1.1   Describing Ensembles

In the same way that we like to deal with classes of objects instead of individual objects, we will deal with classes of ensembles instead of individual ensembles.

Attributes can describe the constituent objects and subensembles of an ensemble. Invariant constraints may relate constituents with *self* of the ensemble to elaborate the relationship between the two. The relationship between an ensemble and its constituents may be thought of as subsuming a particular sense of the *PartOf* relation.

Additional attributes may describe features that apply to the cluster of constituents as a whole; e.g., the number of constituents. We can also capture information that applies to each of the constituents. Consider a fleet of ships that is represented by an ensemble. The individual ships share the direction in which they are heading. Thus, *direction* can be introduced as an attribute of the fleet itself.

When an ensemble has nonconstituent attributes, it may have a "life of its own". This permits development of a state-transition model. As an example, we can maintain in a fleet an attribute that records the distance of the fleet to its home port. This allows us, for example, to introduce states *nearTheHomePort*, *remoteFromTheHome-Port*, and *farAwayFromTheHomePort*, along with the transition *refuel* that refers to these attributes.

If an ensemble has been equipped with a state-transition model, we can also describe ensemble-to-ensemble and/or ensemble-to-object interactions. For example, an ensemble *fleet* may communicate with ensemble *homeFleet* representing the different home ports of the ships in the fleet. An interaction initiated by *homeFleet* could represent a command for the ships in the fleet to dock into their respective home ports. An example of an ensemble-to-constituent interaction would be the fleet giving a directive specifically to one of its ships.

9.1.2 Summary Definition

1. An *ensemble* is an object with other objects and/or subensembles as its functional constituents.

2. A constituent is a part of at least one and at most one ensemble. (Thus the constituent-ensemble relationship is *not* transitive.)

3. An ensemble mediates all interaction between constituents and entities outside the ensemble.

4. Constituents may interact among each other. In other words, constituents may bear *acquaintance* relations among one another, but not among objects outside their ensembles.

5. An ensemble is responsible for the construction and deletion of constituents.

9.1.3   Examples

We use double-vectors to denote ensemble constituents. For example, we can describe a bank as an ensemble, with its branches (and possibly other entities) as constituents:

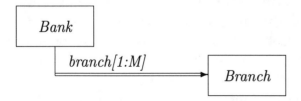

ATM machines may also be described as ensembles. Properties that we have previously described as attributes may be relabeled as constituents:

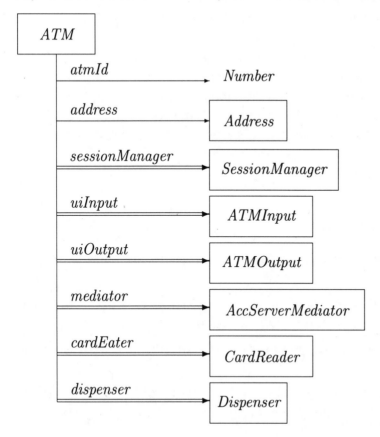

In order for a constituent to "talk" to its enclosing ensemble, the constituent needs to have a handle on this ensemble. This applies to any constituent. Thus we can create a class *Constituent* with the attribute *constituentOf* of domain *Any*. We can then introduce a subclass *ATMConstituent* where the domain is refined to *ATM*, and then use *ATMConstituent* as a mixin class. For instance, we can intersect a generic *Input* class with *ATMConstituent* to produce our *ATMInput* (or a superclass version of it); similarly for the other constituents. We show *ATMConstituent* as a mixin with *Input* to yield *ATMInput*.

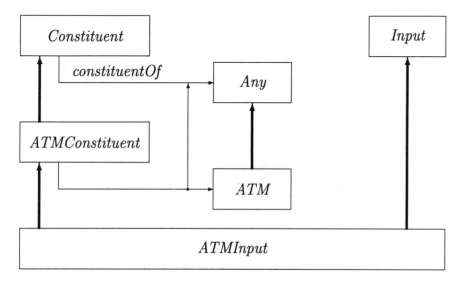

Similarly, we may consider an ATM to be a constituent of a branch:

(Note that the zero lower multiplicity bound still allows branches not to have an ATM.)

Whether it is wise to see ATMs as constituents of branches is another matter. If we do, all interaction between an ATM and external entities, such as nonlocal accounts, other banks, etc., will have to be mediated by the branch. This will entail exposing and exporting part of the ATM functionality to its branch.

9.2   Exposing Constituents

Constituent encapsulation shields the complexity of the inside world of an ensemble. However, sometimes it is necessary or desirable to partially expose the behavior component of a particular constituent.

We do not need special notational apparatus to do this. An ensemble (like any object) can have multiple disjoint transition networks. Exposure of (part of) a constituent can be achieved by "copying" and "elevating" a coherent part of a transition network of a constituent as a behavior component of the ensemble. The copied fragment must be adjusted for the fact that the ensemble itself does not do the work, but instead *forwards* incoming triggers and messages to the delegated constituent. Similarly, an event produced by the constituent directed to an external recipient must be modified such that it is directed instead to the ensemble. The ensemble will take care of the subsequent transmission to the intended external recipient.

As an example, consider a vacuum cleaner with constituents *switch* and *engine*:

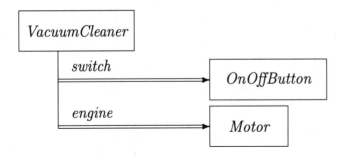

The class *OnOffButton* is a subclass of the class *Button* with generic transition network:

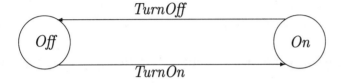

This transition network is generic in the sense that both transitions are uncommitted to what they control. For example, the *TurnOn* transition is not more than:

Turn On		
guard	action	{event}
TurnOn		

Off — [table] → *On*

In general, we do not know how a button is turned on. *TurnOn* is a placeholder for an incoming event in the guard. Similarly, we do not know what device will be affected by the TurnOn transition.

The subclass *OnOffButton* of the class *Button* will know more about the situation in which it participates, so we may specialize the transition. Let us assume that it has an attribute *vcEngine* representing the motor of the vacuum cleaner. Consequently, its *Turn On* transition can be refined into:

Turn On		
guard	action	{event}
TurnOn		*OnEngine* *(vcEngine)*

Off — [table] → *On*

We assume that the motor has a transition network with a transition *OnEngine* in order to respond to the event *OnEngine(vcEngine)*.

We may finally return to the main issue of partially exporting the transition network of the *OnOffButton* constituent to the *VacuumCleaner* ensemble. Instead of turning on a button (which can be deep down inside a vacuum cleaner), the vacuum cleaner itself is turned on. This should forward the proper effect to the *OnOffButton* constituent. Thus, we can give the vacuum cleaner a transition network:

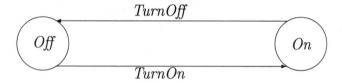

However, these transitions are merely forwarding activities. For example, the *TurnOn* transition expands into:

Turn On		
guard	action	{event}
TurnOn		*TurnOn (switch)*

Off ———————————————————————————————→ *On*

9.3   Other Decomposition Constructs

9.3.1   Aggregation

Several analysis methods approach decomposition by describing "aggregates" that are defined using *PartOf* relations. *PartOf(q, p)* stands for the notion that an object *q* is in some sense a component of another object *p*. These methods treat a *PartOf* connection as an intrinsic concept to model applications and domains.

Unfortunately, *PartOf* is in practice quite underdefined. Mathematicians usually assume that *PartOf* is transitive. Transitivity means:

PartOf(a, b) and *PartOf(b, c)* implies *PartOf(a, c)*.

However, can we entertain the following?

> Plato's stomach is part of Plato, and
> Plato is part of the Greek population, thus
> Plato's stomach is part of the Greek population.

One can object that this example is not fair. *PartOf* has been used here in two different senses, physical *PartOf* and a version of metaphorical *PartOf*. This kind of error is easy to make, especially when in large systems involving multiple analysts. Most cases do not include quite as obvious misnomers as seen in this example.

Without care, *PartOf* might mean nothing more than "is somehow related to". Nearly any use invites clarification. Do we want *PartOf* to be transitive? If so, are we prepared to do transitivity inference? Will our development tools help us enforce transitivity? Will an implementation realizing *PartOf* enforce and exploit transitivity?

Rumbaugh et al [192] provide a more specific interpretation of aggregates: If *p* is an aggregate of *q1, q2, ..., qn*, then there is a behavioral connection between *p* and its constituents (possibly recursively so). To achieve a particular operation *O* on *p*, *p* will forward this operation *O* to its components *qi*, and will perhaps perform some integration operation. This requires that all elements reachable from an aggregate via the transitive closure of the *PartOf* relationship should support this operation.

As an example, consider asking a physical entity e for its weight. When e knows that it is composed of $f1$, $f2$, and $f3$, it can ask for their weights and reply with the sum of their answers. Similarly, consider the task of copying a chapter. A chapter consists of sections. A section consists of paragraphs . . . consists of characters. Thus when all the notions in this chain support the notion of copying, then chapters can be copied "by transitivity".

This version of aggregation still leaves open several matters of interpretation. Circularity is certainly out. But what about a component being part of more than one aggregate (apart from being implied by transitivity)? Do we want that? Does the destruction of an aggregate imply the destruction of the components? Does the destruction of a component imply the destruction of the aggregate?

Ensembles were defined to provide answers to such questions:

- The constituent-to-ensemble relationship is explicitly *not* transitive. Ensembles introduce abstraction layers. The constituents of layer $N + 1$ reside in layer N and certainly do *not* reside also in layer $N - 1$.

- While an ensemble manages construction and deletion of constituents, the issue of whether a constituent is a *physical* part of the ensemble is otherwise incidental. If this fact happens to contribute to the model, it must be expressed separately.

- Ensembles must explicitly forward events to constituents. Ensembles thus allow but do not require transitive propagation of operations. The development of models that do maintain transitivity remains a useful option in appropriate situations.

9.3.2 Subsystems

Ensembles are closer to the notion of subsystems developed by Wirfs-Brock et al [230], who motivate them in a similar fashion. However, they treat subsystems as pure analysis constructs, without any implementation consequences:

> A *subsystem* is a set of . . . classes (and possibly other subsystems) collaborating to fulfill a common set of responsibilities. . . .

> Subsystems are a concept used to simplify a design. The complexity of a large application can be dealt with by first identifying subsystems within it, and treating those subsystems as classes....
>
> Subsystems are only conceptual entities; they do not exist during execution.

We take the opposite position about implementation consequences for ensembles. Like all analysis constructs, particular ensembles introduced in the analysis phase may indeed be "compiled away" in a subsequent design phase. However, ensembles with regular attributes in addition to constituent attributes can persist into the implementation and become "managerial" objects. In fact, ensembles may be seen as declarative analysis-level versions of the communication-closed layered compositional OO design constructs that play a central role in Part II (or vice versa). The encapsulation and forwarding properties of ensembles (which are not necessarily shared by subsystem notions) play central roles in the design phase.

Still, the notion of a subsystem bears a useful additional connotation with respect to development task decomposition, without commitment to other definitional aspects of ensembles. We will continue to use the term when highlighting this sense of decomposition.

9.4   Ensembles as Systems

Since we have defined an ensemble to be an object (with additional features) and since an object has a single thread of control, we may wonder whether we can model an entire *system* faithfully as an ensemble. Consider the example of a *Branch* ensemble having multiple *ATM*s as constituents. How do we ensure with this setup that multiple interactions can occur at the same time?

We give two answers. First, we can simply expose appropriate parts of the transition networks of the ATMs through the *branch*es to a *bank*. Alternatively, we can add to the class *Branch* an attribute *user* with the same multiplicity *[0:M]* as for *atm* and we express through a constraint that $user_i$ interacts with atm_i. The users may be modeled explicitly as "stubs".

9.5 Summary

Ensembles are generally "large" encapsulated objects with a connotation of internal parallelism. They are similar in nature to subsystems. Ensembles introduce multiple layers of abstraction necessary for dealing with large target systems. These multiple layers of abstraction complement the bottom-up flavor of the OO paradigm with a top-down component. This allows a divide-and-conquer development strategy where multiple analysts deal with relatively independent subsystems.

Ensembles encapsulate their constituents. Inner objects and subensembles cannot directly interact with external entities. Ensembles have the exclusive responsibility to create and delete their constituents.

9.6 Further Reading

Ensembles were introduced in [75]. Much of Booch's [39] treatment of "decomposition" may be seen as an account of ensemble definition. Subsystems are given ample attention in [230], [203] and [121]. Other methods (especially Rumbaugh et al [192]) postpone subsystem development to the design phase. Alternative high-level class constructs that are less geared toward problem decomposition are discussed in [89].

9.7 Exercises

1. Discuss whether the following pairs of notions can be in the ensemble – constituent relation:

   (a) A hand and a finger.
   (b) A country and a capital.
   (c) IBM and its marketing department (assume that it has one).
   (d) USA and its defense forces.
   (e) The USA government and its defense forces.
   (f) A bicycle and a wheel.
   (g) The 20th century and 1950.
   (h) Your feet and a smell.
   (i) A keyboard and a key.
   (j) A billiard ball and spherical.

2. Formulate some ensemble – constituent pairs in the domain of banks.

3. Formulate some ensemble – constituent pairs in the domain of airline reservation systems.

4. Describe a fragment of a transition network of an ATM that must be exposed to a branch when we consider an ATM to be a constituent of a branch.

5. An architecture of a system may be seen as consisting of a high level decomposition in functional subsystems. What role, if any, could ensembles play in architectural descriptions? (Consider that sometimes a distinction is made between logical architecture and physical architecture.)

6. We have been critical regarding aggregates and its *PartOf* relationship. Investigate a domain with which you are familiar and see how *PartOf* can play a role in it. Is *PartOf* transitive in this domain? If so, what are the ramifications? How would *PartOf* be handled in the design? In the implementation?

Chapter 10

Constructing a System Model

In this chapter, we illustrate the synthesis of a target system model using the building blocks described in previous chapters.

The reader may wonder whether such an activity is necessary and, moreover, whether such an activity is still "analysis" or a transgression into the computational realm of design. It cannot be denied that constructing a model of an intended system has the flavor of design, at least to the extent that some commitments are made with respect to (logical) system architecture. At the same time, the relative concreteness of a model is an advantage for all parties involved. Analysts are forced to think through the demands of the customer from yet another perspective. The validity of a model can be checked by having analysts and customers mentally execute scenarios. Designers will obtain an abstract model that may be transformed into an executable realization.

We will present a "vertical slice" of an OO analysis, in a sequence corresponding to steps described in more detail in Chapter 12. We discuss:

1. A requirements fragment.
2. A few scenarios (use cases).
3. A few subsystems.
4. A vocabulary.
5. A precise expansion of some elements in the vocabulary.
6. A model consisting of (prototypical) instances, specialized classes, ensembles and relationships, and a class interaction diagram that summarizes object interactions.

10.1   Requirements Fragment

We envision an ATM transaction menu that will be pulled up by a customer using a certain designated key. The menu will list several transaction services the branch offers. We will discuss several choices: an automated payments service, automatic overflow management, and overdraft protection. The customer will select one and run through a series of submenus to clarify and describe a specific transaction. We assume the usual (*circa* 1993) ATM hardware configuration, minimally including a numeric keypad and a small CRT.

ATM as a subsystem refers to the user interface events on the actual ATM machine. The actions of putting in a card, collection and verification of same, plus entering the PIN number as additional verification of account person validity are examples. The transactions available on an ATM include deposits, withdrawals, balance verification and so on. In our vertical slice of the ATM subsystem, we will discuss card and PIN entry verification and the section of the menu system dealing with our set of transactions.

Bank as a subsystem is a repository for data and an agent of events from the perspective of the ATM subsystem. In this example, we will look at the data and events centered around the three transactions being modeled, automated payment service, automatic overflow management, and overdraft protection. The bank will play a server role in a client/server relationship, where the ATM is the client and the bank is the server. The bank will also maintain a registry of all account verifications involved in transactions as well as registering billing for the three services.

Automated payments service.   A customer can pay bills through an automated payment plan. The automated payment service offers a series of submenus by which the customer can initiate a payment plan where fixed amount and variable amount bills are paid automatically. The latter can occur by empowering a recipient to specify an amount due. The customer will be able to set time and amount constraints on all automated payments.

When clients select the automated payment service, they are asked to key in the account number of a payment recipient. Once this is verified, a client specifies fixed or variable payment, the timing of the payment (e.g., one time only, biweekly, weekly, monthly, yearly, any time), and if appropriate, the payment amount or a maximum limit amount. A series of submenus will be provided to further refine these choices if necessary. For example, if the customer specifies variable monthly, the customer would have an opportunity to set a payment date and to set a payment amount limit (a payment would have to be under this amount). After everything has been verified, the client will be asked to specify a start time (now, or some future date).

The bank plays a central role in the automated payment service. It will manage payments from the checking account on the appropriate designated dates. It will register and track all variable payment amounts, including registering the appropriate amount from the recipient, checking it against any constraints and paying it on the designated date (an event-driven transaction). The bank will also make regular or one-time-only payments of customer-stipulated amounts to designated recipients on designated dates (a stipulated transaction).

Automatic overflow management. Customers may specify an account as a recipient of a payment using an automatic overflow management menu series. This enables a customer's savings account, another checking account, a child's trust account, a money market account, etc., to be the recipient of overflow amounts in the checking account. The client would enter a maximum checking account balance that, when reached, would trigger an automatic payment of the overage into the specified account.

The bank will again manage checking account balance constraints for automatic overflow management. This time a transaction resulting in a maximum overage will result in a triggered withdrawal/deposit into the designated account (wherever that may be).

Overdraft protection plan. A customer's checking account may be paid from a designated savings account in order to maintain a minimum balance. The client would enter an account number that acts as the "protector" account (i.e., the account that will pay the checking account each time a transaction would bring the balance below the minimum). Provided the protector fund continues to be well endowed with money, the balance will never fall below the minimum. This account will, of course, be verified. Then the minimum checking balance will be entered. If a pending transaction will put the account balance below this figure (which could be $500 or $0.05 or whatever), the designated "protector" account will immediately transfer funds up to the specified minimum maintenance amount.

The bank will keep track of the account checking balance and the balance minimum (and maximum if it exists). It will also keep track of the designated "protector" account balance. Additionally, it will register any transactions coming in against the checking account. If a transaction will put the checking account balance below its minimum, the transaction registry will immediately notify and withdraw the correct balance from the "protector" account. If the "protector" account does not have the necessary funds, it will register the notification for later action.

When the protector account does not have enough money to maintain the minimum checking balance, it will register this situation. When funds are available, it will immediately transfer the amount necessary to maintain the minimum if the condition still exists. An error will be registered as soon as the minimum is not maintained. When a transaction occurs and there is not enough in the checking account *and* the protector account cannot cover the minimum, an error will be registered leading to a charge by the bank for the overdraft. This will proceed on a transaction-by-transaction basis. When the protector account again has money it will automatically check the checking account balance and replenish it to the specified minimum.

A customer may "protect" the protector account. An example of this might be a checking account that is protected by another checking account, which in turn is protected by a trust account. Protection "cycles" where an account is protected by another account which is protected by the first account will not be allowed.

10.2   Use Cases

The narrative in the previous section explains the functionality to be supported in a high-level fashion, perhaps as produced by a marketing department. A first step in analysis is to extract scenarios, or *use cases* that describe the behavior of a system from an external user's perspective. (A user need not be human. It might be another system as well.) Use cases were introduced by Jacobson [120, 121], who describes them as follows:

> A use case is a specific way of using the system by using some part of the functionality. Each use case constitutes a complete course of events initiated by an actor and it specifies the interaction that takes place between an actor and the system. A use case is thus a special sequence of related transactions performed by an actor and the system in a dialogue. The collected use cases specify all the existing ways of using the system.

There are two forms of use cases. The ones illustrated here have the form of *linear sequences* or *timethreads* [45] describing the course of typical system-context interactions. An alternative version gives the interactions in the form of a *tree*. The branch points correspond to choices made by the user, with alternative continuations chosen by the intended system. These are more accurate for capturing all possibilities, and are necessary for capturing worst case performance requirements. The sequential format eliminates "pathological" continuations and is more likely to illustrate how a user's intention is to be achieved.

We provide minimal sketches of the three principal use cases. The details are mainly dreamed up, educated guesses that are not strictly justified by the requirements. In reality, approval from a customer for such extensions is to be obtained early on to avoid more costly rework in a later stage.

10.2.1 Automated Payment Service

1. Customer puts card into ATM card slot and enters PIN number.
2. Card verified and main menu presented.
3. Customer selects the transaction services menu and the corresponding menu is displayed.
4. Customer selects "automated payment service" and is prompted for the recipient's account number.
5. Customer enters recipient's account number.
6. Account verified and a menu with payment schedules is presented.
7. Customer selects monthly payment schedule from one-time, biweekly, weekly, bimonthly, monthly, yearly, etc., and a submenu refining the payment schedule is presented.
8. Customer provides the day of the month for the periodic payment. A submenu asking for an amount comes up with options such as a fixed amount or a maximum amount.
9. Customer selects the maximum amount option and provides as the maximum, $75. A menu asking for the start date comes up with options such as "now" or a supplied future date. (Choosing a maximum amount signifies that this is a variable payment amount and that the recipient will supply the required amount. The date will be used as the payment date. The recipient must supply the amount of payment by this date. If a recipient specifies a payment above the maximum amount, only the maximum will be paid.)
10. Customer selects "now" as the start date.
11. Transaction is verified and approved and the main menu is displayed.

10.2.2   Automatic Overflow Management

1. Same as steps 1 and 2 in the first use case.

2. Customer selects "transaction services" menu and the corresponding menu is displayed.

3. Customer selects "automatic overflow management" and is prompted for an overflow account number.

4. Customer enters overflow account number.

5. Account verified.

6. Customer enters a maximum balance in checking account. This maximum balance cannot be less or equal to a minimum balance established on the account. (A customer request for a maximum balance just $1 over the minimum balance would be allowed with this constraint. The customer may have to be constrained to a greater difference.)

7. Customer may select start date as "now" or fill in date.

8. Transaction is verified and approved.

9. Customer selects "main menu" or "exit".

10.2.3   Overdraft Protection

1. Same as steps 1 and 2 in the first use case.

2. Customer selects "transaction services".

3. Customer selects "overdraft protection", and is prompted for the choices of "bank" or "protector account".

4. Customer selects "protector account".

5. Customer enters protector account number.

6. Account verified.

7. Customer enters minimum balance in checking account. This cannot be more or equal to a maximum balance established on the account.

8. Customer selects "now" as start date.

9. Transaction is verified and approved.

10. Customer selects "main menu" or "exit".

10.3 Subsystems

We use templates for structuring the predominantly English descriptions. These "structured" reformulations of a requirements document help prepare for more precise graphical descriptions.

10.3.1 ATM Subsystem

Parent system(s)
> The ATM system that consists of the sum of the physical machinery and our software component.

Internal subsystems
> Communication input system
> Communication output system
> Deposit control system
> Customer card control system
> Dispenser control system
> Bank communication system
> Other account entities

Generic functionality
> Controls the interactions between a customer and either the bank to which the ATM belongs or a third party financial institution.

Clients of subsystem
> Customers,
> Service personnel

Servers of subsystem
> Customers,
> Service personnel,
> Bank system and other account entities.

Other subsystems
> (None)

10.3.2   Bank Subsystem

Parent system(s)
>   A Bank system encompassing the central bank offices and all the branches. It includes all the distributed hardware and software that makes up the bank's automated system.

Internal subsystems
>   Account tracking system
>   Deposit control
>   Withdrawal control
>   Communication notification
>   Communication input/output system
>   Gateway communication system
>   Payment calendar control
>   Billing control

Generic functionality
>   Data repository for account and billing information.
>   Communicates with other account system entities.
>   Acts as the transaction manager for the client.

Clients of subsystem
>   ATM
>   Customer

Servers of subsystem
>   (None)

Other subsystems
>   (None)

10.4 Vocabulary

A *vocabulary* superficially corresponds to a data dictionary. However, while a data dictionary prepares for the definition of data structures, a vocabulary prepares for the definitions of classes and related constructs.

We provide structured descriptions of some classes as preparation for their characterization in our graphic formalism. (We omit for now similar treatments of ensembles, relations, and parametric instances.) Later on, in design, we will reformulate graphic notations in our textual **ODL** design language, which will in turn be reformulated into a target programming language. All these reformulations force us to rethink, each time from a different perspective, what the task is and how it is to be solved.

10.4.1 Client Class

Parent class(es)
> Person

Generic functionality
> Uses ATM, produces checks, receives statements, etc.

Clients of class
> (None)

Servers of class
> (None)

Other interaction classes
> Statement, Check, ...

Salient features
> name, ssn, address, ...

Salient states
> standing: [new, below average, average, above average, excellent]

Salient transitions
> change address, add account, close account, change standing

10.4.2 Account Class

Parent class(es)
> (None)

Generic functionality

> This is a record of financial assets. The usual operations, including deposit, withdrawal, balance inquiry are supported in addition to advanced actions.

Clients of class

> Customer, ATM, Other accounts

Servers of class

> Bank, Other accounts

Other interaction classes

> ATM, Other accounts

Salient features

> clientId, type, balance, balance constraints, date and type of transaction

Salient states

> new, open, closed, constrained

Salient transitions

> created, ongoing transactions, limiting

10.4.3   Menu Class

Parent class(es)

> Main menu

Generic functionality

> The menu subsystem is the user interface for the customer. It has a series of question and/or answers and information to be conveyed to the customer.

Clients of class

> Customer

Servers of class

> Account

Other interaction classes

> Account, Client, Customer

Salient features

> transaction type menu, questions, answers, dates, submenu items

Salient states

> question, answer, informational

Salient transitions

> query, information collecting, display, traversal

10.5   Classes

A systematic attack on class specifications would describe in turn each relevant class, providing for each a static and dynamic characterization. Instead, we proceed by elaborating material in a "natural" way, driven by the use cases. These examples illustrate how an analyst may traverse the analysis space in an associative manner. A CASE tool would help track and order these activities.

To begin, we exploit and extend the description of an ATM as given in Section 5.3.1. The following fragment of the transition network is relevant for dealing with our use cases:

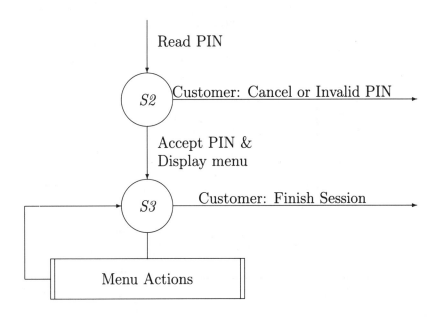

In the *S2 – S3* transition, we can do more than just display the general menu. Since the ATM card has been read successfully and a correct PIN has been provided, the owner of the card (the client) may be determined. Other information, including which bank issued the card and which branch is the "home" of the client may be determined as well. At this point, a session log is created that contains the client/customer, the date-time, and all transactions. All these initializations are done by *InitAtmSession*. Each menu choice in *S3* by the customer will lead into a subtransition network that will ultimately lead back to *S3*:

Accept PIN		
guard	action	{event}
OK(PINInfo)	InitAtmSession DisplayMenu	

S2 —— S3

10.5.1 Automated Payment Service

When the customer has chosen the Automated Payment Service (APS) option, an instance is created that describes the desired payment service. There are two similar, but slightly different services; one in which the paying client determines a fixed amount that should be transferred each time, and the other one in which the recipient stipulates each time what the to-be-transferred amount should be:

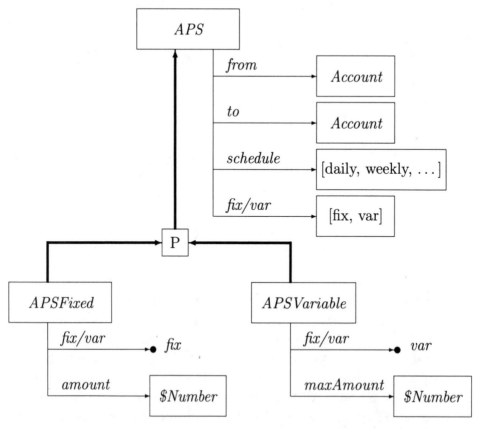

The class structure bundles commonalities in the class APS. This allows us to create two subclasses that represent, respectively, the fixed and variable payment schedules. The subclasses *APSFixed* and *APSVariable* exclude each other (on the *fix/var* attribute), and together form a partitioning of *APS*. The two classes also differ in whether a fixed amount or a maximum amount is indicated per transfer.

Fixed Automatic Schedule

Next we deal with the machinery that will trigger the proper transfers, starting with the fixed case. For each automatic schedule, an instance of FAS (Fixed Automatic Schedule) is created:

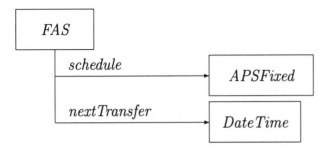

An instance of this class has a clock triggered transition that will rejuvenate itself at each activation. The initial value of the attribute *nextTransfer* will be obtained from the customer during the ATM interaction. The transition network of a *FAS* is:

Create Transaction		
guard	action	{event}
self.nextTransfer	*CreateTransfer*	
$< \$DateTime\$$	*ResetNextTransfer*	

The expression $\$DateTime\$$ in the guard refers to the current time. When the current time has progressed beyond the time indicated by *nextTransfer* the transition Create Transaction will fire up. The activity *ResetNextTransfer* expands into the description:

$$nextTransfer' = nextTransfer + self.schedule.schedule$$

The *CreateTransfer* activity may consist of creating an instance of the class *Transfer* introduced in Section 3.6:

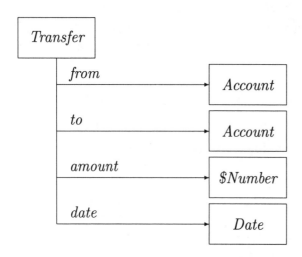

Create Transfer has access to all the information to properly initialize a new instance of *Transfer*. A naive transition network for *Transfer* illustrates how the transaction can be effectuated:

		Adjust-Accounts		
→ S1 —	guard	action	{event}	— S2 →
	True	*Subt(self.from, self.amount)* *Add(self.to, self.amount)*		

This approach assumes that the *Account* class transition network supports a *Subt(ract)* and an *Add* transition.

An instance of *Transfer* is prototypical of transient objects. It has been initialized when it is entering *S1*, it executes during the *S1 – S2* transition, and then it disappears.

This story is a simplification. System and/or network failures have not been dealt with. Also, logging of a transfer (in addition to logs maintained by the accounts) has been omitted. Observe as well that we have ignored the little detail of how to handle the situation when an account has insufficient funds for a transfer. When we discuss the overdraft protection use case, we will expand the transition network of *Transfer* to be more realistic.

Variable Automatic Schedule

The VAS (Variable Automatic Schedule) is similar to the FAS:

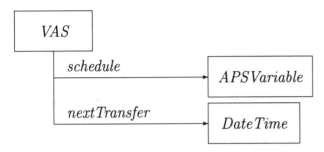

Again we have a similar transition network:

Create Transaction		
guard	action	{event}
self.nextTransfer < *$DateTime$*	*CreateTransfer* *ResetNextTransfer*	

The only difference is that the action *CreateTransfer* must access the *self.to*-account through a service transition invocation of the form

    nextPaymentFrom(self.to, self.from)

in order to determine what to fill in for *amount* in a *Transfer* instance. Thus we assume that a certain subclass of *Account* supports the *nextPaymentFrom* transition as a service that produces the amount to be transferred by the requesting account.

    In summary, the transition subnetwork of *ATM* that deals with this use case either needs to generate an instance of *APSFixed* together with an instance of *FAS* for the case of fixed periodic payments, or needs to generate an instance of *APSVariable* together with an instance of *VAS* for the case of variable payments.

10.5.2   Automatic Overflow Management

We assume here that the customer has set up a session with an ATM and that a subtransition network has been entered as a result of selecting the Automatic Overflow

Management option. The use case requires the customer to provide an overflow account and a maximum amount to be maintained by the account. A reasonable choice for recording this information is to add optional attributes to *Account*:

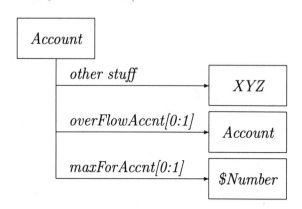

Instead of adding these optional attributes, we could have created a subclass of *Account*, such as *AccountWithOverflowManagement*, and added these fixed attributes to this subclass. The customer's regular account would be discontinued after copying over all attributes into a new instance of *AccountWithOverflowManagement*.

The desired functionality is obtained by adding the following transition network:

Transfer Overflow		
guard	action	{event}
self.balance > self.maxForAccnt	*CreateTransfer*	

The action *CreateTransfer* again has access to all the information to initialize an instance of *Transfer* that will take care of the actual operation. The amount to be transferred is obviously:

   $self.balance - self.maxForAccnt.$

10.5.3 Overdraft Protection

An account must be protected so that it cannot fall below a certain level. The level is determined by the bank as a default or can be strengthened by the client. For example, a limit set by a bank for a checking account is usually $0. The limit can be negative as is the case for credit lines. However, a client can stipulate that an overdraft protection service should be activated at a higher level than the bank's limit, for instance to avoid penalties. At the same time a level specified by a customer should be less than an overflow level, if this service is used. Thus, we have as an invariant:

bank-minimum-level ≤ client-minimum-level < client-overflow-level.

This service will work provided a protecting account is able to transfer funds. Since a protecting account may itself be protected, we will model a transfer from a protecting account as a request that is generated when a balance falls below either the minimum level specified by the client or the minimum level specified by the bank.

We are assuming that an *Account* has an attribute *bankMin* that expresses the minimum set by the bank and an optional attribute *clientMin* that expresses the minimum specified by the client. By adding an optional protecting account, we obtain:

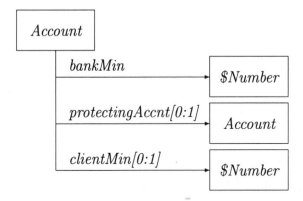

In order to model the desired behavior, we revisit the transition network of a *Transfer*. The guard in the Adjust-Accounts transition must be strengthened and the transition must be embedded in a network.

To simplify the diagrams, we ignore a minimum specified by a client. Thus the overdraft protection service will be triggered here only when the minimum specified by the bank would be surpassed. By strengthening the guard from *True* into:

(self.from.balance − self.from.bankMin) ≥ self.amount

we get the guarantee that the Adjust-Accounts transition does not produce an overdraft. The resulting transition network is as follows:

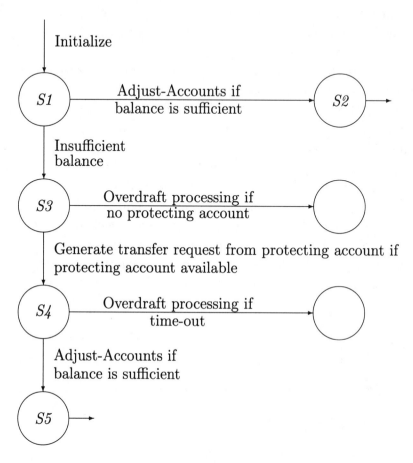

The dynamic waiting in state *S4* may be surprising. But remember that while doing analysis, the desired functionality is described concisely without worrying about performance.

In summary, the transition subnetwork of *ATM* that deals with this use case needs to fill in the optional attributes into an *account* in order to start the service.

10.5.4   Account

Several extensions to class *Account* have already been described. Here, we will look at the extensions that must be made in order for an account to be the recipient of automated payments.

First we give the class *Account* the optional attribute *nextCharge*. This attribute associates for each account in the set what its next payment should be. This information is accessed periodically via the service transition *nextPaymentFrom*. We omit the mechanism that determines the amount that is to be transferred for every account in the set and for every pay period:

An example transition specifies that every pay period, requests from accounts that have automated variable periodic payments are serviced:

nextPaymentFrom		
guard	action	{event}
nxtPmtFrm *(account)*	$Py' =$ charge in list for *account*	*reply(Py')*

10.6 Ensembles

We have many ensembles in our domain of interest. For example, we have so far been quite casual regarding accounts. We have suggested that accounts are residing in an unstructured "ocean". To be more realistic, we could have made distinctions between locally maintained accounts, accounts belonging to the American Bank, or another bank's accounts. These distinctions enable different services to be invoked for different types of accounts.

10.6.1 ATM

In Section 9.1.3 we described an ATM from an ensemble perspective. Here, we will add some details, beginning with a few new properties necessary to support the use cases. First, class *ATM* must be equipped with the following new attributes:

stripData, the information read in from an ATM card.

PIN, the data provided by the customer for authentication.

customer, the client that has initiated a session.

account, an account of a client; either the account for which overflow management is to be installed or the account for which overdraft protection is to be installed.

All use cases are realized via subtransition networks that start in *S3* and that lead back to *S3*. They all follow the pattern of:

1. Obtain the relevant information from the customer.

2. Validate the data if appropriate and/or have the customer confirm choices.

3. Generate new objects if necessary, as is the case for the automated payment service.

4. Assign the information obtained to attributes of objects.

5. Abort the subnetwork at the customer's request or because the customer cannot provide valid data.

Ensemble Properties

So far, our characterizations in the dynamic model have been high level, essentially ignoring the details where ensembles have to be acknowledged. For instance, in the transition network of an ATM in Chapter 6, we wrote bluntly:

> Take in card,
> Read strip &
> Display PIN request

At the same time, we described an ATM as an ensemble with constituents (among others):

> *ATMInput,*
> *ATMOutput,*
> *CardReader.*

A more careful and precise elaboration of "Take in card" requires describing these activities through interactions via events between an *atm* and its constituents.

We will illustrate an interaction inside an *ATM* ensemble, using the *Idle – S1* transition from Section 5.3.1.

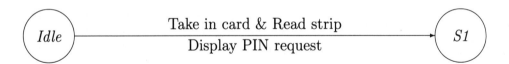

None of the actions on this transition are actually performed by the *ATM* ensemble. They are controlled by its constituents. The *ATM* ensemble itself need not to be involved in manipulating the card. The only data of interest to the *ATM* is the strip information. The display operation is delegated to another constituent. Consequently, we arrive at the following interactions with the constituents:

Idle	Get strip data & Display PIN request			S1
	guard	action	{event}	
	Get(stripInfo)		*Out(PINRequest)*	

We assume here that the expectation *Get(stripInfo)* is matched by an event generated by the *ATMInput* constituent, and dually the *Out(PINRequest)* will be picked up by the *ATMOutput* constituent.

10.7 Model

Although the context has been quite sketchy, we have assembled most of the salient ingredients of a model of an ATM.

10.7.1 Parametric Instances

Constructing a model requires the definition of some (parametric) instances. The use cases apply to any ATM and to any eligible set of accounts. A minimal model consists only of *ATM*s and *Accounts*. *ATM*s may be described as parametric instances:

In order to flesh out the model, we must provide at least stubs for the constituents of *atm_X*. We leave this as an exercise. Additionally, the constituents of *atm_X* and the *atm_X* ensemble itself have to be "welded" together. Their interactions should be described as point to point communications instead of broadcasted events. For details, see the interaction diagrams in Section 6.3 where they have been introduced and Section 6.4.1 where they have been applied to an ATM.

The next step is to add parametric instances of *Account*, adjoining all relevant classes, ensemble, and relationship descriptions.

The account *account_X* will play the role of the primary account selected by the customer for respective uses cases. Similarly, we will have *account_Y* as recipient for periodic payments and *account_Z* for overflow account and protector account.

10.7.2   Use Case Satisfaction

The final step of analysis is model validation. However, machine execution of the model is not possible. Transition actions in the networks have not been formulated as algorithms but are instead in English (sometimes as structured English precondition and postcondition formulations).

To show that the model satisfies the use case scenarios, we may role play the objects in mental walk-throughs. The use cases we formulated earlier are only the bare minimum. Exception situations and corner cases have to be investigated. How does the model behave when a customer indicates that the recipient account is the same account as the one that will be charged for the automated payment service? Is it acceptable to have automated payment services between two pairs of accounts in both directions?

Stress testing the model may reveal ambiguities or incompleteness in the requirements. Identifying these errors in an early stage will save substantial repair costs later. Prototyping efforts may be employed when there are doubts about correctness. These activities may result in the iteration of various analysis tasks, especially when analysis (or development generally) has been performed in vertical slices.

10.8 Summary

In this chapter, we have outlined an approach to the construction of a model for a desired system using notions developed in the previous chapters. The phase in which semiformal classes, ensembles, and relationships are developed is preceded with a phase that relies on structured English to describe use cases, subsystems and a vocabulary. Of course, we do *not* claim that these two phases (and their subactivities) necessarily be performed in a breadth-first, waterfall manner. Vertical slices and iterations can be done as necessary (see Chapter 12).

The model produced by an analysis relies on carefully constructed building blocks. When classes have been defined with reuse in mind, then they often need to be subclassed to fit the needs of a particular target system (see Chapter 8).

10.9 Exercises

1. Provide the subtransition networks of an ATM that deal with the three use cases. They start in *S3* and lead back into *S3*; see Section 10.6.1.

2. Assume that we have extended the use case for automated payment service such that the customer can supply optionally an expiration date for the service. Extend the models to capture this additional functionality.

3. We simplified the modeling of the overdraft protection use case. We omitted a client-specified minimum level. We also ignored the fact that a protecting account, which cannot replenish another account but which obtains funds later, should "remember" its obligation. Extend the models that we presented to deal with these omissions.

4. Modify the overdraft protection use case such that members of Congress cannot subscribe to this service. Expand the models to detail what happens when an overdraft occurs. Introduce different categories of clients where the different categories are penalized differently for overdrafts. Make sure that members of Congress always get the most severe penalties.

5. An account can play the role of a protector account provided it is owned by the client that sets up an overdraft service. Give the details of the transition network (of an ATM?) that enforces this constraint. An account cannot protect itself, which is a special case of circular protection links. Where is this constraint formulated in the models?

6. Expand the ATM model to include other services.

7. Construct a distributed bank model.

8. Devise the "ultimate" bank services model – the one that replaces the ATM. (It might use interactive television from your home, and include new services such as registering and paying everything automatically with no customer intervention, the five minute home loan interview without paperwork, etc.).

Chapter 11

Other Requirements

The notions and notations developed thus far aim at capturing the intended functionality of the target system. We have used "functionality" in a narrow sense, excluding performance specifications, resource specifications, etc. For instance, we can describe the functionality of a subsystem only by stating that it performs a *sort* operation, while omitting a commitment regarding the resources, the number of compute servers, the performance, upper bounds on processing times, etc. In this chapter, we discuss the treatment of these so-called "non-functional requirements".

11.1   Resources

Resource constraints refer to the resources that are available to the executing target system. They do not refer to constraints that might apply to the *development* effort of that system.

There are many kinds of constraints, ranging from number and type of underlying compute servers, availability and capabilities of primary and secondary storage, accessibility of networks and their capabilities, and on up to the assumed nature of system infrastructure software.

All these constraints pass right through from the initial requirements phase to the design phase. For example, compute server constraints are explicitly addressed during the design phase. Other existing resource constraints must be satisfied somewhere and sometime during design and/or implementation.

However, it is possible that details brought out by the analysis yield the insight that there is a mismatch between resources that will be available to the target system and the demands of the system. Having too many available resources can be dealt with easily, but is unusual. Having not enough resources requires backtracking and resolution at the level of the requirements specifications.

11.2   Timing

Timing constraints are usually referred to as *real-time* constraints. A timing constraint can be formulated for phenomena at the system-context boundary. Here are some examples:

1. A dial tone must be produced within 0.2 seconds after the phone has been taken of the hook.

2. After a customer has inserted an ATM card in an ATM, the customer must be prompted for the PIN within 0.5 seconds.

3. When a customer has not responded within 30 seconds with a PIN, a reminder is displayed. The session is terminated when the customer has not responded within 45 seconds after the display of the reminder.

4. The card number – PIN combination is to be validated within 5 seconds.

5. After the XYZ subsystem is turned off, the pump will continue until the temperature drops, but for no longer than 5 minutes.

We may classify these constraints into two categories (cf., [70]):

Performance: Certain actions executed by the system as a response to a stimulus from the outside, must be completed within a certain time window. Items 1, 2, and 4 in the preceding list are examples of performance constraints.

Alertness: The system (or a component) should resume control when an external agent (for instance another system) does not respond/reply within a certain amount of time. Items 3 and 5 in the list are alertness constraints.

If we look at the system and its context from a bird's-eye view, we see that performance and alertness timing constraints reduce to the same notion. When the system does not satisfy a performance requirement, the context will be alerted and will take appropriate actions. Dually, when the context does not perform from the system's perspective, a system's alertness mechanism must jump in.

System-context interaction speed is also subject to performance-based timing constraints. For example:

1. Events in a stream are separated by at least 0.03 seconds.

   This constraint indicates that a recipient of the event stream has a lower bound on its ability to process the events, and thus that the generator must not be too *fast*. This illustrates that lower bounds on time windows sometimes have to be specified.

2. Continuous one-way reliable data exchange must be at least 3 gigabits per second.

   This expresses a performance constraint for both parties in an interaction.

Timing constraints are formulated for the demands of a particular system. This prescribes that notations for capturing these constraints should be adjoined to target system specific notions.

11.2.1 Annotating Use Cases

Use cases are obvious candidates for timing constraint annotations. For example, we can annotate a modified fragment of a use case from the previous chapter. The notation $\{x\}$ denotes a state of affairs at time x.

- Customer puts card into ATM card slot $\{a\}$. The ATM will read the magnetic strip. The next step occurs when the strip can be read.

- Customer is prompted for PIN number $\{b\}$;
  $b - a \leq 0.1s$.

- Customer enters 4-digit PIN number $\{c\}$;
  $c - b \leq 1m$.

- Card verified and presentation of main menu $\{d\}$;
  $d - c \leq 0.1s$.

- . . .

11.2.2 Annotating Transitions

Timing constraints described in use cases must be propagated into transition networks. However, to keep separate reusable generic classes and their transition networks from target system-specific classes and their transition networks, we must extend only the latter.

Let's have a closer look at a simple version of a telephone use case called *PhoneSession* from a switch control perspective. A corresponding transition network fragment is depicted in tabular notation:

init state	action	result state
phone on hook	take phone off hook	phone off hook
phone off hook	provide dial tone	dial tone
dial tone	process digit	wait for next digit
wait for next digit	process digit	wait for next digit

We may want to express the requirement that the transition *provide dial tone* should take at most 0.2 seconds. This is an example of a performance constraint. To be more precise, we put a bound on the time that can expire between leaving the *phone off hook* state and entering the *dial tone* state. This transition may imply interaction with third-party objects, which in turn may trigger other activities; nonetheless, the transition has to reach its goal state in 0.2 seconds. We could use the following notation (where *poh* stands for *phone off hook*, and *dt* for *dial tone*):

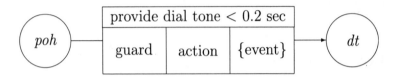

As an alternative notation, we may attach time labels to the arcs leaving and entering states, and then capture the same constraint using an expression that refers to the labels:

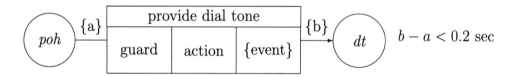

11.2.3   Annotating Transition Sequences

The second notation scales up when we need to put a bound on a sequence of transitions. Consider an initialization transition network that contains, for example, two variant sequences:

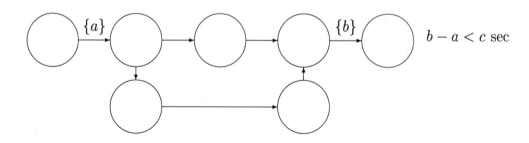

11.2.4   Annotating States

The guards of the *process digit* transitions depend on the occurrence of an external event, namely, a customer selecting a (next) digit. We want to provide for a time-out when the customer does not come up with a (next) digit. This is an example of an alertness constraint. A bound should be placed on waiting in the originating states of these transitions. For instance, a customer may be required to select the first digit within a minute, and each subsequent digit within 10 seconds (*dt* stands again for *dial tone*, *wfnd* stands for *wait for next digit*):

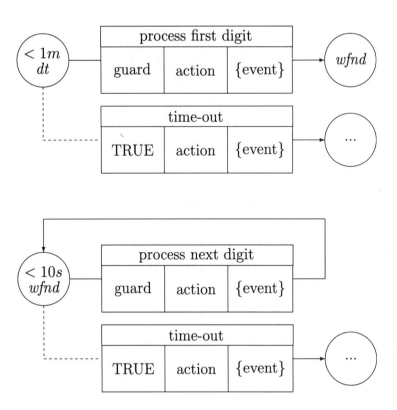

Timing constraints within the states specify that associated guards (which depend on events that describe the arrival of a digit) should be satisfied within a certain time window. (These diagrams are oversimplified in that a last digit of a number is recognized through a time-out and that special short phone numbers are not recognized.)

Timing constraints within states are not necessarily associated with outbound transitions that depend on events. For example, we can have an object m that monitors an aspect of object p, where a guard in a transition in the network of m refers to the state of affairs of p. When the condition in the guard is not satisfied for too long a period, a time-out transition takes over. More specifically, consider a power plant that operates according to its own logic. To improve the safety of the plant, we can have a monitor object m that watches over sensor p readings. Normal functioning of the sensor p would entail that monitor m make a transition within a particular time frame. If not, a time-out transition springs into action.

For another example, we revisit a fragment of the transition network of an ATM given in Section 6.4.1:

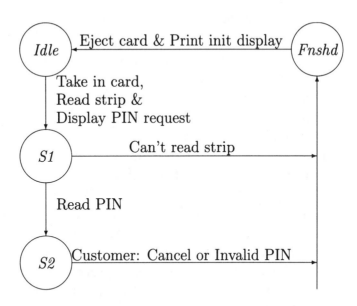

Recall that the *Idle – S1* transition has been modeled in Section 10.6.1 to generate an event targeted at the *ATMOutput* constituent. The *atm* ensemble expects to obtain from its *ATMInput* constituent a PIN in its *S1 – S2* Read PIN transition as detailed in Section 6.4.1.

Suppose that the requirements document specifies that the customer must provide the PIN within a certain time span. This requirement can be accounted for by adding another time-out transition from *S1* to *Fnshd*. This parallels the *Can't read strip* transition and depends on a time limit in *S1*:

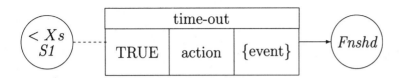

11.2.5 Constraint Failures

We began by extending a sequential use case with timing annotations. These extensions exposed the incompleteness of the use case since no remedial actions have been specified when time constraints are violated. This is acceptable for the specification of user-system interaction, but needs remedial action when "closing off" the requirements. One may want to be specific about how badly the system behaves when a timing constraint is not met, taking into account total breakdown versus gradual degradation and everything in between.

Constraints may be annotated with some indication of the consequences of failure. For ease of use, these constraints and consequences may be organized into general categories. For example, Jacobson et al [121] provide several classifications of constraints in real-time systems. A distinction is made between *hard* deadlines and *soft* deadlines. Not meeting a hard deadline results in a disaster. An example is a control system for an aerodynamically unstable plane. Not meeting a soft deadline results in a degradation of service. A slowly responding ATM is an example. They also make the distinction between critical, noncritical, and nonessential services. Critical services have hard deadlines. Noncritical and nonessential services both have soft deadlines. They differ in that a "nonessential process may miss its deadlines without any effect in the near future, but may have an effect in the long term if not executed (for example, maintenance and bookkeeping functions)."

11.3   Other Constraints

Boehm [36] (see also Davis [70], chapter 5) mentions the following categories of other constraints: portability, reliability, efficiency, human engineering, testability, understandability, modifiability. These are refined into fifteen subcategories including self-containedness, robustness, integrity, and conciseness. We have nothing to add here at the level of analysis, but do address associated design criteria in Chapter 15.

11.4   Summary

Many non-functional requirements pass through analysis and are input to the design and/or the implementation phases.

Timing requirements may be classified into *performance* and *alertness* constraints. A performance constraint indicates that a certain operation by the system is to be completed in a certain time window. An alertness constraint indicates that a system should resume control when an external event does not occur within a certain time window.

11.5   Further Reading

Jacobson et al [121] further categorize time constraints in real-time systems, including for example, those between periodic and aperiodic processes.

Hoogeboom and Halang [115] argue that time should play a more explicit role in analysis and development. They propose that processors be equipped with radio receivers to replace the notion of local time by the "awareness" of global time. They also propose that tasks be scheduled in the same way as done in our society, using reservations for time slots, priorities, etc. It is hard to disagree with the advantages they list:

- More problem oriented, since the problem is stated in terms of time. Therefore, it reflects the user's way of thinking.
- Enhanced predictability. No unpredictable waiting periods due to delay statements of synchronization operations.
- Improved dependability by checking and early conflict resolution.
- Synchronization and scheduling are treated within the same framework.

11.6   Exercises

1. We have equipped an *atm* ensemble with a *dispenser* constituent. Assume that the requirements document specifies that the customer has to take dispensed bills within y seconds. Otherwise, the *dispenser* will reabsorb these bills and generate an appropriate alert. Model a *dispenser* and its transition network in enough detail to capture this functionality.
2. Model a pump subsystem in which, when the subsystem is turned off, the pump will continue until the temperature drops to a threshold, but for no longer than 5 minutes.

Chapter 12

The Analysis Process

How does one proceed from the requirements to the design input?

In previous chapters, we have been discussing analysis notions and notations, culminating in the construction of a model of a target system. In this chapter, we will concentrate on the process dimension of OOA. We start off by investigating more general software development process concepts. We describe the OO analysis process abstractly, making it independent of particular tasks and developers. We informally present a partially ordered set of analysis activities within this framework. We then illustrate how OOA notions themselves can be applied to the more precise description of fragments of this generic OOA process. We compare the results to alternative approaches, and finally discuss prospects for corresponding tools.

12.1   Software Development Process

The notion of a "software development process" can be interpreted in several ways:

1. It can refer to the actual behaviors of a team of analysts, designers, implementors, and maintainers working on a particular development task.

    This process emerges (provided the organization has a certain discipline) from a process plan, as described in (2) below. Such a cooperative activity can be assisted by tools that have knowledge about a particular development paradigm, that capture the output of team members, that mediate their interactions, that do version control, that do progress monitoring, etc.

2. It can also refer to a particular plan made for a certain development task.

Such a plan would prescribe an intended process execution as outlined in version (1). A process plan is guided by the process as defined by the paradigm used, as in (3) below, or by features of the task at hand, by corporate policies, by human and other resources, etc. Such a plan would be the basis for progress monitoring. It can be used to allocate resources, to help decide what to do in case of plan execution deviations, etc. Again we can envisage tools that assist in representing plans, deadlines, dependencies, critical paths, etc. Such tools could, of course, interact with those in version (1).

3. It can refer as well to generic, recommended, broad-brush scenarios for doing software development.

   These scenarios may be seen as providing inspiration for setting up development plans as in (2). Alternatively, these development process scenarios can act as constraints on those plans.

There are also intermediate interpretations. For instance, a generic, broad brush scenario can be refined by a commitment to a given analysis paradigm. In turn, such a paradigm-specific process description can be narrowed to accommodate the specific properties of an application domain and/or of policies defined by a corporation.

Standard accounts ([91, 198], and especially [188]) describe the software development process in a generally similar fashion. Their treatment of the development process is paradigm neutral. As a result, these authors describe the development process only in large-granularity components including analysis, design, implementation, compilation, debugging, etc. Our commitment to the OO paradigm allows us to be more specific. In particular, we will "open up" the OO analysis phase in this chapter. (We will do the same for the design phase in Chapter 15.)

12.2 Default Sequence of Steps

In this section, we elaborate on a default sequence of steps for OO analysis:

1. Obtain "complete" requirements.
2. Describe system-context interaction.
3. Delineate subsystems.
4. Develop vocabulary by identifying instances with their classes, ensembles, and relationships.

5. Elaborate classes and relationships by defining their generic static structure and describing their generic dynamic dimension.

6. Construct a model in which the dynamics of objects are wired together.

These steps are connected by transformation – elaboration relationships. The output of the last step, the model, feeds naturally into the design phase.

Backtracking may occur at any time. Choices made upstream may be revised on the basis of insights gathered downstream. Tool support is obviously invaluable to help decide what must be scrapped and what can be salvaged. All steps combined can also be iterated to incorporate feedback from the customer.

12.2.1 Requirements

Whenever a requirements document already exists, the requirements step can be by-passed. It has been argued (e.g., by Ward and Brackett [225]) that the analysis phase encompasses the acquisition of the requirements as well. This would entail extracting the requirements from the customer while transcribing them into the analysis formalisms. Although this is possible, it is not necessarily recommended. Reformulating a "complete" initial requirements document allows checks on these requirements.

The notion of completeness is relative. A natural language description is usually too imprecise or too cumbersome to yield a watertight system characterization. In addition there may be aspects of the requirements that cannot be formulated because customers simply do not know what they want. Those aspects, for example, user interfaces, will have to be elucidated by prototyping.

12.2.2 System-Context Interaction

The behavior description is, of course, a core element of the requirements. Since the requirements language is usually free-form, any appropriate formalism can be employed. If it has not been done already, prototypical interaction sequences (use cases) between the context and the target system should be detailed. Corner cases and exception cases can be useful as well.

12.2.3 Subsystem Delineation

Splitting up a target system into weakly interacting subsystems is the next challenge. This step is intrinsically heuristic. An intended automatization of a manual system may adopt decompositions that have been already introduced. For example:

· Acquire data / Process data / Return response.
· Ordering / Manufacturing / Delivery / Planning / Accounting.
· User interface / System logic / Persistent data.

These can all be possibilities for subsystem delineation.

We must be prepared to revisit decisions made in this phase, either on the basis of subsequent interaction with the client or on the basis of newer insights obtained downstream.

Subsystems are candidates for mapping into ensembles. We will introduce another bundling notion, clusters, in Part II. Subsystems and clusters may or may not coincide. Subsystems represent a bundling of entities that are cohesive in a logical sense. Clustering represents the physical cohesion of objects that will reside within a process on a compute server. Accounts are an example of objects belonging to a subsystem of a bank that can be scattered physically in a distributed design and implementation.

Multiple subsystems create multiple options – breadth first, depth first, or any combination in between. With multiple analysts, it is attractive to work partially breadth first, where each analyst is responsible for one or more subsystems.

12.2.4   Vocabulary Development

Vocabulary development may be performed for each subsystem. When multiple analysts are involved and/or when a single analyst has introduced synonyms, several merging phases may be required to remove duplicates and synonyms.

An initial step involves the identification of classes whose instances will make up the system. There are many approaches. Several of the following categories are based on those described by Firesmith [92].

Abbott's noun approach.   This process relies on a requirements document and more specifically on a description of prototypical system – context interaction sequences. As described in Chapter 3, objects and their classes are identified by underlining nouns, pronouns, and noun phrases. Individual (parametric) objects are located by noun phrases that refer to unique entities such as *sensor number 5, the fifth sensor*. Verbs and verb phrases can be used to get an initial understanding of the operations associated with the objects found.

This technique may yield false positives and worse, may fail to locate relevant classes. Another problem is that a requirements text contains an abundance of noun phrases. The previous sentence, for example, contains four noun phrases:

· another problem,

> · a requirements text,
> · noun phrases,
> · an abundance of noun phrases.

Thus one needs to prune judiciously using this approach. Nevertheless, the technique provides a fertile starting point.

Structured approach. This technique has the following variants:

- A context diagram shows the external entities with which a software system must interface. Each external entity that is a terminator in the diagram corresponds to an individual object or class. This approach yields almost no false positive identifications, according to Firesmith [92].

- A data flow diagram (DFD) depicts processes, flows of data, and data stores. A data store can be identified as an object or a class. Processes associated with a data store can give a hint of the operations to be supported by the corresponding object.

Using pre-existing DFDs is attractive from a cost perspective, but as observed in Firesmith [92], they often have the wrong scope: "Pieces of the same abstract object or class are often on several DFDs." Developing object-oriented DFDs is recommended only when "you have to" (e.g., for contractual or political reasons).[1]

State approach. When a state of affairs is mentioned in the requirements document, a candidate object may be used that exhibits that state. Since one object may support multiple states, we may have to merge candidate objects identified by this approach. This approach may sound counterintuitive given the presentation sequence of the previous chapters. Object identification precedes the development of transition networks and thus precedes the description of states in these transition networks. However, when "state" is used in an imprecise sense, this approach may lead to the identification of useful classes.

---

[1]A reviewer of this book was a bit more adamant: "DFDs, by the admission of the very people who use them, are useless except to develop some kind of mysterious cult understanding. That data stores can be identified as objects of classes is absolutely wrong on so many levels of abstraction that I can barely count them. First, classes should be locales of behavior: the behavioral coupling in a DFD does not manifest itself in data stores. Second, classes reflect stable abstractions of the application domain; if they do not, then all these claims of OO supporting long-term maintenance are for naught... Bringing up DFDs here is just stupid. Just say no!"

Attribute approach. This follows the same pattern as the previous approach. As stated in Firesmith [92]: "For each data abstraction, identify the corresponding ...class of which it is an attribute." A data dictionary, if one happens to be available, might serve as a crude source of inspiration.

Operation approach. Another variant on the same theme and from the same source is: "For each functional abstraction, identify the corresponding ...class of which it is an operation."

Relationship approaches. Three variants are mentioned in Firesmith [92]:

- An entity in entity-relation diagrams may be seen as a first approximation of an object/class.
- Similarly, if there is a semantic net description of a domain, the nodes in these nets can be identified as candidate objects/classes.
- Again, if by some miracle there are message/interaction diagrams, their nodes can be identified as candidates.

Firesmith [92] observes that the construction of the last two diagrams relies on some early insight into at least some of the relevant objects/classes. CRC cards [22] provide a more direct and fruitful vehicle for eliciting object relationships and collaborations.

Decomposition approach. When large objects are found, we may want to look for component objects. The issue of whether a large object can be given the status of an ensemble may be ignored at this stage. Components can have different appearances including spatial *PartOf*, temporal *PartOf*, and the many versions of metaphorical *PartOf*.

Reuse approach. This entails investigating repositories that capture the ingredients of earlier and similar systems. We can obtain inspiration from class libraries (possibly produced by a domain analysis) and/or *frameworks*. Frameworks are organized sets of classes and related constructs, usually self-contained hierarchies, that intentionally fall short of specifying those subclasses needed for particular systems and applications. They are skeletons that must be supplemented by system-specific subclasses and operations. A framework can be an overall "wrapper" or it can be a structure for a major subresponsibility such as persistence or graphical user interaction (see Chapters 13 and 15).

Abstraction approach. If "mechanical" approaches fail, we must rely on original thinking. A requirements document and auxiliary sources of domain knowledge must be scrutinized for the identification of unique and subsequently prototypical objects and their relationships.

Firesmith [92] suggests looking for the following kinds of items (or sets of them):

· Aggregates or devices.
· Persons or roles.
· Organizations.
· Locations.
· Events.
· Interactions.

Shlaer and Mellor [203] present a similar list:

· Tangible objects, things that exist in the physical world.
· Roles, purposes or assignments of people, pieces of equipment, or organizations.
· Incidents, some happening or occurrence.
· Interactions, associations between objects.
· Specification objects that capture rules, standards, or quality criteria.

In a new domain, an OO analyst has a great amount of freedom to pick and choose candidate objects, classes, and relationships. Since not much is at stake at such an early stage, it pays to play around. Mapping physical entities onto objects and physical events onto events is an obvious choice. However, an analyst also has the freedom to objectify physical or abstract events. Fitness for use is the general guideline. Minimality of notions, orthogonality of concepts, naturalness, and unbundledness of functionality are obviously desirable although potentially conflicting desiderata.

In this early stage, it is better to have false positives that will be weeded out in subsequent refinements than it is to overlook key concepts. Although we may ultimately need (parametric) instances in the last step of the analysis phase (model construction), every object should be generalized into a class, even when the model contains only one instance of a class.

12.2.5 Class and relation elaboration

An overview of this phase is represented in the diagram introduced in Chapter 2:

	inside object	between objects
static	attribute constraint	relationship acquaintanceship
dynamic	state transition	interaction causal connection

This table is enclosed in a hidden quantifier:

```
For every identified class do:
    Fill in the entries of the table
```

In a naive interpretation, we would for each class in turn completely fill in this table. The right-hand entries in the table already imply that this is not feasible. We need to have some overview of the collection of classes in the system to describe relationships and inheritance. Similarly, it is useful to have a preliminary insight into potential interaction partners when the interaction capabilities of class instances are formulated. A more realistic approach for this phase is captured by:

```
For every entry of the table do:
    For each class do:
        Elaborate the class as prescribed by the table entry
```

In what sequence do we traverse the entries in the table? There is no right answer. As we have seen, static and dynamic descriptions are strongly intertwined. To summarize:

- Attributes define an overall universe representing the cartesian product of the attribute value domains.
- Constraints define a subuniverse space.
- State predicates describe disjoint subspaces that correspond to the states in transition networks.
- A guard in a transition further narrows a state subspace. When multiple transitions emanate from a state, their guards will define disjoint subspaces inside that state space.
- An action on a transition yields a state that is consistent with the properties that define the target state.

Still, as discussed in Chapter 2, we prefer to go from left to right in the first row and then the second row. (See Section 12.4 for alternative traversals suggested by other methodologists.) However, inheritance cuts across all steps. Elaborations and models constructed during any of these activities may reveal a commonality in structure and behavior between two or more classes. This commonality can be factored out by a (multiple) inheritance relationship between classes. Such commonalities can also emerge with respect to classes residing in a library of analysis concepts.

Class Statics

The vocabulary development phase produces candidate classes and relationships. After selecting concise and evocative names we must describe each class with attributes. Although each class must have a unique name, classes should be distinguishable on the basis of their attribute characterizations. A rule of thumb is if two classes have identical attributes, then they are most likely the same. (We have seen exceptions in Chapters 3 and 5.)

An attribute expresses an essential definitional feature that is shared by all instances of a class. A minimal characterization of an attribute consists of the value domain of the attribute and a name that explains the role or relationship that an attribute value has with respect to the instance to which it belongs. Multivalued attributes may be annotated with multiplicity characterizations. Defaults for an attribute value and/or multiplicity description can be formulated in this phase as well. Constraints can restrict attribute value combinations and/or refer to multiplicity descriptions.

Relationships

Relationships help capture target system-specific knowledge by describing connections among different objects. Relationships may also be used to modify descriptions in the previous step. For example, when an attribute has a multiplicity range that includes zero, one may eliminate the attribute and represent this information as a relationship instead.

Class Dynamics

A transition network can be rigorously developed for a prototypical class instance as soon as the static attribute characterization is available. Postponing transition specifications until after inheritance class connections are established sometimes produces an initial transition network "for free" via inheritance.

States and transitions are dual notions. Whether one enumerates and defines the states or a mixture of the two depends on the available data. Beyond its name, a state is preferably defined in terms of a predicate on the space of value combinations of the attributes. An operation on a transition is preferably defined not only by its name but also by preconditions and postconditions.

Interaction

"Hard-wiring" interaction connections between prototypical class instances should be avoided. Object interactions may instead be described through relationships that can later be captured as attributes (or not) as the target system model is constructed.

Synchronous interaction may be described on the server side with an interface description that details what is expected from the client and what, if anything, will be delivered. This may consist of signature descriptions, preconditions and postconditions. Similarly, on the client side, a dual description should be formulated to describe the data to be sent to the server and what is expected from the server. Asynchronous interaction proceeds in a similar fashion, via descriptions of events, their producers, and consumers.

12.2.6   Model Construction

The previous activities provide the key building blocks for assembling a model of the target system. The overall structure, the architecture, is guided by:

- The architecture of a similar, previously developed system, if any.
- A generic framework, if any applies.
- A specific framework (such as a user interface) that can play the role of a generic framework, if any can be found.
- An ensemble object that can represent the whole system.
- A family of ensembles or objects that can represent the whole system in a "democratic" fashion.

The model is subsequently constructed by recursively filling in the details of this architecture up to the level at which it becomes obvious that the design phase can construct a computational realization of this descriptive model.

When objects are chosen to interact with each other, we must ascertain that the mutual expectations and obligations for events and for client-server interactions match. If necessary, application-specific subclasses must be introduced to pin down interaction partner commitments at this stage.

Model construction may reveal that areas are underconstrained, inconsistent, or simply ill defined. If interaction with the customer does not resolve this situation, prototyping may be used to gather more insights into such unresolved areas.

12.3   OO Analysis of the OO Analysis Process

The presentation in this section is in a sense a *meta* activity. Meta is an ambiguous notion that needs clarification. We will *not* use OOA to describe OAN syntax. Neither will we describe the semantics of the OOA constructs. Instead we will sketch the pragmatic dimension of the OO analysis process. Of course, we will avoid the process aspects that are team- and project-specific. We will limit ourselves to the abstract, generic interpretation as defined in Section 12.1.

We stated earlier that a development activity may change the requirements. New insights can be obtained that will fill in omissions, add additional constraints, eliminate constraints, or replace existing constraints with others. We ignore this aspect of the analysis process and focus on the transformation of some frozen version of the requirements into an analysis model of the target system. However our model does have a traceability infrastructure for dealing with changes to the requirements.

The first step of an analysis process demands that we obtain requirements and complete them as necessary. In our case, we want to describe the OOA process, so we can refer to the previous section describing default steps and activities as the requirements document for this enterprise. Subsequently, we ought to provide for system-context interaction, subsystem delineation and vocabulary development. However, we will bypass these steps. Our abstraction level eliminates the analyst. We cannot effectively discuss system-context interaction or model construction. Additionally, the OOA process is too abstract to allow subsystems to be distinguished. The vocabulary consists of concepts such as class, relationship, instance, attribute, constraint, transition network, state, transition, etc., so we can go straight into class elaboration.

12.3.1   Graphical Overview

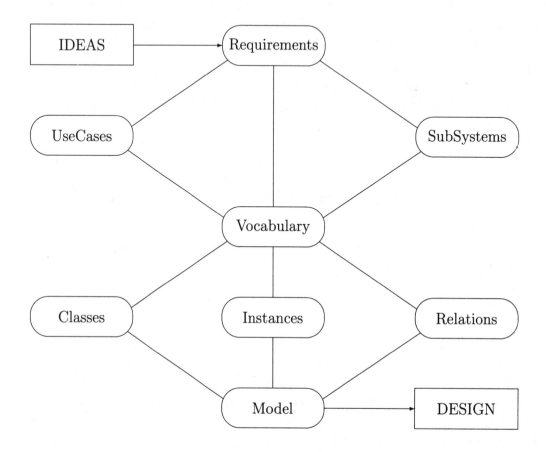

This diagram may be interpreted as follows:

Boxes. The IDEAS box represents external input to the analysis process. The DE-SIGN box denotes the next phase in the development process.

Ovals: The ovals denote the artifacts that are constructed in the analysis process. If complete requirements are initially available then the Requirements oval resides outside the analysis process boundary as well.

Horizontal arcs. These arcs represent input and output dependencies.

Other lines. The other lines in the diagram denote dependencies between the artifacts. For example, a class definition depends on at least one item in the vocabulary and similarly the model depends on classes, instances and relations. Phrased differently, an item lower in the diagram is obtained through *elaboration* of an item or items higher up in the diagram.

This diagram resembles a class interaction diagram. But while the arcs in an interaction diagram represent synchronous or asynchronous object interaction capabilities, those lines here denote "manual" interventions by analysts. During analysis, we reformulate and expand an informal set of requirements into a more formal description. This transformation is done gradually. UseCases, SubSystems and Vocabulary are still informal in the sense that they rely on natural language, but at the same time they structure the characterizations by providing templates. The crossover point is in the elaboration of the items in the Vocabulary into items in Classes, Instances, and Relations.

These items may be further expanded. For example, class development may be represented using the following diagram:

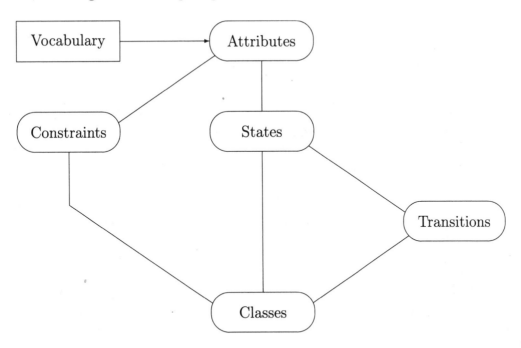

The diagrams contain a few simplifications. For example, "Vocabulary" represents several different kinds of categories – classes, ensembles, relationships and their instances. Also, the main diagram does not capture a validation step in which a constructed model is checked to ascertain that it satisfies the behaviors expressed by the use cases.

We have *not* explicitly represented the introduction of inheritance connections among classes and relationships via abstraction and specialization. Abstraction of commonalities among classes and relationships may be performed at any time. Consequently, this operation is global to all the elaboration activities depicted in the diagrams. Specialization occurs after a preliminary version of a class or relationship has been formulated and it is recognized that the intended class is already partially realized. Thus this operation can be associated with the behavior of the class *Class*.

12.3.2   Statics

Since *analysis* is a key concept for us, we start with the class *Analysis*. An instance of class *Analysis* is a repository for a particular analysis task.

When an *Analysis* instance is created, a *requirements* attribute must be initialized with information that has been "chopped up" into a sequence of "bite-size" fragments labeled *Text**. Preferably, each *Text** fragment embodies a single idea, in the form of a *Figure*, *Table*, or simple *Text*.

These requirements fragments are described as things to be elaborated. Elaboration of analysis fragments is the core notion that will be expanded when we address the dynamic dimension of these classes.

An *agenda* attribute registers the elaboration tasks still remaining for a particular analysis project. This attribute will be initialized as a copy of the *requirements* attribute. During the course of analysis, it will be elaborated to include other instances of class *AComp* (Analysis Component).

An *instances* attribute refers to identified stable instances of classes, ensembles and relations. The corresponding classes and relations themselves are represented through attributes *classes* and *relations*. Most other attributes are self explanatory. The associated classes will be further detailed as we proceed.

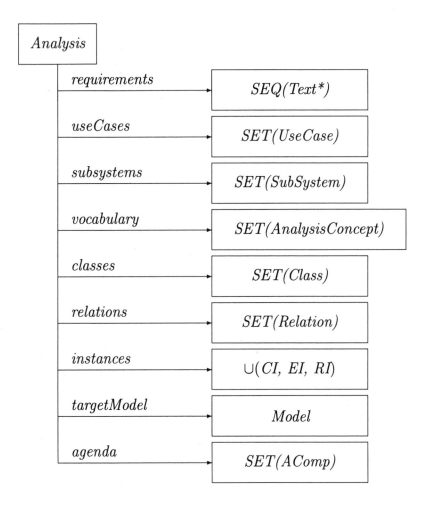

In order to establish trace links between the constituents of an analysis, we introduce the four classes *AComp, ACompL, ACompR,* and *ACompLR.*

The class *AComp* captures overall commonalities among *Text*, UseCase, SubSystem, AnalysisConcept, Class* and *Relation*. We represent the traceability connections with the attributes *elaborates* and *elaboratedIn*. Alternatively, we could have introduced a binary relationship *Elaborate*.

Most constituents have both backward and forward elaboration links. However the *requirements* captured in *Text** do not have backward links, and a *Model*, which brings everything together, does not have any elaboration links.

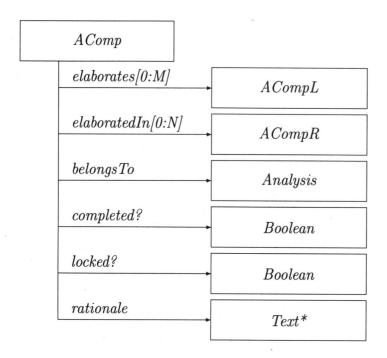

Where:

> *belongsTo* provides a backward reference to the instance of *Analysis* to which this
> artifact item belongs.

> *rationale* allows registration of why a particular elaboration is chosen.

> *completed?* records whether the current component is considered to be complete.

> *locked?* is superfluous for the task at hand, but could be used by a CASE tool to
> prevent contention across multiple analysts.

Class *AComp* is refined into *ACompLR* via *ACompL* and *ACompR*. Classes *ACompL*
and *ACompR* differ only in whether they *must* have predecessors or successors. This
refinement captures the idea that *ACompL* instances must have predecessors, that
ACompR instances must have successors, and that *ACompLR* instances must have
both elaboration chains.

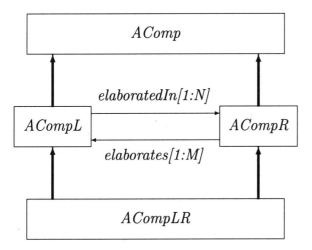

When we create an instance of *ACompLR* (and hence an instance of *ACompR*) we may not yet know what its successors will be. Thus we must give its *elaboratedIn* attribute a dummy value and add this artifact onto the agenda to ascertain that this attribute will be filled in properly later.

The *requirements* (of class *Text**) represent the start of the traceability chain:

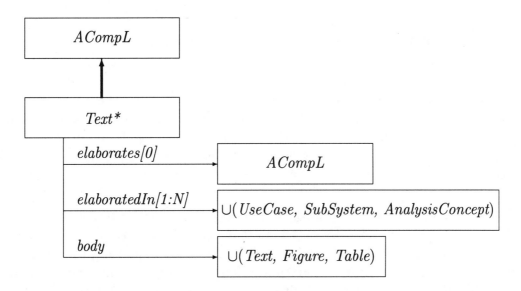

An instance of the class *UseCase* describes in a pseudo-formal way a prototypical interaction sequence with a target system:

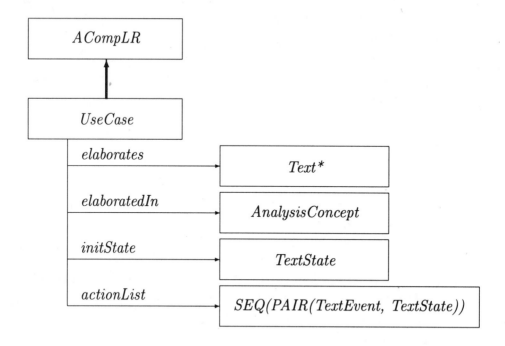

Where:

> *actionList* describes a *UseCase* as a sequence of the form:
> $< Event_1, State_1 >< Event_2, State_2 > \ldots < Event_n, State_n >$.

> *initState* provides a characterization of the initial state of the interaction sequence. An instance of *TextState* is text that explains a particular external state of affairs in which someone/something can act, yielding an instance of *TextEvent* upon which the system can act, which will yield yet another instance of *TextState*.

The class *SubSystem* is used to introduce decompositions of the target system. To simplify the situation, we call the target system itself a *SubSystem*. Its parent attribute would simply be missing; this effect is achieved by exploiting the permitted zero multiplicity of the *parentSystem* attribute. The setup of this multiplicity description permits a *SubSystem* to be a constituent of more than one subsystem. Whether this freedom is to be exploited or, alternatively, whether the subsystem hierarchy should be a tree is up to the analyst.

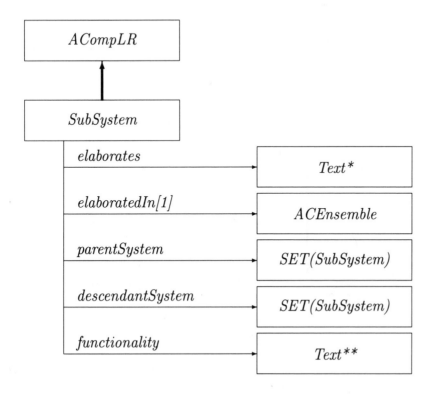

The *Text*** class captures structured text to annotate a subsystem, much as we provided for annotations in the class *UseCase*. We will use *Text*** in other classes as well. To provide more guidance for annotations, we could define specialized versions of *Text*** that correspond to context-specific templates.

The *vocabulary* attribute in class *Analysis* is a set of *AnalysisConcept*s. The class *AnalysisConcept* captures the commonalities of, and is partitioned by, the classes *AC-Class, ACEnsemble, ACRelationship, ACCI, ACEI* and *ACRI. ACClass, ACEnsemble*, and *ACRelationship* provide structured but not yet formal descriptions of their respective classes, ensemble classes, and relationships. *ACCI, ACEI* and *ACRI* capture the kinds of instances (*CI, RI,* and *EI*, respectively) in the realm of the target system. The inheritance structure of these classes exploits the fact that an ensemble has been conceptualized as a special instance.

The only work done inside *AnalysisConcept* is that eligible instances of the attribute value restrictions of *elaborates* and *elaboratedIn* are constrained:

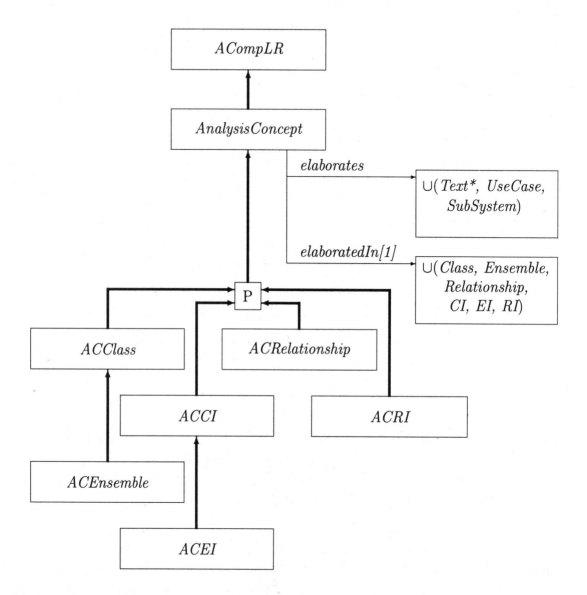

*AnalysisConcept*s provide focused descriptions of the constituents of an analysis. Of the six (indirect) subclasses of *AnalysisConcept*, we give the diagrammatic expansions of only *ACClass* and *ACCI*, along with the the associated class *Class*. (The others follow similarly.) A class description in *ACClass* is captured textually in *Text*** and formally in a *Class*. Distinguished *instances* are recorded as *ACCI*s. Class *ACCI* includes the attribute *instanceOf* providing an upward reference to the corresponding *ACClass*.

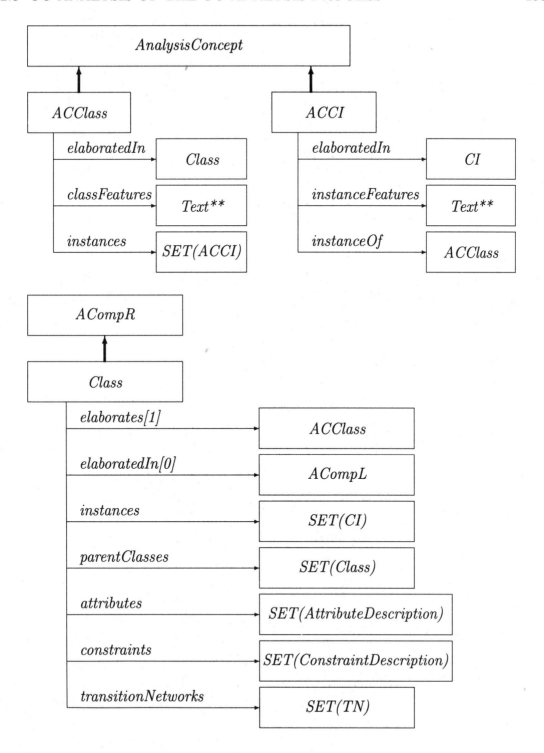

Note the similarity between class *Class* and the metaclass framework discussed in Chapter 8.

The binary inheritance relationship between classes is absorbed in the *Class* attribute *parentClass*. Alternatively, we could have used an *Inherit* relationship:

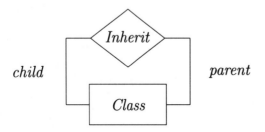

Elaboration of the other classes needed in class *Class* requires commitment to particular representations of class features. A first approximation of the class *AttributeDescription* has the form:

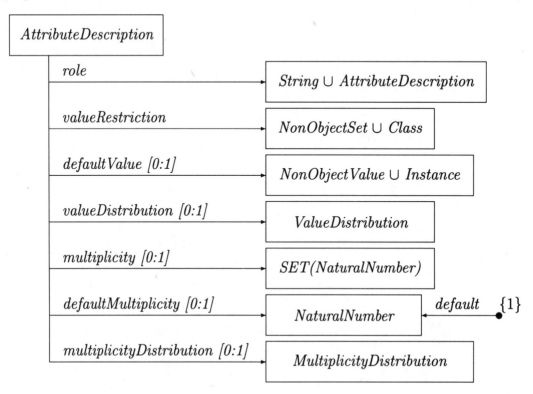

Where:

role is either a descriptive name for the attribute or a reference to an attribute in a parent class that is made more specific.

valueRestriction is a description of a class from which instances can be attribute values or a description of non-object values.

defaultValue is the default value or a probability description of attribute values.

multiplicity is a "repetition count" of the attribute.

defaultMultiplicity is a default count or a probability description of the multiplicity feature.

ValueDistribution is either a set of pairs of the form (value, probability) or a genuine probability distribution function describing the distribution of values.

MultiplicityDistribution similarly describes the probability distribution of multiplicities.

Rather than digressing into other representational matters, we present the other *Class*-related classes only as brief sketches:

ConstraintDescription represents constraints using a formal characterization of a formal language such as the predicate calculus. In short, a constraint consists of an expression in which attributes and optionally *self* occur as parameters.

TN represents transition networks. Its main attributes are *states* with domain *State*, and *transitions*, with domain *Transition*. Constraints should express that states and guards in a *TN* are disjoint unless the class has multiple *TN*s.

Transition represents transitions within *TN*s. The class has the attributes *fromState*, *toState, name, guard, action*, and *event* among others.

State represents states within *TN*s. The class has attributes including a characteristic name and an expression that refers to the value domains. The expression should demarcate a nonempty subset in the cartesian product spanned by the value domains.

CI represents class instances in terms of attribute values, etc., based on the above
representations.

All the components of the analysis are used for the construction of a model. Instances
and classes are specialized, if necessary, to express object interaction commitments.
A model consists of a set of instances corresponding to stable objects, and a set of
classes and relationships that act as generators for transient entities:

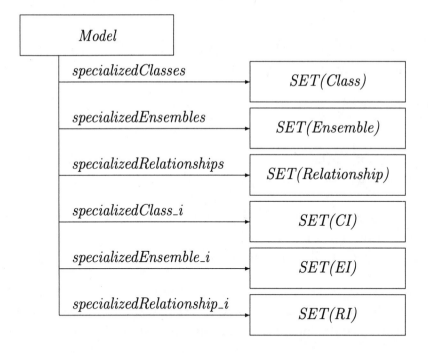

The attributes in the class *Model* suggest that we do not use classes, relationships,
etc., as is, but instead use refined or specialized versions. This is a consequence of
our philosophy that the classes, relationships, etc., originally developed should be
generalized, as if they were the result of a domain analysis. Then they must be
specialized to fit the needs of an intended system. We elaborate on the nature of
these specializations while discussing the dynamic view.

12.3.3 Dynamics

We will present some fragments of the transition networks associated with these classes. Every analysis activity starts by selecting an item from the *agenda* attribute inside an instance of *Analysis*. A random choice from this agenda would be:

Select Agenda Item		
guard	action	event
TRUE *Fetch-task-for (client)*	select random element and remove from agenda	*return-to* (client, selected-element)

(For simplicity, we ignore empty agendas, and temporarily ignore check-out operations on selected agenda elements.)

The agenda selection operation may be refined in several ways. At a minimum, random selection could be replaced with mechanisms allowing the analyst to select which tasks to pick from the agenda. Other policies may be supported by making certain tasks "invisible" and/or only accessible in particular ways. For example:

- A top-down approach for the treatment of subsystems and ensembles would require that these be elaborated first.

- A reuse policy might require searching for relevant analysis artifacts in a domain-specific library before an analyst addresses a particular task.

For the class *AComp* we can set up the following minimal transition network:

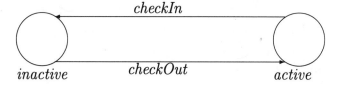

The *checkOut* transition can be triggered by the *selectAgendaItem* transition inside *Analysis*. Alternatively, it can be invoked as a client-server operation in the action part of *selectAgendaItem*. The guard in *checkOut* can depend on whether an instance of *AComp* has its *locked?* attribute set; if not, it can be set in the action part. This transition network may be extended in the (indirect) subclasses of *AComp*. For example, the class *ACompR* may support transition:

create A Successor		
guard	action	{event}
TRUE		
Elaborate	*create-instance-vr (ElaboratedIn)*	

(*active* state)

The expression *create-instance-vr(ElaboratedIn)* creates an instance of the value restriction of the attribute *elaboratedIn*. Inside the class *ACompR* the value restriction is the class *ACompL*, but for an instance of *UseCase* we would obtain an instance of *AnalysisConcept*.

The newly created instance should also be added to the value restriction of the attribute *elaboratedIn*. The instance construction operation should additionally be extended in order to initialize attributes. For example, the *elaborates* attribute can be given as its value the identity of the object that instigates its creation.

We can extend this transition network further for subclasses of *AnalysisConcept*. For example, in the class *UseCase* we can introduce transitions that set the values of the attributes *initState* and *actionList* via interaction with an analyst:

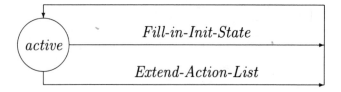

Although an analyst would have to take the initiative to select such a transition, the transition could help the analyst by displaying templates identifying the information to be provided by the analyst. These templates would be defined by the attributes in *UseCase*.

Most of the transition networks for other classes can be patterned similarly. For example, a transition network for *Class* should have a transition that helps the analyst fill in attribute values. The backward elaboration pointers give access to the relevant semantic information. The value domain of such an attribute helps to define an acquisition template.

An exception is the transition network for the class *Model*. In a sense, we need all the power of the OOA process inside a *Model* since we have to customize classes to join their interaction patterns together. While a generic class can specify a communication unilaterally via an event, a prototypical instance of a specialized class should be equipped with the knowledge of its communication partners. Either we must introduce acquaintance relationship instances and provide "hooks" inside objects that consult such relationship instances to figure out what the communication partners are, or we must bypass the indirection of acquaintance relationships and "hard-wire" knowledge of the communication partner inside the objects.

12.4   Alternative Processes

To place this version of the analysis process in perspective, we sketch the analysis procedures proposed by some other methodologists.

Gibson gives the five steps of Object Behavior Analysis (OBA) [97] as follows:

1. Understand the application; identify behaviors.
2. Derive objects using the behavioral perspective.
3. Start classifying objects.
4. Identify relationships among objects.
5. Model processes.

Ignoring the preliminary aspects of step (1) we can plot these steps in our table:

	inside object	between objects
static	Derive objects (2)	Classify objects (3) Identify relations (4)
dynamic	Identify behavior (1)	Model processes (5)

In contrast, the OOA method of Shlaer et al [200, 201] and the OSA method of Embley et al [89] move from left to right first in the top row and then in the bottom row, although the vertical separation is less apparent in [89]. A similar route is followed by Coad and Yourdan [57]:

> Rather than jumping right into a study of functions and sequencing, the OOA analyst first focuses on Objects, Structures, Attributes (and Instance Connections) – and then finally gets around to a consideration of Services (and Message Connections).

The OMT method of Rumbaugh et al [192] describes a quite elaborate sequence of steps. Still, interpretations of each can be seen in the process described in this chapter:

Object Modeling
- Identify objects and classes.
- Prepare a data dictionary.
- Identify associations (including aggregations) between objects.
- Identify attributes of objects and links.
- Organize and simplify object classes using inheritance.
- Verify that access paths exist for likely queries.
- Iterate and refine the model.
- Group classes into modules.

Dynamic Modeling
- Prepare scenarios of typical interaction sequences.
- Identify events between objects.
- Prepare an event trace for each scenario.
- Build state diagrams.
- Match events between objects to verify consistency.

Functional Modeling
- Identify input and output values.
- Build data flow diagrams showing functional dependency.
- Describe functions.
- Identify constraints.
- Specify optimization criteria.

12.5 Tools

Analysis tools may be classified along several dimensions:

Tool integration. Is the tool a stand-alone point tool or is it (potentially) integrated in a set of tools that covers the life cycle?

Data integration. Are the artifacts produced by a customer stored in a proprietary database or in a format that is compatible with emerging standards?

Control integration. Is the tool able to generate events to be picked up by other tools? Dually is the tool able to respond to events generated by other tools?

Team support. Does the tool support only a single user or are the proper hooks in place to support teams?

Minimality. Is the tool extensible? Is the tool customizable? Does the tool support capturing metrics? Does the tool have the flexibility to support and guide novices but at the same time does not impede experts? Does the tool support the (OOA) process in the multiple interpretations outlined in Section 12.1?

Interface. Can the user interface be adjusted to provide a consistent appearance with other tools?

This shopping list is daunting, as has been observed by Humphrey [117]: "Such comprehensive environments will likely be very large, possibly rivaling or even surpassing the largest operating systems."

There are not as yet many tools that support OO analysis (although surprisingly many vendors claim their tools to be in some ill-specified sense OO-ish). Cadre has a product that implements the OOA method of Shlaer and Mellor [200, 203]. Rational has a product called ROSE that implements the method of Booch [39]. This tool supports analysis as well as design. Hewlett-Packard has developed an in house prototype of Embley's et al [89] OSA. The companies MarkV and ProtoSoft have developed meta-tools providing generic support for classes, relationships, transition diagrams, interaction diagrams, etc. These are highly parameterized so that the notions and graphical representations of "any" method can be emulated.

12.6   Summary

A software development process is guided by broad scenarios, particular plans, and situation-dependent factors. A generic recommended scenario for the OO analysis phase includes default steps:

1. Obtain "complete" requirements.
2. Describe system-context interaction.
3. Delineate subsystems.
4. Develop vocabulary by identifying instances with their classes, ensembles and relationships.
5. Elaborate classes and relationships by defining their generic static structure and describing their generic dynamic dimension.
6. Construct a model in which the dynamics of objects are wired together.

"Flow of control" in this space is uncommitted. Thus whether breadth-first descending or vertical slicing is done depends on the features of a particular task and the prescription of a risk analysis.

   We illustrated this analysis process by applying it to itself, and also in Chapter 10 where we applied it to the construction of an ATM system.

12.7   Exercises

1. The classes *Class, Ensemble, Relationship, CI, EI,* and *RI* share the property that the *elaborates* attribute is single-valued. They share as well that the *elaboratedIn* attribute is absent. Introduce an abstract class that factors out this commonality and integrate this class in the other classes. Hunt for other opportunities for abstraction.
2. Expand the undefined and underdefined classes in the OOA process model, including those indicated by summations.

Chapter 13

Domain Analysis

Previous chapters have concentrated on analysis methods resulting in the clarification of the requirements of a particular target system. However, often, a system may be seen as an element of a stream of products. If so, we can investigate their common features. Such a domain characterization can then be leveraged for each system to be developed.

Target-specific OO analysis techniques often generate models with applicability stretching beyond the needs of the system(s) under consideration, and thus intrinsically incorporate at least some form and extent of domain analysis. However, the notion of domain analysis as a distinguishable enterprise remains an immature topic, in need of considerable development. In this chapter, we survey general views, models, and variants of domain analysis, along with their consequences for reuse.

There are several ways to define "domain". For example, Berard [26] gives two characterizations:

1. A collection of current and future (software) applications that share a set of common characteristics.
2. A well-defined set of characteristics that accurately, narrowly, and completely describe a family of problems for which computer application solutions are being, and will be sought.

A founder, if not the founder, of domain analysis is Neighbors [164, 165]. He wrote in 1980:

> The key to reusable software is captured in domain analysis in that it stresses the reusability of analysis and design, not code.

13.1   Models

The scope of a domain investigation can vary widely. A definition of domain analysis formulated by Prieto-Diaz [217] elucidates its purpose as:

> ... a process by which information used in developing software systems is identified, captured, and organized with the purpose of making it reusable when creating new systems.

Arango and Prieto-Diaz [16] present a model of domain analysis summarized in the following SADT diagram:

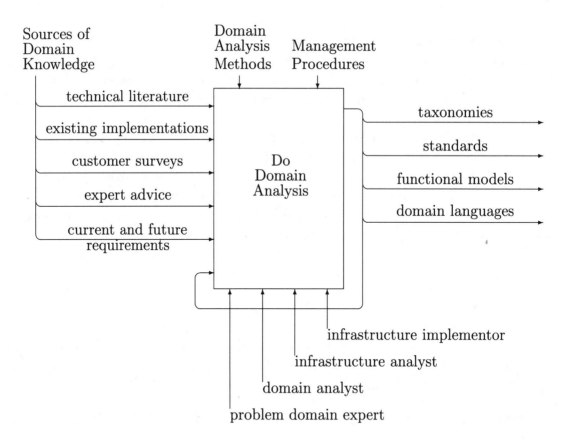

This model describes domain analysis as an activity that takes multiple sources of input, produces many different kinds of output, and is heavily parameterized. For example, one parameter is the development paradigm (e.g., SA, Jackson, OO). Raw domain knowledge from any relevant source is taken as input. Participants in the process can be, among others, domain experts and analysts. Outputs are (semi)formalized concepts, domain processes, standards, logical architectures, etc. Subsequent activities produce generic design fragments, frameworks, etc.

While this account gives an inspiring initial insight into domain analysis, it is not the full story. Several refinements are presented next.

13.1.1 Product Definition Domain Analysis

When a product is seen as part of a new or an existing stream of products, the domain of this product stream may itself be studied. This study will in general go beyond technical aspects of the product. For example, strategic alignment, longer term marketing aspects, product positioning, risk analysis, common look-and-feel, covering a diversity of product features, etc., will play a role in conjunction with investigations of generic terminology, logical architectures, reliability standards, and other general considerations.

Such a study may be seen as a domain analysis. It involves a multidisciplinary team. Consequently a nonformal language is the *lingua franca*. A software development paradigm, such as OO, is unlikely to play a prominent role here.

13.1.2 Requirements Domain Analysis

When there is enough confidence that a stream of products can be produced, one may want to factor out the commonalities in the multiple analyses that must be done for each product. Thus one may want to do a *conceptual* domain analysis that yields common ground for each specific analysis. OO analysis notions lend themselves for capturing generic concepts at multiple levels of granularity. Ensembles, subensembles, classes, and generic relationships are all candidates for describing an application domain.

While we can use the *notions* and notations from an OO analysis method for requirements domain analysis, we have to adjust the process dimension. We cannot rely on a system-specific requirements document as input to the process. Instead, we have to take in any relevant features from the documentation that describe the commonality of the products. Experts and customers may be tapped, as suggested in the generic diagram. However, the situation differs from the diagram in that people have to be primed for more specific and detailed information. The output side differs as well because the process stops earlier; no model is to be constructed. Instead, generic classes, relationships, ensembles, etc., are produced. These may be organized into one or more OO *frameworks* that may be specialized to the needs of particular systems.

For example, many of the ATM examples in previous chapters are not geared to any specific system. To the extent to which these descriptions are realistic, they are contributions to an OO domain analysis of "ATMs for banks". Our model of the OOA process in Chapter 12 represents an even better example of this form of domain analysis. This model abstracted across different development styles and contexts. It did not culminate in a particular target model, but only those model components forming a basis for any OOA process.

Domain Engineering

A requirements domain analysis may lead to an OO domain engineering effort. This entails the construction of design fragments of the generic elements identified by a requirements domain analysis. These designs can be implemented and added to a domain-specific code library.

13.1.3   Generator Domain Analysis

When a stable domain serves as the basis of a product line or market segment, one may consider constructing a generator for a particular domain. This generator may then be used to automatically build (parts of) any of a series of related products. Relational database systems are an example of a mature, stable domain where it is quite conceivable to perform a generator type domain analysis. The query language, platform, operating system and windowing environment would be main parameters for such a relational database builder.

The analysis performed for the construction of such a meta-program may be seen as a third version of the notion of domain analysis. One may assume for such an enterprise not only that the domain is stable and well understood, but also that domain specific design and/or code libraries are available.

One may even step one level higher. For example, the Rose system (Reuse Of Software Elements) [146, 147] was an experimental meta-meta-program that assisted in capturing domain knowledge and design know-how for the domain.

13.2 Reuse

Domain analysis is not a one-shot affair. Product definitions evolve continuously. The development of a particular system that exploits previously accumulated domain knowledge can be the source for new insights about the domain that adds to or refines codified domain knowledge. In analogy to the emergence of domain-specific code libraries, we foresee the development of domain-specific analysis concept repositories, linked ultimately to code via domain-specific design repositories. The following diagram describes the interactions:

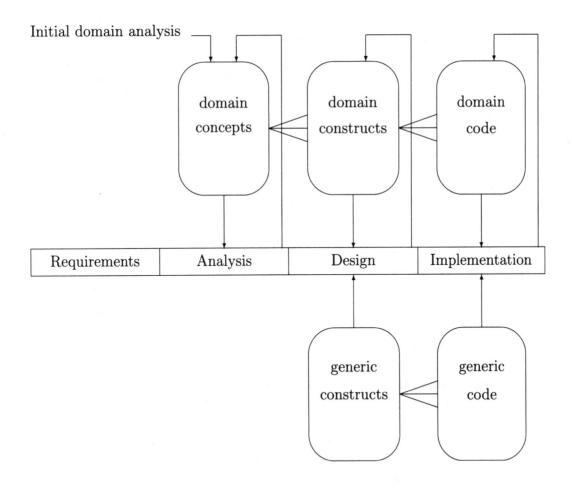

Functional model components are the primary outputs of a domain analysis. The feedback loops describe/prescribe that the outputs of the different phases are to be abstracted and added to the domain repositories. The "bird-feet" lines in the diagram that are attached to the repositories express their interconnections. For example, a domain analysis concept can have multiple realizations in the design repository. Similarly, a domain construct can have multiple realizations in the corresponding code repository, where each realization satisfies different auxiliary requirement trade-offs.

Domain analysis is the spearhead for disciplined reuse in software development. This is quite obvious for the generator version of domain analysis, but applies as well to the two weaker versions. An organization for system development will be complemented, when cost effective, by an organization that maintains and manages domain-specific repositories. OO analysis has much to offer to domain analysis from a technical perspective. However the sociological, cultural and organizational problems of realizing a cost effective reuse program that underlies our diagram extend beyond the technical dimension (see, among others [183]). As discussed in Chapter 15, these obstacles are more easily conquered at the OO design and implementation levels. This has led to the widespread adoption of reuse-based strategies in OO design and programming efforts. However, these practices remain incomplete without equally prevalent adoption of a reuse-based engineering discipline at the requirements and analysis levels.

13.3   Summary

While OO analysis is focused on the features and functionality of a single system to be generated, a domain analysis focuses on the common and variant features across a family of systems. At least three versions of domain analysis may be distinguished: (1) at the level of product definitions, (2) at the level of analysis of the proto-products, and (3) at the level of the analysis for a generator of applications in the domain. Because of the informality of version (1), the OO paradigm plays a less significant role there than in versions (2) and (3).

To ensure the reusability of the domain models produced, domain analysts use diverse sources of domain knowledge. These sources provide information on the range of potential systems in the domain. While all domain analysis methods involve extraction of terminology and identification of a common domain language, the OO domain analysis method accomplishes this task through identification of classes, relationships and behaviors. Such domain models may translate into reusable frameworks.

In a reuse strategy the domain analysis work-products must be maintained and enhanced over many systems. The domain analysis repository contains domain models that form the basis of subsequent systems analysis activities.

13.4 Further Reading

The state of the art in domain analysis is concisely formulated in a Domain Analysis Working Group Report from a workshop held in 1991 [217]. Many open questions are formulated in this document. The great diversity of perspectives suggests that domain analysis is still in an embryonic stage with substantial potential for further developments.

13.5 Exercises

1. Revisit the previous chapters and identify which of those specific notions, notations, and procedures can be reused for a domain analysis.
2. Perform a domain analysis in any of the interpretations of this chapter for a domain with which you are familiar.

Chapter 14

The Grady Experience

Above all else, the goal of analysis is human understanding of systems and their problem domains.

In a recent study [100], Grady identified cost components of software development across the whole lifecycle, including maintenance and functionality enhancements. The cost percentages assigned to the different components stem from a combination of educated guesses and empirical data obtained from inside and outside of Hewlett-Packard:

Component	Percentage
Program understanding	27%
Requirements analysis	24%
Design	18%
Implementation	18%
Testing	13%

Grady estimates that 27% of the total cost must be attributed to "program understanding". This is a separate component from requirements analysis, design, implementation, and testing. It represents the efforts of analyzing what existing artifacts are all about before remedial actions can be taken in the case of bug fixes, or, in other cases, before functionality extensions can be performed.

One may wonder why the program understanding component absorbs such a large fraction of costs. A glimpse of an explanation may be found in another set of data presented in [100]. Each of the four other components were further split into two categories: *Work*, the effort spent during the first time in the cycle; and *Rework*, the accumulated efforts from all the other iterations.

The following table demonstrates that rework plus program understanding accounts for 60% of costs. These contribute little to the implementation efforts. Assuming that code size correlates with coding effort, the code grows as a result of rework by about $\frac{1}{4}$.

Component	Work	Rework
Requirements analysis	7%	17%
Design	7%	11%
Implementation	14%	4%
Testing	12%	1%

We conjecture that the key to the substantial program understanding component resides in the initial efforts. The initial analysis, design and implementation efforts have the ratio 1:1:2. We surmise that implementations start before the task is sufficiently understood and before a reasonable design has been constructed. Once an initial implementation has been obtained, the damage is done. The analysis and design outputs are insufficient guides for maintaining and enhancing the system.

Grady's account of the cost components is somewhat tentative. Still we recommend that the reader go back to the beginning of Part I.

Part II

Design

Chapter 15

From Analysis to Design

The goal of the design phase is to generate a description of how to synthesize software objects that behave in accord with analysis models and meet all other system requirements. This phase is a set of activities with:

Input: Functional, resource, and performance requirements.

Output: A specification providing a complete plan for implementing the system.

Techniques: Transformation, refinement, reification, composition.

Analysts see objects as descriptions of required properties and behavior. Designers view objects as *computational* entities which realize the desired properties in a manner that may be readily implemented using common object-oriented programming languages and tools. In this way, design serves as a bridge between analysis activities that describe those properties a system should possess, and implementation activities that describe the language and environment-dependent manner in which it is constructed.

15.1 Continuity

The border between analysis and design is often filled with discontinuities in non-object-oriented approaches to development. Designers sometimes use analysis information in only the most general ways and reanalyze the problem at hand from a computational perspective using different techniques and strategies than that of analysis.

analysis. This can even apply to object-oriented design. When OOD is preceded by non-OO analysis, much of the design phase should be preceded by a secondary analysis using the methods described in Part I to establish declarative structure.

One of the most attractive features of a uniform object-oriented approach to software development is *structural continuity*. The basic decomposition of a system into objects retains its general form from analysis through design and into implementation. Structural continuity is both an empirical observation (i.e., something that appears to hold widely across object-oriented development efforts) and a guiding principle for design methods. Even though their perspectives, methods, and goals differ, object-oriented analysts, designers, and implementors maintain the same overall orientation. They employ the same concepts and terminology for describing objects, classes, behaviors, inheritance, etc. This simplifies and streamlines the development process.

From a designer's point of view, many of the structures and descriptions that we have been calling analysis *models* in Part I may be thought of as declarative software *designs*. In Part II we assume that the main declarative aspects of a system model/design have been constructed using the methods described in Part I. Part II is "merely" about computational concerns. However, the continuity principle also ensures that OOA models may be refined and restructured during the design phase without the need for painful back-translation when reconciling designs with specifications. The border between design and implementation is also guided by continuity. Program designs should be tuned and restructured on the basis of experimentation, monitoring, and feedback with executable code.

Among the best tools for assessing the need for improvements at all levels is prototyping. We will show how OOD methods can accommodate the creation of prototypes that reflect only those transformations and details already committed. These steps may then be revisited after experimenting with the tentative system.

Exploitation of continuity results in a design process that is robust in the face of errors, suboptimal constructions, and other snags. Any design process that relies on the omniscience and perfection of analysts is doomed to failure. Methods must allow for analysis models to have occasional gaps and imperfections. Constraints and opportunities that stem from computational concerns can strengthen, complete, or override those seen from a declarative perspective. Similarly, analysts (even domain analysts) may not always recognize and exploit common design idioms, reusable components, and applications frameworks. Regardless of these considerations, the diversity of OO constructs allows many concepts to be described in any of several nearly equivalent ways. In the following chapters, we present several alternative strategies for expressing various analysis constructs. The best choice from a design perspective need not mesh with that from analysis.

For these reasons, designers should be prepared for the possibility of new insights, corrections, and improvements throughout the development process. Designers sometimes introduce new classes, refactor class hierarchies, and intertransform constructs in the process of meeting other goals. The methods described in Part II allow these manipulations to be phrased in ways that maintain contact with the original OOA models.

Reviews

Continuity also streamlines *traceability* from a software process management perspective. When design refinements are intrinsically keyed to OOA models, they are much easier to keep track of than otherwise. However, achieving this is by no means automatic, especially when analysis groups differ from design groups. Traceability requires a high degree of interaction and frequent reviews, mainly during the early stages of design.

During such reviews, designers should try to anticipate points at which models run into computational feasibility problems, cases where model incompleteness leads to ambiguities, class structures that are known to lead to software quality problems, and so on. Analysts must be prepared to defend, fill in, and/or revise their decisions.

There are many ways to structure this review process. One is to follow IBIS procedures [60] in which review points are raised as well-formed *issues*. For each issue there may be one or more *positions*. Each position may in turn have one or more *rationales*. Issues, positions, and rationales may all lead to other nested issues. These may ultimately lead to a set of decisions, actions, or other outcomes. Maintaining a record of such reviews in this structured form enhances traceability.

15.2 Transformation

15.2.1 Inputs

Object-oriented design methods exploit continuity while proceeding from a declarative to a procedural point of view. This process may be seen as a series of transformations from the inputs to the outputs of the design process. The most important input considerations *from* analysis are of the same general form as those described in Chapter 2 as analysis *inputs*. While the headings are the same, the details are substantially more refined, and reflect the products of OOA activities.

Functionality: The purpose of the system, as described by (multiple) declarative models of objects, classes, relations, states, transitions, interactions, etc.

Resource: The computational substrate on which the system will be built.

Performance: The expected response times of the system.

Miscellaneous: Auxiliary constraints including:

Software quality requirements concerning reliability, modularity, safety, cohesion, testability, understandability, reusability, and extensibility.

Lifecycle requirements for system evolution, demanding design allowances for reimplementation, repair, extension, and related adaptations necessary for coping with future requirements.

Compatibility requirements governing interactions with other systems, subsystems, and components (most typically non-OO ones) through constrained interfaces.

15.2.2 Process Criteria

We describe design activities as a series of transformations. However, we cannot prescribe fully algorithmic transformation schemes. The spectrum of transformations includes a few utterly mechanical translations, some involving guided (but not fully predetermined) series of refinements, some providing a wide range of options that must be chosen using situation-specific criteria (this is the most typical case), and some for which we can only provide general advice about how to connect initial and final conditions. The structure of these transformations relies on criteria common to the design of *any* transformational process, including:

- Group all transformations into meaningful, tractable phases with well-defined inputs, outputs, and separation of concerns.
- Obey logical dependencies. Do not schedule a step until its prerequisites are complete.
- Keep downstream options open. Avoid premature commitments to nonessential details.
- Operate on the most general representation possible for any transformation, thus minimizing redundancies resulting from similar operations on special cases.

- Output refinements and restructurings using the same representational framework as their inputs.

For example, requirements may be handed to a designer in sizable chunks, or even all at once. However, because of their intrinsic dependencies, design activities attempting to deal with these requirements must be in part sequential. It is impossible to assign resources to objects and manage their use until resource demands are at least approximately determined by establishing representational and computational properties. It is similarly impossible to address performance issues until these mappings are known. Sequentiality does not, however, imply that *all* activities within one subphase should be performed before all in the next.

While we use these criteria for guiding the overall design process, they also govern the architecture of just about any transformational system. Examples include compiler design, simulation system design, and computer vision processing system design.

15.2.3 Phases and Activities

The three major categories of input from analysis subdivide focal design issues in a natural way. We can expand on these groupings to better characterize them from a design perspective:

Functional design: Definition of representational and algorithmic properties of classes obeying the declarative constraints specified within OOA models.

Physical design: Mapping of objects to processors, processes, storage, and communication channels, along with design of facilities to manage these resources.

Performance design: Reconciliation of functionality and resource mappings to meet performance requirements when expressed using the target implementation languages, tools, configurations, etc.

The distinctions between functional, physical, and performance phases help capture different concerns and activities within design. While this is a reasonable way of classifying well-accepted *object-oriented* design practices, it differs from traditional approaches in a number of respects. For example, there is no separation between "coarse" and "detailed" design. Our presentation actually begins by discussing some small granularity issues, and our performance design methods consider both in-the-small and in-the-large performance factors. Thus, these categories focus more on the goals of design than their granularities. Similarly, we do not focus on (logical) "architectural design" *per se*. OOA models already specify much of the logical structure of systems. While many aspects of this structure may be modified during design, their general forms are established through declarative modeling.

We summarize some highlights of this process in the accompanying diagram. (It has the same interpretation as those of Chapter 12).

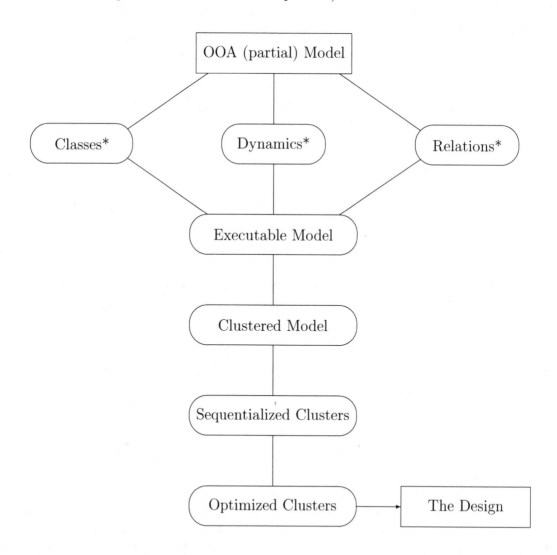

The basic framework admits several variations. For example, functional design may be interleaved with parts of OOA by dealing with subsystems or other coarse-grained components as they become available. Design activities may be subdivided among designers working concurrently and semi-independently. Performance design and implementation activities may be similarly distributed and pipelined. Also, design of the general form, policies, and infrastructure of many physical system matters may proceed at nearly any point.

15.2.4 Object Definitions and Models

Even though OOA is a declarative activity, analysts implicitly or explicitly adopt some kind of underlying abstract computation framework. Designers must ultimately replace this framework with one that is more easily supported by implementation languages, tools, and systems. Thus, not only must designers transform abstractly defined objects into concretely implementable ones, they must also transform the underlying processing and communication structure. This may be clarified by separating out the underlying computational models used in OOA from the ways analysts describe objects:

- Objects possess logical states and attributes, relations to other objects, and dynamic capabilities that may alter these across time.

- Each object is a member of some class. All objects of a particular class possess the same static and dynamic features, but may be in different states.

- Each object is a potentially active, autonomous sequential agent, performing at most one activity at a time.

- Objects communicate by generating events. The nature of event generation varies, and may include point to point messages and nonspecific requests issued via blocking, nonblocking, and timed protocols.

- Events may trigger transitions, new events, and/or the construction of new objects.

We have seen in Part I that most OOA practices implicitly or explicitly assume that every object is an "active" agent residing in its own processor. This framework would be pretty easy to deal with in design if a system were targeted for a massively parallel MIMD computer supporting exactly this computational model. But this is not a reality. These days, practical systems must occupy many fewer processors than objects. This means that objects must be packed into a relatively small number of interacting processes.

For both conceptual and pragmatic reasons, it is useful to think about a model that pushes this to an extreme, and packs *all* objects into a single program. This computational model is captured in the notion of a single-process object-oriented supervisory kernel. A kernel is the virtual machine that supports object computation. It specifies how objects are constructed and managed, how events are scheduled, and how communication is arranged.

The pragmatic utility of this model is that, unlike the massively parallel version, a single-process kernel may actually be implemented without engaging in many of the design issues described in Part II (cf., [216]).

15.2.5   Prototype Interpreters

An operational high-level kernel serves not only as a concrete implementation of a computational reference model, but also as an interpretive prototype simulator useful for experimenting with preliminary designs.

Prototypes may be implemented using techniques common to any single-process simulator or interpreter. The basic idea is to create a single active computational agent that receives all events in some kind of queue. When conditions allow, it pulls an event off the queue and performs the indicated actions on behalf of the simulated objects. In this way, all conceptually active objects may be simulated passively, at the expense of creating an all-powerful super-object forever repeating the following steps:

- Take from the queue any action that has all of its triggering constraints satisfied and process it:

  - If it is an object construction event, create a new (passive) object with the required initial states and attributes.

  - Else if it is an elementary state change operation on a primitive object, then directly compute it.

  - Else place on the queue all component events listed in the body of the transition.

This is actually just a variation on the computational structure implicit in OOA object models. (Compare the figure on page 99.) It assumes that *all* state changes, etc., are explicitly described in a computational fashion. But instead of empowering all objects to perform their own transitions and communicate with others, this model forces the single super-object to behave as if it were composed of all others, and to communicate only with itself via the queue.

The single-process nature of this interpreter allows it to be constructed without dealing with concurrency, distribution, and encapsulation issues that otherwise complicate design. However, this is a highly simplified model. A more complete version would need to address several other issues described in Part II, including:

Dispatching: Translating an event into the corresponding operation of a particular object.

Queuing: Keeping track of the conditions allowing operations to be triggered.

Conversion: Translation of more complex constructs (e.g., client-server interactions) into the simple format demanded by the model, or, equivalently, incorporating extensions that directly accommodate these.

Object management: Controlling storage and other resources consumed by simulated objects.

Symbolic analysis: Evaluating constraints, types, and annotations placed on objects, classes, relations, events, etc., before or during simulation.

Efficiency: Selection of algorithms that allow acceptable performance of functioning interpreters.

Many other design and implementation issues must be faced during the construction of such an interpreter. For large software development projects, efforts to do so are repaid with the ability to test preliminary designs. For smaller efforts, this model, even if not implemented, remains a useful conceptual tool for approaching and organizing design efforts.

While very generally stated, the features of this model are not engraved in stone. A preliminary design step is to agree on those details that might impact the overall approach taken in designing individual classes. This may then serve as a computational *reference model* for design. For example, the reference model may be severely constrained when the system is required to be implemented as a single program written in a single language. In this case, the language's own run-time kernel (or an abstraction thereof) may be substituted for the interpreter.

This view of prototype-compatible design does not cover *all* uses of prototypes. For example, prototyping the look and feel of a user interface is best carried out through side efforts experimenting directly with a Smalltalk environment, or with a C++ system using the InterViews toolkit [142], or whatever.

15.2.6   Translating Notations

The language of analysis is that of models and notations geared toward the goals of the analysis phase centering on the description of what systems do (not how they do it), written in a way that is meant to be complete, yet humanly understandable by both customers and designers.

Designers need to recast analysis models to enable further transformation of the declarative information supplied by OOA, while also supporting expression of computational and representational information important to implementors. Neither the graphical and textual notations of analysis, nor the implementation-dependent notations of common object-oriented programming languages suffice to describe this effectively. The computational aspects of design become tractable only by introduction of a notation that can capture analysis concepts on the one side, and implementation constructs on the other.

These considerations are not restricted to matters of software design. Electronics design increasingly relies on textual notations such as VHDL [144] to express the detailed structures and properties of designs while still abstracting over physical layouts and electrical characteristics. However, there are no universally or even commonly accepted intermediate languages for software design. In the case of systems-level object-oriented design, there are few such languages at all, and none that seem particularly well-suited to our goals of supporting (relatively) simple translation of analysis models on the one hand, and (relatively) language-independent design on the other. So, for the purposes of this book, we have reluctantly concocted an intermediate language (ODL) as a vehicle for expressing basic design notions. Like OAN, ODL is intended to be a very lightweight veneer that is easily converted to other notations and languages. We do not in any way insist that ODL be used when following the design methods described in Part II, but we need something concrete and specific to get across the main ideas. However, this book is not "about" OAN and ODL. You do not have to take the syntax as seriously as we sometimes do. In the course of reading

OAN Construct	ODL Construct
Instance (ch. 3, 8)	new (ch. 16)
Parametric Instance (ch. 8)	new, unique (ch. 17)
Class (ch. 3)	class (ch. 16)
Attribute (ch. 3)	fn (ch. 17)
Qualifier (ch. 3)	Qualifier (ch. 17)
Constraint (ch. 3)	inv (ch. 17)
Multiplicity (ch. 3)	opt, SET, ... (ch. 17-18)
Default (ch. 3)	generator ops (ch. 16-17)
Relationship (ch. 4)	class, fn, ... (ch. 18)
Relation Instance (ch. 4)	new, class, fn, ... (ch. 18)
Parametric Relation Instance (ch. 4)	inv, ... (ch. 18)
Generic Class (ch. 4)	class[T] (ch. 16, 18)
Set (ch. 4)	class, SET[T], ... (ch. 18)
State (ch. 5)	fn (ch. 17,19)
Initial State (ch. 5)	init (ch. 17)
Final State (ch. 5)	delete (ch. 24)
Transition Guard (ch. 5, 6)	when (ch. 19)
Transition Action (ch. 5, 6)	==>, { *calls* } (ch. 16-20)
Transition Event (ch. 5, 6)	==>, { *sends* } (ch. 16-20)
Service (ch. 5, 6)	op (ch. 20)
Exception (ch. 5, 6)	reply, ... (ch. 20)
Message Queuing (ch. 6)	pend (ch. 19)
Acquaintance (ch. 6)	fn, arguments, class, ... (ch. 16-18)
Subclass (ch. 7)	is, ... (ch. 16)
Partition (ch. 7)	oneOf, ... (ch. 17)
Metaclass (ch. 8)	class, generator, ... (ch. 18, 22)
Ensemble (ch. 9)	class (ch. 16-22)
Ensemble Constituent (ch. 9)	local, own (ch. 17)
Timing Constraint (ch. 11)	@ ... (ch. 19-20)

Table 15.1: Translations from Analysis to Design

examples, you ought to be able to jot down similar constructions using your favorite notation.

While translation from OOA to OOD declarative form is straightforward, there are few recipes. As listed in Table 15.1 (a preview of translation mechanics discussed in Part II), several options are usually available. Even so, the transformational nature of design maintains backwards compatibility. Design measures result in classes, operations, etc., whose basic structural characteristics remain representable in OAN. The principle of structural continuity implies that most graphical OOA models are also graphical *design* tools, at least for the declarative aspects of design. However, our increasing computational focus leads to decreased reliance on OAN.

ODL shares many features with commonly used object-oriented programming languages. It differs from programming languages in its ability to describe the properties of objects and operations, in addition to their representational and computational structure. Also, ODL retains from our analysis models the ability to describe parallelism and system architecture without having to commit to the extra-linguistic tools and systems typically required for their implementation. (This fact represents the most fundamental reason for using ODL in this book. The current state of languages, tools, and services for implementing such notions otherwise precludes a uniform treatment of underlying design concepts.) Still, ODL is very small and primitive, as OO notations go. These properties sometimes lead to awkwardness, but also lead to transparent translation to OO programming and tool constructions. We will exemplify translations to C++ and C++-based tools as we progress toward program design issues.

15.2.7 Active Objects

Design notations and corresponding methods for objects that may indeed be active, process-like entities denoted by our analysis models differ in several respects from those focused only on passive objects manipulated within a single OO program. Because these concerns *may* come into play even when objects are ultimately implemented as passive entities, we will not often distinguish the two until we need to. As a preview for those experienced in OO design of passive objects, we briefly characterize here some of the more notable differences in constructs and emphasis. Details will, of course, follow in later chapters.

Autonomy.   Because they are autonomous independent agents, the "membranes" separating the insides from the outsides of active objects are better defined than those for passive objects. For example, active objects are sometimes ultimately placed on different processors. There cannot be any representation dependencies, references to "shared memory", or commitment to other single-process constructions at least until it is known where different objects will physically reside. Similarly, it is usually a bad idea to claim that one active object is representationally embedded within another. Design methods arrange connections among helper objects rather than "embedded subobjects". The existence of links connecting one object to others thus forms important design information, even when these links can never be directly accessed by other objects and do not form parts of visible interfaces. Another consequence is that there are fewer opportunities for simultaneously subclassing both interfaces and implementations.

Thus, many design steps that form natural components of passive object design must be restructured. We resist premature commitments to sequentialization, representation, and other computational strategies that support declarative properties. The resulting practices may, however, be seen as extensions of the classic design goal of avoiding premature optimizations (i.e., counter-optimizations) of any form.

Communication.   Interactions may include combinations of one-way message sends and synchronized bidirectional exchanges. Designs relying on one-way asynchronous messages and other protocols built from them are often qualitatively different than sequential programs employing only procedural invocation.

As in our analysis models, we treat the issue of whether an operation should reply to a sender as a property of the receiving object. Clients *must* wait for the reply in any interaction defined using a bidirectional, procedural operation. One-way message sends may be either synchronous or asynchronous. In one-way communication, synchronicity refers the sending and reception of messages. *All* one-way messages are asynchronous with respect to their *effects*. In synchronous one-way schemes (as found, e.g., in **Ada** rendezvous constructs) a sender must wait until the receiver is able to accept a message. In asynchronous schemes (as found in most distributed processing toolkits), a sender may always generate a message. The message may be buffered by the communications media until it is accepted. There are intermediate forms as well. For example, even in asynchronous schemes, senders may need to wait for a channel over which to send a message. Channel availability may depend on the readiness of a dispatcher that resolves and routes requests. Conversely, in synchronous systems, receiver objects may possess queuing mechanisms allowing them to essentially always accept messages. Thus, we have been and will continue conservatively construing one-way messages as generally asynchronous. Adding synchronicity properties does not change the logic of resulting designs, but may lead to stronger guarantees about event sequencing and timing.

Coordination.   Interaction protocols for common services and bookkeeping responsibilities must be specifically designed. Routing, dispatching, and polymorphism support may also be under "manual" control. In addition to other computational and construction details, synchronization and control mechanisms must be specified and implemented. In particular, the design of joint actions involving synchronized transitions among possibly many objects requires transformations that eliminate potential interference, establish protocols to coordinate transitions among participating autonomous objects, and provide recovery mechanisms allowing one object or operation to fail without causing the entire system to fail.

15.3   Design Phases

This section provides an overview of principal phases, activities, concepts, and issues described in Part II of this book. Part II is structured similarly to Part I, although many details are not strictly parallel to those of Part I. The core chapters 17-20 parallel chapters 3-6 describing the four basic components of OOA models. However, dynamic computational issues play a far more central role in design, and thus permeate all other discussions.

15.3.1   Functional Design

The initial focus of design is to move from the world of description to that of computation. In the terminology that we will adopt for Part II, OOA descriptions are *abstract*. They describe attributes and constraints without completely indicating how it is that objects represent and maintain them. OOA dynamic models are similarly abstract. They describe the conditions and effects of state transitions and interactions without fully committing to algorithmic or representational details.

Abstract Classes

Abstract classes are the translation units of OOA information into a form suitable for other design activities. An abstract class is a kind of summary model, that may be used in the analysis phase as well as design (see Chapter 6). One or more abstract classes bring together descriptions of attributes, relations, states, transitions, events, and interaction protocols for an analysis-level class, while also propelling further design activities.

A near-synonym for "abstract" is *black-box*. Analysis models describe the outsides of objects without saying much about what the insides ought to look like. Abstract classes and operations are valuable tools for design too. Abstract classes at the design level may also represent constraints that are decidedly "abstract" but of interest only to designers, not analysts. They may describe the nature of objects introduced solely for behind-the-scenes design purposes and to fill in other gaps.

It is sometimes necessary to recast analysis information into different constructs and idioms in order to meet design goals. Analysis models do not address the nature of classes as software artifacts. Other class architecture requirements are implicitly or explicitly present during the functional design phase. We explore these issues a bit further later on in this chapter.

Concrete Classes

Among the primary tasks of functional design is *reification*, the synthesis of internal representational and algorithmic specifications that meet the declarative constraints of analysis models, along with other software-based criteria. This is the most time-consuming and creative aspect of the design process. Designers must choose among the multitude of available idioms to find those that best reflect the abstract specifications and other design goals. They must ensure that software quality criteria are met by paying attention to well-known pitfalls including aliasing and interference.

For each abstract class, a design must define one or more *concrete* classes that define the inner details of objects that fulfill the promises laid out in the abstract versions. These concrete classes may be introduced without disrupting the abstract characterizations. Any concrete class defines one particular, specialized way of obtaining the properties defined in an abstract class. Thus, concrete classes may be defined as *subclasses* of abstract ones. Because of subclassing, the abstract versions may continue to be used in the course of other design activities, without introducing any dependencies on how these classes are actually composed. Design also *introduces* a number of classes for the purpose of organizing and managing relationships, constraints, and interactions between other objects.

Compositional Design

Essentially all OO methods for synthesizing internal class properties are *compositional*. Objects obtain their static and dynamic properties by aggregating, delegating, inheriting, and coordinating those of other objects. The basic idea of compositional design is to build complex objects and operations out of simpler ones. This can take many forms, falling between two extremes:

Property-driven composition.   Property-driven composition begins when you are given an abstract characterization of a class. You must then find some components that make good on it. Typical steps include:

1. A set of attributes and behavior is described as an abstract class.
2. Other candidate components supporting at least some of the required properties are found or created.
3. The declarative constraints of the complex entity are restated in terms of combinations or sequences of those of the identified components.
4. A concrete version of the complex entity is then defined to access, coordinate, and/or extend the components.

Management-driven composition.   In management-driven composition, you are given information about how a number of other objects may be related and/or how they may interact. This information is just as "abstract" as OOA class descriptions, but is focused on relations rather than individuals. The design goal is to find ways of representing and managing relations and interactions. Typical steps include:

1. A set of relations, constraints, services, management chores, or interaction protocols is determined for a given set of objects.
2. A class or set of classes is defined to represent and track participant object information. Instances of these classes serve as "agents" for the components.
3. Constraints and protocols are localized within the agent classes.
4. Abstract characterizations, external interfaces, inheritance relations, etc., are defined for the agent classes.

These approaches are almost opposite perspectives on the same process of bridging external interfaces and internal affairs through managed composition. Most designs involve at least some aspects of both perspectives. For the moment, we emphasize only the compositional basis of both views. Abstract objects become software objects when built out of other software components. Conversely, groups of related components can be brought together under an abstract interface.

Bottom-up Methods

The compositional object-oriented design process differs significantly from that of classic "structured" methods. In those approaches, the design phase is normally a top-down refinement process starting with crude structural design, followed by module design, and then detailed design. OO strategies sometimes amount to the reverse of this.

OOA models already provide top-down decomposition of a system into constructs akin to abstract classes. Designers may define associated concrete classes in a more productive bottom-up fashion.

Assuming the existence of good analysis models, there is no absolute necessity that design methods be bottom-up. Top-down analysis models specify both complex and simple classes, operations, etc. It is possible to start off designing details of complex objects and to worry about components later. But there are a number of compelling reasons for working up from the simple to the complex as the default strategy:

Internal reuse: Smaller scale components tend to be usable in many different roles across a system. If they are not designed once, up front, it is very likely that similar, but not identical classes will be designed (perhaps by different designers) for many of these roles. This is a waste of everyone's time, a source of incompatibilities, and a barrier to further reusability.

Layering: A different label for internal reuse is "layering" (or "superimposition"). Higher level, coarser-grained classes may be layered on top of collections of simpler ones. When the underlying classes are addressed first, other designers may in turn build off this richer base, without worrying about the feasibility of underlying details.

External reuse: If components are useful in multiple roles within one system, it is likely that they will be reusable in other applications as well. It often pays to design such components more carefully to make them usable in broader contexts than those required for the applications immediately at hand. It is technically easier in OO frameworks to tune a general component for a particular application than to generalize a special-purpose one.

Imported components: Components created for relatively general and/or elementary purposes are more likely to be available than those for specialized subsystems. If available, complex classes can be designed to use them.

One pass design: Detailed characterizations of the attributes and behaviors of complex objects are often dependent on properties of components. If these are known, further design activities need not be interrupted or postponed. Simple safeguards within foundational objects minimize chances of making design errors stemming from assumptions that a component can do something that it cannot, and improve run-time safety.

Testability: Unit tests may be designed for individual components without considering their application contexts.

Known primitives: Analysts get to pick their own "primitives". But all software objects must ultimately be tied to the workings of elementary software objects such as booleans, integers, etc. Sometimes this involves an annoying amount of attention to such details. There is a compensating advantage: Because this bottommost level is essentially constant across different programming languages, systems, and platforms, designers have a known starting point for composing classes.

These considerations lead to tactics that are highly reminiscent of those used in other design enterprises. The combination of top-down analysis and compositional design has been a winning strategy in a variety of engineering endeavors, especially electronics design. As discussed by Cox [64], many aspects of object-oriented software design parallel those of circuit design. A circuit is designed by composing (most typically via standard interconnection strategies) various elementary devices, each of which is described in terms of its interface, and is often available in different versions.

Identifying components.   Bottom-up composition first involves the identification and design of those elementary classes necessary in the construction of others. This is not quite as glamorous as larger scale design activities. But one of the general claims of OO approaches is that class-based methods *scale* across small and large granularity problems.

Pure bottom-up design is most straightforward for very basic and/or general components. It is easy to identify at least some of the analysis model entities that serve as the most fundamental building blocks in a system. They are the ones that do not make any reference at all to any others in the definitions of their static and dynamic properties. After defining these, attention can be turned to classes that depend only on elementary ones, and then in turn these, and so on. All of this can usually be surmised through an informal definitional dependency analysis noting which classes definitionally rely on which others. Of course, it is not the least bit necessary, or even desirable, to proceed exactly in this order.

Preliminary models often lack detailed consideration of the lowest levels of component structure. They sometimes omit descriptions of such components all together, leaving them to designers, who may in turn pass the buck down to implementors. In other cases, they may describe features in unstructured terms, rather than as encapsulated classes. In others, analysts may have failed to notice how the definition of an elementary class or two could simplify treatment of several complex ones.

Some of these situations may be avoided through reviews of analysis models, especially with domain analysts who are familiar with tactics used in related software efforts. Others will require a bit of backtracking while in the midst of dealing with other components. Experience gained while designing various classes may lead to refactorings, new encapsulations, and other simplifications that are sometimes difficult to predict in advance.

Identifying frameworks. In addition to pure bottom-up sweeps, self-contained hierarchies may be isolated for special attention. These frameworks are useful not only as subsystem- or system-independent components, but also as tools in helping shape the conceptual underpinnings of a system development effort. Frameworks may be viewed as partial "theories" of particular domains, problems, and plans of attack. Early selection of frameworks helps guide application design. It ensures that different designers view similar problems appearing in different parts of a system in similar ways.

Scaling up. The ultimate in bottom-up compositional design is *megaprogramming* [226], the piecing together of large systems into huge ones. Similar methods apply but, of course, at much different scales. Many of the safeguards that allow smaller scale composition to proceed smoothly become unavailable, and strategies must be created to "glue" large, otherwise incompatible megaobjects together in a useful fashion.

15.3.2   Physical Design

The task of physical design is to map a set of software objects onto a set of physical objects.

Typical OO systems cannot enjoy the simplicities of either of our extreme computational models, "one object per processor" or "all objects in one process". Most systems need to reside in some middle ground of this continuum, in which all analysis-level objects are grouped into some number of coarse-grained active objects, or *clusters*. Each cluster contains some (usually large) number of objects sharing a CPU, an address space, and other physical resources.

Clusters themselves map easily into contemporary system *process* structures. In fact, our active object model is nearly identical to standard models of system processes. Thus, another way of viewing the design process is that in functional design, we assume *every* object, from the tiniest boolean object on up, can be implemented as a self-contained system process. For purposes of functional design we would like to stay away from physical mappings as long as reasonable. With few exceptions, these concerns do not impact the basic structure of classes and objects described by analysis models. It is not terribly productive to deal with these constraints until the computational properties of a system are at least approximately known.

In physical system design, we remedy the illusion that the system can be implemented using arbitrarily many processes. There are two principal phases of physical design. First, objects must be mapped to clusters. Second, the management facilities required to support these objects and clusters must be designed and/or employed.

Nearly all systems are constructed with the help of support tools and services that make specific commitments about how clusters are put together, managed, and allowed to communicate. These allow for ultimate transformation into a range of software architectures.

15.3.3   Performance Design

Systems design activities result in a two-tiered architecture. The system as a whole may be viewed in terms of the interactions of a relatively small number of coarse-grained cluster objects. Each of the clusters is in turn a *program*, usually written in a standard sequential OO programming language along with associated tools allowing communication to other clusters.

Performance design mainly involves transformations of the "second-class" passive objects forced to reside within programs. Design activities involve both accommodation and tuning:

Passivation. Intrinsically concurrent properties and mechanisms such as synchronization and triggering need to be either eliminated or simulated by objects residing in sequential environments and programmed using standard OO languages.

Optimization. Numerous measures are available to recast or otherwise tune classes and operations to meet performance requirements. Optimization and tuning involve interplay between designers and implementors.

15.4 Design Criteria

The central notion of a class at the design level is wonderfully flexible and powerful. Classes form a natural focal point for organizing diverse descriptive, representational, and computational properties. The ways in which these properties are conceptually viewed often governs the basic plan of attack for functional design.

We focus on design techniques associated with several different conceptual perspectives on the nature and roles of classes and objects. The different perspectives normally correspond to OOA models that stress particular features of objects. Often, multiple perspectives may be applied to the same OOA model. Designs can look very different depending on which sets of techniques are employed.

We will encounter some general principles for designing classes, as well as some particular idiomatic constructions representing known (small-, medium- or large-scale) architectures that may be applied to common design problems. We focus primarily on the former. We cannot describe all of the OO design architectures, patterns, and idioms that you are likely to need or run into. We restrict ourselves to surveys of some general forms. Still, we frequently discuss multiple alternative paths to a design solution, sometimes at the expense of presenting idioms and constructs that are closer to the level of neat tricks than of principled, stepwise developments. OO design has not matured to the point where we can fully rationalize, evaluate, or even categorize these strategies. Indeed, some people think that the situation-specific nature of design all but precludes development of comprehensive theories and accounts.

We describe many constructs, idioms, and strategies available for transforming analysis constructs into software. While we provide a few hints and guides for using them, we do not include explicit answers for questions such as, "Which strategy is best for representing relationship R?", "Should M be written as a blocking or nonblocking operation?", and so on. Most such questions cannot be answered. Few strategies and constructions are always right. Their appropriateness depends on how they fit into other design goals and criteria, that may differ from those of analysis. This notion that *models* are to be transformed into software *components* places a different perspective on some standard quality notions.

The most central criteria revolve around *compositionality*. Compositional design is simplest when the construction of one class depends only on the abstract class specifications of its components, not their internal structures. In a compositional design framework, just about every class should be designed to be amenable for use as a component by others. In the remainder of this section, we survey a few more specific criteria and concerns that may serve as guides for deciding among different OO methods and constructions. We will also preview some of their implications for choosing among design idioms and transformations, leaving others for later.

15.4.1   Coupling

The most well-known design guidelines for enhancing composition revolve around the issue of *coupling*. An operation, object, set of objects, class, or set of classes that minimizes demands on the computational environment is said to have low coupling with respect to that environment. Decoupled entities are normally easiest to compose. Coupling is a very broad concept, and may be partitioned along several dimensions.

Representational coupling.   Classes should not depend on the specific representational and computational details of one another. The central tactic of defining and using abstract classes stems from the idea that composite classes and actions should minimize dependencies on irrelevant representational and computational details. These concerns lead to the routine exploitation of *interoperability* and *black-box reuse*.

Complex objects need not be dependent on, or even know about, the representational and computational details of other components, as long as they do the right thing. Common abstract class descriptions may cover a range of interoperable implementations. This solves several related design problems:

Interchangeable parts: New components may be swapped for old ones without disrupting other classes.

Multiple representations: Different versions of the same kind of component may work best in different parts of the system. There is no reason at all to settle on just one version. Unlike most *modular* design strategies, OOD facilitates coexistence of multiple implementations of the same capabilities.

Prototype evolution: During prototype development, classes can be thrown together in the most haphazard way, even as nonfunctional stubs, in order to get something executable for evaluation. These classes may then be replaced with more serious versions in an incremental fashion.

System evolution: Very often, evolutionary software changes can be isolated by reimplementing a few classes that preserve the same interface to the rest of the system, but differ vastly in internal details. For example, persistent storage management may be recast to use a different database service.

Performance tuning: Poorly performing classes can be identified and replaced, again, without disruption. In this way, prototype evolution, performance tuning, repair, and evolution are all performed using the same fundamental strategy of component replacement.

Extensibility: There may be several levels of subclasses that all preserve the same interface but add upon each other's mechanics. Creation of a subclass rather than an interoperable sibling class is an attractive option for tuning, evolution, and replacement.

External components: Existing systems that we cannot (or will not) implement may be described via ordinary classes, but with implementation details that are beyond our control.

Standardization: It is both easier and more productive for a company or group to standardize on interfaces than on internal details. Some people predict eventual industry-wide standardization of many object-oriented component specifications.

Testability: Representation-independent test suites may be constructed for entire sets of classes.

Frameworks: Medium-scale, multipurpose, reusable class hierarchies that depend only on the abstract interfaces of various components have proven to be valuable tools for simplifying and accelerating further design. The frameworks themselves are never touched. Different applications are constructed by defining particular versions of the abstract components. Generally, just about *any* hierarchy of abstractly defined classes is a candidate framework. However, only those few that turn out to be useful across different applications and contexts deserve the title.

We are fanatical about eliminating representational coupling, especially at the lowest levels of class design. We are concerned about the design of systems that might be built using multiple heterogeneous platforms, operating systems, and configurations. We take careful, even tedious, measures early in the design process to guarantee avoidance of low-level representational dependencies.

These concerns extend upward. The other side of interoperable subclasses is *black-box reuse*. We encourage the use of pure composition rather than certain subclassing strategies. Black-box composition is a means of routinely minimizing representational coupling.

Value coupling.　Classes should be written so that operations are as independent as possible on the particular values of attributes. This is a natural practice in OOD. Generally, superclasses define attributes and behaviors without committing to particular values. Whenever necessary or desirable, subclasses and related constructs may then define special cases for special values and conditions. Parameterization constructs (e.g., generic classes) provide similar opportunities for removing such dependencies.

Subclass coupling.　Beyond minimizing the dependence of one class on how other classes support various features, components may be designed to reduce dependence on whether these features are present at all. This is another view of the notion that preconditions should never be overstated.

Attributes and arguments should always be defined using the *least* specific (i.e., most abstract) class type that is guaranteed to have the right attributes and behavior. For example, if some `print`[1] operation just prints a `name` attribute, then even though it might be "intended" for use in printing `Client` names, it may as well accept any `Person` object, assuming that `Person`s have names and class `Client` is a subclass of class `Person`. This may in turn lead you to abstract out yet simpler and more general superclasses. For example, you might decide to create a class `NamedObject` as a superclass of `Person` and/or other classes.

Other consequences of subclass coupling include the following.

---

[1]For clarity and emphasis, we continue to use *this font* for OOA level names but `this font` for OOD level names.

Subclass independence: Decreasing the granularity of classes by imposing new superclasses introduces a different form of coupling. Classes become less dependent on each other, but more dependent on the details of a class hierarchy itself. This is not at all bad, but sometimes results in the design of components that are unusable outside of an otherwise irrelevant class hierarchy. The use of shallow hierarchies, as well as exploitation of generic, parameterized class mechanisms can remove unnecessary dependencies. Also, special "flattened" versions of classes may be defined. These pull together all inherited information in one class, allowing it to be used stand-alone.

Subclass extensibility: Superclasses may be defined only in terms of base properties, which are then specialized in subclasses. Applications need not know which particular subclass they are using. But abstraction of the "right" properties can be hard. Superclass descriptions need to be strong enough to be usable by other classes as arguments and components. But they also need to be weak and general enough to allow definition of subclasses that extend and refine these properties in all useful directions.

Subclass performance: Inheritance may be used as an optimization technique. By constructing classes ensuring that general-purpose algorithms are always available, but employing special ones when additional constraints hold, both performance and integrity criteria can be met. When efficiency requirements overwhelm others, optimization via subclassing can be further exploited to improve performance, although sometimes at the expense of additional, undesirable coupling.

Identity coupling. A real danger in OOD is the potential proliferation of "connection" attributes within classes. These connections maintain communication channels with other objects. The more objects and classes that one object needs to know about, the more dependent it is on the details of its environment.

There are several remedies. For example, when one object requires some service, it often does not need to know exactly who provides this service. We would rather not have to keep track of the targets (recipients) of service messages, especially when they may change, or when discovering the "best" service provider is a nontrivial matter. We attack this at several levels, from exploitation of basic *dispatching* mechanisms to the design of higher granularity mediator objects.

Protocol coupling. A sender of any message (or, equivalently, generator of an event) should require only those effects and communication of effects minimally necessary. For example, send-and-forget one-way message passing places the lowest possible demands on the objects performing the operations, since it does not assume anything about when operation effects hold, or even require that notification be sent back to senders indicating completion. We will also discuss constructs that allow objects to interact without hard-wiring either the identities or the operations invoked on the other objects. A similar tactic is to build mediator objects that enforce particular protocols among objects who do not otherwise know how to respond to each other.

Minimization of identity and protocol coupling is the design analog of analysis-level postponement of the definition of interaction partners (Chapter 6). However, identity and protocol coupling are *not* always all bad from a computational perspective. Perhaps the ultimate decoupled system is a relational database, where (from an OO view) objects are just represented in terms of their attributes and relations, and centralized systems (database managers) coordinate all state changes without any independent communication between the objects whatsoever. While this may or may not be a good way to manage persistent storage, it is far too centralized to serve as a reasonable model of most software systems. Object-oriented designs distribute knowledge and coordination across a system, generally at the lowest level that it can be reasonably managed. This requires compromises between localization and centralization through intermediate levels of identity and protocol coupling.

Code coupling. The definition of concrete operations should be decoupled from the contexts in which they are employed. This requirement is most obvious and critical when classes are designed for possible use in concurrent execution environments. Here, the internal characteristics of an operation may be identical across different classes and subclasses, but the situations under which these actions are triggered may differ significantly.

For example, in a concurrent environment a request to get an item from a List may be postponed until an item becomes available. In a sequential environment, it may result in an exceptional condition. However, we would like to describe the details of how the item is obtained in the case when the list is not empty in the same way across both situations. We will focus on the design of classes that are assumed to be usable in concurrent settings. However, many will need to become sequentialized.

15.4.2 Cohesion

The other side of minimizing *demands* is minimizing *features*. This is related to the familiar software engineering concept of *cohesion*. A class that maintains, localizes, and protects only those features necessary to perform its primary role is said to have high cohesion.

Objects should provide "just enough" functionality and support features necessary to serve their intended roles. While there is often some leeway in deciding among core primitive attributes and operations, objects need not be burdened with the responsibility of supporting derived operations that can be performed *with* them, rather than *by* them. This enables additional superimposed layers to control components in different ways.

Strengthening features. The most common strategy for minimizing features is to enhance the guaranteed properties of those that remain as core attributes. For behavioral features, this often corresponds to the notion of strengthening postconditions.

Encapsulation. Encapsulation is the meeting point between coupling and cohesion. Objects in design contain features that support advertised functionality, but hide the underlying mechanisms so that other objects cannot reach in and corrupt them. This kind of encapsulation is among the central defining features of the object-oriented approach. But it is not an *automatic* consequence of OOD, and is among the hardest things to get just right. Well-designed classes are as open as possible, so that others may use them for diverse applications, but not so open that others may abuse them.

15.4.3 Reliability

Correctness is, of course, of paramount importance. However, objects must also be designed to be robust with respect to internal design and implementation errors leading to run-time faults, misuse (errors by clients), and failures of other objects on which they rely.

Several alternative strategies are available for each case. They need to be tailored to the situations at hand. In addition to the kinds of errors usually addressed in OOA, computational concerns lead to the following problems. Several are just different views of the same phenomena.

· A message has no valid receiver.

- A message is sent to the "wrong" receiver.
- An object receives a message it cannot handle.
- An object receives a message with value argument that it cannot handle.
- A client obtains a result that it cannot handle.
- An invoked bidirectional operation never replies.
- A received request never executes.
- An object reaches an illegal (undefined) state.
- An object cannot be constructed.
- An object cannot be killed.
- An object forever waits for an event that never occurs.
- An operation triggers "by accident".
- A supposedly "dead" object wakes up.

Error policies. Of course, the best policy for dealing with errors is avoidance. Error avoidance is mainly a static design-time issue that ensures that no action is ever performed unless all of its preconditions hold. In principle, many errors are avoidable via program verification. But we do not foresee the existence of full OO verification tools and techniques in the near future.

Descriptions of the diagnosis and recovery of unpreventable errors should be part of any OOA model. Communications failures, deadlocks, and so on may be accommodated using time-outs, recoveries off history logs, or whatever means specified. Design activities may introduce other opportunities for failure. In most cases, the best strategy is to backtrack to Part I of this book and reanalyze conditions and actions, including:

- Inaction (ignoring errors).
- Logging faulty attempts.
- Notifying other objects about failures.
- Notifying people about failures.
- Multi-level notification protocols based on severity.
- Notification protocols at multiple levels of centralization.
- Retrying an operation again with different arguments, etc.
- Postponement, usually by requeuing failed operations.
- Time-outs on waits for operations.
- Redirecting a message to a different receiver.
- Conditional continuation based on error values, etc.
- Termination of operation sequences.

· Rollbacks to undo the incomplete effects of a failed operation.
· Re-initializing or reconstructing failed objects.
· Re-initializing or reconstructing the entire system.
· Self-destruction.

15.4.4 Human Factors

Like all software constructs, classes are written both for machine and human consumption. To be usable (and reusable), classes must be retrievable, readable, understandable, convenient, general, and so on. These properties rest in part on the availability of good tools to help designers find, understand, and integrate other classes, as well as the availability of documentation, tracing mechanisms, etc. But even the best tools and documentation are useless unless classes are designed with these factors in mind.

15.4.5 Conservatism

First, do no harm. Some OOD constructs and idioms are novel, esoteric-looking, and/or technically demanding. These are balanced with notions aimed at enhancing the chances that designs will be correct, reliable, maintainable, traceable, testable, understandable, and reusable. This emphasis distinguishes our account from many other standard treatments of OOD. We strive to integrate descriptive and computational approaches, sometimes to the point of awkwardness, but always with the intention of providing maximal guidance for designing classes in a conservative, correct fashion.

The key components of this approach are those that *integrate* descriptive and computational information, mainly via steps linking abstract and concrete classes. We should note that this approach does have some limitations. It can limit the design space. Some concrete class designs may obey abstract constraints, but maintain properties in ways that we cannot describe. We sometimes avoid this by limiting the kinds of descriptive properties attached to abstract classes.

15.5 Managing Design

Good design requires good management of constituent activities and developers. While general software development process management strategies are outside the scope of this book, we note in this section a few aspects that are special to OO design and development efforts, especially those surrounding roles and practices enhancing component reuse. They apply equally well across most phases and levels of design and implementation. We will not bother to distinguish them within this context.

15.5.1   Roles

Development roles may be assigned according to the kinds of entities that need to be designed and implemented. These may include classes, process management services, interprocess communication services, programs, code-generating tools, simulators, test suites, performance monitors, documentation, installation manuals, and so on. There are also partitioning strategies that cut across these task-based categorizations. Different individuals or teams may be assigned responsibility for tasks associated with different *subsystems* identified in the analysis or design phase. This is common practice in any development effort. Alternatively, people may be assigned responsibility for developing related *classes* and/or *tools* that need to be built regardless of their use in any particular subsystem.

These categorizations sometimes conflict. An increasingly prevalent compromise is to perform most assignments by subsystem and/or task, but also to assign people or teams to *reuse management* and/or *tool management* efforts that operate in close coordination with other teams.

In an ideal version of this partitioning, individuals performing subsystem and application development engage in pure *design with reuse* methods. All development builds on top of reusable components and tools developed and maintained by other teams. At the same time, newly developed components are fed back into the reuse effort. This may be pushed to extremes for routine applications development. Individuals assigned to create miscellaneous small applications may do so solely by connecting existing components in new ways. This would be facilitated by the use of special graphical OO programming languages that construct programs by compiling interconnection graphs.

Support Teams

Tool management and reuse management teams are motivated and structured along the same lines, and are even commonly rolled together as the responsibility of a single team or individual. In both cases, implementation of the current system may progress most rapidly if the teams are involved very early in the system development process, so that support software is ready when needed.

The differences between OO tools and OO class libraries can be a little subtle, and perhaps not even worth defining with respect to management efforts. For example, a tool that *generates* classes for custom user interfaces is often interchangeable with an application framework providing operations on abstract `Window`, `Button`, etc., classes that may be customized through composition and subclassing. The availability of one might govern whether and how to develop the other. Here, for example, the optimal solution might be to have both an applications framework and a tool that quickly generates common cases within that framework.

A vague but more useful distinction is separation of general-purpose tools and classes from domain-specific ones.

General-purpose software might include user interface classes and tools, inter-process communication tools, basic collection classes, system interface classes, and instrumentation tools. For these, teams and individuals may spend more time in acquisition and evaluation of externally obtainable components than in creating new ones. They may become the local experts in the use of this software, and provide training and consulting to others. Cases in which general-purpose classes and tools are required, but not available, may lead to side channel development efforts that are sponsored by several ongoing applications projects.

Domain-specific software supports a line of products, but not any one of them *per se*, for example, application classes (e.g., for banking), tools generating class stubs obeying particular error protocols, and classes and tools supporting authentication protocols. Most domain-specific efforts are constructive rather than evaluative. Building such classes and tools during the course of development of any one project represents an investment in the future.

15.5.2 Managing Reuse and Tools

Reuse management should be an ongoing concern. For any particular project, a reuse team should be involved early in the development process. Members help identify components and chart out reusability prospects. These efforts are facets of *domain analysis*, as described in Chapter 13.

Regardless of whether they address general-purpose or specialized software, and whether they are centered around tools or components, the basic goals in support management are similar: To prevent people from needlessly re-creating designs and implementations, to provide people with a means of profiting from the efforts of others, and to encourage people to create components and tools that may be reused by others.

Problems emerge when individuals do not think to reuse classes before designing or implementing them. Without care, many essentially identical classes may be defined using different names and conventions in different parts of the system. Among other problems, none of these are typically as good as those that would be produced from a well-managed reuse program. Support efforts may include:

- Identifying potentially reusable components.
- Evaluating component quality and suitability for reuse.
- Importing components developed elsewhere.
- Developing software "glue" to facilitate composition of different components.
- Providing support tools for browsing, understanding, and using components.
- Coordinating feedback, annotations, bug reports, etc.
- Integrating different media and notations.
- Developing components projected for use across multiple projects.
- Training others in the use of existing components.

Controlling Components

The control of reusable components extends techniques common to other software coordination efforts. Tools and techniques should address both reuse-specific and other supportive roles, including:

Version control: Central tracking of versions, tests, and usage histories.

Format standards: Tools maintaining standard formats for designs, code, documentation, etc.

Updates: Protocols and tools for error reports, change requests, suggested improvements, resubmissions, and replacements, along with subsequent release notices.

Annotations: Feedback and commentary from component users accessible to other potential and actual users. Usage notes remain among the best means for communicating client-side documentation.

Retrieval: Clients cannot reuse components if they cannot find them. Components may be retrievable using any plausible path. These include the standard inheritance-based paths, those specified by interface, by functional category, by keywords, and so on.

Browsing: A standard browsing system for models, designs, code, graphics, documentation, etc.

Metrics: Basic metrics (e.g., numbers of classes, subclasses, operations) may be collected to summarize sets of related components.

Ownership protocols: Responsibility for a class or set of classes may be assigned to a principal "owner", who may or may not also be an actual designer. If a component passes from a team to a reusable library, ownership may also pass to the reuse team.

Access control: During development, classes should be available to developers, but not others. Access control strategies prevent potential users of a class from obtaining and/or attempting to modify premature versions.

Configuration control: Components destined to work in specific products, releases, platforms, etc., must be so marked and maintained.

Release management: Tools to gather software, documentation, etc., in preparation for particular releases.

Testing: Test histories, test generators, testing and integration protocols, etc.

Generators: Standardization of formats, approaches, and policies is facilitated by tools that help semiautomatically generate parts of design descriptions, for example, those that help ensure conformance to selected error handling policies.

Design checkers: Tools for checking whether designs meet standards and other criteria.

Program development: Compilers, debuggers, editors, etc.

Tool integration. It is unlikely that you will find single integrated tool sets that contain all of this functionality, in addition to integrated support for OOA methods (Chapter 12) and requirements and domain analysis. In the future, integrated tools may be available supporting traceability and version management of all artifacts across all development phases, team (policy) support, prototype interpreters, and indexed access to libraries of analysis, design and code components.

However, less extensive solutions fare reasonably well, especially for small and medium efforts. For example, as reported in [77], a successful medical software product produced in 18 months by a team of eight relied only on a single-user OOA drawing tool and a C++ compiler. Still, they expect more than 80% reuse for a follow-on project.

Evaluating Components

Criteria and protocols need to be established for assigning, accepting, revising, replacing, and removing components. General criteria may be based on the quality concerns described earlier in this chapter. However, such criteria are notoriously difficult to apply to individual components. Beyond simply observable qualities such as tests and testability, few automatic checkoffs are always applicable. This leads to the widespread adoption of *review* (inspection) procedures.

There are many kinds of reviews, including blind inspections, joint walk-throughs, and comparisons of multiple independent designs. These procedures are well described in standard texts on software process management (e.g., [117]). They apply equally well to OO development and to reuse management. Such efforts may be operationalized via *certification* policies and procedures describing those steps that must be taken for any component to be certified for general reuse. These normally include some combination of requirements for testing, review, and assessment via metrics.

Evaluating Use

Reuse and tool management efforts and their clients should themselves be evaluated. This is a difficult issue. Metrics for evaluating how effectively people have reused classes and exploited tools remain controversial. Worse, many standard "productivity" measures (e.g., lines of code generated per programmer) sometimes *counterindicate* effective reuse. Much care and judgment is needed in evaluating developers within this framework.

15.6 Summary

Ideally, object-oriented design methods and practices seamlessly mesh with those of analysis. This is a byproduct of more general continuities inherent in object-oriented software development. These ideals may be approximated by arranging that design subphases and activities respect these continuities. Design may be approached as a series of *transformations* dealing with functional, resource, and performance requirements. At a technical level, transformation is often only a metaphor, not a series of blind mechanical translations. But even so, transformational logic leads to the formulation of a default strategy that is structured enough to be useful, yet flexible enough to support countless situation-specific variations.

Whether it is focused on the description of object properties, behaviors, relationships, or interactions, design is primarily a compositional process. Complex classes rely on simpler ones for many of their static and dynamic features. Since OOA models already provide descriptive accounts of high-level class organization, the design process may employ more productive bottom-up methods. OO design is also *idiomatic*. Class-based design frameworks are almost *too* flexible. Different idiomatic approaches to the same problem often lead to different design solutions.

Criteria for evaluating such solutions resemble those established for any other software artifact. There are many criteria to choose from, and few ways to measure any one of them. We consider them to be most valuable in guiding the design process itself, rather than as metrics for gauging the quality of individual classes, although they may certainly play a part in this as well.

Creating distinct reuse and/or tool management teams is a central factor in making good on the high productivity reputation of the OO paradigm.

15.7 Further Reading

Different authors differently categorize the borders or lack thereof between analysis and design; see, for example, Monarchi and Puhr [162], Dasgupta [67], and Potts [182] for summaries.

The compositional OO approach to the design of active objects is perhaps most closely associated with the work of Tsichritzis, Nierstrasz, and colleagues at Geneva; see, for example, [168].

Berard [26] and Meyer [157] provide alternative characterizations of coupling and related OO software quality criteria. Reuse-oriented software process management is discussed by several authors in the collection edited by Biggerstaff and Perlis [32].

Design interpreters may be constructed using simulation, logic programming, and constraint propagation techniques, including those found in OO constraint systems such as Garnet [163].

More formal computational models of active objects might be based on abstract process models including CCS [159], π-calculus [160], and the Chemical Abstract Machine [30], on algebraic frameworks (e.g., [227]), or on concurrent constraint systems (e.g., [194]). Alternative conceptualizations include models treating all objects as sets of storage locations accessed and controlled by multiple processes [54, 15, 133].

15.8 Exercises

1. Compare the approach described in this chapter with that of other transformational systems with which you are familiar; e.g., compilers, computer vision systems.

2. Describe how and why our OO kernel and reference model differs from those used in discrete event simulation systems.

3. Sequentially pipelined activities sometimes stall. Describe some possible stall points in a pipelined analysis-design-implementation process framework and how to deal with them.

4. In Chapter 5, we started using constructs (e.g., event generation) that are not classically considered to be *black box*. Why do you think we still characterize them as abstract from a design perspective?

5. Explain the difference between function composition and object composition.

6. We did not list "generality" *per se* as an independent component design criterion. Should we have?

7. List similarities and differences between:

   (a) An `Integer` object and a *nail*.
   (b) A `PullDownMenu` object and a *hot water faucet knob*.
   (c) An `AccountList` object and a *refrigerator*.
   (d) Reusable *software* and reusable *hardware*.

8. Why do lines-of-code metrics sometimes counterindicate reuse? Do they *always* do so?

Chapter 16

Description and Computation

In this chapter, we introduce technical details surrounding functional class design. The basic strategy is to collect analysis information describing class features and tie them together as abstract classes. The computational side of these classes is designed through the definition and use of other components. We illustrate with a few ridiculously simple classes.

16.1 Translating Analysis Models

Analysis models define features and constraints using constructs that describe properties of objects, but are not themselves objects. This *descriptive* information forms the basis for abstract classes. For example, a simple Counter may be described as an object that always possesses a count property, as well as operations (transitions) such as clear that change that property. This class might be described via OAN models including:

clear counter		
guard	action	{event}
TRUE	$count' = 0$	
clear		

NZ ——— [table] ———→ Zero

The `count` property is a *value* attribute that describes the state of an object. On the other hand, an instance of class `Counter` is of course an object, and not just a property *per se*, even though it only reflects a single interesting property and supports state transitions that alter that single property. This would be true even if we designed a `Counter` class in which no other object could ever "know about" the `count` property.

While we must proceed toward a computationally-based view of objects in OOD, we do not want to lose such declarative information. Maintaining both descriptive and procedural information at the design level increases the chances that computational specifications are correct by construction.

We accommodate this in **ODL** by supporting the notion of an *abstract class* that collects static and dynamic information, and recasts it in a form more readily amenable to other design activities. In simple cases, abstract classes just describe a set of value properties, and how they change with transitions. We may collect OOA descriptions pertaining to counter objects and the events they respond to as follows:

```
class Counter
  fn count: int;
    inv count >= 0

  fn isZero: bool = (count = 0);
    init isZero = true

  op clear ==> isZero' end

  op inc   ==> count' = count + 1 end

  op dec   when isZero then  % no effect %
           else count' = count - 1 end
end
```

[We will postpone describing most syntactic details of **ODL** for a while, and pretend that you are following along. But try to figure it out. We try to keep **ODL** examples down to the smallest self-contained constructions that illustrate the main ideas.]

Even though it looks somewhat computational in flavor, this abstract class declaration is really just descriptive. It says that counter objects are entities that may be ascribed an integer-valued `count` property. Other constraints and operations are described with respect to that attribute. Simple status inspectors such as `isZero` summarize an aspect of the state as a boolean indicator value.

16.1.1 Attributes

We declare **OAN** attributes as *functions*. The `count` declaration in no way means that any counter object "directly" maintains any kind of integer-like internal representation, only that it needs to report the state in integer form when asked. For example, a counter could be implemented by pushing and popping random items onto some kind of stack. The number of items on the stack would correspond to the count, and could be so reported.

At the same time, we would like to ensure that these abstract properties actually hold for any software counter object. We will do so by mandating that implemented versions of classes indeed support descriptive functions such as `count`. Of course, it is possible to perform object-oriented design without explicitly incorporating such descriptive techniques. In other words, we *could* just implement an integer-based or stack-based counter without bothering to tie them explicitly to descriptions of what they are supposed to do. Among other disadvantages, this would break all continuity and traceability with respect to analysis models.

16.1.2 Domains

In **ODL**, we provide a very small set of predefined value types (principally `bool`, `int`, `real`, `char`; see Chapter 17) for use in the definition of abstract classes. We keep this small to facilitate the transition from specification to implementation. Value domains are treated very differently than classes of objects in **ODL**. Values are "more abstract" than objects. For example, the `bool` value `true` has no identity, cannot be changed into another value, and does not itself communicate with other objects. It is a raw description. An *object* with a boolean property does have an identity, may be able to mutate state, and may partake in interactions with other objects.

The differences between value-based and object-based perspectives are most evident in the separation of ordinary value types from equally ordinary *objects* whose only role is to maintain such values in the usual ways. For example, we may define *class* `Bool` as:

```
class Bool
  fn val: bool;
  op t!: ()     ==> val' = true end
  op f!: ()     ==> val' = false end
  op set(newVal: bool): () ==> val' = newVal end
end
```

A Bool object always has a bool state of being true or false. But since it is an object, it may change its state. Of course, we can design objects that *do not* change their states too. We will design quite a few of those.

Some ODL details: We often use capitalization conventions as in this example, with lower-case for value types (bool) and capitalization (Bool) for classes. It is a bit confusing at first, but makes things easier later. The characters "?" and "!" are acceptable as parts of names. We sometimes use the former for simple "self-describing" attributes, and the latter for "self-describing" commands. As a degenerate case, we use just "?" itself as a name for value attributes of "basic" classes maintaining values of predefined value types, and drop the intervening "." on access. Thus, to cut down verbosity, we alias the Bool val attribute as just "?". For any boolean object aBool, saying aBool? gets its current value.

16.1.3   Dynamics

Classes Counter and Bool contain examples of the two basic ODL dynamic constructs:

Functions: A fn is a "value sensor", or "attribute inspector" that reports state information without otherwise disrupting an object. (The keyword fn is optional.)

Operations: An op is an event-driven transition (or "method"), identified by its associated input event (message) name and signature. It may be either a one-way operation or a bidirectional operation that guarantees to reply to its sender (and to "block" its sender until it does so). Declarations of blocking operations include an indication of the kind of entity returned. When ops do not return a particular result but only return synchronization, this is marked with "()". When they do, the results may either be given a name within the declaration or as a shorthand, treated anonymously and replyed. We will consider further variations and refinements of ops in Chapter 20.

Procedure-style (blocking) interaction is a reasonable way to describe elementary operations on elementary classes such as `Bool`. Even though an operation such as `f!` is not very "interactive" or bidirectional, we stick with established conventions when dealing with basic classes such as `Bool`. In contrast, the `Counter` class declared `inc`, `dec`, and `clear` as one-way operations. We could have chosen otherwise in both cases.

Effects

Operations may be characterized abstractly by listing their *effects* using the syntax `==>` *expr* `end`, where *expr* is any descriptive expression. The prime (as in `val'`) indicates the state *after* the transition has completed.

Effects are the main translation constructs for **OAN** *action* and *event* descriptions, as well as simple state changes. For example, the effects for `t!` and `f!` correspond to the transition network:

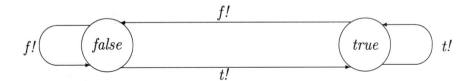

As is the case in analysis (see Chapter 5), the nature of effect descriptions can be a bit arbitrary. With any luck, analysis models have provided descriptions that are "complete" while still suppressing "irrelevant" details. It is more than common for effect statements to be described via textual annotations rather than these slightly more formal specifications. We will most often use the more structured versions, since it makes further manipulations and transformations easier to describe and illustrate. However, the methods can be used with whatever degree of precision and formality you can obtain from analysis models. The more precisely effects can be described, the easier it is to transform them into executable code. At some point, at some level, this kind of translation needs to be performed.

16.1.4   Services

Cohesion and Layering

There are many ways to define classes like `Bool`. Nothing absolutely forces the definition of a given operation as primitively available within a class. Matters of relative primitiveness are often judgment calls in class design. The set of operations defined for a class should, on the one hand, be minimally complete, describing only those transitions that cannot be defined in terms of others. On the other hand, usability concerns lead to the definition of operations that make common client-side usages simple to express. Pragmatics argue for hiding enough detail that operations may be efficiently implemented without introducing observable dependencies. For example, we might prefer to express `Bool::set` as the sole primitive, and then define `t!` and `f!` in terms of `set`, or even to define all of them in terms of a `toggle` primitive. (As here, we use "*class*::*op*" when necessary to distinguish the version of *op* defined in *class*.)

The tactic of defining basic classes to have minimal yet complete interfaces, and then adding functionality via layered operations rather than mangling existing classes is sometimes called *extension by addition* [103]. It is a good way of enhancing the maintainability and evolvability of designs. It places some pressure on getting the "little" things in a set of class designs right to begin with.

Some heuristics may guide such decisions. If an operation can be phrased as a sequence of other defined, accessible operations on its targets, it should not be listed as an operation of any one of the associated classes. This rule may be balanced with the goal of minimizing arguments to operations.

Service Operations

The simplest kind of layering is the definition of service operations. Operations may accept and/or return either state or object information as message "arguments" and "results". Also, operations need not be listed within classes if they obtain their effects by coordinating others that *are* received by participants. For example, we may have a service transition described for some unrelated object:

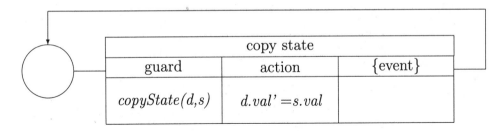

set to inverse		
guard	action	{event}
invertSet(d,v)	*d.val' =not v*	

This might correspond to **ODL** operation:

```
op invertSet(dest: Bool, v: bool) ==> dest'? = ~v end
```

Because it was not embedded in a class, this operation may even be considered as a "top-level" utility procedure. Actually, in **ODL** we do not consider *any* operation to be truly receiverless. All top-level operations are assumed to be owned by objects of class System. However, we will describe them as receiverless until we get a chance to describe the necessary mechanics (Chapter 18). For another example:

copy state		
guard	action	{event}
copyState(d,s)	*d.val' =s.val*	

This corresponds to **ODL** operation:

```
op copyState(dest: Bool, src: Bool) ==> dest'? = src? end
```

These operations use combinations of "pass by description" or, more familiarly, "call by value" (as seen in the value v:bool), as well as "pass by participation" or "call by reference" (as seen in dest:Bool) to exchange information. There is a big difference between the two. A value argument represents a raw state value that need not be attached to a particular object. An object argument lists a participant in a transition. The participant is not in any sense "transmitted" or "copied" somewhere. Instead, the operation is given *access* to the indicated object. A better term (that we will routinely use) is *link*. The operation is provided with a "communications link" to each participating object. Other roughly equivalent terms include "port", "capability", "reference", and "pointer". Use of participant arguments is the most common way of transmitting and representing transient OOA *acquaintance* relations. (We investigate alternatives in Chapter 18.)

These differences represent the familiar territory of value versus reference arguments in many non-OO programming languages and systems. The reason for belaboring them here is that participation in events has a much broader *design* significance in OOD than elsewhere. When you have access to an object, you might send it messages, change its state, capture its identity for later use, and so on. When all you have is a description, you cannot necessarily do any of these things. This is a more pervasive issue than implementation-level rules for keeping track of "variables" versus "expressions" in procedural programming languages.

16.2   From Abstract to Concrete

16.2.1   Concrete Operations

Effect descriptions may include references to other operations. For example, we could have described the previous operation in terms of raw manipulations on `Bool`. It is conceivable (but very unlikely) that the **OAN** models already did this:

copy state version 2		
guard	action	{event}
copyState(d,s)	*d.set(s.val)*	

```
op copyState_2(dest: Bool, src: Bool) ==> dest.set(src?)' end
```

Composite operation definitions such as `copyState_2` are more like "scripts" than descriptions of raw state changes. Because of this, we need not ascribe them as a properties of `Bool` objects per se, but instead as "application" operations that happen to use `Bool`s.

Mentioning a primed operation inside another effect means *only* that its effects hold. For example, the effect,

```
    dest.set(src?)'
```

indicates that the effect of `copyState_2` is just the same as the effect listed under **set** with the indicated substitutions. It does *not* say whether the effect is actually obtained by invoking `set`. But it does provide a very strong hint about the computations that would meet the effects constraints. The hint may be exploited later, or not. Among other benefits, this "as if" interpretation of action specifications allows recovery from insufficient abstraction in analysis models and other class designs.

Reification

Given the form and content of operation `copyState_2`, we do not have to limit ourselves to purely declarative definitions. The script seems to tell us *how* to obtain the desired state changes. We are free to commit to those hints and bind constructs to *concrete* definitions by actually "coding-in" the subevents listed in the effects description:

```
op copyState_2(dest: Bool, src: Bool) { dest.set(src?) }
```

We have just performed our first (albeit trivial) *reification* from an abstract to a concrete definition. By binding a code body (within braces) to the operation, we find ourselves actually specifying computation, rather than effects. While things are not generally *quite* so easy, the ways in which we will list and refine effects often lead to at least one natural computational definition.

It may seem odd that we were able to define *concrete* operations on *abstract* objects. Our `Bool` declaration just listed the abstract properties (or "capabilities") of boolean objects, without saying how they are implemented. For purposes of defining `copyState`, it does not matter how the objects are implemented, as long as they possess the indicated states and operations. It makes no sense at all to introduce such dependencies on internal matters. An essential OO design rule is that participant arguments and other links should *always* be specified in terms of the most abstract black-box class characterization available.

Concrete operation definitions are not at all replacements for abstract ones. The two provide different kinds of information that happen to look almost identical. But the abstract versions are written from the perspective of analysis – *what*, not *how* – while the concrete ones are from the perspective of implementation – *how*, not *what*. (For brevity of examples, we will sometimes list both bindings and effects in the same declaration.)

Concrete definitions are also different than abstract ones in that they are *maximal*. The operation will perform the stated actions and nothing more. Abstract declarations are on the other hand *minimal*. They require that the operation will obtain at least the stated effects. Other unlisted actions are OK as long as they do not conflict. This enables further refinement in subclasses and operation overrides.

16.2.2   Concrete Classes

Primitives

There might be several ways of implementing boolean objects. For example, interfaces to mechanical switches fulfill this description. However, at this bottommost level, we almost always rely on built-in software primitives for concrete representations. For each elementary type, we will assume the existence of a *default* primitively available subclass that implements it. We further abuse capitalization conventions, and denote primitively available implementations using an all upper-case notation:

```
class BOOL is Bool
  fn val: bool            { % magic % }
  op t!: ()               { % magic % }
  op f!: ()               { % magic % }
  op set(newVal: bool): () { % magic % }
end
```

[ODL details: "is" declares a class as a subclass. The predefined class `Any` serves as the root of the inheritance hierarchy. It has no attributes or behavior, and is thus defined as `class Any end`. All other classes declared without an `is` clause are treated as subclasses of `Any`. All features declared in any superclass hold in a subclass. Features may be strengthened via redeclaration.]

Again, the capitalization conventions are a bit confusing, but prevent massive awkwardness of expression. To recap, `bool` is the type of raw boolean state values, `Bool` is the type of mutable boolean objects, and `BOOL` is the default implementation of these objects. More descriptive names might be *boolean-state-value*, *mutable-boolean-object-type* and *default-primitively-implemented-mutable-boolean-object-type*. We also use these conventions for `int`, `Int`, and `INT`, and similarly for `real` and `char`.

The term *default* has some significance here. Actually, we should have defined classes `MC68KSmalltalkBool`, `VAXCBool`, and so on, to reflect the fact that different interoperable representations are available on different machines, systems and languages. But this would be pretty silly and useless. We use the all-caps form to denote the default version of a primitive object type on the platform implementing the object.

If this bottom-feeding sounds overly implementational and/or paranoid to you, be comforted that now that we have laid down tactics for eliminating representation dependence, we will not have to think about these precautions very much.

Concrete Classes as Subclasses

The class BOOL is declared as a *subclass* of Bool, since it obeys all of the characteristics of Bool, but also declares additional (computational) characteristics owing to the binding of features to computational actions (that in this case are undefinable in ODL since they are considered magically primitive).

This is a very different use of inheritance than seen in Part I, where subclassing was employed only to relate the properties of different classes. It is, however, thoroughly reasonable, and meets the definitions of ·Chapter 7 if the notion of "property" is extended to include computational and representational features. Class BOOL does possess all of the properties of Bool, but is further constrained by commitments about particular ways of representing and computing things. Another way of saying this is that class BOOL *conforms* to Bool. Any other object or operation demanding something with the properties of Bool could surely use a BOOL object.

Construction

Unlike abstract classes, concrete classes are directly, deterministically *instantiable*. Rather than just describing properties, concrete classes fill in all of the information necessary to represent and compute software objects obeying the stated properties. We specify object construction in ODL by *binding* all undefined attributes in a "**new**" statement. As a minor simplification, when there is only one such attribute we just omit naming it:

```
...
b1: Bool := new BOOL(false);
b2: Bool := new BOOL(true);
copyState(b1, b2);
```

[In examples, "..." means "something has been left out here that must be filled in for the example to make sense". In this case, the *context* of the statements has been omitted. They should be encased in some other operation.]

16.3   Composing Classes

State types, abstract classes, and concrete classes (e.g., respectively, `bool`, `Bool`, and `BOOL`) may be used to define other classes and objects. For a tiny example, suppose we need to define lamps possessing only a simple toggle switch:

```
class Lamp
  fn on: bool init= false;
  op flip ==> on' = ~on end
end
```

[Initial condition constraints may be specified using `init=`.]

Lamps seem to be related to boolean objects, but are not subclasses of `Bool`. However, we can still *use* a `Bool` to describe compositional details:

```
class CompositeLamp is Lamp
  local switch: Bool;
  inv on = switch?
  op flip ==> invertSet(switch, switch?)' end
end
```

The `switch` declares that each lamp knows of, communicates with, and/or otherwise accesses a `Bool` object. For both better and worse, our notation does not quite capture the OOA conceptual differences between *partOf*, *brotherOf*, or any other relationship. They are all expressed via the same link constructs.

16.3.1   Invariants

Invariant, or `inv` statements declare constraints that must hold across all states during an object's existence. The declaration `inv on = switch.val` says that the `on` state attribute always has the same value as `switch`'s `val`. This almost, but does not quite say that the state of the lamp should be computed by inspecting the state of the switch. More generally, such `inv` constraints represent *contracts* between two objects that must be maintained across all computation. The `inv` helps further clarify the nature of the relationship (link) between `Lamps` and `Bools`. In OAN, this relational invariant might indeed be specified using a parametric relation instance.

In `CompositeLamp`, we also replaced the effects description of `flip` with one that is equivalent to the original, but now more clearly delegates responsibility for handling the transition to the underlying component. Delegation of tasks and subtasks is among the chief reasons for using composition in the first place. The `CompositeLamp` need not know any of the details about how to meet the listed effects of `flip` if it knows of other objects and operations that do.

16.3.2 Composites as Ensembles

The `CompositeLamp` declaration does *not* say that a `CompositeLamp` object has a "physically embedded" `Bool` object, only that it "knows of" and (here, exclusively) exploits one. Avoiding, or at least postponing, the issue of representational embeddedness is a key tactic in successful compositional design. Just as blind acceptance of *PartOf* leads to problems in analysis (Chapter 9), blind representational embedding leads to problems in design. (In Chapter 23, we introduce qualifier `packed` to express embeddings, but only as a consequence of physical design considerations.)

However, we do want to claim that access to the `Bool` object is internal to the `Lamp`, and not part of its interface. Such `locals` differ from regular "public" `fns` in that they are accessible only internally to the object. The fact that `CompositeLamps` employ a `Bool` is irrelevant to any other objects that may interact with them. Suppressing this fact from the interface reduces coupling.

In ODL, any attribute or operation may be declared as strictly internal via qualifier `local`. This indicates the presence of an attribute without the presence of a public access function, thus supporting basic OO encapsulation rules that hide internal matters from other objects. If one object wants to do something with another, it must somehow determine its identity and issue a publicly listed message to it. If for some reason we did want to make the `switch` visible to other objects in `CompositeLamp`, we would have to add a non-`local` `fn` to access it. The use of `local` does not, however, commit to concrete details. Access to the `switch` might still be arranged through some kind of computation rather than direct binding (see Chapter 17).

These tactics are closer to the spirit of OOA methods than they might first appear. In Chapter 4, we noted that basic attributes might be construed as *relations* between objects and value domains. In design, object-based relations are links. Components that help support basic attributes are related to their hosts via `fns` describing private links. However, this similarity also leads to a difference. In design, all but the very most primitive objects are explicitly composite. Thus, even "simple" software objects are more like the *ensembles* described in Chapter 9 than the unprotected classes described in Chapter 3.

The *routine* commitment to hiding internal features represents a second difference between OOA and OOD. Many OOA models are too trusting. They list attributes for other *people* to look at. In design, we list the same kinds of attributes, but take special precautions to ensure that other software objects cannot mangle them. We trust other software less than people. Actually, we do not trust anyone. But we can list the `switch` object here on paper, knowing that you cannot reach onto the page and directly modify `switch` to turn off the lamp by your side. Without a membrane to protect it, other software objects may well be able to "reach into" some poor hapless `Lamp` and do just that.

For example, compare the **OAN** description of `CompositeLamp` with that of the `VacuumCleaner` example from Chapter 9:

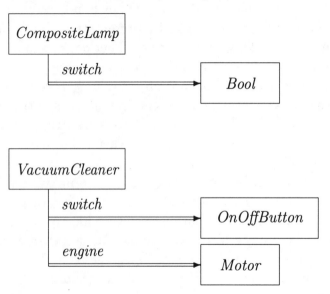

Even though the component of `CompositeLamp` is much less interesting than those of `VacuumCleaner`, the same construction strategies apply. Conversely, private `local` links provide the first step in translating the constituents of OOA-level ensembles. Generally, **OAN** "double vectors" translate into `own` links, a special stronger version of `local` described in Chapter 17. (In fact, `own` would be appropriate even in the present example.)

16.3.3   Concrete Composites

The `CompositeLamp` declaration is still incomplete. It does not represent components or bind actions, it just describes them. As always, there are many ways to define concrete versions, but the obvious one is `LampV1`:

```
class LampV1 is CompositeLamp
  local switch: Bool <>
  on: bool { switch? }
  op flip { invertSet(switch, switch?) }
end
```

[We normally give concrete classes names ending in V*n*, where *n* is a "concrete version number".]

In ODL, all links within concrete classes defined using "<>" must be bound to other objects during construction. Here, any fresh `Bool` object in a `false` state would do:

```
myLamp := new LampV1(switch := new BOOL(false));
```

Constructors may be wrapped within other operations and classes to better hide details, control initialization, maintain defaults, and keep track of instances. Note that constructors form the exception to privacy rules for `locals`. Constructors must be able to attach links while initializing objects.

16.4 Controlling Transitions

A *semaphore* may be described as an object with a boolean state attribute `locked`, a `wait` operation that blocks while `locked` is false and then atomically sets it to true, and a `signal` operation to set it back to false. This may be represented as:

```
class Semaphore
  fn locked: bool init= false;
  op wait: ()   when ~locked then locked' else pend end
  op signal: () ==>  ~locked' end
end
```

The definition of classes such as `Semaphore` hinges on the fact that the reception of a message such as `wait` does not always immediately lead to the execution of the corresponding actions. In ODL, the conditions under which the message may trigger are listed in `when` clauses, which serve as the OOD translation of OOA guards and state-dependent transition specifications. (None of our previous `Bool`-based examples happened to require state-based guards for any operations.) These `when` guards are purely descriptive tools, just like effects. In fact "==> *eff*" is shorthand for "`when` `ready` then *eff*", where `ready` is the topmost level of state abstraction (see Chapter 5).

Here, the class definition says that **Semaphore** objects must **pend wait** message until they reach an unlocked state. Any number of **wait** messages may be **pending** at any given time.

In ODL, **when** constructs must cover all cases (i.e., there must be a trailing **else** clause, along with possibly several intervening **elsewhen**s). However, delays are not the only possible alternative outcome. For example, in the **Counter** class described at the beginning of this chapter, we just ignored **dec** when the internal count was zero. For illustration, we can recast this using the ODL "outer" form of **when** that lists together all operations that may be triggered in a given state. The two easily intertranslatable forms respectively emphasize the required internal conditions versus the triggering input events in OAN transitions:

```
class Counter ...
  when isZero then
    op dec: () ==> end
  else
    op dec: () ==> count' = count - 1 end
  end
end
```

The lack of any effect in the first clause allows the **dec** message to be ignored when the count is already zero. (To ensure this, the effect should state **count' = count.**)

To demonstrate the interplay here, note that by turning the empty effect to "pend", and changing the nonblocking **inc** and **dec** operations into (renamed) blocking forms, a **Counter** can be transformed into another common construct, the **CountingSemaphore**:

```
class CountingSemaphore ...
  op signal: () ==> count' = count + 1 end
  op wait: () when ~isZero then count' = count - 1 else pend end
end
```

16.4.1   Concrete Transitions

Concrete code bodies must faithfully mirror both effects and synchronization conditions. In ODL, concrete actions within curly braces are assumed to be *atomic* with respect to external clients, and performed without interruption. In the same way that it is impossible for the effects of both a **Semaphore wait** and **signal** operation to hold true simultaneously, we ensure that it is impossible for both a `wait` and a `signal` operation to execute simultaneously. For example, a more concrete `Semaphore` class may be defined as follows:

```
class SemaphoreV1 is Semaphore
  local l: Bool <>
  local op set_l_true { l.t! }

  locked: bool  { l? }
  op wait: ()   { if ~l? then set_l_true else pend end }
  op signal: () { l.f! }
end
```

For illustration, we broke out the concrete action `set_l_true` from the condition under which it is triggered. While overkill here, this commonly useful tactic enables the separate design and development of actions and their synchronization conditions, as well as the reuse of the same action within different conditions and operations. For convenience, we also sometimes write intermediate forms that are concrete in some effects but not in guards or in alternative clauses. For example:

```
op wait: () when ~locked then { set_l_true } else pend end
```

At some point, the `whens` and `pends` need to be transformed (see Chapter 19).

16.4.2 Parallelism

Of course, atomicity of actions within each object does not at all preclude concurrency of *groups* of objects controlled by a single host. Since essentially all design-level classes may have the definitional characteristics of analysis-level ensembles, just about *any* object may harbor the forms of parallelism described in Chapter 9. For example, consider a class that maintains two counts and has an operation for incrementing both at once:

```
class DoubleCounter
  locals  c1: Counter <>;  c2: Counter <> end
  fn count1: int { c1.count }
  fn count2: int { c2.count }
  op incboth: () ==> count1'' = count1 + 1, count2'' = count2 + 1
                 { c1.inc; c2.inc } end
end
```

[Sets of local declarations may be grouped together, as here. Also, for expediency, this class collapses abstract and concrete versions. We will sometimes mix descriptions like this while demonstrating abstract and concrete features at once.]

Recall that the original Counter class defined inc as a one-way (nonblocking) operation. Thus, the incboth operation here may issue both requests without waiting for replies from either of them. The subactions may be executed independently and concurrently. One-way sends serve as a translation of OAN send-and-forget messages listed in the *Events* box of transition descriptions. They may also be used to obtain multiple independent "simultaneous" logical transitions.

Here, because inc is nonblocking, the incboth operation cannot itself contain any guarantees about *when* the desired effects hold, only that they will take place *sometime* after the operation triggers. This may be all that is desired. Such effects are indicated in ODL using a double-prime to mean "eventually".

16.5   Generic Classes

Generic (or parametric) classes are those that define a whole family of related classes, differing only in matters concerning one or more types that are used as arguments to the class declarations. Generic classes are most useful for defining various "collections" including those described in Chapter 18.

In ODL, generic classes and operations defined on them are declared with one or more type parameters within [...]. These classes may be instantiated by supplying actual types. We maintain the convention of giving upper case names to generic classes and operations. Generic classes may be subclassed in parametric or instantiated form. For example:

```
class STACK[T]
  fn length: init= 0;
  fn empty: bool = (length = 0);
  fn top: opt T;
  op push(x: T): () ==> top' = x, length' = length + 1 end
  op pop  when ~empty then length' = length - 1 end
end

op clear[T](s: STACK[T]) ==> s.empty'
    { while ~s.empty do s.pop end } end
```

```
class REVERSIBLE_STACK[T] is STACK[T] ...
  op reverse; ...
end

class WindowStack is STACK[Window] ...
  fn currentlyDisplayed: bool;
end

op display(s: STACK[Window]);
```

Here, push and clear are operations defined on *any* kind of stack, while display is defined only on stacks of Window objects.

16.6   Generating Instances

ODL classes *describe* objects. Like OAN models, they list attributes, dynamics, required initial conditions and invariants. Classes themselves do not define the facilities, rules, and related processing needed to *generate* objects of a given class.

Managing construction is a classic trade-off between flexibility and encapsulation. For maximum flexibility, we would like to be able to construct concrete objects by just asking that a set of links be attached in the desired way within some newly generated software entity. For maximum reliability and security, we would like to restrict the rights of other objects to create new instances while simultaneously gathering up all construction policies, defaults, and related processing in one place, to make it easy to evaluate correctness. For illustration, we adopt constructs and policies that are compatible with a range of conventions commonly seen in OO systems, from free-form binding to the mandated use of arbitrary forms of metaclasses.

We assume that a new operation is associated with each concrete class. The new operation has the special argument syntax of accepting pairs of bindings (or simple state values in the case of primitives). However, if a class specifies one or more generator class(es), then new is disabled at top level, and is only available from within these generators. The effect of mandating uniform metaclass-based generators may be obtained using the policy of *always* specifying one generator per concrete class. We will increasingly add further capabilities to such generators.

Even though they are not really parts of the target classes, generators are intimately tied to them. They must ensure that all stated invariants and initial conditions

hold. For example, we may add a class that hides the messy details of making new
LampV1 objects:

```
class LampV1 is Lamp ...
  generator LampV1Gen
end

class LampV1Gen ...
  op mk(initstate: bool) l: unique LampV1 {
    l := new LampV1(switch := new BOOL(initstate)) }
end
```

By convention, we usually call basic constructor-wrapper operations "mk". As discussed in Chapter 17, "unique" here indicates that each invocation generates a different instance as its result.

Note that the constructor in this example needs to commit to a particular concrete
version of Bool (just the default BOOL) to actually create the inner component. It
could not have listed it as just Bool since Bool is an abstract class, and we need a
concrete object. Our *list all types as abstractly as possible* design rule requires that
we almost always postpone selection of linked concrete object types to constructors.

Multiple Constructors

This rule also implies that we may have several *different* generator classes, or just
different constructive operations in the same generator for LampV1 objects, each making a different choice about concrete components. For any given class, there may be
several reasonable ways to construct objects. For example:

```
class LampV1Gen ...
  op dflt: unique LampV1 {
    reply new LampV1(switch := new BOOL(false)) }
  op clone(x: LampV1): unique LampV1 {
    reply new LampV1(switch = new BOOL(x.on)) }
end
```

Defaults.   Because generator classes are responsible for construction, they are also
responsible for maintaining information about *default* initial conditions described in
OOA models. The managed objects themselves need not know anything about default
settings. Thus, default information normally associated with the target classes in
OOA models usually translates into generator class design.

Cloning. A `clone` (also known as "deep copy" or "copy-constructor") operation is sometimes useful. This constructor makes a new object with the same observable properties as its argument.

16.6.1 Abstracting Interfaces

Our `LampV1Gen` class provides a set of concrete operations special to `LampV1` objects. To reflect the fact that there are many ways to represent Lamps concretely, we can elevate our manager declaration into one that holds for any Lamp manager class:

```
class LampGen
  fn defaultInitState: bool init= false;
  op setDefault(b: bool): () ==> defaultInitState' = b end
  op dflt                 q: unique Lamp ==> q.on = defaultInitState end
  op mk(initstate: bool)  q: unique Lamp ==> q.on = initstate end
  op clone(p: Lamp)       q: unique Lamp ==> q.on = p.on end
end
```

```
class LampV1Gen is LampGen ... end
```

All of the operations are now expressed abstractly. They may be implemented in different ways in concrete subclasses. This chain of transformations is almost the reverse of property-driven design. Instead of starting with some properties, and then finding concrete classes to make good on them, we started with some concrete chores to be supported, and derived a common property-based interface. (For the sake of brevity, we will often use **new** expressions or isolated construction procedures in future examples, with the understanding that they should be grouped into appropriate generator classes that may in turn be given abstract interfaces.)

16.6.2 Dispatching

We will further examine the role of OO *dispatching* (message binding, resolution, and routing) in Chapter 21. But this is a good opportunity to introduce some issues that dispatching is meant to solve.

The encapsulation of construction within generators leads to a new design problem. When we were content to just use **new**, we imagined that there was a supervisor object sitting there to "catch" the request and do the right thing. But when construction details are encapsulated within special classes, any client wishing to create a new `LampV1` object must know of a generator object out there willing to make one. However, this introduces object coupling. We do not want to mandate hard-wired knowledge of generators inside clients. We remedy this via special dispatching policies that support a simple form of "call by role", or "object dispatching". This is one way to further postpone resolution of acquaintance relations (see Chapter 6).

The basic idea of object dispatching is for a supervisor object to accept a message nonspecifically addressed to *any* object of a given class, and then to route it to some particular object (of its choosing) that can service it. We may just assume "random routing" that arbitrarily selects any object of the required type. (We will later describe how to attain more selective policies.) In ODL we indicate these requests using "$":

```
op lampUser  {  local l: Lamp := LampGen$dflt; ... }
```

Object dispatching liberates designs from undue object identity coupling. In fact, it may be possible to fully replace all identity-based communication with strategies in which clients provide only the necessary descriptive properties of target objects rather than their identities. However, the cost of doing so often makes this option thoroughly impractical. For example, consider the descriptive measures needed for a `CompositeLamp` object to identify the `Bool` object that serves as its `switch` every time it performs `flip`.

16.7 Design for Testability

Even though testing issues are more bound to the implementation phase than to design, many design methods are centered around the notion of *design for testability*, bridging OOA models with computational designs. These methods increase the likelihood that class designs solve the *right problem*, and that class operations execute in the *right way*.

The implementation of every concrete class ought to obey the constraints described by its abstract superclass(es). So far, we have focused on transformations and refinements that enhance the likelihood that concrete classes are correct with respect to these abstract specifications. However, the work involved in transforming textual and approximate descriptions into executable expressions is also repaid in the design of unit tests for classes. The opposite also applies, perhaps even more so. In practice, writing self-tests at the same time that classes are designed is a productive way to *discover* well-specified constraints, effects, and the like.

A set of tests may be designed relating each abstract class to any and all concrete subclasses. Two principal kinds of tests, constraint checks and trace checks, may be mixed and matched as needed.

16.7.1 Constraint Checks

Invariant ("inv") constraints may be codified as self-check functions. These may in turn be used as run-time assertions within test suites and/or placed in code attached to run-time exceptions within concrete classes themselves. For every concrete class, you might define an operation `invCheck` that collects and evaluates all computable invariants for the class. For example, `CounterV1::invCheck` should check that `count >= 0`. Invariants need not be readily or even feasibly computable within a class. However many are, and most others may be approximated for testing purposes.

An `invCheck` operation might be invoked only during testing. But it may also be invoked during system execution, especially after particularly tricky operations. It might even be invoked by a daemon object that periodically inspects system integrity. Constructors inside generator classes also form convenient places to define many tests. Constructors create new objects that must:

- have all "<>" links bound to suitable objects
- obey all `inv` constraints
- obey all `init` conditions.

We have already seen how constructors may be grouped into manager classes. Beyond their organizational role, the *effects* descriptions of their component constructor operations help to describe the minimal requirements of construction across a set of subclasses.

Outside of constructors, invariant expressions and qualifiers may be checked by evaluating them at the beginning and/or end of any or all concrete operations. While these invariants may be temporarily broken within the body of any operations, each concrete action body has the obligation to patch constraints back together. This reflects the guarantee that if the invariant holds before the operation fires, then it still holds on completion. Class invariants are the same as *loop invariants* (see, e.g., [101]) except they extend across different operations, rather than parts of a single operation. (In fact, if object computation is conceptualized in terms of the event driven loop of Chapter 15, these notions may be treated as equivalent.)

16.7.2   Trace Checks

Similar remarks hold for effects defined using "==>" for abstract operations. However, since effects may refer to both "before" and "after" states of participant objects, they cannot be evaluated automatically. It is usually easy to define associated test functions manually by keeping track of initial and final properties of interest in a driver routine.

The idea of checking the effects of a single operation may be extended to sequences of operations, or *traces*. The most useful tactics for self-tests are *constant* traces, *equivalent* traces, and *simulation* traces. In Chapter 20 we describe bookkeeping classes for keeping track of tasks and sets of operations. These may also be used as a locus for defining such tests.

Constant Traces

A constant trace is one that is claimed to propel an object across a sequence of operations that lead it back to a state having the same properties from which it began. (This is almost always the exact same abstract state.) For example:

```
op flipTwice(l: Lamp) ==> l.on' = l.on
   { l.flip; l.flip } end


op pushPop[T](s: STACK[T], x: T)
   ==> (s.length = s.length') /\ (s.empty \/ (s.top' = s.top))
   { s.push(x); s.pop } end
```

The fact that these checks must be defined as "tests" rather than "specifications" in ODL shows one of the essential differences between structured OO notations and specification languages in which such properties are often specifiable as "axioms". Also, as is the case for invariant checks, tests need not exhaustively evaluate all properties to be effective. They need only check properties and approximations of properties of interest.

Equivalent Paths

An equivalent-paths trace establishes two different sequences that are claimed to have the same total effect on abstract state. These are just like checks for algebraic identities; e.g., the commutativity of addition generates the test $a + b = b + a$. For example:

```
op add12(b: Int, d1: int, d2: int)  { b.add(d1); b.add(d2) }

op add21(b: Int, d1: int, d2: int)  { b.add(d2); b.add(d1) }

op test(b: Int, d1: int, d2: int): bool {
    b2 := new INT(b?);
    add12(b, d1, d2); add21(b2, d1, d2);
    reply b? = b2? }
```

Interaction diagrams and use cases from analysis may provide requirements and hints about useful tests. Any time there are two different paths from one state to another, a test procedure can be constructed to check that the two paths actually have equivalent effect. Applying these ideas to nonblocking one-way operations takes more work. You must be certain that transitions are completed before checking for their effects. Notification techniques (see Chapter 22) may be of use.

Simulation Traces

Other testing strategies are more appropriate for objects that rely on interfaces to foreign, external hardware and/or software. External entities not only have mechanics that cannot be controlled, but they also generate sequences of events that cannot be predicted in advance. For example, an ATMCustomer may be defined as a software object, but it contains attributes derived from entities defined as pure external interfaces (e.g., the number of seconds since the last key press). Such externally derived state information may be simulated in order to propel and assist design, prototyping, and testing efforts for ATMCustomer and all other objects with which it communicates. For example, a subclass SimulatedATMCustomer may be constructed that somehow generates appropriate patterns of attributes.

Two main techniques are used for designing simulated objects. The first is to generate states in accord with use cases described in OOA models. These are variants of trace tests, providing scenarios for which known results should hold.

The second is to generate attributes randomly. However, these must be generated in accord with all class invariants and other constraints. This can be very difficult. A more tractable approach is to simulate raw input events coming from the external entities. This is normally easier since such events are much less constrained, so are amenable to simple pseudorandom generation. It is better since it also tests responses to external events, rather than just laying attributes into place. This is potentially useful in preliminary assessments of performance and alertness requirements.

As a matter of policy, designers may create a `SimulatedExt` for every externally implemented class `Ext`. This then allows dependent classes such as `ATMCustomer` to be tested without the need for a random simulation-based subclass.

16.8   Transformation and Composition

We have focused on a set of design strategies linking abstract and concrete design. These tactics and constructs form most of the basis for transformational, compositional design. Although we will see a lot of variations and twists, we can now narrow down the steps a bit from our previous characterizations.

Define abstraction: Collect from analysis models the central properties and operations defined for a class. Transcribe and transform this into an abstract class declaration describing types, constraints, and effects.

Define composition: Re-express these features in terms of the properties and behaviors of other components, leading to a composite (sub)class declaration. Do this in as many ways as you like, forming any number of composites that have the same abstract features.

Define computation: For each composite class, create one or more concrete (sub)classes by transforming properties and effects into delegated values and scripted actions, and by specifying construction details.

These steps need not, and most often should not, be attached to the same class declaration. Subclassing may be used to reflect the fact that there are many possible ways to represent and compute features, and we have chosen only one of them. This is most clearly important for capturing the differences between abstract and concrete declarations.

The distinction between abstract and concrete classes is a case where aesthetics and good design coincide. No one likes to look at the ugly details of concrete class declarations such as `LampV1`. Similarly, other client classes and applications need not, and should not, know about these internal matters. Once the feasibility of one or more concrete definitions has been established, they need not be revisited for purposes of functional design. Most further design matters deal only with the abstract versions.

The starting point for these transformations depends on details of analysis models. For example, a class such as `Counter` is most likely defined solely in terms of abstract declarative properties. But the analysis description of `VacuumCleaner` included some compositional and computational details. So, from a property-driven view, the middle "composition without computation" stage is only sometimes useful. For example, we skipped it entirely for `Semaphore`, and will for many others. In the fairly common case in which the transformation from composite to concrete classes is just about completely constrained (i.e., when there is only one sensible translation from effects to actions), it makes little difference whether they are defined separately or combined into the same class. Sometimes, a code body *is* nearly its own best specification.

Rational Reconstruction

This abstract-to-concrete scenario is an overly idealistic view of design. When analysis models are weak or incomplete, actual design practice is exactly the reverse of this strategy. Designers often first construct a concrete class that seems to do the right thing, and then later abstract away nonessential internals and retrospectively rationalize decisions, ultimately resulting in an abstract class. This is the tactic we used in arriving at abstract interfaces for generator classes.

Even though this is common, it is useful to act as though you are always following the abstract-to-concrete strategies. This is a bit silly, but it is a recommended practice across just about all design efforts (see, especially Parnas and Clements[181]), software or otherwise. In particular, *failing* to rationally reconstruct an abstract interface for a concrete class can be a serious error, since it binds all further classes to concrete details that will almost surely change as classes and applications evolve.

16.9   Summary

Class design is triggered by a group of OOA models collected into design-level abstract declarations. The design of associated concrete classes and operations employs a transformational approach focused on *composition* – arranging that other objects be used to obtain desired functionality, and *reification* – finding courses of action that obtain the required effects.

16.10   Further Reading

Similar OO design notations appropriate for active objects include DisCo [124] and Hybrid [166]. Alternatives include *actor* systems [233] and direct use of parallel OO languages such as POOL [9] or distributed ones such as emerald [185]. Several formal specification systems have been altered to be more applicable to OO methods; see for example, descriptions of OO extensions to Z in [210], to VDM in [229], and to Larch in [135]. Methods based on formal specification tend to place an even stronger emphasis on refinement and reification techniques than described in this chapter. Jones [127] describes methods that integrate ideas from formal methods and process calculus. Johnson and Russo [125] provide examples and case studies of abstract class and framework design. Ossher, Harrison, and colleagues [103, 173] further investigate extension by addition as a design policy.

Our treatment of attributes as functions is similar to that supported in CLOS [35] and Iris [93]. The overly careful distinction between values and links is similar to that of impure functional languages such as ML [228]. The use of guards as specification and design constructs was pioneered by Dijkstra [80]. The broadening of postconditions to effects that reference other effects (which is intrinsic to structures involving subclassing) appears to have been introduced (in a different context) in [148]. Helm et al [107] introduced the notion of constraints as contracts between objects; see also Meyer [157] and Delcambre et al [78]. Our use of object generators is similar to that of emerald [185]. The language BETA [132, 149] presents an alternative framework for localization and embedding.

16.11   Exercises

1. Explain the difference between an interface and a listing of attributes.

2. Instead of treating OOA attributes as *functions*, why don't we just say that attributes are "directly represented" inside objects?

3. If this is *object*-oriented design, why do we sometimes define operations "outside" of objects?

4. Should the Lamp class have been reworked to be a *subclass* of Bool?

5. Design an abstract VacuumCleaner class. Refer to other OOA details listed in Chapter 9. Then design a corresponding concrete class.

6. Design one or more RefrigeratorDoor classes.

7. Is it really an appropriate use of inheritance to say that BOOL is Bool?

8. Design a constraint test and a trace test for class Semaphore.

Chapter 17

Attributes in Design

This chapter further details mechanisms for declaratively and computationally describing attributes, concentrating mainly on scalable in-the-small methods and concerns. We start by distinguishing types, qualifiers, and constraints within the context of ODL (feel free to skim these sections), and then discuss some strategies for designing concrete classes that meet these declarative constraints.

17.1 Defining Attributes

17.1.1 Value Types

One way to conceptualize a value is as "anything that may be passed along a wire". Actual objects are not values. Computers cannot be squeezed through wires. However, descriptions of objects *are* values.

You can assume the existence of any set of value types you like.[1] We will use only a small number of value types, and thus maintain some contact with things that can be easily supported across a wide range of languages, tools, and systems. We restrict all low-level dependencies to the interpretation of state values within messages. (In heterogeneous distributed systems, these assumptions might be supported through the use of tools that interconvert message formats.) With only a bit of awkwardness, all *class* designs can be made independent of such details.

We predefine types `bool`, `int`, `real`, `char`, `time`, `blob`. The types of object links are also values. "Void", written as "()" and perhaps best pronounced as "synch", is a

---

[1]Including no types at all other than those describing links. See Chapter 20 for the mechanics.

reply type describing bidirectional operations that do not bear results. (We will also introduce *named* synchronization replies in Chapter 20.) We distinguish a `time` type to avoid commitments about its form (e.g., integer or real). We use literals such as `30ms` and `2y3d` as values. The strange type `blob` (a now-common acronym for Binary Large OBjects) is non-first-class type used only to refer to *uninterpretable* hunks of bits.

We do not assume any particular bounds on numerical types. You may wish to do so, and could even tie them to common low-level constructs such as `sixteenBitInt`. But it is probably a better idea to express such things via constraints, and leave out the lowest level mappings until necessary.

Fixed sized vectors (arrays) of types are denoted using syntax *type*`[`*capacity*`]`, where *capacity* is the number of elements; for example, an attribute `name:char[20]`. Elements are indexed starting at zero. The `[...]` syntax is analogous to that for generic classes. However, unlike similar **ARRAY** collections (Chapter 18), we take these vector types as pure values, without any underlying object structure. We use them almost exclusively to describe string constants. Literals of any `char` vector type may be indicated as quoted strings `"like this"`.

Later in this chapter, we also illustrate a `record` (tuple) type used for structuring large sets of descriptions within messages. Messages themselves are in turn definable as value records.

We use value types extensively for describing and transmitting state information. But we do so within this very limited framework. We avoid the definition of, for example, sequence or set types. We will see how to define *classes* that obtain the desired effects. For example, to minimize implementation surprises, we reluctantly avoid even variable-length string types. A `String` *class* may be used in order to avoid the silly, horrible limitations of types such as `char[20]`. But we will postpone doing so for a while.

17.1.2 Links

Classes describe families of related objects. But class information attached to object attributes does not refer to classes *per se*, but instead to *connections to objects*. The value of a link is the *identity* (ID) of the object on the other side of the link. You might think of an ID as some kind of pointer value. (It has been said that OO is the living proof that you can solve any problem by adding another pointer.)

In **ODL** we work only with *typed* IDs, meaning that *a* class membership must be specified whenever an ID is used. Since objects may conform to more than one class, this class specification need not be unique. It may declare a superclass of the most specific class describing the object. However, this declaration can then be used as a design-time safety measure to guide usage. Types are used as a convenient way of recording the assumed attributes and operations of an object on the other side of a link. Clients are generally restricted to only invoke operations that are listed in the class definition of the declared type.

As we will see, not *every* construct is statically checkable within the restricted framework of standard OO type systems. While this is a major hindrance at the analysis level, the use of simply checkable type signature information is a major asset at the design level. Types describe constraints in the most "lightweight" possible fashion and communicate them to other designers, thus reducing possibilities for design error. They enable partial mechanical coherence checking of designs. Situations in which simple checking fails alert designers to possibly fragile constructions. The same remarks hold for additional constraints, invariants, and effects. But here, prospects for mechanical checking are slim. Still, they make it easier to perform reliable concrete design, they are often easier to communicate to others than vague textual descriptions, and they help partially automate testing and other checks.

17.1.3 Objects

Objects themselves are considered to be either purely, magically primitive (e.g., BOOL) or purely composed of links to others. There are no in-betweens. This is essentially the Smalltalk [99] model of objects. To illustrate some differences between values and objects, consider introducing a class allowing the use of values in contexts demanding object types. For example:

```
class RealVal  val: fixed real <> end
```

The main difference between a RealVal and a real is that an instance of RealVal has an identity. Two RealVals, r1 and r2 that both hold the val 3.14159 (so r1.val = r2.val) are still distinguishable via the test of whether r1 = r2. The *value* 3.14159 is the same no matter how many times you write it down (create an instance). But as cast in an object framework, each instance is detectably different. The fact that value types are "unlocated" is one reason we describe them as "more abstract" than objects. Value frameworks abstract over our definitional feature of objects (see Chapter 1) requiring that instances be uniquely identifiable.

17.1.4   Enumerations

The equivalents of enumerated types are intertwined with the ODL oneOf subclassing constraint. For example, instead of declaring an enumeration type voltageLevel with elements activeVoltage and ground, we might define:

```
class VoltageLevel                      fn level: real; end
class ActiveVoltage is VoltageLevel inv level ~= 0.0 end
class Ground is VoltageLevel            inv level = 0.0   end

inv VoltageLevel = oneOf(ActiveVoltage, Ground)
```

In ODL the C = oneOf(...) construct limits the subclasses of C to those in the list. It declares that the mentioned subclasses completely and exclusively cover the superclass. This is the ODL version of *partitioning* specifications (Chapter 7).

Restricting subclassability via oneOf trades off extensibility for precision and the ability to reason about cases. Only the listed subclasses may be defined. But this is often exactly what is needed and/or what an OOA model specified. Note however that even if a set of subclasses covers a type, each of these may be further subclassed. For example, ActiveVoltage could be subclassed into PositiveVoltage and NegativeVoltage. A set of classes that is exclusive but does not cover may be declared by defining an Other class, as described in Chapter 7. We do not use a special design notation for cases in which subclasses nonexclusively cover the superclass.

It is an easy matter to transform simple enumerations into this framework. Restricted class declarations contain all of the expressive power of enumerations, and more. Since they are classes, each of the "enumerated elements" may have additional properties, such as level in the current example.

17.1.5   Qualifiers

Value and object types are used in defining fns. These constructs serve as the basic translation mechanisms for OOA-level attributes, and may be annotated with the following qualifiers. Qualifiers are *descriptive* restrictions. Their effects are not always mechanically checkable. For example, uniqueness of attributes normally cannot be checked by simple observation. Behind-the-scenes design rules and/or run-time processing are needed to ensure that duplicate values are not present across objects. Just listing the qualifier cannot generate these mechanisms automatically.

`fixed`, meaning that the value remains constant (although perhaps different for each instance) during the lifetime of the entity.

`common`, meaning that the value must be the same for all instances of this entity.

`unique`, meaning that the value of the attribute differs across all entities.

`opt`, meaning that the `fn` need not be defined/connected at all.

`own`, short for `local fixed unique`.

Outside of `opt`, **ODL** does not include multiplicity notation. Multivalued **OAN** attributes are translated using SETs or other collections described in more detail in Chapter 18.

The "scope" of any qualifier or constraint is that of the enclosing entity (including top-level, classes, and operations). In particular, qualifiers attached to op arguments, locals, and results apply per-invocation. For example, qualifying an op result as unique indicates that each invocation generates a unique result.

Constancy

Constancy declarations lie at the intersection of several annotation constructs. For example, the following all have the same meaning:

```
votingAge: fixed int = 18;
votingAge: common fixed int = 18;
votingAge: fixed int;   init votingAge = 18
votingAge: fixed int init= 18;
votingAge: int;   inv votingAge = 18
votingAge: int = 18;
```

The fact that an attribute cannot change aids later design and implementation. For example, when object link attributes are declared as `fixed`, this means that two or more objects bear an immutable, hard-wired relation to one another (see Chapter 18).

However, qualification must be done with care. There is a difference between the observation that an attribute does not happen to change, and the requirement that it logically cannot change. Applying `fixed` in the former case is a design error. It precludes declaration of perfectly reasonable subclasses in which the attribute *could* meaningfully assume different values, even if it happens not to in the superclass. On the other hand, failing to qualify an attribute as `fixed` when a class depends on its constancy is an easy way to generate inadvertent subclassing errors.

Uniqueness

The best way to represent OOA-level uniqueness claims is to use **ODL** *unique* qualifiers. Parametric instances (Chapter 8) are explicitly unique. Other uniqueness claims
are often explicit or implicit in **OAN** models. For example, a bank branch may have
a `mgr: unique Manager`. Also, models may somehow claim or imply that a given
object must be the sole member of a given class.

These issues come up in pure design contexts as well. A design may ensure that
there is only (at most) one live instance of a particular class. For example, it may
require that *exactly one* `AccountNumberMaker` object reside on a system. We mean
"require" in the sense that correctness of the system as a whole can be guaranteed
only if there are not multiple instances that may interfere with each other, as opposed
to a (possibly better) design that will work OK if there is one, but also if there are
more than one.

System-wide uniqueness may be indicated via top-level uniqueness constraints,
and supported by the appropriate computational devices. For example:

```
class AccountNumberMaker
  generator AccountNumberMakerGen
  own id: Int <> init id? = 0
  op newNumber: unique int { id.inc; reply id? }
end

class AccountNumberMakerGen
  theInstance: opt AccountNumberMaker;
  op mk: AccountNumberMaker {
    if null(theInstance) then
       theInstance := new AccountNumberMaker(id := new INT(0)) end;
    reply theInstance }
end

theAccountNumberMaker: fixed unique AccountNumberMaker :=
  AccountNumberMakerGen$mk;
```

Here, the generator class accepts the maintenance of uniqueness as its responsibility.
However, there is a limit to the declarative specification of these matters. For example,
we *also* should have claimed that `AccountNumberMakerGen` was unique. This leads
to infinite regression. Ultimately, system construction *policies* must be invoked in
order to ensure conformance. This is a general consequence of any kind of generator

or metaclass framework. We may define generator-generators, generator-generator-generators, *ad infinitum*. At some point, correctness relies on disciplined usage of `new`.

In this example, we used `unique` at the `AccountNumberMaker` level to ensure that the results of each `newNumber` invocation were in turn unique. Our simplistic implementation required this tactic, since it had no other way of guaranteeing that the sequence numbers would not conflict with others. Similar considerations apply to other attributes and functions qualified as `unique`. Again, the easiest (and sometimes only) way to ensure uniqueness of values is centralization. Centralization is, in turn easiest to guarantee through the use of `unique` instances. Ultimately, uniqueness of instances is a system-wide construction policy issue.

Own Attributes

The `own` qualifier for `id` is very useful in the `AccountNumberMaker` class. It claims that the `Int` component supporting the class is *fully* under the control of an `AccountNumberMaker` object. The component is unique to the instance. The link is never revealed to any other object, so no other object can modify it. The link is never rebound to a different component. To emphasize their hiddenness, we sometimes give `owned` objects names starting with underscores. Listing components as `own` is almost always the best way of translating ensemble *constituents* (Chapter 9).

In general, the more links that can be declared as `own`, the safer the design. Classes possessing only nonexported `own` links form decoupled *communication-closed* layered structures that are easier to reason about, implement, and reuse. In fact, non-owned links should be considered exceptional cases for "elementary" classes and attributes.

Optional Attributes

ODL attributes that are subject to redefinition and/or undefinition must ultimately be declared via *binding* rather than computational definition. Non-`fixed` attributes may be rebound to different values *only* by their owners. All `opt` attributes may be unbound using the common but deceptive, `p := null`. (This is deceptive because it makes `null` look like a value or object of some sort, which it is not. It is a dynamic multiplicity indicator.) Predicate `null(p)` is true if `p` is not connected. Optional attributes default to being unbound (`null`).

17.1.6   Constraints

There are two kinds of attribute constraints in ODL:

> `inv` *expr* constraints placing restrictions on perhaps many attributes that hold throughout the lifetime of the entity. As a shorthand, *decl* = *expr*, denotes an equality `inv` "in line" with the declaration.

> `init` *expr* constraints specifying conditions that must hold on initialization. As a shorthand *decl* `init=` *expr* provides an initial equality constraint "in line" with the declaration.

The ODL sublanguage used to specify invariants and initial conditions (as well as effects and other constraints) is somewhat limited. We call expressions involving state-preserving `fns` (attributes) *inspections*. We mandate that all constraints be expressed as read-only inspections. This ensures that we are not specifying transitions when we think we are just declaring properties. We need good reason to believe that constraints may be concretely checked in ways that do not unintentionally affect the states of the objects they describe.

Value inspections in `inv` and other constraints consist of the usual boolean, relational, and arithmetic functions on values. We use operators common to most programming languages, including "~" for *not*, "/\\" for *and*, "\\/" for *or*, "=>" for *implies*, and "~=" for *not equal* ("/\\" and "\\/" are treated as short-circuiting). Also, series of expressions inside constraints may be separated by commas, denoting conjunction (*and*). Comma-separation is usually more readable because of lower precedence. Inspections may also contain `if` constructs and references to other functions.

Among many other applications, constraints may be used to help declare state discriminators that are based on particular settings or combinations of other attributes. It is useful to define each such state mentioned in analysis models as a simple boolean `fn` of the same name that is true when the object is in that state. For example:

```
class Account ...
  currentBalance: real;
  overdrawn: bool = ( currentBalance < 0.0 );
end
```

These functions may take arguments, as in:

```
class Lamp ...
  fn hasStatus(b: bool): bool = ( on = b )
end
```

It is often appropriate to declare them as top-level functions. For example:

```
fn bothOn(a: Lamp, b: Lamp): bool = ( a.on /\ b.on )
```

Identity and Equality Constraints

When applied to links, "=" is the identity comparison operator, telling whether two links are connected to the same object. The fact that we can test whether any two links refer to the same object means that *every* object in a system must have a different identity.

Thus, there is no logical need to declare "id numbers" or other unique keys as properties (e.g., accountNumber in class Account). However, we will often still do so, in part for pragmatic reasons. Unless the system will live in a 100% self-contained object-oriented environment, it will sometimes need to interact with other database packages, communications services, and the like that do not understand or preserve object identity and thus require that some kind of "manual" identification strategy be used. This occurs even when interacting with foreign OO systems that use different identity representation schemes than those in the target system implementation. In such cases, we will need to veil pass-by-participation under pass-by-description protocols. Manual identification schemes are well suited for such roles. Using those that have already been specified by OOA models avoids having to create them artificially. Also, per-class identifiers are substantially easier to maintain as unique than global ones.

Comparing two links with "=" only tests whether the links refer to the same object. It is an error to use an identity test to discover whether two possibly different objects both provide some service or share some state characteristic. However, if you want a function saying whether two objects have the same descriptive features, then you will have to write it yourself. We cannot predefine these. It is very common to only want to count selected features (e.g., keys) when testing for state equality. In fact, it is often necessary to write *families* of equality functions reporting equality with respect to various criteria. For example, there might be a function sameCoordinates to test that two points have the same x,y values, and a function sameColor to test that they have the same displayed color, and perhaps a function SameCoordinatesAndColor, and so on.

State equality is in the eye of the beholder in designs with subclassing. For example, two instances of a class `Point` that does not declare a `color` attribute could only be equal with respect to coordinates. Two objects of subclass `ColoredPoint` could be equal with respect to any of these three functions. A `Point` compared against a `ColoredPoint` may be equal with respect to coordinates, but not others. You need to know which sense you mean in any particular case. A good ounce of prevention is *never* to define a function just called `equal`. There are just too many senses of "equal" for one function to represent. Similar remarks hold for `lessThan` and other functions that compare two objects.

17.2   Concrete Attributes

Attributes in concrete classes must be defined via either *binding* or *computation*. The choice is made in ODL by either listing an attribute as "`<>`", meaning that the value must be bound at construction, or defining it in "`{...}`" brackets, meaning that it is computed.

Bound (or "stored") attributes differ from computed ones in that they may be *rebound* (if non-`fixed`) and/or *unbound* (if `opt`). For simplicity and conformance to most implementation languages, we require that computationally defined attributes and operations not have their definitions rebound, unbound, or otherwise dynamically modified. The only way in which their values may change over time is by internally accessing properties of one or more mutable *objects*. The effects of rebinding may be had in this way, but the logistics are a bit harder.

Of course, ODL supports the usual `if`, `while`, etc., statements needed to evaluate concrete attributes. You can declare local objects, conditionals, loops, and so on. Because we push OO conventions down to the bottom, operations on simple integers, etc., look more like those in other languages that uniformly distinguish values from objects (e.g., ML and forth) than procedural code. This is an acquired taste at best:

```
op factorial(n: int): int    {
   local f: Int := new INT(1);
   local i: Int := new INT(n);
   while i? > 0 do f.mul(i?); i.dec end;
   reply f? }
```

ODL `local` value fns may be used to provide a more conventional veneer:

```
op factorial(n: int): int    {
    local f: int := 1;
    local i: int := n;
    while i > 0 do f := f * i; i := i - 1 end;
    reply f }
```

17.2.1 Representation

The mechanics of stored links differ from those of stored value attributes. Stored links may be represented transparently as "slots". For example:

```
class Elevator ...
    local door: ElevatorDoor <>              % stored
    doorButton: DoorButton { door.button } % computed
    op replaceDoor(newDoor: ElevatorDoor)  % rebind
        { door := newDoor }
end
```

The same declaration patterns hold for value attributes:

```
class Elevator ...
    isMoving: bool <>                        % stored
    doorOpen: bool { door.isOpen }           % computed
    op move { isMoving := true; ... }        % rebind
end
```

However, any non-fixed stored value attribute depends on some kind of *object* to maintain state information. As a default mechanics-level strategy, we assume that stored value attributes expand into functions that access (via "?") and reset (via set(val)) the states of automatically defined objects of corresponding types (e.g., Bool objects for bool values). The underlying links are given the same names as the functions, but with a leading underscore. For example, the listed declaration may be treated as if it were:

```
class Elevator ...
    own  _isMoving: Bool <>
    isMoving: bool { _isMoving? }
    op move { _isMoving.set(true); ... }
end
```

Alternatively, updates could be performed by binding the links to fresh objects with the indicated initial values; it does not much matter. In any such scheme, "stored" value attributes are provided with computational definitions referring to underlying objects. These links may be initialized in constructors via explicit binding or, by convention, implicit linkage to a new object of the corresponding default concrete subclass:

```
class ElevatorGen ...
  op mk: unique Elevator {
      reply new Elevator(isMoving := false ...) }
end
```

The net effect of these conventions is to allow value attributes to appear to be "directly represented" within objects whenever it is convenient to do so. However, by making these conventions explicit, we also facilitate bindings of values to "smarter" objects when necessary. For example, `isMoving` might instead be defined to extract the value of an object of a special subclass of `Bool` that shadows state changes on persistent media or notifies an indicator lamp object when its state is changed. The ideas may be scaled to any value-like attribute type.

Optional Attributes

Because computational definitions may not be rebound or unbound, `opt` attributes must be defined through binding, not computation. For optional value attributes, this requires similar representational maneuvering. We do not specify a default strategy.

There are many ways to declare and represent optionality that might make sense in particular cases. These may be defined manually. For example, an optional attribute might be transformed to two `fns`; `attr:A` to hold the value, and `hasAttr:bool` to tell whether it is logically bound or not. Alternatively, an `int` attribute that should logically never be negative may be given a negative value to indicate unboundedness.

17.2.2   Concrete Inspections

Both our analysis models and our design-level constraint annotations treat attributes such as `aBool.val` and `aLamp.on` as "directly" sensed and knowable both within and among objects.

In software, generally, the only way for one object to determine the state of another is to ask and be told. Thus, in design, a value attribute is construed as a "function call". In this way, information that looks "static" in analysis must be communicated via simple dynamics. For example, the `on` value in `Lamp` objects is obtained by invoking `val` for the `switch` component, ultimately obtaining a value. Objects even "ask themselves" what their states are. Essentially all software objects are "reflective" and "self aware" at least in this limited sense. We exploit this more in design than in analysis.

Even though we must handle this information dynamically, it is vitally important to maintain the implicit assumption that an object's listed attributes may be determined without otherwise disrupting the object. Doing otherwise would mean that the logical state of an object would change in the act of ascertaining it. Any design that includes such actions has low *a priori* chances of being correct.

This leads to the design rule that the concrete definitions of state sensor functions (attributes) cannot ever cause state changes visible from other potential client objects. In other words, they must be *state-preserving*, in a somewhat stronger sense than the otherwise similar notion of service transitions. They must behave as if no transitions are performed at all.

However, to be picky, concrete `fns` are *never* computationally pure. They induce "microstates" in objects while computing and returning answers to function queries. Our design rules boil down to the requirements that the computational necessity of these microstates should never impact abstract functionality (see Chapter 19).

Note that "state preservation" is defined with respect to *descriptive* information. Concretely defining a function to perform some internal processing that could never have any effect visible to other objects is consistent with this view, although intrinsically slightly dangerous. A classic example is a `Point` implementation that uses standard rectangular coordinates for internal representation, but also caches the values of its polar coordinates whenever asked so that it may more quickly report them if asked again.

17.2.3 Examples

Objects such as `MailingLabels` simply maintain several loosely related attributes. The classes consist of set/get interfaces, with a value reporter and a value replacer operation for each property listed in the analysis model:

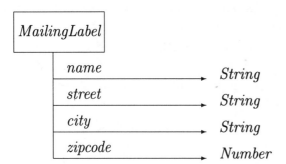

```
class String80 s: char[80] end
class MailingLabel
  name: fixed String80;
  street: String80;
  city: String80;
  zipcode: int;
  op setStreet(newSt: String80) ==> street' = newSt end
  op setCity(newC: String80) ==> city' = newC end
  op setZip(newZ: int) ==> zip' = newZ end
end
```

Concrete versions are most often constructed by hooking up attributes to more primitive objects that provide the required functionality. A simple default-strategy class is:

```
class MailingLabelV1 is MailingLabel
  name: fixed String80 <>
  street: String80 <>
  city: String80 <>
  zipcode: int <>
  op setStreet(newSt: String80) { street := newSt }
  ...
end
```

```
op mkMailingLabelV1(n: String80, s:String80, c: String80, z: int):
 unique MailingLabelV1 {
   reply new MailingLabelV1(name:=n, street:=s, city:=c, zip:=z) }
```

Manual control over internals may obtained in a tedious but straightforward fashion:

```
class MailingLabelV2 is MailingLabel
  own _name:Name <>;
  own _street:String80 <>;
  own _city:String80 <>;
  own _zip:Int <>

  name: String80 { _name? }
  street: String80 { _street? }
  city: String80 { _city? }
  zip: String80  { _zip? }
  op setStreet(newSt: String80) { _street.set(newSt) }
  ...
end

op mkMailingLabelV2(n: String80, s:String80, c: String80, z: int):
 unique MailingLabelV1 {
  reply new MailingLabelV2(
    _name := new NameV1(_nm := new STRING80(n)),
    _street := new STRING80(s),
    _city := new STRING80(c),
    _zip := new INT(z)) }
```

Here, we have assumed the definition of a little `Name` class that holds `char[80]`'s for use as names, perhaps also supporting operations for finding middle initials, etc. We could have created similar classes for the other components.

Similar translations may be applied to most of the OOA class descriptions from Chapter 3. For example, the *Bank* class:

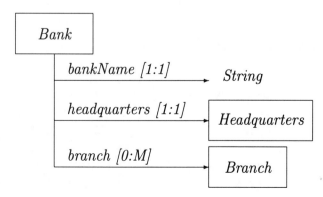

```
class Bank
  bankName: String80;
  local headquarters: Headquarters;
  local branch: SET[Branch];
end
```

We used the default visibility commitments here. We listed the `headquarters` and `branch` attributes as private links and the `name` as a public attribute. In this abstract version, we avoid computational and representational commitments. A corresponding concrete class can nail this down, perhaps as:

```
class BankV1 is Bank
  bankName: String80 <>
  local headquarters: Headquarters <>
  local branchInfo: BranchInfo <>
  local branch: SET[Branch] { branchInfo.getBranches(bankName) }
end
```

17.3   Views

A general term for a class that renames or exports restricted properties of another is a *view*. By adding renaming-based views, a concrete class may be repackaged to obey a variety of abstract interfaces expected by different clients. Views are often employed as retrospective techniques that allow already-existing components to be used in new ways.[2] Among the most common applications is to create a secondary interface for one or more classes to remove incompatibilities with other software. For example:

```
class DB_CompatibleAccountV2 is DB_CompatibleAccount ...
  local acct: Account;
  num: int { acct.acctNumber }
  op add(amt: Cash) { acct.credit(amt) }
end
```

---

[2]More formally inclined readers might notice that views provide a way to define arbitrary homomorphisms among classes, albeit in a "second-class" fashion. We have no way of expressing the abstract properties of these homomorphisms.

We have created a view simply in order to rename properties and operations to those expected by some other clients. Renaming-based views are among the best means of supplying "glue" that allow classes developed for different purposes, or obtained from different libraries, to be used together.

Unrestricted views may be created to allow use of values in contexts demanding object types. We used this tactic earlier in defining the `RealVal` and `String80` classes.

More importantly for present purposes, views provide mechanics to restrict, protect, and package components to meet abstract constraints on host attributes. Thus they serve as vehicles to implement forwarding and encapsulation properties of both OOA-level ensembles and the smaller ensemble-like classes that pervade design.

17.3.1 Restricting Operations

Our predefined value-maintaining classes (`Int`, `Bool`, `Real Char`) possess all of the usual update operations (`set`, `add`, etc.) definable for objects maintaining the corresponding values.

Some of these operations may be nonsensical when predefined object types are used in support of new classes. It is necessary to think through the legal and meaningful operations that are supported, even (or especially) for simple property-holding classes. Classes holding values with restricted operations may be defined manually by listing the operations in full.

For example, we may wish to restrict objects representing account balances to have a current dollar value that is initially zero, and to limit operations to those that add and subtract other values to the current value (corresponding to deposits and withdrawals), as well as to adjust by a multiplicative constant (in order to add interest and the like). "Looser" and/or inappropriate operations (e.g., `set`, `div`) need not be supported. This could be expressed abstractly as:

```
class Balance
  val: real init= 0.0;
  op add(c: real) ==> val' = val + c end
  op sub(c: real) ==> val' = val - c end
  op mul(r: real) ==> val' = val * r end
end
```

A concrete class may be defined as a view of a built-in class:

```
class BalanceV1 is Balance
  own _val: Real <>
  val: real { _val? }
  op add(c: real)  { _val.add(c) }
  op sub(c: real)  { _val.sub(c) }
  op mul(r: real)  { _val.mul(r) }
end
```

The definition of a class such as `Balance` mostly serves to protect against accidental misuse, not abuse. For example, it *is* possible for another object to reset a balance to a completely different value by first subtracting out the current value, and then adding in a new one. However, if nothing else, the restricted constructs advertise standard usage and practice.

17.3.2   Restricting Values

The descriptive value types defined in our basic framework do not provide any "active" protection for maintaining constrained, structured, or interdependent properties; for example, the fact that a *probability* value must be between zero and one. Views provide a locus for the infrastructure necessary to ensure that simple values and states stay within prescribed restrictions.

State values may be constrained by creating and using a *class* describing immutable objects. Such a class consists only of `fns` describing `fixed` (or otherwise constant) attributes, along with invariants among them. Because there is no way to change the state of such objects, they have the same pragmatic role in transmitting state information as simple values. For example:

```
class ProbabilityValue
  val: fixed real;  inv 0.0 <= val, val <= 1.0
end
```

```
class ProbabilityValueV1 is ProbabilityValue
  own _val: Real <>
  val: real { _val? }
end
```

For objects that do not change state, it is obviously crucial to get their construction right. An abstract generator interface and appropriate subclasses might be defined as follows. We intentionally skirt error processing for now, and simply use a value of zero if the argument is out of range in `mk`:

```
class ProbabilityValueGen
  local fn inRange(r: real): bool = (0.0 <= r /\ r <= 1.0);
  defaultProb: real init= 0.05;
  op setDefault(r: real) when inRange(r) then defaultProb' = r else end
  op mk(r: real) q: unique ProbabilityValue
     when inRange(r) then q.val = r else q.val = 0.0 end
  op dflt q: unique ProbabilityValue ==> q.val = defaultProb end
  op clone(p: ProbabilityValue) q: unique ProbabilityValue
     ==> q.val = p.val end
end


class ProbabilityValueV1Gen is ProbabilityValueGen ...
  op mk(r: real): unique ProbabilityValueV1 ...;
end
```

17.3.3 Restricting Mutability

Similar techniques apply to stateful classes. For example, a mutable `Probability`
class and associated utilities may be defined as follows. To again postpone error
handling issues, we make things easy for ourselves by failing to require any action
when numbers are out of bounds.

```
class Probability
  val: real;
  local inRange(x: real): bool = (0.0 <= x /\ x <= 1.0);
  inv inRange(val)
  op set(r: real): () when inRange(r) then val' = r else end
end

class ProbabilityV1 is Probability
  own _val: Real <>
  local inRange(x: real): bool { 0.0 <= x /\ x <= 1.0 }
  val: real { _val? }
  op set(r: real) { if inRange(r) then _val.set(r) end }
end

op copy(dest: Probability, src: Probability) { dest.set(src.val) }

class ProbabilityGen  op mk ...; end
```

Changing state by rebinding objects.   A different concrete design strategy is to construct a class that rebinds a `ProbabilityValue` on each `set`:

```
class ProbabilityV2 is Probability
  local p: ProbabilityValue <>
  val: real { p.val? }
  op set(r: real) { if inRange(r) then p := ProbabilityValueGen$mk(r) end }
end
```

This "write once" strategy guarantees that bottommost entities are never mutated. Links are instead rebound to fresh immutable objects. This sometimes simplifies their management.

Combinations.   Value and operation restrictions may, of course, be combined. For example, if a savings account balance should never be negative, this could be reflected in an associated class:

```
class SavingsBalance ...
  val: real;  inv val >= 0.0
  op sub(c: real)
    when c <= val then val' = val - c else % error % end
end
```

These strategies provide more understandable, safer, and better encapsulated class definitions than ones supporting `set` and `get` interfaces to read and write values. Rather than just giving in at this lowest level and treating value-maintaining objects as read/write "variables" in the procedural programming sense, it pays off to model them like any other object, in terms of required properties and transitions. In practice, OOA models rarely do this, so the task is left to design.

17.3.4   Wrappers

Consider a class that provides a view of a *single* operation on a *single* object in order to give it different characteristics. For example, suppose for some reason we need to use a `Lamp` object, but instead of invoking `flip`, we would like to just call it `call`. We could do this with a little view class:

```
class LampWrapper
  local l: Lamp <>
  op call: () { l.flip }
end
...
wrapper := new LampWrapper(l := myLamp);
wrapper.call;
```

Given just this example, it may be hard to believe that classes such as `LampWrapper` turn out to be useful technical tools. *Wrappers* are perhaps not the most intuitive OOD construct, but they are among the most versatile for technical manipulations. It is easy to generate them automatically. First define abstract class:

```
class Wrapper
  op call: ();
  op send;
end
```

For convenience, we provide both a blocking (`call`) and one-way (`send`) version of each, so clients may use either form. In **ODL** we define a macro[3] `WRAP` that defines an appropriate subclass and also instantiates a corresponding instance. For example:

```
wrapper := WRAP(myLamp.flip);
```

automatically generates something like the following.

```
class Thunk9063 is Wrapper
  local object: fixed Lamp <>
  op call: () { object.flip }
  op send { object.flip }
end

wrapper := new Thunk9063(object := myLamp);
```

---

[3] *Macros* are tiny software development tools expressible inside a language. Our macros might be replaced either by external tools or by adding corresponding syntax to the language *per se*. Some constructs that we describe as macros might be considered "basic" in other systems, and vice versa. Also note that many of our macros are *very* smart. We make no claims that they are implementable via text replacement mechanisms.

When we are using classes as tools for organizing attributes, constraints and operations, their definitions tend to be focused on computational matters rather than properties and descriptions. But not a lot can be said about a wrapper. Every concrete subclass of `Wrapper` does something completely different when `call` is invoked. This makes it harder for wrapper users to predict effects of invocations. For this reason, more rigidly specified view classes are preferable to wrappers whenever something more *can* be said about operations.

But in a different sense, wrappers *enhance* design safety. A wrapper user cannot get at any of the other operations the underlying object may possess, and thus cannot generate unexpected message sequences. In this way, wrappers serve as pure "operation ports" that are untied to particular objects. One difference between OOD and other distributed processing frameworks is that in OO, object links are basic and operation ports are derived, while in otherwise similar systems such as **Hermes** [211], something close to the opposite holds. This style may be emulated using wrappers and views.

17.4 Exports

Objects should not export links to other objects as public attributes or as arguments or results of other operations unless it is logically necessary to do so in order to enable further communication.

It is both an abstraction error and a pragmatic invitation for disaster for an object to return a link to a helper object when it is asked simply to report the value of some attribute. If identities are never revealed to other objects, then others cannot (directly) send them inappropriate messages.

Consider, for example, a `Square` class built using `Points`:

```
class Point
  x: real;
  y: real;
  op shiftX(v: real): () ==> x' = x + v end
  op shiftY(v: real): () ==> y' = y + v end
end
```

```
class Square
  local lowerLeft: Point;
  local upperRight: Point;
  inv upperRight.x > lowerLeft.x,
      upperRight.x - lowerLeft.x = upperRight.y - lowerLeft.y
  op shiftHorizontally(offset: real): ()
      ==> lowerLeft.x' = lowerLeft.x + offset end
end
```

This class contains no provisions for other objects to determine the coordinates of the square. Clearly, some are needed. The *wrong* way to do this is:

```
class BadSquare ...
  lowerLeftPt: Point { lowerLeft }
end
```

```
op abuse(s: BadSquare)  { s.lowerLeftPt.shiftY(1000.0) }
```

The client (`abuse`) changed the lower left point in a way that almost surely broke the squareness invariant. Moreover, this construction is *conceptually* wrong in this context. The identity of the `lowerLeft` point is not the value of the attribute. In fact, since it is not listed as `fixed`, the link might sometime be rebound to a different `Point` object that still maintains the listed invariants. The attribute function should instead reveal the indicated logical state information, not the helper object itself. There are several ways to do this.

17.4.1 Forwarding

A simple but sometimes tedious approach is to expand out and forward all relevant value attributes. This is the same technique seen in Chapter 9 for exposing partial transition networks for constituents. For example:

```
class Square_2
  lowerLeftX: real;
  lowerLeftY: real;
  upperRightX: real;
  upperRightY: real;
  inv upperRightX > lowerLeftX ...
end
```

A concrete class could still use `Point` objects internally:

```
class Square_2V1 is Square_2 ...
  own lowerLeft: Point <>
  lowerLeftX: real { lowerLeft.x }
end
```

The argument (rather than attribute/result) version of this is to parameterize oper-ations to receive a set of value parameters that transmits the state information. The receiver might use this information to make a local copy of the object, and work off that:

```
op moveCursor(xcoord: real, ycoord: real) {
   local p: Point := new PointV1...; ... }

class SquareV2 is Square ...
  op moveToLowerLeft {
    moveCursor(lowerLeft.x, lowerLeft.y) }
end
```

17.4.2   Description Records

Tedious attribute-by-attribute forwarding may be replaced with aggregate description records that transmit all relevant information about objects in a more structured fashion. In ODL we use an immutable record framework for such purposes:

```
record pointDescription(xcoord: real, ycoord: real);

class Point2 is Point
  xc: Real; yc: Real;
  x: real { xc? } ...
  fn description =  pointDescription(x, y);
end

class SquareV3 is Square ...
  own lowerLeft: Point <>
  lowerLeft: pointDescription { lowerLeft.description }
end
```

In ODL, `records` have the same form as messages themselves. They are used only to simplify and structure message transmissions. If it is necessary to hold or manipulate them, then corresponding *objects* and their classes must be defined.

Definition of `description` functions across classes in a system can be an effective preliminary step in establishing mechanisms that save descriptions of objects on persistent media (see Chapter 22). They also help standardize the forms of state descriptions that are decoded into objects by receivers. For example, a Square class may itself support:

```
record SquareDescription(ll: PointDescription, ur: PointDescription);

class SquareV3b is Square ...
  description: squareDescription  =
    squareDescription(lowerLeft.description, upperRight.description)
end
```

These may be even further standardized to achieve compatibility with external software. For example, descriptions could be structured according to the ASN.1 [172] standard.

17.4.3 Copying

Another common solution is to return copies (clones) of internally held objects. For example:

```
class PointV3 is Point
  xc: Real; yc: Real;
  x: real { xc? } ...
end



class SquareV4 is Square ...
  lowerLeftPt: unique Point {
    new PointV3(xc := new REAL(lowerLeft.x),
                yc := new REAL(lowerLeft.y)) }
end
```

Sending copies as arguments to other operations can be an effective way of avoiding situations where clients try to send messages via links obtained as arguments. The two-sided version of this protocol is *copy-in/copy-out* passing in which the server sends back a newly created object that the client may then bind.

The difference between copy-based protocols and simply exporting links is that even though the original and the copy have the same state, they are not the same object. Receivers cannot depend on messages to these copies having any consequences with respect to their originators. This is one way of interpreting our conventions for passing pure values. Even though passing a `real` might ultimately be implemented using a local `REAL` object, the receiver knows that it cannot exploit this object's identity.

17.4.4 Views

An intermediate solution is to construct read-only views of exported objects. For example (collapsing abstract and concrete versions of classes for the sake of brevity):

```
class PointVal
  locals _x: Real <>;  _y: Real <>; end
  x: fixed real { _x? }
  y: fixed real { _y? }
end

class Point3 ...
  own xc: Real <>;  own yc: Real <>
  coordinates: PointVal { new PointValV1(_x := xc, _y := yc) }
end

class Square5 ...
  own lowerLeft: Point3 <>
  lowerLeftPt: PointVal  { lowerLeft.coordinates }
end
```

Since `lowerLeft` is never rebound in `Square5`, the attribute functions of `PointVal` views will always report the current values, not just those that held at the point of construction. Yet objects that hold these views are unable to modify them. Views thus serve as *capabilities*. Objects holding views may perform only those operations that are forwarded out. It is easy to generalize this scheme to provide views of *any* subset of properties, not just status attributes. For example, a view could be constructed to only allow clients to modify x coordinates, not y. These capabilities/views may even be constructed and managed by a central service.

17.4.5   Exports and Delegation

While it is a bad idea to export links as stand-ins for attributes, objects may sometimes send local links to other helper objects in the course of operations. It is for this reason that we have not "syntactically" mandated that own links not be exported. We will in further discussions merely assume that a no-export policy or its equivalent is maintained.

"Equivalent" here means that objects may well send out own links as arguments to other "trusted" helper functions, operations, and objects that responsibly assist in their maintenance without further exporting them or interfering with other operations. Pure inspection fns may always be invoked in this way. While intrinsically somewhat dangerous, other exports are occasionally difficult to avoid.

Trustworthiness of helpers is another way of talking about their correctness with respect to a given need and context. For example, a Balance object might delegate interest updates to an InterestMgr via the message im.update(_val). The decision to export own link _val represents a measure of trust that the operation performs the intended service. If this sense of safety and correctness of a helper is not ascertainable, then more conservative measures are called for. Adaptations of other standard measures are available. Among other possibilities, the Balance object could send a clone of the _val, and later copy the state of the clone back to _val. Alternatively, the InterestMgr::update operation could be recast to receive and return values. The clients themselves may then update the appropriate objects. A more extreme option is for the Balance to perform all interest computations itself. However, this needlessly duplicates the functionality of InterestMgr and adds to the complexity of the Balance class.

Measures based on the safety and correctness of individual operations suffice for localized, small-scale use. Unlike most methods described in this chapter, they do not always scale well. We describe more extensive and "heavyweight" measures ensuring safe exclusive control over arbitrary exported linked objects in Chapter 22.

17.4.6   Screening Functions

Especially when attributes are in any way hidden, exceptional interaction conditions often may be avoided by exporting "screening functions" in addition to status indicators.

Some operations contain **when** conditions that refer solely to unchanging properties of their arguments. To avoid exceptions, clients should be able to determine whether the arguments they intend to send are indeed legal. Illegal cases may include out-of-range numerical values, unbound **opt** links, and objects that do not obey **inv** constraints with one another. To prevent clients from sending bad arguments, receivers may provide them with the means to determine themselves whether they are OK. Objects may *advertise* preconditions by exporting guard screening functions that clients may invoke before committing. This pulls responsibility for dealing with errors up one level from the receiver to the sender:

```
class Probability ...
  fn inRange(x: real): bool { 0.0 <= x /\ x <= 1.0}
end

op user(p: Probability, r: real)  {
  if p.inRange(r) then p.set(r) else ... end }
```

However, even with such arrangements, the operations must still contain exception mechanics (see Chapter 20) unless *all* clients obey the protocol. This may be enforced by design rules and tools. Another way to assign responsibility for value argument screening is to phrase arguments in terms of simple constrained value-holding classes. This localizes most error situations to those surrounding (failed) object construction, which is sometimes a more convenient base for defining error protocols than elsewhere.

17.5   Composition and Inheritance

We have so far in this chapter focused on compositional layering mechanism to form concrete classes that obey declarative constraints. Subclassing strategies provide both extensions and alternatives.

The most important intuitive guideline for subclassing at the design level is *substitutability*. It must be possible to substitute a subclass instance everywhere a superclass type is listed in a system, and still have everything operate correctly with respect to superclass guarantees. Hence, as described in Chapter 7, it is OK for subclasses to add or strengthen properties listed in the superclass, but never to delete, contradict, or weaken them.

17.5.1 Extending Operations

Subclassing is, of course, the natural technique to employ when a class requires *extended* rather than restricted views of primitives. For example, in later chapters we will need versions of simple classes that may be lockable, may notify other objects when they change state, and so on. In some applications (see Chapter 22) nearly every class should contain one or more standardized notification protocols. These may be defined in a familiar fashion. For example:

```
class ShadowedReal is Real
  local db: PersistentStore;
  local op notifyOfChange ==> db.notify(self, val)'' end
  op set(r: real): () ==> val' = r, notifyOfChange' end
end
```

17.5.2 Concrete Subclassing

It is very common for one concrete class to be a subclass of some abstract class, and additionally to share internal strategies with another related concrete class. This provides an opportunity to pit the compositional designs we have so far been using against multiple inheritance designs. For example, consider an `AdjustableLamp` class:

```
class AdjustableLamp is Lamp
  brightness: real;
  op adjust(delta: real) ==> brightness' = brightness + delta end
end
```

One way to construct a concrete class `AdjustableLampV1` is as a subclass of `AdjustableLamp` that happens to contain a `LampV1` as an internal component to which it delegates most properties and operations:

```
class AdjustableLampV1 is AdjustableLamp   % composition
  own l: LampV1 <>
  own br: Real <>
  on: bool                   { l.on }
  op flip                    { l.flip }
  brightness: real           { br? }
  op adjust(delta: real) { br.add(delta) }
end
```

A second version says that `AdjustableLampV2` is both a concrete subclass of `Adjust-ableLamp` and also an "extension" subclass of `LampV1`, since it employs the same kinds internal components and adds one more:

```
class AdjustableLampV2 is AdjustableLamp, LampV1 % concrete inheritance
  own br: Real <>
  brightness: real        { br? }
  op adjust(delta: real) { br.add(delta) }
end
```

This second sense of inheritance, *concrete subclassing*, is the most common form of inheritance employed in object-oriented programming. It is a simple way to combine the effects of compositional design with abstract subclassing, thus adding to the innumerable ways to express *PartOf*.

   Concrete inheritance can also lead to more concise class descriptions than does the manual combination of composition and property inheritance. Listing delegations in a composition-based strategy is tedious and inelegant looking. To remedy this just a bit in **ODL**, we use a macro **FORWARD(obj)** that declares forwarders for *all* operations supported **obj**, and a parameterized version that forwards only the indicated operations. (We describe some further variants in Chapter 22.) For example:

```
class AdjustableLampV1 is AdjustableLamp ...
  l: LampV1;  FORWARD(l, on, flip);
end
```

In the remainder of this section, we survey issues leading us to downplay the use of concrete subclassing for many design problems.

Black-box reuse.   Our initial example of `AdjustableLampV1` was (for illustrative purposes) suboptimal. There is no reason at all that a concrete `AdjustableLamp` class should be linked to a concrete `LampV1` object. Indeed, declaring it so breaks our design rule that links should be declared with respect to *abstract* classes rather than concrete ones. It is clear that *any* kind of `Lamp` would be OK as a component. A constructor for `AdjustableLamp` should be free to pick the one it wants:

```
class AdjustableLampV1a is AdjustableLamp ...
  l: Lamp <>   % not LampV1
end
```

```
op mkAdjustableLampV1a: unique AdjustableLampV1a {
   reply new AdjustableLampV1a(l := LampGen$dflt, br := new REAL(0.0)) }
```

This level of decoupling is impossible with concrete subclassing. Our `Adjustable-LampV2` class must always use exactly the same representation as `LampV1`.

Embedding.   There are several conceptual interpretations and programming language support mechanisms for concrete subclassing. In most schemes (e.g., [208]) a concrete subclass is construed as somehow containing an "embedded" instance of a superclass. However, this does not provide a simple handle for later (in this case) independently placing simple `Lamps` and the `AdjustableLamps` built upon them in different processes, if required. While this is perhaps a silly idea in the present example, larger designs encounter serious problems. Commitments about whether one object should be `packed` representationally within another are physical design issues, and should be addressed as such (see Chapter 23).

Renamings and restrictions.   A subclass cannot change the name of a property declared in its superclass(es). Also, it is just plain wrong for a subclass to somehow "cancel" properties or operations listed in its superclasses. Both of these break the substitutability relation that forms the heart of subclassing in design. However, these effects are easy to obtain using composition. In fact, most of our restricted value classes use exactly this strategy. For example, we simply cannot force a computer to directly accommodate a simple concrete `Balance` type, which only supports `add`, etc. We must restrict the more general capabilities of `Reals`, which *are* directly supportable via `REAL` and/or other classes, in order to design concrete versions of this "simpler" class.

Inner invocations.   Subclassing allows the creation of actions with "inner" self-invocations, in which the sense of the self-invocation changes in subclasses. This is an intrinsically self-recursive idiom. Here the subclass intersperses new work between the actions defined in the superclass version. This must be prearranged, usually via subclassing strategies of the form:

```
class A
  op middle { }
  op m { print(" begin "); self.middle; print(" end ") }
end
```

```
class SubA is A
  op middle { print(" middle ") }
end
```

Here, (new SubA).m prints "begin" "middle" and "end" (although perhaps not in this order, since they were defined as one-way sends in this example). This is because the self-invocation to middle in A::m is taken to refer to the currently overridden version, not the one in A. In OO systems, the class identity of self is defined to covary with the subclass being declared. The effects are most noticeable when self-referential computations are invoked.

It is easy to define such recursive invocation structures using subclassing. However, the same effects may be obtained in a sometimes clearer fashion via explicit layering. Here, a new layer may be created simply by redefining m as a top-level operation. It need/should not know anything about how the parts work, just how to coordinate them. While we are at it, we could break out a slightly better interface:

```
class AA
  op pre;  op middle;  op post;
end
```

```
op m(a: AA) { a.pre; a.middle; a.post }
```

```
class A is AA
  op middle { }
  op pre     { print(" begin ") }
  op post    { print(" end ") }
end
```

```
class SubA is AA
  a: A;  FORWARD(a, pre, post);
  op middle { print(" middle ") }
end
```

Probably the most common cases where inner operations appear most natural are *default* scripted actions listed in superclasses. Like m here, these default actions are intrinsically coordination-based, defining higher-level operations as scripts of more primitive class operations, each of which may be redefined in subclasses. However, layering these scripts on top of classes rather than within them generally leads to more extensible designs.

Mixins.   Consider a slight recasting of our lamp example, this time using the *mixin* class Adjustable. This class provides independent functions for adjusting magnitudes, untied to Lamps:

```
class Adjustable
  magnitude: real init= 0;
  op adjust(delta: real) ==> magnitude' = magnitude + delta end
end
```

```
class AdjustableLamp_2 is Adjustable, Lamp end
```

Classes such as Adjustable are nearly useless by themselves, but readily combine with others to form new specializations. Mixin-style multiple inheritance, like all multiple inheritance designs, is simplest when the properties described in each class are completely independent from those of the others. In these cases, simple composition suffices to create concrete versions:

```
class AdjustableLamp_2V1 is AdjustableLamp_2
  own adj: Adjustable <>; own l: Lamp <>;
  FORWARD(adj); FORWARD(l);
end
```

A similar version using concrete subclassing for either or both ancestors would run into the same issues as simple concrete inheritance. Moreover, when multiply inherited properties do interact, it is generally necessary to handcraft special versions of relevant operations. For example, if adjusting the magnitude down to zero should automatically turn off the lamp, this interaction would need to be hand-crafted (perhaps using notifications between adj and l; see Chapter 22).

17.5.3   Subclassing and White Box Reuse

Black-box composition is generally a safer strategy than either concrete composition or concrete subclassing. The new class uses the other as a mere component, so it has no special privileges to any internals. This makes it impossible for the new class to redefine things in ways that inadvertently break invariants.

Further, both layered composition and subclassing may be distinguished from forms of differential design in which bits and pieces of definitions in one class are reused and reworked in white-box fashion in another. These do not usually coincide. When they do not, *neither* disciplined subclassing nor composition is appropriate. However, pragmatic concerns make it very tempting to abuse one of these techniques.

In a sense, the *right* tool for this job is *cut-and-paste* reuse, in which definitions from one class are lifted and edited for use in another. However, the disadvantages of such practices are obvious. Among other problems, if the original version is discovered to be incorrect, it becomes very difficult to trace all of the others that are equally wrong.

There *is* a good solution, adopted in several OO languages. A design and programming system can itself facilitate and control white-box reuse-with-modification by providing a means for logically cutting and pasting the internals of one concrete class inside another, along with the convention that definitions mentioned as different in the new class replace those in the other. (A nearly equivalent strategy is used in languages (e.g., POOL [9]) that explicitly maintain two separate kinds of inheritance hierarchies, one for properties, and the other for reused code.)

For example, suppose we need to design a lamp that only has two brightness settings:

```
class DiscretelyAdjustableLamp is Lamp
  brightness: int;
  op adjustUp ==> brightness' = 269 end
  op adjustDown ==> brightness' = 54 end
end

class DiscretelyAdjustableLampV1 is DiscretelyAdjustableLamp
  opens AdjustableLampV1
  op adjustUp { br.set(269) }
  op adjustDown  { br.set(54) }
  local op adjust(delta: int)
end
```

The `opens` clause says that the listed parts of the class(es) are logically copied into the current declaration (subject to overrides) without saying *anything* about subclassing relations. It need only be used when performing white-box reuse that mangles the internals of the other class in a way that does not preserve subclassing relations. This was done here because the `AdjustableLampV1::adjust` operation does not deal with absolute settings, only relative ones. There is no other direct way to unconditionally set the brightness to a particular value. Also, since the `adjust` operation is not a part of the `DiscretelyAdjustableLamp` interface, it is redeclared as `local`. (This is safer than deleting it outright.)

The advantages such facilities are mainly (and importantly) *managerial*. They have the same effects as cut-and-paste-and-modify, but help track modifications by linking constructions to their ultimate sources. This ensures that if a definition is changed, the effects are felt in all other classes that use it.

These methods do *not* introduce *object* access issues. The opened objects themselves are not being accessed, just their declarative and definitional structures. Similarly, invariant and effect information found in the `opened` class cannot be reused. Usage is limited to concrete characteristics.

The whole idea of white-box reuse is to modify component and subcomponent code to do things they were never intended to do. When either pure composition or pure subclassing suffice, they are far better options. The hard work, guarantees, tests, and so on that others have already put into the design of these components may then be exploited.

For example, in the present case, a `DiscretelyAdjustableLampV2` class could be constructed to use a `AdjustableLampV1` as a component, while additionally keeping track of the current brightness settings via other attributes. In this way, it can send the appropriate value to `adjust` to implement `adjustUp` and `adjustDown`. This layering might or might not lead to a slower implementation. If it does, encapsulation boundaries may broken in a more thoughtful way in later design steps dealing explicitly with performance issues (see Chapter 25).

17.6 Summary

Being careful about the occasional subtleties of simple attributes is the first step in reliable class design. We refine OOA-level descriptions to reflect distinctions that make a difference in software. We introduced a number of *design restrictions*, including strong typing and state-preserving inspection rules. Even "elementary" classes include attributes that must be dynamically constrained by restricting value ranges, mutability, and exports. Inheritance and composition mechanisms may collide in designs using concrete subclassing. This is generally avoided through the use of abstract subclassing plus composition.

17.7   Further Reading

OO methods for dealing with attributes share commonalities with those based on abstract data types (ADTs); see Liskov [145]. Cook [62] describes some differences between OO and ADT methods.

Many slightly different constructs have been termed "views" and several other view-like constructs have been described; see, e.g., [2, 196, 98, 81]. Constructs similar to wrappers have been termed *thunks* [1] and *envelopes* [63]. They are also mappable to *closures* in Smalltalk [99]. Communication-closed layers form a central role in many distributed design frameworks; see, for example, [15].

The use of compositional methods rather than concrete subclassing is discussed more fully by Raj and Levy [184]. Inheritance in active objects is discussed in [94] and references therein.

17.8   Exercises

1. Design one or more `Date` classes that would serve the needs of *Date*s as used throughout Part I.

2. Design one or more `Cash` classes that could serve as a translation of *$Number* from Part I. Use or revise `Balance`.

3. Should `bcd` (binary coded decimal) be a primitive value type? Why/why not?

4. Describe three additional ways to represent the OOA notion of an optional value attribute.

5. Design generator classes for `MailingLabels`.

6. Why should built-in concrete classes such as `INT` support a mutable `add(x:int)` operation that adds `x` to the current state value? Would it be better to just support `set(x:int)`?

7. Design a class for immutable `Complex` numbers. Create a view of `Complex` to reimplement `Point`.

8. Give an example of a case in which an object cannot provide argument screening precondition functions because it cannot compute them.

9. Design abstract and concrete `CheckingAccount` subclasses of the `Account` class. Design the concrete versions using (a) composition (b) concrete subclassing.

10. An alternative to defining value-based views would be to enhance the primitive value system. This might then allow us to write `type probability = real where 0.0 <= probability <= 1.0 end`. Why is it better to define *classes* instead?

11. Build a tool that accepts range-restricted value descriptions (e.g., in the form listed in the previous question) and automatically generates (a) an abstract immutable class, (b) a default concrete subclass, (c) an abstract mutable class, and (d) a default concrete subclass, all obeying conventions of your choosing.

Chapter 18

Relationships in Design

In this chapter, we describe objects that track, collect, and maintain other objects. In previous chapters of Part II, we normally assumed that we were dealing with OOA models that mentioned only the abstract attributes and associated properties of particular classes, operations, or sets of classes. The design methods focused on the transformation of this information into composite and concrete class definitions meeting these properties. Another view focuses on their relations to other objects. Relations describe objects solely in terms of "who they know".

In many ways, relational information forms the complement of property-based abstract class information. Pure abstract classes list only `fns` and `ops` without necessarily revealing anything about internal connections. Pure relationships list only links, without necessarily revealing anything about properties and behaviors of the groups of objects when considered as a whole. In relational design, we often add properties and behaviors to the interfaces of classes holding known links, rather than finding component objects that help satisfy a known interface.

18.1 Relationships

OOA models may describe relationships in either of two ways. Relational models discussed in Chapter 4 explicitly specify relations such as *SisterOf*, *WorksFor*, *UsedBy*, and so on, connecting particular objects. Also, OOA class descriptions may describe links to objects as intrinsic attributes. For example, a `Face` class may list attribute `nose:Nose`. This represents a connection to a `Nose` object that is constrained to play a certain role in its `Face`.

All relationships (as well as composite objects) are described in ODL using the same basic link constructs. Declaring that some class X has a y:Y attribute or link means only that each X object "knows about" or "may directly communicate with" an object of class Y. This cannot capture the different senses in which different objects may be connected. Semantically meaningful relations such as *SisterOf* can only be established by convention, by naming strategies, by qualifiers and annotations, and, mostly, by usage.

There are many ways to capture static relationship information, depending on how it is structured and used. In fact, there are at least as many strategies as there are "linked data structures" and associated techniques, as extended by subclassing and other OO constructs. We will describe only a few of the most common and useful points on the design space resulting from considerations including:

- the arity of the relation
- whether the relation is intensionally or extensionally defined
- the cardinalities of the domains
- whether it is functional (at most one target per source) in either direction
- whether relationship instances have properties beyond those of participants
- whether the whole relationship has properties beyond those of instances
- whether participants must determine which relations they are members of
- whether participants ever directly communicate with each other
- whether participants must determine the identities of other participants
- whether nonparticipants communicate with members via the relation
- whether membership is nonoptional for objects of certain subclasses
- whether membership may be transient
- how entry and exit conditions of transient relations are controlled
- whether participants may control which relations they are in
- whether membership must be explicitly tracked or logged, and if so, how
- whether the relationship still holds if one or more participants change.

18.1.1 Relational Classes

A good starting point is to declare each element of a relationship as an instance of a *class* with `fixed` object link attributes. For example, the ownership relation between clients and accounts is:

```
class ClientAccountTuple % or 'class Own'
  local cl: fixed Client;
  local acct: fixed Account;
end
```

The entire aggregate relationship itself could then be defined as a SET of such tuples.

However, this is by itself a pretty useless design. The class has no external interface at all. No other object may communicate with members of ClientAccountTuple. Such classes are "abstract" in a very different sense than the abstract classes we have previously encountered. They represent abstract linkages, relationships, and/or interaction potentials between objects. We will sometimes use the phrase "pure relational" to denote this kind of class.

Adding properties.   If a relational class exists in order to help other objects keep track of relationships, it may contain an interface that "gives away" the identities of participants. It may also contain any other properties and constraints of interest. A variant of the original may be defined as a subclass:

```
class ClientAccount
  client: Client;
  account: Account;
  inv account.ownerID = client.clientID
  lastAccess: Date;
  op markAccess(d: Date) ==> sameDate(lastAccess', d) end
end
```

```
class ClientAccountV1 is ClientAccount
  client: Client  <>
  account: Account <>
  own lastAccessDate: Date <>
  op markAccess(d: Date) { lastAccessDate.set(d) }
end
```

Classes such as `ClientAccount` expand on a simple relationship to localize attributes and operations, and to isolate and manage object interaction. For example, the difference between abstract and concrete versions may be exploited when hiding database retrieves behind the veneer of an interoperable relational class.

Back-links. While simplest and nicest, these relational class declarations do not make allowances for objects to directly "know" what relations they are in (i.e., here, for clients to know their accounts). If this is necessary, we might *additionally* declare that such relational objects serve as conditionally bound link attributes of their participants. We may also add predicates that allow one member to report whether it is related to another:

```
class Client_1
  r: opt ClientAccount;
  fn owns(a: Account): bool  = (~null(r) /\ r.account = a);
end
```

(and/or similarly for `Account`). This is one translation of:

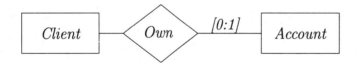

Cross references. The previous strategy only works for *[0:1]* and *[1:1]* relationships. If each `Client` may own an unbounded number of accounts, then the links and back-links must be defined as collections, for example:

```
class Client_2
  r: fixed SET[ClientAccount];
  accts: fixed SET[Account];
end
```

Conditional links. If a relationship is accessible only via its participants, if it possesses no other attributes, if there is no other reason to track it externally, and if the relationship is *[1:1]* or *[0:1]* for each participant, then there is no need to declare a relational class at all. Instead, each participant may declare a conditionally bound link attribute to the others, perhaps along with state attributes that keep track of whether the relation is in effect:

```
class Client_3 ...
  isOwner: bool;
  acct: opt Account;
  inv isOwner => ~null(acct)
end
```

Unconditional links. If objects of one class are uniformly and necessarily related to those of another and there is no other need to keep track of the relation separately, the relation may be declared using regular link attributes. For example, say that accounts are intrinsically required to be owned by particular clients, so that it is impossible to have an account without an owner. This implies that `Account_2` is *itself* a sort of relational class in addition to its other properties:

```
class Account_2 ...
  owner: fixed Client;
end
```

Subclassing. If only special kinds of objects are related to others, they may be split away and described as subclasses. For example, if only some kinds of accounts have owners, we could make `OwnedAccount` a subclass of (ownerless) class `Account`.

Rebindable Links. If the form of the relation must always hold, but one of the participants may vary, then the link need not be declared as `fixed`. For example, declaring just `owner:Client` means that an account always has an owner, but that it might be owned by different clients during its lifetime.

Generics. Specific relational classes may be subsumed under generic classes. For example, at an extreme, any relationship linking any two objects of the same class could be described parametrically via:

```
class PAIR[T]
  first:  T;
  second: T;
end
```

```
class ParentChild is PAIR[Person] ... end
```

This level of abstraction can impair understandability. Here, for example, we would probably like to label the two participants as `parent:Person` and `child:Person` rather than just `first` and `second`. Luckily, both effects may be had at once through *views*:

```
class ParentChild parent: Person; child: Person end
class ParentChildAsPAIR is PAIR[Person]
  local pc: ParentChild;
  first: Person  { pc.parent }
  second: Person { pc.child }
end
```

18.1.2 Relations versus Subclasses

Relational designs focus on relations among objects. Inheritance is a relation among classes. The two concepts should not be confused. Relational classes may look superficially similar to multiply inherited classes. However, relational classes describe internal connections, without a commitment to visible properties, while (abstract) multiple inheritance describes properties, without a commitment to composition. Sometimes these may be mixed and matched, but it is worth getting the options straight. For example, it might be tempting to express the ownership relation as:

```
class CA is Client, Account end
```

This declaration says that all objects of class `CA` have all the characteristics of accounts as well as all those of clients. Thus, `CA` objects have `interestRate` properties, can perform `deposit` operations, but also have `lastName`s, `clientID`s, and so on. This is surely not what is intended. It is never a good idea to express such relationships as multiply inherited classes unless by rare chance *all* properties and operations defined on all of the component classes may be inherited meaningfully.

18.1.3 Constraints on Relations

Relation specifications may include `inv` constraints representing *contracts* [107] between their members. For example, a relationship may include the constraint that the client ID number of a person's checking and savings accounts must be the same. Or a user interface specification may say the open/closed status of a cash dispenser door matches that of a displayed door-icon. These might be specified at the OOA level explicitly via constraints, or implicitly via parametric relations (Chapter 4).

Note that parametric (generic) relational classes are not the same as OOA-level parametric relation instances. The latter are typically used to indicate constraints on elements of other classes. For example, the *Family* class in Chapter 4 might look like:

```
class Family ...
  parent: Person;
  child: Person;
  inv parent.isCustodianOf(child)
end
```

Simple static measures occasionally suffice to maintain invariants. Some relational constraints and dependencies may be satisfied by designing classes that share links to the same source object. For example, a good way to ensure that all accounts held by a person report the same client number is to have them all share links to the same client object, and delegate requests to get the client ID through the sole object whose job is to maintain it. As long as the constructors and participants ensure that the links are properly shared, all is well. This technique is just the time-honored practice of reducing a value equality constraint to a link equality constraint. Assuming `fixed` links and/or other precautions, this need be established only once:

```
class AccountPair ...
  savings: fixed SavingsAccount <>
  checking: fixed CheckingAccount <>

  inv savings.owner = checking.owner % rely on constructor to establish
  inv savings.clientID = checking.clientID % implied by owner equality
end

op mkAccountPair(c: Client): AccountPair {
  reply new AccountPair(
     savings := new SavingsAccount(... owner := c ...),
     checking := new CheckingAccount(... owner := c ...)) }
```

Such strategies fail when the constraints carry dynamic consequences (i.e., lead to transitions in any of the participants). For example, if there were some action that each account needed to perform if the client ID changed, this must be actively coordinated using the methods described later in this chapter and in Chapter 22.

18.2   Collections

SETs and related classes are often used to represent collections of objects all of which satisfy some property or relation. Many different collection classes may be defined, each differing in interface and policies for keeping track of objects. These serve both as tools for expressing multiplicity features described in analysis models, and also as bases for many manager classes.

The general forms of these classes are not unique to object-oriented design. They are similar to constructs used to describe and specify groupings within other design approaches (see, e.g., [126]). As usual, there is nothing very special about the precise definitions of the classes we list here. They are ones that are most commonly found to be useful. We do not make much of a commitment about the exact form of these classes or of their inheritance relations in following discussions, but we need them to exemplify designs using collections.

18.2.1   Sets

Sets are usually the best way to translate *[0:N]* attributes described in OOA models, as well as collections of relational tuples and other groupings. As discussed in Chapter 4, analysts might use set notation for such purposes, in which case essentially no transformation is necessary. A generic class SET supports properties size and membership predicate has, as well as operations to add, remove, and perform operations on elements:

```
class SET[T]
   size: int;                    %    number of elements
   empty: bool              =    size = 0;
   fn has(item: Any): bool;  %    true if item is in set
   op put(item: T): ()       ==> has(item)' end
   op remove(item: T): ()    ==> ~has(item)' end
   op applyC(p: WRAPPER1[T]); %    call p on all elements
   op applyS(p: WRAPPER1[T]); %    send p to all elements
end
```

Parameterized Wrappers

New forms of wrappers are referenced in applyC and applyS. These invoke (either in call or send mode) the same operation for each element of a set. The associated wrappers take an argument, thus allowing the passing of arguments through to the inner operations:

```
class WRAPPER1[T]
  op call(t: T): ();
  op send(t: T);
end
```

We assume a `WRAP1` macro that creates the right kind of wrapper and instantiates it. This then allows:

```
op print(s: SET[MailingLabel]): () { s.applyC(WRAP1(print(#1))) }
```

[We use "#n" as a placeholder for macro argument number n.]

A `WRAPPER2` may be defined similarly for two-argument operations, and so on. Special versions may also be defined to wrap procedures and functions classified on result type in addition to argument type. We will sometimes do this. For example, a `PREDWRAPPER1` is a `WRAPPER1`-like class that wraps its actions within `fn pred: bool`, so it can transmit a boolean result back to its sender. Such basic macros cover the most common need for holding operations as objects. But there are as many kinds of wrappers as there are relational classes and operations. They cannot *all* be generated mechanically.

Extensions

Any number of auxiliary operations may be defined on top of set classes. For example, set union and difference might be supported in a *mutable* fashion:

```
op putAll[T](dest: SET[T], other: SET[T]): ();
  % add all elements of other into dest
  % i.e., set dest to (dest U other)
op removeAll[T](dest: SET[T], other: SET[T]): ();
  % remove all elements of other from dest
  % i.e., set dest to (dest \ other)
```

Refinements of set classes may be defined through subclassing. For example, special versions of sets might guarantee that `applyC` traverses elements in an order based on some kind of key values. It is also convenient to define less powerful *super*classes. In particular, defining `PUT_ONLY_SET` that supports only `has` and `put` is a useful way of to ensure that items are never removed or otherwise touched.

Associated concrete classes may be based on hash tables, linked lists, balanced trees, and so on. It is often useful and convenient to implement the `applyS` and `applyC` operations as *multicasts* (see Chapter 22).

Examples

A SET may be used in translating the *Hand* class described in Chapter 3:

```
class Hand ...
  thumb: Finger;
  fingers: SET[Finger];
  inv fingers.size <= 6, fingers.has(thumb)
end
```

The SET[SET[Student]] in the following version of the *School* class results from the mixture of *[1:M]* and explicit set constructs:

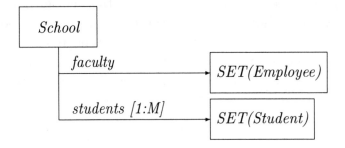

```
class School ...
  faculty:  SET[Employee];
  students: SET[SET[Student]];
end
```

The simplest relation-holder is just a set whose elements are relational objects. Other status operations may then be added. For example:

```
class ParentChildSet is SET[ParentChild] ...
  op put(pc: ParentChild);
  fn hasParent(p: Any): bool;
  fn hasChild(c: Any): bool;
end
```

18.2.2   Other Collections

Bags.   BAG classes support the same operations as SET, but possess bag (multiset) semantics. For SETs, multiple insertions of the same object result in only a single occurrence, while in BAGs, multiple insertions result in multiple occurrences. Both SETs and BAGs may be defined to be subclasses of a simple COLLECTION that makes no guarantees one way or the other.

Buffers and queues.   A useful variant of a bag is a buffer, supporting only put, take, empty, and full. The take operation removes and returns *any* arbitrary element:

```
class BUFFER[T]
   empty: bool;        % false if can take
   full: bool;         % false if can put
   op put(item: T): (); % insert an item
   op take item: T;    % take any item
end
```

Unbounded versions may be defined as subclasses for which full is constantly false. (The same technique may be used to create possibly bounded SETs and BAGs.) Subclasses of BUFFER may strengthen the guarantees of take. In particular, a QUEUE promises that take returns the least recently inserted item (i.e., maintains FIFO policies).

Maps.   MAPs represent sets of pairs of objects in which the first element of each pair is unique and serves as a "key" for the second. They support the same features (on pairs) as SET, plus a function at that accepts a key, and returns the corresponding element or is null if there is no such key. (We will describe a better way to phrase this operation, via named replies, in Chapter 20.) For example:

```
class Employees
   boss: Employee;
   ssns: MAP[Name, SSN];
   inv ssns.at(boss.name) = boss.ssn
end
```

A useful variant is an EQUIV_MAP, which guarantees that keys and contents have a one-to-one relation, and supports an unmap(cont) to return the first element, given the second.

Tables.   Tables are special versions of maps from integer values to contents. They are common replacements for SETs when there is a need for clients to be able to access individual elements through indices. A useful subclass supports traversal:

```
class TABLE[T]
  size: int;                        % number of elements
  empty: bool;                      % true if size = 0
  has(index: int): bool;            % true if item with index is in table
  op put(item: T): int;             % put item anywhere, return its index
  op remove(index: int);            % unbind item at index
  op at(index: int): opt T;         % return item at index
  op atput(index: int, item: T):(); % rebind item at index
end
```

```
class TRAVERSABLE_TABLE[T] is TABLE[T]
  lowest: int;                      % minimum bound index
  highest: int;                     % maximum bound index
  op next(index: int): int;         % next bound index
end
```

These may be used, for example, in:

```
class Entries
  v: TABLE[Account];
  fn accountExists(acctNum: int): bool { ~null(v.at(acctNum)) }
end
```

```
op printAll(t: TRAVERSABLE_TABLE[Employee]) {
  local i:int := t.lowest;
  while i <= t.highest do print(t.at(i)); i := t.next(i) end }
```

There are several other idioms for arranging traversal. An alternative strategy illustrated later is to define *iterator* objects with operations that reveal the "current" element of a particular collection object, as well as those that step to the next (or previous or whatever) element on request.

Arrays.   Arrays are constant-sized, contiguously accessible tables of (opt) objects, supporting usage such as:

```
class Balances
  v: ARRAY[Balance];
  op printAll { local i: int := 0;
    while i < v.size do print(v.at(i)); i := i + 1 end }
end
```

Multidimensional arrays may be declared as `ARRAY[ARRAY[T]]`. Alternatively, special cases (e.g., `MATRIX`) may be defined directly. `ARRAY`s may also be used to translate bounded OOA multiplicities. For example, the *Hand* example might be recast as:

```
class Hand ...
  fingers: ARRAY[Finger];
  inv fingers.size = 6
end
```

Sequences. `SEQ` classes represent sequences (lists). `SEQ` supports `has` and `size`, plus `hd` and `tl`, and operations `prepend`, `append`, and `concat`. For example:

```
class Book ...
  ch: SEQ[Chapter];
  inv ch.hd.number = 1
end
```

A mutable string class may be defined as:

```
class String is SEQ[Char] ...
  op toUpperCase; % transform all chars to upper case
end
```

An immutable version may be defined as:

```
class CharVal val: fixed Char; end
class StringVal is IMMUTABLE_SEQ[CharVal] ... end
```

where `IMMUTABLE_SEQ` is a superclass defining only `fns`, not mutating operations.

Sequences as Per-Object Relations

Rather than treating the elements as parts of a structured collection, sequential ordering may be represented as a relationship between individual objects. For example, if each `Chapter` object intrinsically bears an *is-followed-by* relation with another, this could be expressed through:

```
class Chapter ...
  next: opt Chapter;
end

class Book ...
  firstChapter: Chapter;
end
```

This may be refined a bit by segregating those objects that *are* followed by others versus the (only) one that is not:

```
class Chapter_2 ... end
class FinalChapter is Chapter_2 ... end
class LinkedChapter is Chapter_2
  local next: Chapter;
end
```

However, this does not apply if any given object may need to change its status from linked to unlinked or vice versa (e.g., if a new final chapter is added, making the old one nonfinal). Alternatively, the links may be wrapped "around" the objects rather than "within" them:

```
class Chapter_3 ... end
class ChapterLink
  local ch: Chapter_3;
  local next: opt ChapterLink;
end
```

This is a common strategy for designing the internal structure of concrete SEQ, SET, etc., classes. Note that this loses subclassing. For example, if `Chapter` objects have `title` attributes, then so do `LinkedChapters`. But for `ChapterLink` objects, the `Chapter` is treated as an internal component. The attributes are not automatically propagated (although this could be done manually via forwarding).

Active Data Structures

Elements of a sequence or other collection may include protocols for collaborating on various tasks. For example, suppose we would like to be able to send a `printBook` message to *any* `Chapter` object in a book, and still have the book printed in chapter order:

```
class Chapter_4 ...
  locals prev: opt Chapter_4; next: opt Chapter_4; end
  op printBook {
    if ~null(prev) then prev.printBook else self.printAndPropagate end }
  op printAndPropagate {
    Printer$print(self); if ~null(next) then next.printAndPropagate end }
end
```

In this case, there may be no need to create a Book class representing all members of the relation. This is only attractive when group (relation) membership need not be otherwise managed or tracked.

There are as many such designs as there are operations on data structures. This example is an "active doubly linked list". Similar configurations and algorithms may be based on trees, hypercubes, and other graph structures (see, e.g., [123]).

18.2.3 Repositories

Repositories (or "containers") are collections that take an active role in protecting and maintaining their elements. These structures provide footholds for establishing storage, persistence, and database management. From an analysis perspective, repositories are collections that are also ensembles. They are also crosses between collections and generators. Like collections, they keep track of all members in some structured fashion. Like generators, they include operations that cause new objects to be constructed. A repository class may be defined to maintain all objects of interest in a particular class or set of classes, as well as associated constructors and other bookkeeping functions. For example:

```
class ActiveAccounts
  accts: SET[Account];
  syslog: TransactionLog;
  acctErrorHandler: AccountErrorHandler;
  ...
  op mkAccount(initBalance: real...) a: unique Account {
    a := ...; accts.put(a); }
  op deactivate(a: Account): () { accts.remove(a) }
  op overdrawnAccounts(s: SET[Account]); % place all overdrawn accts into s
end
```

Classes such as `ActiveAccounts` have all the makings of database services that maintain, report on, and serve as the primary interface for collections of objects. For example, we could extend this to include the general purpose:

```
op select(s: SET[Account], pred: AcctPredicate);
   % add all accts obeying predicate into s
```

Many object-oriented databases use constructs of this general form [18]. They differ across dimensions such as whether managers are designed to keep track of all versus some elements of one concrete class, one abstract class, one hierarchy, and so on. They also differ in how they collect, traverse, and present the component objects.

Most repositories are based on `SET`s. In Chapter 3, we noted that *classes* may be viewed as descriptions of sets of objects, all sharing some of the same properties. A repository using a `SET` to keep track of a group of objects, all of the same concrete class, may be seen as a concrete translation (or variant, or extension) of a metaclass (see Chapter 8).

Reifying Class Descriptions

Besides tracking objects, metaclass-like repositories may be able to answer questions about their properties. For example, they might support a check to see if all contained objects possess a given attribute:

```
class ActiveAccounts_2 ...
   attrs: fixed SET[AttributeDescriptor];
   fn hasAttrib(a: AttributeDescriptor): bool { attrs.has(a) }
end
```

Support for such queries requires that all details of *classes* themselves be reified by creating classes representing the metaclass attributes described in Chapter 8. Representational forms for attribute functions, operations, messages, etc., must be devised. For example:

```
class AttributeDescriptor ...
   name: String;
   args: SEQ[ArgumentDescriptor];
   type: ClassDescriptor;
   quals: SET[AttributeQualifierDescriptor];
end
```

Unless a target implementation language and/or support service already includes all of the background declarations for classes such as `AttributeDescriptor`, an entire framework of such classes and operations must be designed.

We refrain here from providing a full self-descriptive framework for **ODL**. Most practical system design efforts require conformance with possibly conflicting predefined features of existing tools and database facilities (see Chapter 23). For example, such a framework could serve as a basis for a query language built on top of the base system. Similarly, standardized "interface repositories" collecting attribute and service descriptions may be needed in support of dispatching and routing (see Chapter 21). The need to conform to existing database and/or dispatching facilities may limit options and expressiveness.

Exporting Elements

Normally, collections include attributes and operations specifically designed to reveal and track maintained objects. But this need not be so. A repository may be designed to never export the identities of elements:

```
class HiddenActiveAccounts ...
   accts: SET[Account];
   op mkAccount(initBalance: real...) { accts.put(new Account...)}

   op selectivelyApply(predicate: Predicate, action: Action)
      { % do action for all accounts meeting predicate % }
end
...
accts.selectivelyApply(PREDWRAP1(#1.overdrawn), WRAP1(print(#1)));
```

Here, the repository only supplies methods that relay operations to internal objects selected via descriptive predicates, without ever revealing the component objects.

Interception

An alternative design is to retain a form of identity-based communication, but to manufacture pseudo-identities that are then intercepted. A repository agent may pass out arbitrary keys that uniquely identify internal objects. This results in a managed "public" object identity scheme overlaid on top of the "real" internal one. Any kind of ID format (e.g., strings) could be used, with various kinds of `MAPs` performing the translation. To illustrate with integer pseudo-IDs:

```
class KeyedActiveAccounts ...
  tab: TABLE[Account];
  op mkAccount(initBalance: real...): int {
    reply tab.put(new Account...) }
  op addToBalance(key: int, amt: Cash): () {
    local a: Account := tab.at(k);
    if ~null(a) then a.addToBalance(amt) end }
end
```

All access to the internal objects is mediated through the specially generated pseudo-IDs. The agent may then intercept, preprocess, and otherwise manage operation requests to these objects, at the expense of duplicating the entire interface of the contained objects and providing the appropriate forwarding.

18.3 Coordinators

Relational classes and collections are special kinds of encapsulators. They keep track of other objects and may maintain a separate, controlled interface to them. This attitude toward relational classes leads to a number of design strategies that exploit these properties.

The best examples stem from the need to convert top-level operations to other forms. We have distinguished operations that are received by particular objects versus "top-level scripts" that just so happen to employ these objects. For example, we could define operations for our mailing label class like this:

```
class MailingLabelV2 is MailingLabel ...
  op setStreet(newSt: String80) { _street.set(newSt) }
  op setZip(newZip: int)        { _zip.set(newZip) }
  op setCity(newCity: String80) { _city.set(newCity) }
end

op copyAddress(dest: MailingLabel, src: MailingLabel): () {
  dest.setStreet(src.street);
  dest.setCity(src.city);
  dest.setZip(src.zip) }
```

Operations such as `setStreet`, `setCity` and `setZip` differ from `copyAddress` in that they are all received by mailing label objects, while `copyAddress` is an application operation that in turn invokes more primitive operations on its participants.

The use of receiverless operations turns out to be inconvenient in later design. One pragmatic reason is "name space pollution". When a project is constructed by multiple developers, clashes in choices of top-level operation names and the like become inevitable without further precautions. Receivers may be "found" by exploiting the relationship between composite *classes* and composite (scripted) *actions*. Any composite action may be recast as an argumentless operation that is owned by a class with link attributes corresponding to the associated arguments of the original version. For example, we could declare a *class* that directly supported the `copyAddress` operation:

```
class MailingLabelCopier
  local dest: MailingLabel <>
  local src: MailingLabel <>
  op copyAddress: () { dest.setStreet(src.street); ... }
end

c := new MailingLabelCopier(dest := lab1, src := lab2);
c.copyAddress;
```

This example illustrates the fact that operation coordinators may always be built up from relational classes. *Any* free-standing "scripted" operation with one or more participants may be transformed into a coordinator class with a single argumentless action. Thus, our "top-level" operations might be thought of as relational *class* specifications of a particularly simple sort. Free-standing operations and concrete objects are two points on a continuum of conventions and usages:

- Objects may support multiple "entry points", while free-standing operations do just one thing.
- Objects *persist* between their actions, while operations conceptually just "go away" when they are done.
- Objects have identities, while operation invocations do not.
- Operations defined within classes are received by the associated objects, while free-standing ones are conceptually receiverless.
- Among other minor syntactic differences, we bind arguments by-name for objects, but by-position for operations.

There is a lot of middle ground here. Whenever there is a need to manage interaction in a way that defies implementation through a single operation, a composite, relational or collection class may be built or extended.

These classes serve as perhaps more literal translations of *acquaintance* relations described in Chapter 6 than other classes we have so far described. The view and wrapper classes described in Chapter 17 may also be seen as examples of this tactic. In all cases, the conceptual property that distinguishes them from ordinary composite classes is the *relational* nature of link information. Links inside such classes are used to track and manage participants that are not otherwise within the object's exclusive control. In other words, relational objects form layers that are not necessarily or even usually communication-closed.

Conventions and Transformations

Different OO languages and systems have different policies about operation receivership and coordination. While these need not directly impact design strategies, they may influence their expression. Some OO languages (e.g., **CLOS**) and OO databases (e.g., **Iris/OpenODB**) do not (at least normally) directly attach operations to classes at all. In such cases, there is less motivation and support for converting multiparticipant operations into classes. In fact, the reverse transformation is more appealing, and sometimes even necessary. Systems encouraging this style are usually accompanied by lack of access restrictions, enabling more centralized handling of dynamics. However, this also makes it harder to express matters of distribution. In a fully distributed system, it may be difficult or impossible to implement a centralized top-level facility for handling all otherwise receiverless messages.

At the other extreme, some OO languages *require* that all operations be attached to classes. This policy sometimes leads designers to attach operations to the "wrong" classes. For example, it is tempting to attach operations on *pairs* of `MailingLabels` to the `MailingLabel` class itself rather than a coordinator. However, this does not always result in the intended effect. This is the reason we attach all top-level operations to `System` without demanding that `System` be declared as a class in a conventional manner. Transformations may be applied at any time to distribute capabilities among receivers.

Applications

Variants of acquaintance relations and "event stepping stone" classes may be used as single-purpose event coordinators between fixed sets of objects. For example, a class may coordinate the door-sensor-motor interaction from Chapter 6:

```
class DSM ...
  locals
    door: fixed Door <>
    sensor: fixed TempSensor <>
    motor: fixed Motor <>
  end
  op doorOpens { motor.halt }
  op tmpLow    { motor.halt }
end

class Door ...
  local dsm: DSM;
  op openDoor { ...; dsm.doorOpens }
end
```

The DSM class serves as one translation of the oval in:

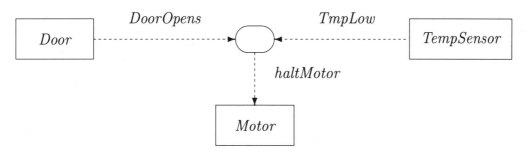

The dynamics of coordinator objects are discussed in more detail in Chapter 22.

18.3.1 Modules

Rather than wrapping up all participants as links, a *module*-like class may hold only the "protocols" for maintaining relations and interactions among particular kinds of objects, leaving the arguments intact. Usually, such classes support a collection of operations that all have exactly the same arguments. For example, to group sets of operations on pairs of MailingLabels:

```
class MailingLabelPairModule ...
  op copyAddress(dest: MailingLabel, src: MailingLabel);
  fn sameName(a: MailingLabel, b: MailingLabel): bool = (a.name = b.name);
end
```

These classes are similar to modules in other design frameworks. They help organize and localize groups of related functionality. They also serve the same conceptual role as generators. In fact, they may be defined in an arbitrarily similar manner to generator classes. The main difference between them is that here, the objects are not only constructed, but also pushed into action. For example:

```
class MailingLabelPairModule ...
  op copy(d: MailingLabel, s: MailingLabel) {
    new MailingLabelCopier(dest := d, src := s).copyAddress }
end
```

This is one way to implement pure "stateless" *service transitions* (Chapter 6) in which the server creates a new object to handle each new request.

For another example, the following coordinator class may be used to translate the *Transfer* relation described (in Chapter 4):

```
class Transfer
  src: fixed Account;
  dest: fixed Account;
  amount: fixed Cash;
  date: fixed Date;

  op transfer; % do the transfer
end
```

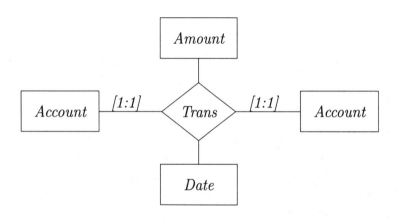

Alternatively, a `transferless` version of `Transfer` might be accepted by a module:

```
class TransferProtocol
  op transfer(t: Transfer); % do the transfer
end
```

Such classes may be scaled up to mediate arbitrarily complex actions. For example:

```
class TrafficLawModule ...
  op encounter(v: Vehicle, s: TrafficLight);
    % if s is red, tell v to stop and tell s to turn green soon, etc.
end
```

Again, these mediators differ from coordinator objects in that they know *only* the protocols, not the participants, which are transmitted as arguments that may change from invocation to invocation. Callers must know of appropriate modules, as well as other co-participants. Alternatively, protocol mediation modules may be seen as **generators** of coordinator objects. Given a protocol and a set of participants, they may construct and set in motion a coordinator.

18.4 Relations versus Composites

There is a continuum from the relational, collection, and coordinator classes described in this chapter to the composite classes described in Chapter 17. In pure relations, only the links and their invariant constraints matter. Providing some kind of interface and behavior for the class is sometimes almost an afterthought. But for property-driven concrete classes, the links are "uninteresting" and exist only in order to provide a mechanism in support of a desired interface. These represent different approaches to the same basic design activity of relating internal characteristics to outward appearances.

Even though they lie on the same continuum, the conceptual differences between OOA-level relations and composites usually have other computational consequences. The best example, which also serves as a prototypical consideration for a range of other issues, is the notion of *copying* instances. Consider the prospects for writing `clone` operations for our `ClientAccountV1`, `School`, `ActiveAccounts`, or `Mailing-LabelCopier` classes.

One way to clone `ClientAccountV1` is through a *deep copy*. This copy makes in turn a clone of the `client`, `account`, `lastAccessDate`, along with any other nested

components, and then makes a new `ClientAccountV1` object with the links bound
to these objects.

This sounds wrong. Cloning makes perfect sense for underlying support components such as `lastAccessDate`. But the overall purpose of the `ClientAccount` class is
to record connections between pre-existing `Client` and `Account` objects, not to make
up new ones. Conceptually, such a cloned object would *not* be a faithful copy. It
represents a different instance of the relation, between two new objects that presum-
ably have the same states as the originals, but are not the same objects. Generating
such clones nearly always leads to trouble. Any other object wanting a copy of a
`ClientAccountV1` probably needs it in order to communicate with the participants,
not to create new ones.

A second problem is more mechanical. A `ClientAccount::clone` requires associated `Client::clone` and `Account::clone` operations. But suppose that `Client`
also had a direct link to the `Account`. Should `Client::clone` make yet another
copy of the `Account` in the process of cloning itself? And what about circular links?
These issues come into play as well when attempting to create description `records`
for relational objects.

Often, the best pragmatic solution is just not to define `clone` operations for relational objects if you do not have to, thus avoiding the issue entirely. Another option
is to rely on *shallow* copies in which the old link bindings are propagated to the newly
created relational objects. Shallow copying of relational objects may be used to implement a form of parallelism. Clients of each copy may pass messages through the
different relation instance objects simultaneously.

Compare this to the idea of cloning `Lamps`, where *deep* copying seems most sensible. Generally, whenever you can qualify a link as `own` (or otherwise communication-
closed) deep copying is the right approach. Other cases require consideration of
situation-specific semantics. These matters reflect the same difficulties with the
metaphors of *PartOf* and related aggregation concepts discussed from an analysis
perspective in Chapter 9. They do not go away in design.

18.5   Summary

Relational and composite classes represent, track, and/or manage groups of other
objects. They may take a wide range of forms, including:

- pure relational classes that maintain only links and invariants

- extended relational classes that maintain additional attributes describing features of the relation and a public interface for accessing them
- "regular" classes and subclasses that embed relational links as attributes
- composite classes that bind other objects in order to obtain their functionality
- views, operation wrappers, and modules that bind other objects in order to coordinate scripted operations.

Collections similarly come in many flavors, and fill many disparate needs in design. SETs are among the foremost tools in the transformation of OOA models. They are usually the right way of dealing with multiplicities and apply-to-all formulations. However, in any particular situation, other collections might better fit semantics.

18.6   Further Reading

The design and implementation of classes representing relations and collections rests on common linked data structures. Knuth [129], Standish [209], Sedgewick [197], and Smith [207] are good references for the underlying data structures and techniques. Many specification languages (e.g., VDM[126]) provide fuller semantics for "standard" collections including SETs. Special relational techniques and approaches (especially those geared toward persistent storage) may be found in the relational and OO database literature, for example, the *ACM SIGMOD* and *IEEE Data Engineering* conference proceedings.

18.7   Exercises

1. List 3 ways to translate the *MaintainedBy* relationship described in Chapter 4.
2. Why does SET::has take an argument of type Any?
3. Why are ARRAYs filled with opt elements?
4. List two differences between design-level SETs and classes.
5. If you want a SET class that provides a means to print its elements, all you need do is write such a subclass. Why is the combination of apply and wrappers often preferable?
6. Design a SET subclass supporting accumulate, which applies a listed operation to all elements and then combines the results in a way described by another argument.

7. Design a full abstract `String` class and two completely different concrete subclasses.

8. Design a generic `ASSOC` class that specializes `MAP`s for cases with `String` keys.

9. The operation-to-class transformation runs in both directions. Describe how to cope with methods that *prohibit* (a) classes (b) multiparameter operations?

10. List two differences between module classes and the kinds of modules found, for example, in `Modula-2`.

Chapter 19

Designing Transitions

19.1 States and Guards

Objects may behave in different ways when they are in different logical states. OOA models usually address this by defining a property that distinguishes states and then defining transitions using conditional logic that refers to this property. These translate into **when**-guarded operations in ODL. In the simplest cases, states and guards reference boolean attributes. For example:

```
class CardEater
  holding: bool init= false;
  latched: bool init= false;
  local beeper: Beeper;
  local cardLatch: CardLatch;
  op unlatch ==> ~latched' end
  op latch   ==>  latched' end
  op eject
    when ~latched /\ holding then
      cardLatch.release', ~holding'
    elsewhen ~latched /\ ~holding then
      beeper.beep'
    else pend end
end
```

An operation may contain any number of logically exclusive **when** clauses. To reduce awkwardness, series of **when** _ **elsewhen** _ **else** _ **end** guards in ODL are treated analogously to if _ elsif _ else _ end constructs in that each guard in the series assumes the negation of all previous guards. However, this does not in any sense imply that they are evaluated sequentially. (They are not "evaluated" at all. Like "inv" and "==>", they are descriptive, not computational constructs.)

In all cases, guards split operations into clauses, each with a state based triggering condition and corresponding actions and/or effect statements. Requests that are received when the object is *not* in any of the action states may be listed as "pending", and are triggerable at some point if and when the object enters the state. If more than one request is present when the object is ready, triggerable requests are processed in some order. The order in which pended requests are processed is a design decision. We assume first-in-first-out processing order as a default. Later examples describe ways of obtaining other disciplines.

Here, an eject request will stay pending until the CardEater is in an unlatched state. When it becomes unlatched, it will either beep or release the card, depending on its current holding state. For example, if a CardEater receives three eject messages from an angry customer while the card is being latched in the course of a transaction, it will eventually, after an unlatch request from some controller object, release the card and then beep twice. Of course, to be more realistic, we probably should have designed it to behave differently.

19.1.1   State Predicates

Guards often refer to macroscopic states defined in terms of particular settings of various attributes. For example, we can transform the version of the ATM machine presented in Chapter 5 that used the following table to describe states:

	Mn	Id	S1	S2	S3	Fi
available?	n	y	y	y	y	y
cardIn?	n	n	y	y	y	y
stripInfo	nil	nil	nil	ok	ok	nil
PINInfo	nil	nil	nil	nil	ok	nil
finished?	n	n	n	n	n	y

These states may be used to guide some of the actions described in Chapters 5 and 6:

```
class ATM
  locals
    available: bool;
    cardIn: bool;
    OKStripInfo: bool;
    OKPINInfo: bool;
    finished: bool;

    fn mn = ~available /\ ~cardIn /\ ~OKStripInfo /\ ~PinInfo /\ ~finished;
    fn id = ... % similar; also s1, s2, s3, fi

    auth: Authenticator;
    stripInfo: opt StripInfo;
    pinInfo: opt PinInfo;
    fn verifyStripInfo(stripInfo): bool ...;
    op ejectAndReinit ... ;
    op displayPinReq: () ... ;
    op displayMenu: () ... ;
  end

  when mn then
    op maintenanceAction(k: MaintReq) ==> mn' end;
    op makeAvailable ==> id' end
  elsewhen id then
    op cardIn(si: StripInfo) ==> stripInfo' = si, s1',
      if verifyStripInfo(stripInfo) then self.stripOK''
      else  self.stripBad'' end end
  elsewhen s1 then
    op stripOK ==>  displayPinReq', s1' end
    op stripBad ==> ejectAndReinit' end
    op kb(pi: PinInfo) ==> pinInfo' = pi, s2', auth.PINCheck(pi,si)'' end
    op cancel ==> ejectAndReinit' end
  elsewhen s2 then
    op pinOK(pi, si) ==> displayMenu', s3' end
    op pinBad(pi, si) ==> ejectAndReinit' end
  ...
  end
end
```

Postcondition predicates referring to states may be considered as shorthands for updates to the corresponding attributes. For example, s3' in pinOK indicates only that OKPINinfo should be set to true, since that is the only difference between s2 and s3.

In this example, the when clauses do not spell out what to do when inappropriate messages occur (for example, receiving cardIn when in state mn). These must be fully laid out in a complete design.

Our clauses only list event-driven transitions. OOA-level transitions that are enabled by internal state-based guards without any corresponding events are here transformed in two different ways:

Expansion: Eventless actions may be "expanded out" under the appropriate conditions. Here, the internal actions that lead from the fi (finished) to id (idle) state are locally triggered via ejectAndReinit whenever the analysis model specifies a transition to fi (which leads in turn to id).

Self-notification: An object may "artificially" send an event to itself that will trigger the corresponding action. Here, the id state generates messages that are caught by self to propel actions triggered when the stripInfo can or cannot be read.

19.1.2   States as Classes

Classes may be used to organize states and transitions. For example, consider yet another lamp design:

```
class VoltageLevel                        fn level: real; end
class ActiveVoltage is VoltageLevel inv level >= 2.5 end
class Ground is VoltageLevel        inv level <  2.5 end
inv VoltageLevel = oneOf(ActiveVoltage, Ground)

class Lamp3 is Lamp
  active: fixed ActiveVoltage;
  ground: fixed Ground;
  switch: VoltageLevel init= ground;
  on: bool = (switch in ActiveVoltage);
  op flip ==> switch' = if on then ground else active end end
end
```

Here, the state change in `flip` is performed by rebinding the `switch` link back and forth between a constant-active object and a constant-ground one described by the "state-classes" `ActiveVoltage` and `Ground`. This might strike you as being analogous to the physical act of throwing an electrical switch. It may also be seen as an instance of delegation in which the lamp uses the object at the other end of `switch` to help compute the `on` attribute. Rebindability of delegates is an often-exploited property of composite objects. Any state change can be performed by some combination of interactions with existing component objects and/or link changes to different objects.

When classes represent macroscopic states, a state value may be described in terms of the class membership of an object on the other side of a link. In ODL, the *obj* in *class* "type test" construct may be used for such purposes, as seen in the `inv` constraint here. This predicate is true when the indicated object possesses all of the features listed in the indicated class. It must be used with care. For example, "x in Any" is true of *any* object.

State Class Controllers

Changing state by changing components is often easiest when the components form little state-class hierarchies that partition logical states. The states-as-classes view is in turn most useful when each state has fixed, but different properties, that *always* covary. These classes thus reify the notion of *state abstraction* described in Chapter 5. For example, we might define a set of classes describing icons for displaying faces as:

```
class FIcon              mouthAngle: int;       eyesOpen: bool;        end
class FState is FIcon   mouthAngle: fixed int; eyesOpen: fixed bool; end
class HappyF is FState inv mouthAngle =  45,  eyesOpen = true;       end
class SleepF is FState inv mouthAngle =   0,  eyesOpen = false;      end
class SadF   is FState inv mouthAngle = -45,  eyesOpen = true;       end

class MutableFIcon is FIcon
  local switch: FState;
  inv mouthAngle = switch.mouthAngle;
  inv eyesOpen   = switch.eyesOpen;
  op happy!    ==> switch' in HappyF end
  happy: bool    = switch  in HappyF;
  op sad!      ==> switch' in SadF end
  ...
end
```

It is useful and sensible here to define an abstract superclass (FIcon) that branches off in two directions, one side for state classes describing immutable objects, and the other for mutable, "controlling" objects. The states and controllers are *not* subclasses of each other, but can be written to share this blander superclass. This way, clients that do not care whether features are mutable or not can accept either.

These designs form good first-level defenses against incomplete or inconsistent attempts to change state. For example, it is impossible to change the state of a FIcon to happy without also changing mouth curvature. In fact, the technique might be seen as a simpler way of expressing dependencies that would be awkward to describe and maintain using inv constraints in the controller itself. In many cases, this leads to relatively simple ways to translate analysis models with complex state logistics. If any or all of the behavior-controlling states can be isolated as classes, it becomes easier to decompose and/or group operations [21].

19.1.3 Delegating State Dependent Behavior

Consider the car cruise control (CCC) example from Chapter 5. This controller just managed the logical states representing otherwise ungiven operations. There are many possible translations into a design form. Suppose the underlying operations have been partitioned into classes, each of which supports some kind of services appropriate to its macroscopic state. For illustrative purposes, we will assume that they support operation controlCruise as a stand-in.

All client components involved with cruise control operations will interact with CCControllers via an intermediary controlling class, CCC. The CCC class itself just controls state transitions by switching among state-classes.

Taking a few liberties to assume that the events with no associated transitions are just ignored, giving transitions nicer names, and omitting most details other than the state logic, we obtain:

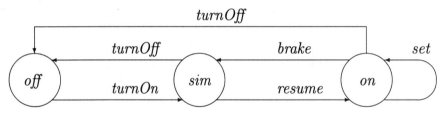

```
class CCController  ...  op controlCruise: (); end

class On  is CCController ... end
class Off is CCController ... end
class SIM is CCController ... end

class CCC
  locals
     switch: CCController; init switch in Off
     desiredSpeed: Int;
     threshold: int = 30;
  end

  op controlCruise: () ==> switch.controlCruise' end

  when switch in Off then
    op turnOn
        when speedSensor.current > threshold then
          desiredSpeed'? = speedSensor.current, switch' in SIM
        else  end
    op resume  ==> end
    op brake   ==> end
    op turnOff ==> end
    op set     ==> end
  elsewhen switch in SIM then
    op turnOn  ==> end
    op resume  ==> switch' in On end
    op brake   ==> end
    op turnOff ==> switch' in Off end
    op set     ==> end
  else % switch in On %
    op turnOn  ==> end
    op resume  ==> end
    op brake   ==> switch' in SIM end
    op turnOff ==> switch' in off end
    op set     ==> desiredSpeed? = speedSensor.current end
  end
end
```

19.2   Atomicity

The analysis models in Part I assume that each object contains a "membrane" that protects and guides processing, causing operations to be atomic and exclusive with respect to observers. Objects noninterruptibly perform at most one publicly listed operation (transition) at a time. Noninterruptibility is one form of state-dependent operation availability. It expresses the constraint that all other operations are unavailable while the object is engaged in some particular action. In design, we normally add internal structure (scripted concrete actions) to obtain the effects of OOA-level transitions, so actions are not "truly" atomic. However, atomicity with respect to external observers generally needs to be maintained to obtain listed transition effects.

These dynamic concerns are mirror-images of structural ones. In the same way that essentially all design-level objects would be viewed as ensembles at the analysis level, essentially all design-level actions would be viewed as scripts (transition sequences). In both cases, external observers must be shielded from these facts unless it is known that adding visible substructure is acceptable.

When analysis models are known to be incomplete and/or inexact, the refinement of transitions into visible smaller-granularity steps may indeed be warranted. For example, an analysis model might have listed *Fly from New York to California* as a single transition, omitting intervening states and transitions including *Drive to Airport, Board Airplane, Reboard in Chicago*, and so on, where each of these may in turn be further subdivided. It is unlikely that the analysis model really intended that the coarse-grained transition be treated as atomic. Moreover, the lack of intervening states precludes descriptions of intervening actions (such as changing flights if one is canceled) that may be needed in this or future systems. These are among the issues that should be addressed during analysis model reviews (Chapter 15). If atomicity is not required, designers may reanalyze, adding appropriate visible states and transitions.

19.2.1   Preemption

Some operations appear to be intrinsically interruptible by clients. Classic examples include operations on multimedia software objects. Multimedia objects are used to manage and control video, audio, and other displays. They commonly require interruptibility in order to break out of (usually hardware-related) "continuous play loops".

Atomicity requirements look problematic in such designs. Without them, one could define a `stop` operation that would allow an object to halt the play or display of its data, and then perhaps do something else. However, this would only be a good idea if it were OK to simply *kill* the object (and then perhaps generate another one). Otherwise, when it returned from the interruption, how would it know that it was supposed to halt? The only answer available from within our framework is that (1) the interruption should modify a state attribute, say, `playing`, and (2) the object should "continuously" (e.g., after every few suboperations) check to see if `playing` remains true.

This is essentially the solution described in Chapter 5. The object may split its chores into little pieces, listening for interrupts between steps. However, this tactic is much too difficult to live with at the design level for systems where cancellation, pausing, and resumption capabilities are routinely required. While one could define operations listing all of the possible listening points, this is very error prone.

As an abbreviation, we can predefine a special pseudo-operation `interrupt` that is considered to be immediately receivable at any time by an object listing it in its interface. The operation immediately places the object in a "listening" mode where it may process new requests, but makes no guarantees that the object is in a particular or even coherent state. However, individual classes may make further guarantees, as established by some kind of low-level hardware or implementation magic. Given this, a prototypical multimedia class might be declared:

```
class Player ...
  data: blob;
  playing: bool;
  op play ==> playing' end
  op interrupt ==> ~playing' end
  op restart;   % seek to beginning
  op resume;    % continue from where left off
end
```

More fine-grained control over interruptible objects may be obtained through layering. For example, the idea of "play until a `trap` signal is received" may be translated by building an object that sets a `Player` in motion and then sends an `interrupt` when it receives message `trap` and the `Player` is `playing`.

As seen here, multimedia objects sometimes need to carry completely uninterpreted bunches of bits. These might include graphics images, video signals, sounds, and so on. In **ODL** we describe these as `blob`s. They are immutable and passed around as copies. However, their inner structures cannot be defined from within

ODL. (If they could be described, they would not be `blobs`.) They may, however, be wrapped up in classes that are then used in a normal way.

19.2.2 Internal Actions

Even in more ordinary designs, interruptibility is not always seen as a liability. For example, the concept of *procedural recursion* is based on the idea that an object may suspend itself inside one procedure by issuing a blocking call for the same procedure, but with different arguments. Resumptions unwind in a stack-based fashion. All state changes effected in the inner call hold when the outer one is resumed. Similarly, an object may want to suspend one operation while it performs another. It is very common to write operations that include internal calls to perform various utility functions.

There is no reason at all to preclude many such constructions as long as designs are clear about their intent. Atomicity need only be maintained with respect to *external* agents. There is a difference between a public operation and an internal reference to something defined as a `local`. In ODL, actions defined within `locals` are always available within otherwise atomic operations. We have been using `locals` in this way routinely.

These inner references cannot go through an object's "outer membrane", so they cannot be treated as possibly externally generated events in which an object just happens to be its own client. Not only are `locals` not part of an external interface, but, in a very real sense, they are not even part of the "controlling" object *per se*. They are components of the "controlled" part of an object. In fact, these local operations might as well belong to other delegated objects, and could be so converted if necessary.

This notion that objects may stand back to investigate and invoke inner features is a form of *reflection*. It is less exotic than it may sound. Reflection is an intrinsic part of guard evaluation. When any object receives a message requesting an operation with a `when` clause, it must evaluate its own state while deciding whether to engage in a corresponding action. Similarly, if an object needs to employ a little utility routine in the midst of some other operation, it may do so without having to act as its own external client. At a mechanical level, this may require that such objects be implemented using a "local control stack". Alternatively, the local wait states and notification techniques described in Chapter 20 may be employed.

An implementation-level view of this distinction is that in a distributed system, `local` access normally corresponds to operations within a process's own address space, and external access corresponds to remote messages. For emphasis and ease of sub-sequent translation, we list any message `m` in which an object explicitly serves as its own external client as `self.m`. Unless a class defines mechanics for interrupting, suspending, and resuming public operations, usage is restricted to one-way sends.

Similarly, we *could* also explicitly list both inner and outer forms of inspective `fns`. But because they are purely state-preserving, we have treated them as usable in either sense. If desired, `locals` may be used to define inner-only versions. For example, in Chapter 17, we mentioned that a `Point` object might cache its polar coordinates when asked about them via an external `fn`, but must be able to inspect its state internally without performing this caching.

19.3   Timing Constraints

In Chapter 11, we discussed specification strategies for bounding the durations of services and transitions. We employ similar strategies in (abstract) design. Any *effect* may include a time-of prefix "@". These may be mixed in expressions with `time` literals indicating elapsed times since operation triggering. For example:

```
class Renderer
  op fastRender(s: Scene): () ==>
    @(diff(displayedLuminance(s), luminance(s)) < 0.1) < 1sec end
  op slowRender(s: Scene): () ==>
    1hr < @(diff(displayedLuminance(s), luminance(s)) < 0.0001) < 2hr end
end
```

This says that the `fastRender` effect occurs within one second of the operation being triggered, and the `slowRender` effect occurs between one and two hours. This notation allows finer specification than possible using our prime and double-prime annotations that indicate effects only at the points of operation completion (prime) and *any* time after triggering (double-prime). This notation may also be used to make stronger claims about the *ordering* of effects.

Time expressions are declarative constraints, which must somehow be met by implementations. To be meaningful, all implementations must conform to the effects, the transit time of messages to and from the objects must be known or bounded, and the `pend` times of messages once received must be known or bounded. Timing constraints are generally only useful in applications in which enough hardware and software properties are hard-wired that such estimates can be realistically achieved.

However, given that they do hold, they may be employed in the design of other classes. For example:

```
class RenderButton ...
  r: Renderer;
  op render { ...
    if battery.estimatedLife < 2hr then
        r.fastRender(currentScene)
    else r.slowRender(currentScene) end ...}
end
```

19.4   Concrete Transitions

The transformation of guarded actions into concretely executable statements can be difficult. A guard may list any number of conditions that must be *simultaneously* true in order for an operation to execute. Unfortunately, guard evaluation and triggering normally involve *sequential* computation (even within distributed frameworks).

This is not a problem for many classes. When guards and effects refer only to *exclusively* controlled properties of the recipient object, attribute evaluations may proceed sequentially. Here, if a state predicate holds true at the beginning of an evaluation sequence, it will still hold true when the operation commences. Guards that look only at nonexported `own` attributes fit this model. Among the most important reasons for using `own` attributes is to ensure simple translation of state transitions into concrete form. For example, a concrete `CardEater` class may be defined as:

```
class CardEaterV1 is CardEater
  own h: Bool <>;  own l: Bool <>
  local beeper: Beeper <>
  local cardLatch: CardLatch <>
  holding: bool { h? }
  latched: bool { l? }
  op unlatch { l.f! }
  op latch   { l.t! }
  op eject {
    if ~l? /\ h? then cardLatch.release; h.f!
    elsif ~l? /\ ~h? then beeper.beep
    else pend end }
end
```

Because the objects representing state information are exclusively held, the guards and actions for `eject` may be computed in a straightforward manner.

However, guards that reference objects that are not under the exclusive control of the receiver object must be handled much more carefully. We postpone discussion of the requisite mechanics to Chapter 22, where we describe the coordination of joint actions in a more general setting.

19.4.1   Self-notifications

Local self-notification techniques can simplify within-object state tracking for transitions that are specified to fire only after only a *set* of microtransitions.

For example, suppose that a specification states that an `ImageCell` object should update its brightness attribute whenever it is sent values from all four of its neighbors. As is typical in such specifications, this description fails to list all possible intermediate states that lead to firing. There may be no substitute to a painstaking decomposition of these states in design. However, minor simplifications may be based on inner self-notifications that allow an object to "tell itself" that a transition is potentially triggerable. In this example, the different combinations of the boolean have$X$ values track all of the possible state configurations that can ultimately lead to firing:

```
class ImageCellV1 is ImageCell
  locals
    brightness: Real;
    northV: Real; southV: Real; eastV: Real; westV: Real;
    haveNorth: Bool; haveSouth: Bool; haveEast: Bool; haveWest: Bool;
    northNbr: ImageCell; southNbr:ImageCell; ...
    op update {
        if haveNorth? /\ haveSouth? /\ haveEast? /\ haveWest? then
           brightness.set((northV? + southV? + eastV? + westV?)/4.0);
           haveNorth.f!; haveSouth.f!; ...
           NorthNbr.SouthVal(brightness?);
           SouthNbr.NorthVal(brightness?); ...
        end }
  end
  op NorthVal(x: real) {
        if ~haveNorth? then northV.set(x); haveNorth.t!; update
        else pend end }
  op SouthVal(x: real); % similar; also EastVal, WestVal
end
```

19.4.2   Queuing

To be implementable, any class containing `pend` operations must be fitted with some kind of buffering mechanism to hold requests that cannot yet be honored. We will approach this by first discussing the design of stand-alone "external" queues that are not treated as parts of the objects using them to maintain requests. Generally, any combination of internal and external queues may be designed to support buffering.

External Queues

Stand-alone queues may be constructed to hold requests serviced by one or more objects. Wrappers may be employed to represent the requests. For example, suppose we wanted to queue up a list of operations to be done later when triggered by a timer or some other event:

```
class Jobs
  q: QUEUE[Wrapper];
  op store(t: Wrapper) { q.put(t) }
  op process { while ~q.empty do q.take.call end }
end
...
jobs.store(WRAP(transfer(acct1, acct2)));
jobs.store(WRAP(print(logfile)));
jobs.process;
```

Untyped events.   In ODL, we use named, typed operations and messages and guards that may refer to their properties. However, sometimes the range of messages (events) that must be received by an object is unknowable or unbounded. When all other tactics fail, this effect can be obtained by adopting much blander and harder to check strategies that employ unconditionally received "message packets" somehow describing the requested operations and arguments. For example:

```
class MessagePacket
  opName: String;
  args: SEQ[Any];
end
```

```
class Agent ...
  q: QUEUE[MessagePacket];
  worker: Worker;
  op msg(m: MessagePacket) {
      if worker.canDo(m.opName) then  worker.do(m)
      else ... q.put(m); end }
end
```

These requests may be manually queued, decoded, and so on. At some level(s) of any distributed system there are agents of this general form, if only those that send and receive packets across a network.

Scheduling

These basic strategies apply to a range of queue-based designs. For example, a printer might be defined using a manually designed "passive" wrapper class that merely reports the text to be printed (perhaps along with other print parameters):

```
class PrintRequest ...  text: ARRAY[Char];  end

class PrinterDaemon
  q: BUFFER[PrintRequest];
  local op print(r: PrintRequest); ...
  op mainLoop { while true do print(q.take) end }
  ...
end

class Printer
  q: BUFFER[PrintRequest];
  daemon: PrinterDaemon;
  op print(m: PrintRequest) { q.put(m) }
end

op mkPrinter p: Printer {
    local printQueue: BUFFER[PrintRequest] := mkBuffer...;
    local printDaemon: PrinterDaemon := new PrinterDaemon(q := printQueue);
    p := new Printer(q:= printQueue, daemon := printDaemon);
    printDaemon.mainLoop;
    reply p }
```

We used BUFFER instead of QUEUE in this example to permit further variations in processing. This opens up additional options for managing and scheduling activities. We could use the same basic design to different effect by defining subclasses of BUFFER[PrintRequest] and/or other changes, including the following:

- The BUFFER::put operation could be reparameterized to send back an explicit acknowledgment to its sender.

- A clause could be added in BUFFER::put to disregard or refuse new requests when the queue is full.

- A "balking" version of the BUFFER::take operation could be defined to always immediately return, sometimes reporting back a sentinel saying that the queue is empty. The print daemon could then do some other work and try again later (see Chapter 20.)

- The queue could be maintained in priority order. Ordering could be based on such properties as:

  1. Increasing page length of the print requests.
  2. Requested priority or deadline as indicated in the PrintRequest.
  3. Time-stamps indicated in the PrintRequest reflecting the time of request.
  4. The sender of the request.
  5. Shortest estimated time to completion.

- Multiple PrintDaemons may be constructed, one per physical printer.

- The buffer might hold several independent queues matched to different kinds (perhaps subclasses) of PrintRequests. This makes it easier for PrintDaemons to share in scheduling chores, take'ing those kinds of requests they service best.

The careful crafting of such policies is a central task in many designs. Common policies may be reflected in the common use of special queue classes across different applications and subsystems. Detailed descriptions of the enormous range of available scheduling policies and techniques are beyond the scope of this book. Other texts describing real-time constraints and scheduling issues from an object-oriented perspective include Levi and Agrawala [140] and Atkinson [17].

Notification techniques (as seen, for example, in `ImageCell`) are also useful in the design of queuing mechanics. The firing of queued messages may be controlled by sending "wake-up" notifications that recheck guards and possibly trigger corresponding actions. One strategy is to check for queued messages after every public operation. Another is to maintain separate queues, and only notify those whose firing conditions are impacted by the operation.

Internal Queues

These strategies may be internalized within individual objects by localizing inside one class the three basic components of queue-based designs:

1. A controller/manager.
2. One or more "passive" (queueless) service components.
3. One or more queues holding unserviced requests.

For example, the `Printer`, `PrintDaemon`, and `BUFFER` serve these roles in the printer design.

Each of these three kinds of components requires attention when translating classes into implementable form. However, they need not be present in each class. The notion of "implementable form" can vary across system architectures, implementation languages, and tools. For example, in Chapters 23 and 24 we will describe the need for *combining* queues of possibly many objects in order to meet resource and performance constraints. Also, the "primitives" and corresponding techniques available for implementing queue mechanics can differ widely. Queue processing may be implemented using simple `Semaphores`, *monitor* constructs, or just about any other similar mechanism available on a system.

We will avoid introducing any particular mechanics until we have addressed the corresponding design issues. However, nearly all approaches are based on refinements of the following basic tactics.

A queue (usually called a "condition queue" or "delay queue") may be associated with each distinct state, including topmost state `ready`. Because of state abstraction, requests associated with each particular (nonabstract) state may be distributed across queues. When an object is quiescent, an incoming message triggers the corresponding operation if it is available in the current state, else it is queued. After every public operation, the queue(s) associated with the current state may be checked. This may entail evaluation of additional guards to ensure that the queued operations are actually triggerable. Guards associated with message arguments and other relational constraints normally cannot be divided among a small finite number of condition queues, so require additional checks on receipt and reinspection.

Queue structure and guard (re)evaluation interact more generally. For example, it is inconceivable to associate a queue with each possible value of an `Account balance`. In Chapter 5, we confined ourselves to only the two states `overdrawn` and `ok`. Correctness may be maintained using an even coarser state mapping at the design level. A single queue may be associated with topmost state `ready`. This queue is checked after each public operation. However, all guards (including current state evaluation) associated with each requested operation must then be rechecked upon inspection. The message is requeued if the guards fail.

Single `ready` queues also simplify handling of messages that arrive when objects are in the midst of other operations. In most systems, incoming messages are queued via preemptive mechanisms. Any requests arriving when an object is not `ready` may be placed on the queue.

Again, because the detailed mechanics for designing and implementing queue processing differ across systems, configurations, tools, and languages, we avoid further commitments. We will continue to use `when` and `pend` to express designs until Chapter 24.

19.5 Summary

Guards control both the *availability* and *choice* of state-dependent behaviors. Attributes, aggregate state functions, and helper classes may be used to organize and maintain logical state information used in guards and effects. Our normal model of object computation assumes that objects are uninterruptible while in the midst of observable operations. Interruptible objects may also be designed, but must be controlled.

Untriggerable requests may wait in per-object queues until objects are ready to deal with them. Special-purpose queues and queuing disciplines may be added on top of this framework. These allow requests to be passed around and manipulated as regular objects.

19.6 Further Reading

Dispatching strategies based on temporal information are discussed by Takashio and Tokoro [214]. The collection [72] includes several descriptions of real-time specification languages and systems containing additional constructs that may be adapted to OO frameworks. Design issues for multimedia objects are presented in several papers in the collections edited by Tsichritzis [218, 219, 220].

19.7 Exercises

1. Design a more serious `CardEater` class.
2. Design all of the simple transitions present in the refrigerator models in Chapters 5 and 6.
3. Finish the ATM controller design.
4. Explain the similarities and differences between state-*classes* and state*Charts*.
5. Convert the `CCC` class to use **when** clauses embedded in op specifications rather than the given "outer" form. Which is easier to understand?
6. Is it sensible for a state-object to tell its controller to change state?
7. Design a `PriorityQueue` suitable for use with a `Printer`.
8. Describe in **ODL** the time constrained *Phone* transitions presented in Chapter 11.

Chapter 20

Interaction Designs

In this chapter, we focus on the design of object interaction scenarios. In previous chapters, we distinguished call/reply-style ops from asynchronous one-way sends. We singled out bidirectional ops in part to obtain a simple foothold on structured bidirectional message passing, as opposed to raw notifications from one object to another.

A synchronized bidirectional op represents the most familiar framework for interaction between objects, procedural invocation. A client asks a server to do something and waits until it is done, obtaining back any results the receiver is willing to provide.

The object-oriented paradigm supports a much richer set of communications strategies and protocols than can be expressed using blocking procedures. In this chapter we discuss several variations, while also demonstrating underlying techniques enabling the design of additional protocols and idioms.

20.1 Callbacks

The most basic form of bidirectional interaction is for some object a to send a one-way message to another object b, who in turn sends back a message to a, and so on.

These designs are often termed *callback* protocols, since the recipient of a message "calls back" its sender by issuing a message to it. They are also very similar to designs based on *continuations* in programming languages such as scheme [1]. In fact, the usages are for most purposes identical. A good example is interaction with a timer:

```
class BeeperTimer
  delayer: Delayer;
  op alarm(secs: time, b: DelayedBeeper) {
     delayer.delay(secs); b.beep };
end

class DelayedBeeper
  t: BeeperTimer;
  op beep ... ;
  op beepAfter(secs: time) { t.alarm(secs, self) }
end
```

Here, the `DelayedBeeper` object is free to do other things after processing `beepAfter`. It is later told by the `BeeperTimer` when it should `beep`.

This is a useful strategy for designing interactions that involve timers of any sort. However, it is difficult to extend this example for such purposes, since the exact message to send back (`beep`) is hard-wired into the definition of the timer. In keeping with the analysis tactics of Chapter 6, this operation should be decoupled so the timer may be used for purposes other than controlling beepers. This can be arranged via wrappers:

```
class Timer ...
  op alarm(secs: time, action: Wrapper) {
      delayer.delay(secs); action.send }
end

class DelayedBeeper ...
  op beepAfter(secs: time) { t.alarm(secs, WRAP(beep)) }
end
```

A beneficial by-product of this wrapping is that the sender does not need to reveal its identity to the receiver. Similarly, if one object replies to a callback argument regardless of who the actual sender of an operation was, then sets of objects may more securely interact, assuming design conventions are set up accordingly.

Callbacks may be "passed through" intermediaries. For example, if we wanted `Dispenser` objects to notify senders when their controlled `DispenserDoors` were opened, we might write it using the abstract classes:

```
class DispenserDoor
  isOpen: bool;
  op close ==> ~isOpen' end
  op raise(ack: Wrapper) ==> isOpen', ack.call' end
end

class Dispenser ...
  door: DispenserDoor;
  op raiseDoor(ack: Wrapper)  ==> door.raise(ack)'' end
end
```

This strategy makes it easier to express designs in which an object delegates tasks to helper objects. The helper, rather than the host may send back any results associated with an operation.

20.1.1　Emulating Procedures

While they may look a bit esoteric, callbacks are actually *lower* level constructs than those underlying standard procedure-style interaction. In fact, it is possible to replace all blocking procedure-style interactions with callbacks. The mechanics for doing so are not much fun, but they are in part automatable through tools. Such maneuvers might even be necessary design steps if the system needs to be implemented using distributed frameworks supporting only one-way primitives.

For a prototypical example, consider an interaction in which an object of some class `Client` requests and receives something from an object of class `Server`. To avoid illustrating too many things at once, we will hard-wire the messages:

```
class Server
  op get: int          { reply 17 }
end

class Client
  op ask(s: Server)    { print(s.get) }
end
```

This may be transformed into:

```
class Server_2
  op get(c: Client_2)  { c.use(17) }
end

class Client_2
  op ask(s: Server_2)  { s.get(self) }
  op use(i: int)       { print(i) }
end
```

The general strategy is to split out each "sequence point" in a series of blocking operations as a separate operation, and then to use callbacks to thread them together. It is the very same idea as using self-propagation messages for looping and/or sequencing operations discussed in Chapter 19. But here, two objects pass the propagations back and forth.

Blocking

Actually, in order to completely mirror procedure semantics, the *wait states* in the receiver must be explicitly tracked. Assuming noninterruptibility, in the first version a Client object gets an int and prints it in a single atomic operation. Our first transformation did not meet this guarantee. The Client could do something else (e.g., start another ask) in between the ask and use. Unless this is known to be acceptable, these operations should be protected with wait-state guards that represent transient forms of *locks* (see Chapter 22):

```
class Client_3
  own waiting: Bool <> init ~waiting?
  . . .
  when ~waiting? then
    op ask(s: Server)  { waiting.t!; s.get(self) }
  else
    op use(i: int)     { print(i); waiting.f! }
  end
end
```

Sometimes protocols may be loosened a bit to allow multiple concurrent operations. If each request and reply also contains a given "task ID", the issuer may keep track of which reply corresponds to which request. For example, using simple integers as IDs:

```
class Client_4
  own tIDGen: Counter <>
  own outstandingRequests: TABLE[Action] <>
  ...
  op ask(s: Server) {
    tIDGen.inc; outstandingRequests.put(new Action...);
    s.get(self, tIDGen.count) }
  op use(i: int, tID: int) {
    outstandingRequests.at(tID).send; ... }
end
```

The use of *time-stamps* rather than task IDs allows actions to be coordinated according to send and/or receive times.

20.1.2   Tracking Services

So far we have taken an object-centric view of interaction. An alternative perspective is to focus on the *services* or tasks being performed rather than the possibly many objects involved in providing them. Since most operations on most objects are designed in support of useful services, this view helps provide conceptual and computational checks on their nature and correctness, especially when using callbacks and other constructs that can be hard to track.

A *timethread* [45] may be defined as a sequence of messages and related processing instigated from a single request to a single object. Timethreads are design-level versions of use cases, event-traces, and scripts. The traversal of a timethread through a set of objects describes a service. Timethreads themselves may be reified. Rather than identifying interactions using task IDs, entire objects may track the different messages supporting a service. For example:

```
class TaskInfo ...
  creationTime: time;
  parentTask: TaskInfo;
  messageLog: SEQ[Message];
  invCheck: bool;
end
```

A new instance of such a class may be created during a service call, and then propagated as an argument for all further messages. New subtask objects may be generated whenever a task "forks" in multiple directions, usually as a result of one-way sends. These may later join the main task. Task bookkeepers are useful for monitoring and debugging these processes. They also provide a means of tracking and controlling service deadlines.

These classes may hold the trace checks described in Chapter 16. A `TaskInfo` object may evaluate sets of per-task invariants that must hold across all points in a service. For example, an authentication service may promise to involve only messages to a predetermined set of objects. Holding the checks in the task itself, rather than in all participating objects, simplifies expression and testing. Some or all participants may then invoke the check during processing.

20.2   Replies

Callbacks and their refinements provide entry points to the design of specific protocols that enhance reliability, security, concurrency, and/or fault-tolerance of bidirectional interaction. A complete survey of such protocols is beyond the scope of this book. (See the further readings.) In this and the next section, we describe common interaction constructions that lie midway between the straitjacket of procedural interaction and the chaos of unstructured one-way sends. We focus first on variations on reply mechanisms, and then on invocations. Of course, designers are by no means obligated to use *all* (or even any) of the described constructs.

20.2.1   Early Replies

Acknowledgments.   Acknowledgment protocols block senders only until messages are triggered. Senders are then free to continue asynchronously. Assuming that the sender is structured to wait for the acknowledgment before proceeding, this is equivalent to a callback-based design in which an `ack` message is sent back to the client before any work is performed:

```
op work(sender: A) { sender.ack; dowork }
```

One application is the support of temporally ordered or *causal* one-way messages. Blocking only until delivery has been acknowledged is a simple way to deal with requirements assuming that messages are received in exactly the same order that they are sent. For example, the specifications for an electronic mail service might require that messages be given serial numbers that reflect (per-site) sending order. In distributed systems using asynchronous sends and where arrival order need not correspond to sending order, some such protocol is required to obtain this guarantee.

The logic of early reply protocols may be extended to allow servers to "release" blocking clients at any point in an operation, not just at the beginning (as with acknowledgments) or the end (as with most service `reply`s). An **ODL** `reply` is different than a "return" statement in most languages in that a `reply` does not terminate the enclosing operation (unless, of course, it is the last statement of an operation). For example, we could rewrite the previous construction as:

```
op work: () { reply; dowork }
```

This construct may be used to obtain *rendezvous* semantics (Chapter 6) even in otherwise asynchronous environments. This is much more convenient than hand-crafting acknowledgment protocols. If necessary, the construct may be implemented by first recasting it into the original callback mechanisms.

Early replies are also useful in data structure update operations that return elements to clients but then asynchronously proceed with internal bookkeeping. For example:

```
class PriorityQueue[T] ...
   locals least: T; op findNextLeast...; end
   op take: T { reply least; findNextLeast }
end
```

20.2.2 Named Replies

Multiple named replies for a blocking procedure allow expression of different kinds of results by giving them labels. Instead of issuing a `reply`, an **ODL** operation may "invoke" different labeled reply forms. Clients must `catch` the corresponding messages. Catch clauses are computational versions of `when` clauses that apply only to wait states on blocking calls. For example:

```
class Slave ...
  op compute(t: Task): done(x: Result), fail(r: Reason)  {
    if canDo(t) then
        done(new Result...)
    else fail(aReason) end }
end
```

```
op useSlave(s: Slave, t: Task) {
    catch s.compute(t)
      op done(x: Result) { use(x) }
      op fail(r: Reason) { print(r) }
    end }
```

Named replies are among the easiest-to-use integrations of procedural and asynchronous interaction constructs. They restrict more general protocols only in that the replies must be caught by senders, not any other objects. They conveniently hide and localize blocking mechanics by creating local operations (e.g., done) that are only valid during particular wait states of other operations. If necessary, these may be implemented via translation into equivalent guarded callback constructs.

Sentinels

Some "abnormal" conditions are expected to occur often. These need not be treated as exceptional events but as likely results of normal interaction protocols. A classic application is for the result of an op to be declared opt. When abnormal conditions occur, the result is unbound. Unboundedness serves as a *sentinel*, indicating that the usual result could not be obtained. For example, MAP::at(key) has its result listed as optional so that it need not return anything when the item is not in the map. Any client of a procedure returning an optional link must be prepared to receive an unbound result. However, named replies provide a more structured mechanism.

```
class MAP[Key, Cont] ...
  op at(k: Key): contents(c: Cont), noSuchKey() { ... }
end
```

Balking

Another application of sentinels is to recast operations that may not be able to return a result at the moment they are invoked because they are not in the right state. Rather than pending, ignoring, or triggering an exception handler, the receiver may just return a notification to the sender. For example, a `Queue` might support a `balkingTake` operation that immediately returns a null result when the buffer is empty. This can simplify designs in which clients poll many such queues. Again, named replies may be employed:

```
class CentralPrintingService ...
  queues: ARRAY[PrintQueue];
  op mainLoop  {
    while true do
      local i: int := 0;
      while i < queues.size do
        catch queues.at(i).balkingTake
          op item(job: PrintRequest) { print(job) }
          op noItem { }
        end;
        i := i + 1
    end end }
end
```

20.2.3 Exceptions

The term *exception* has been applied to a number of variations on the same basic protocol. From our framework, the best way to describe standard exception mechanisms is as a variant of named replies. Named replies provide multiple return points for standard ops. Extensions of this protocol lead to classic exception mechanisms as found, for example, in **Ada**: (1) Exception replies should always terminate the server operation. (2) If a catcher for a reply is not defined in a sender, the sending invocation is canceled, and the process is repeated for *its* sender. (3) If there is no catcher listed in a chain of calls, a system error handler is invoked.

This protocol is easier to use in **ODL** after adding a few conventions: (1) The "normal" reply uses standard `reply` rules. (2) The normal reply is considered to be the only one caught if no others are listed (i.e., if there is no `catch` clause). (3) Intermediaries need not declare uncaught downstream exceptions. The last convention is dangerous but sometimes difficult to avoid in practice. For example:

```
class Probability...
  op set(r: real): (), PrOutOfBounds(p: Probability) {
    if 0.0 <= r /\ r <= 1.0 then _val.set(r); reply
    else PrOutOfBounds(self) end }
end
```

```
op user(p: Probability, x: real): () { p.set(x) }
```

```
op userUser(p: Probability, x: real) {
  catch(user(p, r))
    op PrOutOfBounds(q: Probability) { p.set(0.0) }
  end }
```

Variations on this form of exception mechanism are supported in several object-oriented programming languages and system support tools (e.g., C++, CORBA, Eiffel). For example, in C++, exception messages are declared as instances of *classes*. Otherwise, the protocols are the same.

Exception constructs may be translated into straight messaging form using variants of callback mechanisms. Several schemes exist. All are too messy to detail. Generally, an op declaring a `catch X` may be transformed into a wrapper object with an X operation.

20.3 Invocations

20.3.1 Waiters

Even if an object only supports a blocking version of a resultless operation, a client may still craft a one-way form and invoke it. `Wrappers` may be used to access a blocking procedure in one-way mode. For example, if we wanted to access op `Bool::t!` asynchronously, we could write:

```
op boolUser { ... waiter := WRAP(mybool.t!); waiter.send; ... }
```

The effect of this construction is to create a little object that "waits out" the blocking t! procedure without holding up boolUser. The existence of this transform is one reason why blocking versions of operations tend to be more prevalent than one-way sends. It is much easier to employ this transform than the reverse one. If an object only supports a nonblocking version of an operation, but a client must wait until its effects hold, the only recourse is for the client to poll for these effects itself.

From this viewpoint, a wrapper is a kind of *protocol object*. It encapsulates a certain protocol without having any meaningful role in the actual task being carried out. More general forms of protocol objects are useful whenever the nature of a command or service may be separated completely from situation-specific protocols connecting senders and receivers.

20.3.2 Futures

Suppose a client invokes an operation, but does not want to block waiting for the results until they are actually needed. The best established means for expressing such designs involve *futures*. Several variants exist. We will illustrate a less-than-first-class version that is simply translatable to other **ODL** constructs. The basic idea is to create wrapper objects that wait out procedures, while also blocking *their* callers until they are ready. For example:

```
class ATMTeller
  db: ClientDB;
  op processCredit(cid: clientID, acct: Account, amt: Cash) {
    local c: Client := FUTURE(Client(db.getClient(cid)));
    credit(acct, amt);
    c.notifyAboutCredit(acct, amt) }
end
```

The conceptual view of this is that any actions involving the FUTURE (here, just notifyAboutCredit) are delayed until the invoked procedure (getClient) actually returns. Without futures, we would have had to write a special version of getClient in ClientDB that accepted a callback argument, and then manually factored the processCredit operation to split out the called-back continuation.

Futures themselves suffice as interaction "primitives". All one-way ops may be described as futures waiting on unused dummy objects, and all bidirectional ops may be recast to use futures that are used immediately. Thus, futures may be relied on exclusively for all operations. This is a perfectly fine design option, especially when targeted for the many Lisp-based systems supporting first-class futures as programming constructs. To decide whether to use them, you may wish to examine more detailed and extensive examples of future-based programming (e.g., [50]).

Underlying transformations.   Several transformations are possible. In the easiest, the FUTURE qualifier may be viewed as a macro that expands to use a wrapper class similar to the ones generated via WRAP. This otherwise useless class manages the intervening manipulations. In this particular case:

```
class futureClient453 is Client
  local c: opt Client;
  own ready: Bool <> init ~ready?;
  ...
  op initC(db: Clientdb, cid: clientID) {
     c := db.getClient(cid); ready.t! }
  op notifyAboutCredit(acct: Account, amt: Cash) : ()
     when ready? then { c.notifyAboutCredit(acct, amt) } else pend end
end
op mkFutureClient453 ... % invoke initC % ... ;
```

Parallel sends.   Groups of futures or other waiter objects may be used to obtain the equivalents of "cobegin ... end" constructs common in fine-grained parallel programming languages. An object may construct a number of future objects, each waiting out different computations, and then proceed only when all of them are ready. We discuss such constructions in more detail in Chapter 22.

20.3.3   Time-outs

Time-outs are specified in OOA models to handle a range of possible hardware problems, software errors, and other failures. They also play a role in performance and alertness requirements. The fundamental idea is for a client to send two messages, both of which require replies. One is sent to perform the main operation of interest and the other to a timer. Suppose the main operation replies by issuing operation result, and the timer replies by sending timeout. There are two outcomes:

1. result is received, followed by timeout, in which case the result is used, and the timer ignored.

2. `timeout` is received, followed by `result`. Normally, the time-out leads to some kind of destructive recovery, after which the result can no longer be used, and is therefore ignored.

There are other possibilities; for example, that only `timeout` is *ever* received. But this is generally indistinguishable from the second case. However, it is possible and even necessary to guard against the case that a *previously* requested time-out is received while waiting for the result. It is very convenient if the timer supports a `cancel` operation in order to avoid this. A better solution is to pass and return a time-command ID that uniquely identifies the current time request. All time-outs not carrying the current ID may be ignored. If neither can be arranged, then the object might need to wait out a previous request before proceeding. These actions might be controlled through attributes representing the different wait states. For example:

```
class ServiceUser
  locals
    service: Service;  timer: Timer;
    own gotResult: Bool; init gotResult? = false;
    own timedOut: Bool;  init timedOut? = true;
  end
  op result(r: Result) { gotResult.t!;
    if ~timedOut? then % use r % end }
  op timeout  { timedOut.t!;
    if ~gotResult? then % recover % end }
  op request { if ~timedOut? then timer.cancel end;
    gotResult.f!; timedOut.f!;
    service.svc; timer.alarm(timeOutVal) }
end
```

Finding the right time value to use for time-outs often requires some empirical guidance. Time-out values need to be long enough to give possibly slow and busy servers a chance to reply. However, excessively long time-outs may cause other requests to pile up, forming bottlenecks.

Integrating calls with time-outs. Raw time-out mechanics are not much fun to work with. Time-based processing may be made more usable and at the same time better decoupled via intermediaries that perform these mechanics on behalf of clients. For example, the following sketches a "call with time-out" mechanism employing protocol objects with named replies:

```
class SvcWrapper  op get: Any; end

class TimeOutCaller ...
  op try(svc: SvcWrapper, maxTime: time): Result(a: Any), TimedOut() {
    % variations of above tactics ... % }
end

class Printer_3
  printQueue: QUEUE[PrintRequest];
  op tryToPrint {
    catch TimeOutCaller$try(SVCWRAP(printQueue.take), 10sec)
      op Result(a: Any) { print... }
      op TimedOut { }
    end }
end
```

20.3.4 Alertness

Alertness requirements (Chapter 11) force attention to be paid to the lack of input events that were not even specifically requested in the first place. An object dealing with input events merely expects that input will be forthcoming from the outside world without having set up a software protocol to mandate it.

For example, the digit-processing specification in Chapter 11 contained alertness requirements:

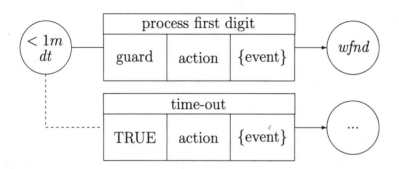

These are somewhat easier to deal with than time-outs tied to other software protocols because there are fewer constraints to get in the way. The core of the design includes:

```
class DigitGrabber ...
  op start { timer.replyAfter(1m, WRAP(reminder)) }
  op digit(c: char) { ...; timer.cancel; ... }
  op reminder { display.printReminder; ... }
end
```

20.4   Control Flow

Combinations of the mechanisms described in this chapter provide alternative strategies for implementing standard control flow constructs. For example, we may design yet another version of a boolean class, this one possessing only "raw behavior" without recourse to values:

```
class TF
  op cond(truePart: Wrapper, falsePart: Wrapper)
     ==> (truePart.send') \/ (falsePart.send') end
end

class True is TF
  op cond(truePart: Wrapper, falsePart: Wrapper) ==> truePart.send' end
end

class False is TF
  op cond(truePart: Wrapper, falsePart: Wrapper) ==> falsePart.send' end
end

class Bool
  local switch: TF;
  val: TF    =  switch;
  op f!      ==> switch' in False end
  op t!      ==> switch' in True  end
  op cond(truePart: Wrapper, falsePart: Wrapper)
           ==> switch.cond(truePart, falsePart)' end
end
```

The effect listed for TF indicates that one or the other effect holds, but without making a commitment to either one. The `True` class promises that only the `truePart` will be invoked; similarly for `False` and `falsePart`. Finally, the mutable `Bool` class can act like either `True` or `False`. These constructs might be used, for example, in a class that either flashed or beeped when asked to indicate an error:

```
class ErrorIndicator ...
  switch: Bool;
  op beep;
  op flash;
  op indicate { switch.cond(WRAP(beep), WRAP(flash)) }
  op setToBeep { switch.t! }
end
```

This example illustrates the fact that flow-of-control statements (e.g., "if") may always be replaced with messages. This is a fine strategy for replacing `if`s inside concrete code bodies with messages. We could have applied it in all previous examples.

In fact, if this logic is carried far enough, there becomes no need for "primitive" value types such as `bool` in OO systems. As here, the "value" *true* might be interpreted as referring to *any* object of a class supporting those operations described in class `True`. (As noted in Chapter 17, abstraction over identity is among the main differences between value and object frameworks.) It is even possible to extend this framework to `int` and other value types [180]. But the mechanics become too messy and impractical to take seriously in everyday design. However, the special case of boolean objects supporting a `cond` operation is very useful and convenient. It forms the heart of several control structure strategies in Smalltalk.

Unifying Constructs

We have seen that the combination of ops, wrappers, subclassing, and guards provide ways of unifying a number of design constructs:

- Bidirectional ops are callbacks to senders protected with wait state guards.
- Attribute fns are special restricted forms of ops.
- Conditionals are wrapper-based operations.
- Values may be described in purely behavioral terms via classes.
- Scripted operations may be encapsulated in their own classes.

These observations are usually of more theoretical than pragmatic utility. Even though they are all related, it is useful to keep constructs separate in order to organize and reason about designs. However, whenever the individual constructs fail to capture design intentions, you can always step up to this level of abstraction and create your own protocols from scratch.

20.5   Summary

The simple notion of object interaction expands into a range of forms, styles, and idioms including the following:

- Callbacks provide fine-grained control over two-party interaction protocols.
- Wrappers allow interaction partners to be statically decoupled.
- Early replies "release" clients from blocking when the results they need are ready.
- Named replies combine the flexibility of different callback channels with the certainty that a call will return to its sender.
- Exceptions provide opportunities to perform nonlocal recovery from errors.
- Futures allow expression of intermediate degrees of client-side blocking.
- Time-outs and other time-based interactions may be used for fault detection and to implement alertness requirements.
- Patterns of messages may be used to replace standard control constructs.

20.6   Further Reading

Nierstrasz [167] surveys of some of the interaction constructs described in this chapter. Several accounts of distributed, concurrent, and parallel design and programming techniques discuss other selected forms and protocols. See, e.g., [211, 17, 12, 11, 123]. ODL named replies are similar to the *termination* construct found in ANSA DPL [3]. Techniques for structuring and using exception protocols are discussed by Burns [46]. Futures play a central role in **ABCL** [233]. Several promising graphical techniques for displaying timethreads are described by Buhr and Casselman [45].

20.7   Exercises

1. Some people advocate that one-way operations should *never* be used, and that bidirectional synchronous communication serve as the basis for all interaction. Give an argument for and against this position.

2. When would it be OK if a `future` were *never* ready?

3. Explain how to devise early reply mechanisms using only an exception construct.

4. In Chapter 18, we mentioned that invoked operations do not have identities, while objects do. Yet we have often added task and message IDs as stand-ins. Should operation identity be primitively supported in OO systems after all?

5. Finish the sketch of the call-with-time-out design.

6. Should "simple" operations on "simple" objects (e.g., `Bool::t!`) really be defined as nonblocking?

7. Design a `whileDo` construct based on `Bool::cond`.

Chapter 21

Dispatching

Any message sent in an OO system may be *dispatched* in any of several senses. At least three separate aspects of dispatching may be distinguished:

1. *Selection* of concrete code associated with an invoked operation for a given object.
2. *Resolution* of the "best matching" version of an operation when two or more are defined.
3. *Routing* of a nonspecific request to a particular object.

Not all senses are directly supported in all OO programming languages and systems. We discuss ways of coping with this later.

Dispatching is a decoupling technique. The three forms of dispatching decouple requests from the corresponding code, versions, and receivers. A *dispatching error* results when an object sends a message that has no valid receiver or corresponding operation. This can occur when there is not a unique best matching action defined for the message name and types of the actual arguments, including the case where no such operation is defined at all, and in the case of object routing, where no eligible recipient exists.

Dispatching errors are among the most difficult problems to plan for. It is inconceivable to write actions that check to see if each and every message could be dispatched and to take evasive action if not. If dispatching errors do occur, the only recourse is to define top-level error recovery facilities, triggered by dispatching mechanisms. Indeed, one of the main reasons for using a strongly typed design language is to avoid this.

Typed OO dispatching adds a safety guarantee to decoupling. Senders are assured that no matter which receiver, version, and code is dispatched, messages result in the desired effects. Thus, dispatching rules are among the mechanisms by which OO systems support subclass *polymorphism*. Because of this, the dynamics of dispatching are dependent on the *declarative* structure of classes and operations.

21.1   Selection

Dispatching mechanisms associated with code selection are essential for basic OO methods. They are usually uncomplicated, simply linking the version of concrete code defined in a class to the appropriate operation name and message.

21.1.1   Refining Operations in Subclasses

To meet basic safety guarantees, subclass versions of operations must obey the rules for refined transitions given in Chapter 7. To briefly recap, subclass versions may weaken preconditions, add actions, and strengthen result guarantees with respect to superclasses.

These requirements occasionally lead to surprising constraints on subclasses and operations. For example, it may appear reasonable to define an `addToBalance` operation in class `Account` of the form:

```
class Account ...
  fn balance: real;
  op addToBalance(v: real) ==> balance' = balance + v end
end
```

Suppose now that while the `balance` attribute in `Account` is numerically unconstrained, subclass `SavingsAccount` adds the constraint that `balance >= 0`. This causes problems. Because `balance + v` might be negative, the `SavingsAccount` `balance` constraint may be broken by the postcondition. Yet the operation cannot be modified to accept only positive values as data and still maintain the subclass justification. Thus, from either perspective, the design is inconsistent.

Several solutions are available. For example, the topmost `Account` class need not define any operations. Different operations with different names and constraints could be associated with different subclasses. However, this eliminates opportunities for polymorphism, thus complicating the design of client classes that interact with different `Account` subclasses.

If one would like to ensure that instances of all `Account` subclasses possess the operation, then the topmost version must be recast. Here, one could define the `Account` version to accept only nonnegative values of v. Subclasses able to accept negative values as well can then weaken the precondition and/or define additional operations. This would be appropriate only if it were logically impossible to define a subclass requiring a *stronger* input constraint. For example, it does not allow definition of a subclass requiring that `v >= transactionFee`.

To allow for arbitrary variation in subclass restrictions, one may adopt a weaker but more general strategy using state abstraction along with a screening function. For example:

```
class Account ...
  fn canAdd(v: real): bool;
  op addToBalance(v: real)
    when canAdd(v) then balance' = balance + v
    else % pend or exception % end
end
```

The `canAdd` predicate defines an abstract state. The screening function may be unconstrained (undefined) in the abstract superclass. Subclasses may then add constraints and concrete definitions. Clients of any subclass of `Account` must be prepared for `canAdd` to be false for any reason whatsoever. A variant of this tactic is to eliminate the guard and then recast `addToBalance` to return a boolean result or named reply reporting whether the operation succeeded or failed. Different subclasses may then differently define the conditions under which the operation reports success.

State abstraction and refinement may be exploited in other situations as well. A subclass may specify refined states that distinguish attribute settings that were lumped together in one superclass state. This may result in two or more versions of an operation being defined in the subclass, each of which obey all superclass guarantees, but in different ways. For example, suppose Q is a special checking account class that charges for transactions only if the balance is under a stated minimum. Q may subdivide the nonoverdrawn state of `Account` into cases of not overdrawn but under minimum balance versus at or over minimum balance. Q may then define two versions of a transaction operation accordingly, distinguished by different guard conditions.

21.1.2 Selection Policies

The details of selection rules may impact how classes and subclasses ultimately become defined in software. Effective use and reuse often relies on more *fine-grained* types than are usually originally present in a design. For example, consider:

```
class X   a: bool;  b: int;   c: real; end
```

```
op useA(p: ?) { if p.a then print("success") end }
```

What type should be listed for **p** in **useA**? Listing **p:X** would be OK. But it might not be the best choice in the long run. It makes **useA** too tightly coupled to **X**. In fact, **useA** would work perfectly well if applied to an object of type:

```
class Y    a: bool;  d: String; end
```

This is a serious limitation to the use of class names in selecting operations. Without evasive action **useA** will be too tightly bound to unnecessary capabilities, hence, less reusable. Solutions hinge on some specific language policies and dispatching mechanisms.

Conformance.   In emerald [185], among other languages, class names do not even matter for type checking and dispatching purposes. Any object of a class with the demanded (name based) properties may be used as an argument to an operation. This is called *conformance*-based typing. It allows "partial" abstract class declarations to be declared retrospectively. For example, we might write:

```
class AThing   a: bool; end
```

```
op useA(a:   AThing)...;
```

Subsequently, **useA** could be invoked with something of class **X** (or rather any concrete subclass of **X**) whether **X** had ever been declared to be a subclass of **AThing** or not. If later, a special form of **useA(p:Y)** were found to be necessary to deal with **Y**s, it could be added. The original version would still be applied for **X**s.

The only disadvantage of pure conformance is that implicit or unstatable invariants and interdependencies may be broken inadvertently. Despite efforts to the contrary, the placement of a group of attributes and operations within a particular class often implies more dependencies than are actually stated. While this is not at all desirable, the possibilities often exist in real designs.

Still, conformance-based strategies are excellent ways to implement systems, since they are so readily extensible and adaptable. But designs based on conformance assumptions can be difficult to transform into OO implementation languages that do not employ conformance-based dispatching. Most do not.

Dynamic lookups. In some OO programming languages, u.useA(x) for some x supporting a and some u of a class supporting useA could be sent without any special precautions or other considerations. In these languages (e.g., Smalltalk [99]) messages are "looked up" dynamically, without the need (or even the provisions) for declared class information. As with conformance, this can be an excellent way to implement systems. However, it is weaker than conformance. Without class information to guide routing, it becomes impossible to specialize useA without embedding type tests inside a single version.

Views. Interfaces to existing classes may be repackaged using views. For example, even without a conformance-based system, we could still define class AThing and useA, but send in an X after creating a class:

```
class XBasedAThing  is AThing
  x: X;  FORWARD(x, a)
end
...
useA(new XBasedAThing(x := myX))
```

This is not always pretty, but is very useful for patching together otherwise incompatible classes and applications. It preserves extensibility while still supporting class-based control of behavior. However, it also complicates object identity issues. An XBasedAThing forwarding messages to an X is not the same object as the inner X.

Refactoring. Even when dealing with systems supporting conformance, dynamic lookups, or dynamic views, the best strategy is to refactor a hierarchy in a way that accommodates less restrictive usage by retrospectively defining new superclasses using the methods described in Chapter 7. This has the advantage of only explicitly defining classes that make some conceptual sense and/or are of known value to client applications. It has the disadvantage of almost always causing further design iteration.

21.2   Resolution

Different versions of operations may be defined inside classes or at top-level in order to deal with *arguments* of different types. Resolution rules are required to determine which version to apply in a particular context. We have been implicitly assuming one of the broadest possible rules, *dynamic closest match* dispatching, which selects the best fitting version defined for the actual participants.

Multiple versions of operations may appear within classes and their subclasses, and/or as sets of ungrouped top-level operations. For simplicity, we will illustrate using top-level cases. For example:

```
op credit(acct: Account, amt: Cash);

op credit(acct: CheckingAccount, amt: Cash);
```

Best-match dispatching follows the logic of *relational* inheritance (Chapter 7). The best version to use corresponds to the "deepest" defined relation/operation among the arguments. Here, when `credit(a, x)` is invoked in some context, if `a` were of class `CheckingAccount` or some subclass thereof, the `credit(CheckingAccount, Cash)` version would be selected. But if `a` were of class `Account` or some subclass of `Account` other than `CheckingAccount`, the `credit(Account, Cash)` version would be selected.

Argument-based operation overriding is sometimes easier to manage than subclassing. It is not necessary to explicitly state which version of which operation is being overridden during declarations, nor even to keep track of which version is overriding which, as long as *some* coherent subclassing relation holds when all versions are considered as a whole. For example, it is often acceptable if neither of two versions overrides the other, but both override a version that might conceptually exist, but because it is never needed, is not defined.

In ODL, the *obj* in *class* construct may be used to indicate and control these mechanics explicitly. Using "in" is not a very good way to *define* operations since it ignores receivers and buries dispatching policies within internals. It is, however, a useful way to *view* them from a client-side perspective. This is especially valuable when checking the consistency of effects across all defined versions of an operation. For example, the combined view of `credit` is:

```
op credit(acct: Account, amt: Cash)
   when acct in CheckingAccount then
      % special version for checking accounts
   elsewhen acct in Account then
      % version for ordinary accounts
   else
      % ''cannot happen''
   end
```

In ODL, each of a series of guards assumes negation of the previous ones. Here, this reduces to the fact that the first listed matching case is selected. In accord with best-match dispatching policies, the subclass cases are listed first, so that the most special applicable version is invoked.

21.2.1 Ambiguity

In Chapter 7, we discussed measures to avoid ambiguity under multiple inheritance. Sets of operations dispatched on multiple arguments can get even more confusing and require similar care. It is possible to declare sets of versions leading to situations where there can be no best match. For example (using CCA and PCA as stand-ins for effects):

```
class PreferredClient is Client ... end

op inspect(c: Client, a: CheckingAccount)  ==> CCA end

op inspect(c: PreferredClient, a: Account) ==> PCA end
```

Neither of these is an override of the other, although both of them are related to the "base" form:

```
op inspect(c: Client, a: Account) ==> CA end
```

None of these versions would be a unique best choice if inspect were invoked with a PreferredClient and a CheckingAccount. It is easiest to see this when these versions are unrolled using when and in. There are *two* ways to do it:

```
op inspect(c: Client, a: Account) % version 1
   when   c in PreferredClient then
     when    a in CheckingAccount then % (*)
     else % a in Account %                   PCA end
   else % c in Client
     when    a in CheckingAccount then CCA
     else % a in Account %                   CA   end end


op inspect(c: Client, a: Account) % version 2
   when    a in CheckingAccount then
     when   c in PreferredClient then % (*)
     else % c in Client %                    CCA end
   else % a in Account
     when   c in PreferredClient then PCA
     else % c in Client %                    CA   end end
```

It is just not clear from the declarations what to write in case (*). The two different unrollings make either PCA or CCA most tempting. While it is surely most reasonable to declare that this case somehow combines the effects of PCA and CCA, no one, least-wise a dumb dispatching rule, can do this for you. Either the design should be completed to cover all cases or else special dispatch resolution rules must be defined (as in CLOS [35]).

21.2.2   Simulating Multiple Dispatch

Most object-oriented programming languages do not support full best-match dispatching rules. As with other caveats we have noted, this can affect the expression of designs, without affecting their logic.

Lack of best-match dispatching is a common source of programming-level errors. Without it, operations may be "unrolled" using type-tests. Another strategy is to transform it to simple selection dispatching. Here we describe the mechanics. These details may be safely ignored unless you need them, although they do demonstrate a model protocol that can be established across different classes for many related purposes.

Double Dispatching.   There is a neat but messy trick that allows multiple dispatching to be simulated perfectly by adding operations to the participant classes, at the expense of protocol coupling. For two-argument operations, this is called *double dispatching*. It extends in a straightforward but horribly awkward way for three or more arguments. This is best illustrated with a bare-bones example. Suppose we have two sets of subclass structures, and multiple versions of some operation f:

```
class A ... end
class SubA is A ... end

class B ... end
class SubB is  B ... end


op f(a: A,     b: B)    { P }
op f(a: SubA, b: SubB) { Q }
op f(a: A,     b: SubB) { R }
```

This setup corresponds to that seen for `Accounts` and `Clients` supporting `inspect` operations. P, Q and R are just stand-ins for the concrete code. A fourth version, f(SubA, B) could be added without changing any of the following logic.

The first step is to *rename* the versions depending on *either* one of the argument types. It does not matter which one, but for ambiguous designs the different choices will result in different behaviors. This is one reason to avoid ambiguous designs. Let's choose B. If we distinguish the versions on the exact B type, we can also recast all SubB declarations as just B. The procedure name will tell us which one to use.

```
op fB(a: A,     b: B) { P }
op fB(a: SubA, b: B) { Q }

op fSubB(a: A, b: B) { R }
```

Because we arranged that the second argument "does not matter" for dispatching purposes, we may now safely embed these inside the A *classes* corresponding to the first argument types:

```
class A ...
  op fB(b: B)     { P }
  op fSubB(b: B) { R }
end
class SubA is A ...
  op fB(b: B)     { Q }
end
```

We could stop here, except that callers would need to know the right versions to invoke, which they do not. But the B's do. We may place the appropriate forwarders in the corresponding classes:

```
class B ...
  op f(a: A) { a.fB(self) }
end

class SubB is B ...
  op f(a: A) { a.fSubB(self) }
end
```

Optionally, a single top-level version may be defined to start things rolling:

```
op f(a: A, b: B) { b.f(a) }
```

21.2.3   Genericity and Dispatching

Selection and resolution rules also come into play with generic classes. There is some leeway between subclassing and parameterization for defining collections and related classes. For example, in Chapter 17, we could have defined a stack as follows:

```
class NonParamStack
  empty: bool;
  op push(x: Any): ();
  op top: Any;
  op pop;
end
```

This would define a stack that could hold instances of any kind of objects whatsoever. This is OK for putting things into a stack, but sometimes less so when they are pulled out. Unless it somehow happens to have additional information, a client looking at the top element does not know anything at all about its capabilities. As far as type information is concerned, it could be anything.

On the other hand, if a client has a STACK[Window], it knows that all elements are Windows. The objects might still be of any subclass of Window; perhaps Bordered-Window, ScrollableWindow or whatever. But they are surely at least Windows. This guarantees that clients can perform window-based operations on all of the objects without having to bother with error-handling details. Parameterized classes are thus generally safer than unrestricted classes and lead to simpler use by clients.

You might think that you could declare something like class WindowStack is NonParamStack to get the same effects through subclassing. But this cannot be done without breaking subclass substitutability rules. The definition of push in NonParamStack indicates that Any kind of object may be pushed onto it. This must be restricted in the subclass to only push Windows. However, then the subclass would not be substitutable.

Type restrictions. For the sake of practical design efforts, we have not listed any restrictions on the type arguments acceptable for generic classes. We adopt the common OO convention that *any* type may match a type parameter, but that instantiating one that leads to undefined behavior is a design error.

We will digress with an example that illustrates some of the resulting issues. Views and parameterized classes are often found together in designs. For example, suppose you need to define ordered sets, where the ordering may be based on *any* kind of key held by any kind of class:

```
class Keyed  key: Any; end

class KeyedSet is SET[Keyed] ...
  op put(x: Keyed) { ... if lessThan(x.key, first.key) then ... end }
end
```

This could be used to hold, say, Accounts, via a view:

```
class KeyedAccount is Keyed
  a: Account;
  key: Balance { a.balance }
end

fn lessThan(x: Balance, y: Balance): bool { x.val < y.val }

myset := new KeyedSet(...);
myset.put(new KeyedAccount(myAcct)); ...
```

This is not as safe as it looks. Because the `KeyedSet` can hold anything viewable as `Keyed`, any particular instance might be filled with just about anything. Maybe that is what you want. But if other such objects return different kinds of keys, then the comparison in `put` may attempt to compare `Balances` to, say, `Bananas`. Most likely you did not even define a version of `lessThan` that compares such things. This would result in a dispatch failure.

This problem is a consequence of the laxness of parameterized type rules. Here, it leads to the insensible notion that you can meaningfully compare *any* two arbitrary objects with a less-than operation, which you cannot.

The simplest way to maximize safety in this and most related situations is to define different kinds of ordered sets based on the types of their keys. The same general construction applies, but controlled by different kinds of `Key` classes, returning types for which less-than functions are known to be defined. More elegant-sounding solutions (if they exist) are hard to obtain without introducing more controversial type apparatus.

21.3   Routing

In Chapter 18, we noted that multiparticipant operations may be transformed into classes. Instead of defining deposits, withdrawals, and inspections as free-standing operations (or worse, as inappropriately received by clients, tellers, or accounts *per se*) they may be defined as the responsibility of corresponding coordinators:

```
class Trans
  op inspect;
  op deposit(amt: Cash); ...
end

class CheckingTrans is Trans... end

class TransV1 is Trans
  generator TransGen1
  locals
    c: fixed Client;  a: fixed Account;  t: fixed Teller;
  end
  op inspect; ...
end
```

```
class CheckingTransV1 is CheckingTrans ...
   generator CTransGen1
end
```

By placing constructors within generators, clients may rely on the third sense of dispatching, object routing, providing the highest level of decoupling:

```
class TransGen1 ...
   op mk(c: Client, a: Account, t: Teller): TransV1;
end

class CTransGen1 ...
   op mk(c: Client, a: CheckingAccount, t: Teller): CheckingTrans;
end

op user {
   t := TransGen1$mk(client1, account402, aTeller);
   t.deposit(100.00); ... }
```

The main limitation of this approach is that clients must know exactly which version of coordinator they wish to construct. Avoiding this entails creation of another top-level operation that uses argument-based dispatching to route construction requests to the appropriate generator, so that clients do not have to do so themselves. Thus, the two forms of dispatching do not always completely substitute for each other.

21.3.1 Routing Structures

Object routing is usually implemented via mediator objects. These can take several forms, including *name servers* and *relays*.

Name Servers. A name server (or ID server) accepts requests describing the kinds of services needed, and returns the identity or other specifier of an object providing the service. For an extremely stripped down example:

```
class IDServer
  p: Printer;  d: Display;
  op getServer(req: Request): Any {
     if req.svc = "print" then reply p else reply d end }
end
```

Of course, the basic idea can and should be extended. The server may hold updatable collections of objects providing different services, maintain descriptions of their interfaces, find the "best-fitting" server for any given request, redirect inquiries to others when a good fit cannot be made, and so on.

These designs have intrinsic static typability problems. For example, the `get-Server` procedure is listed as having a result type only of `Any`, since it returns identities of different kinds of objects corresponding to different kinds of requests. There is no simple way to say anything more specific at the type level. For the sake of safety, clients should be prepared for anything:

```
...
p: Any := reg.getServer("print");
if p in Printer then p.print(myPrintJob) else ... end;
```

Relays.   A relay receives requests and then routes them to designated service objects. For another overly simplified example:

```
class ServiceRelay ...
  m: MAP[ServiceDescription, Server];
  op register(s: ServiceDescription, v: Server) { m.put(s, v) }
  op svcRequest(s: ServiceDescription) {
     if m.has(s) then m.at(s).serve end }
end
```

The main difference between relays and name servers lies in their interfaces. A pure relay silently connects objects, while a pure name server tells one object who it should connect to. They have the same overall function as our object dispatching strategies and amount to manual simulations, extensions, or implementations of them. For example, we could have expressed the name server example directly in ODL as `Printer$print(myPrintJob)`. The reverse transformation is pragmatically valuable. Any design implemented using languages and tools that do not support object dispatching (most do not) needs to be transformed to use manually defined name server and relay objects.

21.3.2   Topologies

Routers and dispatchers of all sorts must keep track of the existences and capabilities of many other objects. The resulting mediation networks may be organized into a number of topologies. It is often preferable to postpone commitments about particular forms to take advantage of those supported by system tools and services.

Central arbitration. In a centrally arbitrated design, only one object or service knows about the entire system. All other objects register themselves and their interfaces with a master "broker". All communication is mediated by this master broker. It forwards all events to the appropriate objects. Backup forwarders may also be present to protect the system against failure of the main broker.

Point-to-point. In a fully distributed, point-to-point design, each object maintains all object and dispatching information for the system, locally resolves messages, and directly sends requests to the appropriate recipients.

Broadcast. Broadcasts offer tremendous simplification of point-to-point strategies. In a broadcast-based design, objects send nonlocal requests to *all* other objects. Recipients simply ignore nonapplicable requests. Objects need not know about nonlocal capabilities at all, at the expense of generating a possibly unacceptable level of message traffic.

Tree-structured. Tree-structured designs represent a midpoint between fully central and fully distributed information. Each object (or an associated helper) knows about one or more routing-tree descendent objects, and routes those requests itself. All other nonlocal requests are sent to a parent object that might either be the recipient, or might know which of its tree descendents to send the message to, or failing these might forward to *its* parent. Various redundancies (e.g., secondary forwarders) may be built into this framework to protect against failures. The general idea of structured distributed OO routing is sometimes called *cooperative dispatching*. Systems developed in such a way are sometimes termed *federated* architectures. The history of network design suggests that as OO systems grow ever bigger and more distributed, such designs will remain among the few tractable options. Even though they possess increased complexity and dynamic overhead, they scale quite well.

Mixtures. Aspects of these strategies may be combined. For example, a system might use point-to-point schemes for most messages, while also employing broadcast or restricted broadcast for others. These decisions might be based in part on physical system issues including communication hardware support and its reliability.

21.4   Summary

Controlling actions by reference to class membership is central to OO dispatching rules. Overriding operations abstractly and/or concretely defined in superclasses provides a means for specializing behaviors that correspond to the special properties of a subclass. Similarly, defining multiple versions of scripted operations on the basis of the class membership of their participants is a way of specializing coordinated actions to deal with special kinds of participants. Without these, extensibility, polymorphism, generality, and the concomitant ability to specialize would be lost.

21.5   Further Reading

Many of the readings noted in Chapter 7 include discussions of polymorphism and dispatching. Argument-based dispatching was pioneered in CLOS [35] and its precursors; see also Shrefl and Keppel [204]. Simulation of multiple dispatch was first described by Ingalls [118]. General routing and communication topologies are discussed in many texts, including Bertsekas and Gallager [31].

21.6   Exercises

1. Operation overriding is often used extensively in design, but not in analysis. Why is this so?

2. Some people think that *obj* in *class* is an evil construct that should not even be present in OO design and programming systems. Give one argument pro and one con.

3. Why is multiple versioning considered to be a better design practice than the use of type tests, even though they can be used to equivalent effect?

4. Explain how to reduce triple dispatching to double dispatching.

5. What is wrong with declaring
   `class Comparable fn lessThan(other: Comparable): bool; end`
   and using it as a basis for defining ORDERED_SETs?

6. Given the fact that relays and name servers of any form can be built, why are typed object routing mechanisms still useful?

Chapter 22

Coordination

22.1 Joint Actions

Coordinator objects introduced in Chapter 18, as well as other composite objects, may not be in "full control" of their operation participants. This complicates translation of guards and effects into concrete form. Generally, any guard evaluating conditions on objects accessed via nonexclusively managed links must ensure that the referenced objects do not change state between the test and the beginning of the operation. Similarly, the coordinator must assure that actions across all participants remain atomic with respect to external observers. Thus, the coordinator must transiently act as an exclusive controller of these objects. A number of approaches are available for carrying this out. To describe them, we must first address the nature of the problems they are intended to solve.

22.1.1 Interference

An intrinsic danger of compositional design is that since we are always building objects by linking together other objects, it is possible to lose track of where any link may actually lead. This creates the potential for *interference*.

Interference occurs when two competing operations or sets of operations are applied to the same object. Generally, any concrete operation that contains the possibility of interference cannot always make good on its abstract effects, and is potentially incorrect. There are two possible results of interference:

Safety Failures: When the individual suboperations of two different actions are interleaved, an object may not end up in the state described by either of their effects, may no longer meet a relational `inv` contract with other objects, and may not be in a legal state at all.

Liveness Failures: When an object sends a blocking message that ultimately blocks `self`, or two or more objects block each other, they lock up.

While these two effects can normally be traded off for one another, neither is the least bit desirable. In both cases, the source of interference may be far removed from sight. Interference may occur when two clients (perhaps oblivious to each other's existence) both try to manipulate the same object. For example, two different `Transaction` objects, both holding a link to the same `Account`, may both be trying to step the account through mutually incompatible operations.

In our design framework, no two objects may interfere with each other if they are interested in a single operation in a single object. Our noninterruptibility rules prevent contention. Sadly enough, these provisions cannot automatically extend to *transactions* in which a *sequence* of operations on possibly many objects must be triggered in a certain way and processed in a certain order, without interleaving any other stray operations. While this is most obviously problematic in systems of concurrently interacting objects, it is just as disastrous in purely sequential designs in which subtasks interfere with the main tasks they are allegedly supporting.

Aliasing

Interference is not restricted to situations involving multiple controlling objects. *Local* interference occurs when a *single* object "inadvertently" tries to use another (perhaps even itself!) in two different roles. This *aliasing* results when two different locally accessible links are attached to the same object. The most obvious forms of aliasing are similar to those found in any system involving references, pointers, or any other link-like construct. For example, in the matrix multiplication routine:

```
op matMul(lft: Matrix, rgt: Matrix, result: Matrix);
```

It may be the case that two or more of `lft`, `rgt`, and `result` are actually connected to the same matrix object. If the usual matrix multiplication algorithm is applied, and `result` *is* bound to the same matrix as either of the sources, the procedure will produce incorrect results.

Aliasing is at least in part a human factors issue. It is just too easy to overlook aliasing possibilities. Often enough, when potential problems are identified, solutions are not hard to come by. Unfortunately, some object-oriented design constructions tend to hide aliasing opportunities. Potential aliasing is hard to discern when arguments or components are of different declared type, but could match the same object. For example, suppose we had:

```
class Account ... end
class SavingsAccount is Account ... end
class CheckingAccount is Account ... end
class BahamaAccount is SavingsAccount, CheckingAccount ... end

op transfer(src: SavingsAccount, dest: CheckingAccount);
```

If the operations on `src` and `dest` within `transfer` interfere with each other, then it would be a very bad idea to invoke `transfer(x,x)`, for some `x:BahamaAccount`. Of course, it may be the case that `transfer` will simply leave `x` in its original state, in which case all would be well. But unless you are alerted to the possibility, you are unlikely to notice that this might be a problem. A similar situation involves aliasing between an argument and a component. For example:

```
class TransactionLog ... end
class SystemLog is TransactionLog ... end
class AccountLog is TransactionLog ... end


class Account ...
   logger: AccountLog;
   op update(... syslog: TransactionLog)  { ...;
      logger.recordBalanceChange;
      syslog.recordTransaction }
end
```

If the `update` operation were invoked with an argument that happened to match an account's own `logger`, there may be two records in the same log, which is probably not what was intended.

Yet another way to mask aliasing opportunities is through relays and other objects that are used as "pass by role" intermediaries. For example, if a dependency manager maintains a set of objects interested in particular change notices, a design may inadvertently result in an object being notified of its own changes. Again, maybe this is OK; maybe not.

Alias Detection

In standard OO systems, any operation has the power to detect simple aliasing (just through a link identity test) and then perform evasive action.

For example, a matrix multiply routine may invoke a slow-but-safe `multiplyIn-Place` procedure when it receives aliased arguments. This idea may be generalized to arbitrary *projections*. Any two-parameter operation, say, `p(a,b)`, may delegate to a special form `p1(ab)` when `a` is known to be the same as `b`. Three-parameter operations (e.g., `q(a,b,c)`) may delegate to two- and one-parameter versions (e.g., `q1(a,bc)`, `q2(ab,c)`, `q3(ac,b)`, `q4(abc)`). This is a bit tedious. But it is also a useful efficiency measure. Actions for aliased cases are often either significantly faster or significantly slower than others. By splitting them out, the best method may be applied to the case at hand.

However, this strategy works only when distinct objects are entirely independent and self-contained, thus sharing no internal links. This is typical, but not definitionally forced for common matrix classes. For example, if one of the arguments to `matMul` were some kind of wrapper or view of another (e.g., if `lft` were of a class that held a link to `rgt` and forwarded all operations to it), then the same problems result even though `lft ~= rgt`.

There *are* ways of specifying classes to (declaratively) preclude aliasing. For matrices, this would first require a set of guarantees stating that no two cells in a single matrix were aliased. For example, a `Matrix` class (or subclass) might include a function to determine whether the identities of two cells are the same:

```
fn eqCell(i: int, j: int, ii: int, jj: int): bool =
   (at(i, j) = at(ii, jj)) = ((i = ii) /\ (j = jj))
```

This version says that the identities of two cells are the same only if the indices are. Another function `allIndependent`, which loops through all possible indices and checks `eqCell`, may then be declared as `inv`. A relational class containing two or three matrices may then rely on these invariants to construct additional functions advertising independence between the cells of different matrices. The complexity of such declarations corresponds to the extensiveness of independence guarantees demanded by standard implementations of `matMul`.

Without such assurance, alias checks via identity tests are *only* definitive when they report `true`. In that case, the two links really are connected to the same object. In all other cases, lack of top-level identity need not imply that two objects are independent and cannot always be used to prevent interference.

22.1.2 Controlling Interference

There cannot be a magical cure for interference. The potential for interference is intrinsic to any system of agents communicating through sharable channels. In special cases, exhaustive static formal analysis of a design might prove it interference-free across all possible executions. However, this is both exceedingly rare and difficult to undertake. Instead, a mixture of prevention, detection, and control must be used. Strategies include centralization, export control, sender rules, sender-receiver protocols, and recovery techniques. We have discussed techniques for centralization (unique objects) and controlling exports (by protecting links, making copies and views, and using collections that never reveal identities of their members) in previous chapters. However, there are limits to these safeguards. It is impossible to remove all link exports without removing all potential for interaction. We address the other methods in turn.

Locking

As a design rule, all senders may promise to access target objects only if they are sure that the targets are under their (temporary) exclusive control. This ensures that all operations on the target objects are atomic and interference-free with respect to all other observers.

Clients may obtain and advertise control by holding *locks*. Clients use lockable objects by first locking, then operating, then releasing. If another client has control over the target, others will wait (blocking on `lock`) until they are done, assuming that all senders play by these rules. After obtaining a lock, one object may issue messages to another with the same confidence about noninterference as does the holder of an unexported `own` link. Objects must release locks immediately when they are no longer needed. Lockable forms of any class are easy to define:

```
class Lockable
  locked: bool;
  op lock: ()   when ~locked then locked' else pend end
  op release: () ==> ~locked' end
end

class LockableX is Lockable, X  end
```

There is often no reason for each object to possess its own lock. The repositories described in Chapter 18 may manage locks for all of their members. Traversable forms may also support collection-wide locking. A single centralized lock manager may even be employed:

```
class LockMgr
  locked(x: Any): bool;
  op lock(x: Any): () when ~locked(x) then locked(x)' else pend end
  op release(x: Any): () ==> ~locked(x)' end
end
```

Note that lock operations are simple renamings of Semaphore operations. Locks may be implemented as views of semaphores. The safest locking protocol is *two phase*, in which all locks for all objects involved in an operation are obtained before any are released (see, e.g., [53] for details).

Nested locking. Locking frameworks are not necessarily effective as defined thus far. Suppose a Square (as in Chapter 17) were of a type that contained exported (shared) links to the inner Point objects. A lock on the square would not gain control over the component points. Interference would still be possible. For this reason, any lock-based framework must also include *nested* locking protocols that are dependent on the linkage details of classes. For example:

```
class LockableSquare is Square ...
  locals lowerLeft: LockablePoint; upperRight: LockablePoint; end
  locked: bool;
  op lock: () when ~locked then lowerLeft.lock',upperRight.lock',locked'
              else pend end
  op release:() ==> ~lowerLeft.locked',~upperRight.locked',~locked' end
end
```

Nested locking requires care. Objects reachable via more than one path should not receive multiple lock requests.

Read and write locks. Regular locks are excessive when clients merely want to inspect their targets (i.e., invoke fns), not try to change them (i.e., invoke ops). Any number of "readers" may coexist without contention or interference. Bottlenecks may be alleviated by differentiating between *read locks* used only for inspections (e.g., in guard evaluation), and *write locks* used in any actions sending state-changing messages. Any number of readers may simultaneously hold read locks, but only one may hold a write lock. Care is needed to implement fair access to both read and write locks (see, e.g., [12] for details). One basic form is as follows:

```
class LockMgr2 ...
  readLocks(x: Any): int;
  writeLocked(x: Any): bool;
  op rLock(x: Any): ()
    when ~writeLocked(x) then readLocks(x)' = readLocks(x) + 1
    else pend end
  op rRelease(x: Any): () ==> readLocks(x)' = readLocks(x) - 1 end
  op wLock(x: Any): ()
    when readLocks(x) = 0 /\ ~writeLocked(x) then writeLocked(x)'
    else pend end
  op wRelease(x: Any): () ==> ~writeLocked(x)' end
end
```

Access Control

Rather than depending on senders to obey locking protocols, receivers may willingly "enslave" themselves to selected "masters". Objects may keep track of their masters and listen only to them. For example:

```
class SlavePoint ...
  locals master: Any;  p: Point; end
  op shiftX(v: real, sender: Any)
    when sender = master then p.shiftX(v)' else % error % end
end
```

Note that SlavePoint is a view of a Point, not a subclass.

The shiftX operation must be supplied a sender argument that must match the master. This may be generalized to support *access control lists* that maintain a *set* of privileged senders. Of course, this design does not in itself provide full security. Without system-level support for this protocol, other objects may be able to send master as an argument and thus obtain access.

Keys.   Unbalanced protection techniques placing nearly all responsibility on either senders or receivers can be fragile. For example, locking depends heavily on the correctness of all message senders in properly obtaining and releasing locks. These protocols may be made more secure by associating keys with locks. The receivers should also know the keys and check them. All other operations can be reparameterized to require keys. For example, using simple locks and integer-based keys generated by some KeyMgr:

```
class LockablePoint3 ...
  locals currentKey: int; p: Point; end
  locked: bool;
  op lock(key: int): ()
     when ~locked then locked', currentKey' = key
     elsewhen key = currentKey then % empty %
     else pend end
  op release(key: int): ()
     when key = currentKey then ~locked'  else % error % end
  op shiftX(v: real, key: int): ()
     when key = currentKey then p.shiftX(v)' else % error % end
end
```

Keys help solve the nested locking problem. The empty effect associated with the condition for a lock request with the same key as already being used allows objects that are reachable from multiple paths to receive multiple lock requests without causing lock-up. Keys thus serve the role of "visit markers" necessary in any linked graph traversal algorithm (see, e.g., [5, 197]).

Smarter keys.   The use of keys alone is not foolproof. A client may tell a third object about a key, allowing the other object to obtain incorrect access. Inappropriate key distribution may be controlled by wrapping view-based classes around the keys themselves. An extreme tactic is to create one-shot key objects that fail to work after a single use. For example, assuming simple integer keys where zero is never a legal key value:

```
class OneShotKey
  own k: Int <>
  own used: Bool <> init ~used?
  op key: int { if ~used? then used.t!; reply k? else reply 0 end }
end
```

Lock operations may then use such objects rather than raw keys. There are many useful variations and improvements. These include support for a fixed number of uses (rather than one), means for requesting additional use once a key has elapsed, sharing keys, "aging" keys on the basis of time rather than use, and operations allowing receivers to revoke locks when necessary. It is, of course, a very bad idea to define a `clone` operation for smart keys. Construction must be managed carefully.

Smart links. There is no conceptual difference between keys, pseudo-IDs, and ordinary links. All are employed to obtain access to particular objects. An entire system based on *smart links* may impose arbitrary security and locking mechanisms "behind the scenes" of normal design efforts. Given the complexity and fragility of access and control mechanisms, this strategy is very attractive for large development efforts.

Forgetting links. Simpler, special-purpose versions of smart keys and links include a set of policies and techniques called *islands* [112]. These partially automate alias-free import/export protocols. The idea is for objects to support a `sendAndNullOutL` operation for each link L that is used when sending components as arguments to operations that form the "bridge" to a set ("island") of alias-propagating objects. The `sendAndNullOutL` operation sends out the current identity, but then unbinds the link so that it may no longer be used by the sender object. It may later be rebound, typically after receiving a message from the original recipient that it may do so. A similar *transfer* operation is supported in **Hermes** [211].

Scaling up. Interference control, access control, and locking mechanisms can become arbitrarily complex. The strategies we have listed in this section are geared more toward accident prevention than protection against malicious invasion. The more hostile the environment and the more critical the consequences of interference, the more elaborate and "heavyweight" need be the protocols. These may include combinations of authentication, multilevel access, certification, encryption, and randomization mechanisms, as provided by system tools and services (see, e.g., [190, 215, 59]).

22.1.3 Managing Interference

Unless proven otherwise, no system is free from safety and/or liveness failures stemming from interference. There is hardly ever a real choice to be had between designing for safety versus liveness. Safety failures normally lead to *undetectable* corruption, but liveness failures lead to deadlock, which is at least in principle detectable, and thus recoverable from.

Detection

Under any of the listed safety measures, potentially interfering operations may cause each other to block forever. Even simple aliasing may suffice to break things:

```
op rotate2(x: LockableSquare, y: LockableSquare) {
  lock(x); lock(y);
    doRotation(x, y);
  release(x); release(y) }

op user(a: LockableSquare) { rotate2(a, a) }
```

Here, the second call to lock on a will block forever. Even an aliasing check of "x=y" in rotate2 would not necessarily repair this if the top-level objects were different but contained shared components with simple nested locks.

Any design using widespread locking should include provisions for dynamically detecting and dealing with deadlock conditions. Some algorithms for doing so are described in [79, 7]. However, deadlock detection is often supported in a much simpler fashion. Objects requesting locks may use time-outs (Chapter 20). They treat the time-out replies as indications of deadlock and initiate the associated recovery measures. This is itself risky, since time-outs may occur for other reasons. But the use of conservative recovery strategies means that false alarms do no more than slow systems down, not cause yet other errors.

Recovery

The most defensible recovery protocol is one in which all modifications to all targets are either *committed* to in the normal case, or *aborted* if deadlock or other failures occur, where aborts leave all objects in their initial states, available for later *retry*. In-between results are not allowed.

These mechanics also apply in many other contexts, including cases in which safety failures happen to be detectable before they do any permanent harm, machines crash, access rights are denied, or software errors are encountered.

In simple cases where actions do not depend on each other, this may be accomplished by storing up all mutative operations (perhaps via a wrapper queue), and then committing by executing the queued operations, or aborting by clearing the queue. The queued operations may be rearranged and optimized before execution. Another set of tractable cases involves operations that have unique "undo" or "antimessage" counterparts that reverse the effects of operations. On failure, a sequence of undo requests may be sent to the participants.

More general transaction control mechanisms save the states of participants before an operation begins and "roll back" objects to these saved states on failure. One way to control such mechanics is to support operations in a mixin class such as:

```
class TransactionParticipant ...
  op beginTransaction(t: TransactionID);
  op commitTransaction(t: TransactionID);
  op abortTransaction(t: TransactionID);
end;
```

However, many situations requiring locking and recovery also involve interactions with database managers or other services that provide particular transaction protocols of their own that must be accommodated. Indeed, for large system designs, it is all but impossible to maintain scattershot selections of methods. Commitment to particular tools, services, conventions, and protocols becomes necessary.

Many transaction support packages exist, but only a few are designed specifically for OO systems. One example is Kala [206]. Kala provides several OO transaction support mechanisms among its other services. Kala deals well with the fact that an object's logical state may be distributed among many other objects connected by links. As we have seen, this fact complicates copying, alias detection, and locking strategies that might be needed in transaction support. Kala addresses this through a mechanism in which each state (or version) of an object may be independently saved without at the same time always recursively saving all linked objects. However, user (programmer) level links are actually "baskets" of lower level links, normally directed at the current versions. These connections can be changed upon transaction commits, rollbacks, and partial rollbacks stemming from failures of nested subtasks.

22.1.4 Joint Action Coordinators

We may finally address the main issue of converting guarded multiparticipant transition specifications into concrete form. *Joint actions* are operations in which state changes in one or more objects lead to coordinated effects in one or more other participants. All transitions involving references to external participants are joint actions,

whether OOA models describe them as such or not. In particular, operations within
relation-based coordinator objects are often of this form. These normally require
transformations that provide "handshaking" to control interference.

We will first describe dynamic coordination using an example that is "all control".
Analysis models and abstract classes may describe effects that occur "automatically",
whenever one or more participating objects are in the proper state. For example, assume an OOA transition that says that a transfer should be started whenever a
checking account is overdrawn, a savings account is underdrawn, and the customer
has requested that the checking account should be automatically transferred. (This is
an illustrative variation of the overdraft protection service described in Chapter 10.)
We may represent this initially in a form that is concrete in actions but not in synchronization control:

```
class TransferMgr
  locals
    ch: fixed Checking; sv: fixed Savings; Cmr: fixed Customer;
    amt: fixed Cash;
    op doTransfer { sv.withdraw(amt); ch.deposit(amt); ... }
  end
  op transfer
    when ch.overdrawn /\ sv.canWithdraw(amt) /\ rqd(Cmr, ch) then
        { doTransfer; self.transfer }
    else pend end
end

op mkTransfer(x: Checking, y: Savings, z: Customer, a: Cash) {
  t := new TransferMgr(ch := x, sv := y, Cmr := z, amt := a);
  t.transfer; }
```

For the moment, we have arranged that the **transfer** operation be "always requested"
by artificially generating operation events and self-propagating them along.

The primary design issue here is that **transfer** cannot be concretely defined by
sequentially testing ch.overdrawn, then sv.canWithdraw(amt), then rqd(Cmr, ch),
and then executing **doTransfer** if all conditions hold. Assuming that none of these
objects are exclusively managed by **TransferMgr**, all may change state between test
time and trigger time.

A second, closely related issue stems from the fact that OOA models require all
effects produced within *action* specifications to be logically atomic. The **Transfer-
Mgr::doTransfer** operation must ensure that both balances are properly updated

before returning. Neither participant may engage in any other activities until this action is complete. Both participants must be under the control of the `TransferMgr` for the duration of the operation.

Unless it can somehow be proven that interference is impossible, dynamic control methods are required to address these problems. Beyond this, a strategy is needed for transforming logical guards into computations. The main alternatives are *polling* and *notifications*. Polling methods are generally poorer, but still sometimes useful.

22.1.5 Polling

In a polling approach, the coordinator for a joint action repeatedly asks participant objects about their states, and then performs the indicated actions if all conditions hold. The self-propagation strategy used at the abstract level may be replaced with a simple loop. Locking is needed in order to freeze participants during testing and/or to control them exclusively during actions. This is facilitated by the use of separate read and write locks.

For example, assuming that the `doTransfer` operation does not send any messages to the `Customer` but only reads its status while evaluating `rqd` in the guard, it may be read locked, while the others are write (or read/write) locked:

```
op transfer {
  while true do
    ch.wLock; sv.wLock; cmr.rLock;
    if ch.overdrawn /\ sv.canWithdraw(amt) /\ rqd(cmr, ch) then
        cmr.rRelease; doTransfer
    else cmr.rRelease  end;
    ch.wRelease; sv.wRelease
  end }
```

Underneath the lock control, this is just a variant of the original specification.

Polling need not require interference protocols if the guards and operations are somehow known not to interfere with other processing. Polling itself can be limited to those intervals when this is known to be true. For example, assuming that no transactions are made at night, a nightly transaction logger that only recorded differences over a 24-hour period could maintain a list of all accounts and their balances, recheck them once per night to discover which ones changed, and write log files accordingly.

22.1.6   Notifications

Polling techniques may test many times for proper conditions before firing. While the number of polling iterations may be bounded in special cases (see [109]), polling is usually both inefficient and unreliable.

Notification-based strategies instead use more efficient event-driven processing. In the case of guards for joint actions, the participants themselves may notify the coordinator that an action may need to be invoked. Notification-based techniques are also more reliable. Assuming queuing, the coordinator can never "miss" an opportunity to trigger an operation.

When participant objects change state in ways that might trigger a joint action, they may send a notification to the coordinator, while perhaps also locking themselves in preparation for possible control. (A usually better option is to wait for the coordinator to issue the lock via a callback sequence.) When there are multiple participants, notification from any one of them can trigger a lock-and-check sequence for the others. For example, using keyed locks:

```
class LockableChecking is Checking ...
   locals mgr: TransferMgr; keyMgr: KeyMgr; end
   op  withdraw(...) { ...
         if overdrawn then
             key := keyMgr.nextKey; self.lock(key); mgr.checkingOvd(key);
         end }
end

class TransferMgrV2 is TransferMgr ...
   op checkingOvd(k: Key) {
      sv.lock(k); cmr.lock(k);
      if sv.canWithdraw(amt) /\ rqd(cmr, ch) then doTransfer end;
      ch.release(k); sv.release(k); cmr.release(k) }

   op savingsOver;      % similar
   op customerApproved; % similar
end
```

The main disadvantage of notification methods is that without planning, they can involve a fair amount of mangling of existing classes in order to insert the right notifications at the right times. To avoid this, classes may be designed to support notifications on any attribute change, as described in Chapter 17. The specific notifications may be added later, even dynamically during execution.

Notification techniques open up a large and varied design space. In the remainder of this section, we survey some common variants.

Unsynchronized Notifications

As with polling, notification techniques do not always require interference control measures. In fact, unless an object must enter a controlled transition or interaction sequence as a result of the state change, it is fine to use simple one-way message passing for notification purposes.

Persistent Conditions

Some triggering conditions are "persistent". Once true, they remain true forever, or at least over the lifetimes of the relevant objects. To stretch an example, suppose that once a customer approved automatic transfer services, they were irrevocable. In this case, only a single notification need be sent to the `TransferMgr`. It would never need to be checked again. However, even this is wasteful. It would be simpler to construct the `TransferMgr` itself only when the customer requested the service.

Objects that check and respond to single persistent conditions are sometimes termed *watches* and *event monitors*. The most common persistent conditions are time-based. Because time increases monotonically, any guard depending on it being after a certain time or after a certain event will stay true persistently.

Periodic actions. When persistent conditions hold on a certain periodic basis, daemons may be constructed to manage the corresponding actions. For example, the following daemon could be used to implement the Automatic Payment Service described in Chapter 10:

```
class PeriodicAction
  period: TimePeriod;
  action: Wrapper;
end
```

```
class TimeTriggerManager
  local s: TABLE[PeriodicAction];
  local t: fixed Timer;
  op alarm(id: int): () {
    if s.has(id) then
        s.at(id).action;
        timer.replyAfter(s.at(id).period, WRAP(alarm(id))) end }
  op put(c: PeriodicAction): int {
    local job: int := s.put(c);
    timer.replyAfter(s.at(job).period, WRAP(alarm(job)));
    reply job }
  op remove(id: int) { s.remove(id) }
end
```

Change Notices

Some joint action specifications require an action whenever an object is changed in *any* way. These changes are difficult to sense by other objects. Particular attribute values are not important, only the fact that they have been changed. For example:

```
class Shape ...
  viewer: Viewer;
  op setX(newX: real) {
    if xCoord ~= newX then ... viewer.redraw; ... end }
end
```

A form of this tactic may be used to translate the `sv.canWithdraw(amt)` condition in `TransferMgr` into notifications. Because the savings account does not know the transfer amount, it should simply notify the `TransferMgr` when its balance changes. The manager may then perform the complete test.

Tools.   A number of specialized frameworks are available for designing classes supporting this general style of change-notice communication. Most graphical and user interface toolkits and frameworks use the *Model-View-Controller* (MVC) approach [99, 131] or any of several minor variations. These provide specific protocols linking change-sources (models), change-audiences (views) and change-instigators (controllers). The frameworks may be applied to nongraphical applications as well.

Special-Purpose Constraint Handlers

Some joint action effects and/or relational constraints are amenable to faster processing than is possible with generic propagation techniques. For example, if a set of Shape objects must always bear a certain geometric relation to each other (e.g., must be spaced uniformly within some region), then changes in any one of them may trigger a special-purpose constraint handler (e.g., a quadratic equation solver; see [108]) that simultaneously changes attributes in all of the constituent objects.

Relays

A single class may be used to mediate notification events among many different sets of objects. Dependency-based designs may be better decoupled and organized through *relay* classes similar to those described in Chapter 21. These maintain sets of connections between objects and mediate their communication. For example:

```
class ViewerRelay ...
  m: MAP[Shape, Viewer];
  op register(s: Shape, v: Viewer) { m.put(s, v) }
  op changeNotice(s: Shape) {
     if m.has(s) then m.at(s).redraw end }
end
```

Relays are exceedingly common and useful designs for coping with input events that may affect varied and changing audiences. Here, change sources need not know the exact identities of their audiences, as long as they know of the appropriate relay object. This technique may be extended to support "pass by interest" protocols in which senders describe the characteristics of audiences and/or the nature of the state change. The relay then determines the best recipient for the message at hand. It is also possible to add more intelligence to relays in order to actively mediate, rather than blindly forward events.

Broadcasters

As should already be obvious, we do not predefine a true *broadcast* primitive in ODL. We instead adopt the more common (and much better supported) view that object-oriented message passing is intrinsically point to point, although often mediated through dispatching and routing. However, the same strategies used for notification relays may be adapted readily to obtain the effects of uncoordinated broadcast.

A relay object can register a *set* of objects that might be interested in receiving some notice and then generate multiple propagation messages. For example:

```
class Rcvr op receive(m: Message); end
class Broadcaster
  members: SET[Rcvr];
  op bcast(m: Message);   % relay msg to all members
  op attach(r: Rcvr);     % add r to rcvrs
  op detach(r: Rcvr);     % delete r from rcvrs
end
```

This may be further refined and extended. For example, the object may offer a filtering service that allows members to receive only those kinds of messages for which they express interest.

Blackboards

An effective merger of polling and notification strategies is to externalize queuing to form a standard buffered producer-consumer design. Notifier (producer) objects send messages to a common queue serving as a "blackboard". The coordinator (consumer) object repeatedly takes these messages and performs the associated actions. In the simplest case, the consumer may just take the form:

```
op mainLoop { while true do msg := blackboard.take; perform(msg); end }
```

The blackboard may actually be split into several queues, perhaps even one per message type. This makes it easier for consumers to control the kinds of messages they are waiting for. Many such designs are discussed by Carriero and Galerntner [51]. These are readily amenable for expression in an object-oriented framework.

Collaboration

The coordination of joint actions does not always require explicit coordinator objects. Each of the participating objects may include protocols for dealing directly with the others. For example, the notification-based version of `TransferMgr` design could be further transformed to allow each of the participants to step the others through a transaction under appropriate conditions. The transformations are similar to those seen for double-dispatching in Chapter 21. For example:

```
class Checking_3 is Checking ...
   locals sv: fixed Savings; cmr: fixed Customer; keyMgr: KeyMgr; end
   op  withdraw(...) { ...
       if overdrawn then
           key := keyMgr.nextKey; sv.lock(key); cmr.lock(key);
           if sv.canWithdraw(amt) /\ rqd(cmr, self) then ... end;
           ...
       end }
end
```

The other classes must be modified accordingly. This eliminates the need for mediation at the expense of extreme identity and protocol coupling among participants, sometimes resulting in designs that are difficult to maintain.

Localizing Constraint Management

When objects are already structurally coupled for other reasons, similar localization techniques may be applied in a less disruptive fashion. Notification techniques may be used to move responsibility for managing class and relational constraints down to component objects rather than their hosts. For example, in our Square class we could define special versions of Point that maintain proper distance from each other whenever either is changed:

```
class DistancedPoint ...
   locals _x: Real <>; _y: Real <>; nbr: DistancedPoint; end
   x: real { _x? }
   y: real { _y? }
   op noPropShiftX(v: real) { _x.add(v); }
   op shiftX(v: real): () { _x.add(v); nbr.noPropShiftX(v); }
end
```

```
class Square_5
   locals lowerLeft: DistancedPoint; upperRight: DistancedPoint; end
   inv upperRight.x > lowerLeft.x,
       upperRight.x - lowerLeft.x = upperRight.y - lowerLeft.y
   inv lowerLeft.nbr = upperRight, upperRight.nbr = lowerLeft
   op shiftHorizontally(offset: real): () { lowerLeft.shiftX(offset); }
end
```

The invocation of `lowerLeft.shiftX` in `shiftHorizontally` maintains all invariants without explicit action on the part of the `Square`. The two forms of `Point::shiftX` (or any of several similar setups) are necessary to prevent looping of notifications.

22.2   Controlling Groups

Group interaction frameworks may be used to translate models usually denoted by *single* classes at the analysis level. These include a number of "master-slave" or "host-helper" designs, in which a controller schedules the actions of a group of worker objects. The normal intent is to hide the fact that these workers exist. These designs represent increasingly larger scale versions of basic delegation techniques.

In most controller designs it is important to ensure that the "outer" controller object appear as a single entity to all outside clients, not as a visible composite of specialists or helpers. This normally requires that none of the internal helpers *ever* "leak" their identities to clients. In many situations, this is arranged merely by ensuring that the controller serve as a barrier, forwarding requests to helpers, and later forwarding back results. A similar practice is to recast bidirectional client-host interactions into those in which the delegate performs a callback to the original client through an anonymous wrapper.

As long as the delegates perform *only* internal operations, there is nothing more to worry about. However, these designs do not intrinsically ensure that operations within slave or helper classes do not send messages that reveal identities to other objects who may thereafter bypass the host and deal directly (and incorrectly) with the helpers. Any message sent from a delegate that includes `self` as an argument could lead to this.

One way to avoid such problems automatically is to arrange that hosts send `self` to delegates as an extra argument for all delegated messages. Delegates then uniformly employ the received `apparentSelf` for all other messages. Some OO languages (e.g., SELF [222]) use variants of this protocol as built-in mechanisms, and to some, this is the only "true" sense of delegation (see, for example, [82, 232]). One obstacle to using this strategy is that the hosts must be prepared to "catch" all messages ordinarily coming back to their delegates in order to redelegate them or do anything else with them. Enabling hosts to do this by adding new public forwarding operations to outer interfaces is at best tedious, especially when delegation links may be rebound. For such reasons, OO languages using such protocols build them into the language proper.

However, as they scale up, these strategies encounter further problems revolving around visibility, identity, and interference. The structures surveyed in the remainder of this section are most appropriate when interactions between controllers and helpers are *communication-closed*. When this does not hold, the architectures and protocols must be modified to employ the kinds of coordination techniques described earlier in this chapter.

22.2.1 Multicast

A *collection* may be distributed among a set of objects, controlled by a single master that scatters requests and then gathers replies. Requests for set membership, etc., may then be *multicast* to all subcollections and run in parallel. The master does not usually need to gather *all* replies. For example, a set membership inquiry may be satisfied when any one of the slave subcollections replies affirmatively.

This idea leads to more general designs in which clients of a master-slave system may sequentially access any number of "answers" to queries, tasks, or problems. These answers may be maintained in a queue or similar collection held by the master, and accessed by clients. A bit of bookkeeping is necessary to keep track of things. For example:

```
class Master
  locals
    slaves: SET[Slave];
    answers: QUEUE[Answer];
    solving: Bool; init ~solving?
    problemID: Int; init problemID? = 0;
    nAnswers: Int;
  end
  op query(p: Problem)
    when ~solving? then {
      solving.t!; clear(answers); nAnswers.clr; problemID.inc;
      slaves.applyS(WRAP1(#1.doProblem(p, problemID?))) }
    else pend end
  op slaveReply(a: Answer, pid: int)
    when solving /\ pid=problemID? then {
      answers.put(a); nAnswers.inc;
      if nAnswers? = slaves.size then solving.f! end }
    else end
  op getNextAnswer: Answer { reply answers.take }
end
```

This design only supports solution of one problem at a time. Multiple problems may be handled by associating different queues with different problems and then reparameterizing things accordingly.

22.2.2   Worker Groups

Such designs may be expressed more easily via the definition of classes describing the higher-level structure and protocols. Worker groups (sometimes called *process groups*) are SETs or other collections of objects that all band together in computing a task or service. Worker groups may have features including:

- Multicast protocols in which a client or controller sends the same message to all members of the group, and then waits for *any* reply, *all* replies, a majority of replies, or a reply meeting some stated predicate.

- Guarantees that multicasts be *causally ordered*. All members of a group should receive the same messages in the same order, as established through sequencing and acknowledgment protocols.

- A set of actions to be taken whenever a worker object enters or leaves a group.

- Consistent methods for detecting failed workers (usually via probes and time-outs) and taking evasive action.

Hiding these details within groups themselves better encapsulates protocol mechanics while also simplifying the design of classes that use them. One such protocol is is *synchronous control*, in which a controller steps other objects through actions in a way that is known to conform to all task dependencies and interaction requirements. For example, the following design solves the `ImageCell` problem (Chapter 19) in a somewhat simpler and possibly more efficient way than our first attempt:

```
class CellStepper ...
  local g: WorkerGroup[ImageCell];
  op step: () {
    g.bcastA(WRAP1(#1.getNorth));
    g.bcastA(WRAP1(#1.getSouth));
    g.bcastA(WRAP1(#1.getEast));
    g.bcastA(WRAP1(#1.getWest));
    g.bcastA(WRAP1(#1.updateBrightness)) }
end
```

We assume here that `WorkerGroup::bcastA` is a multicast protocol that sends a message to all members and then waits for a completion reply from all of them before returning. The `ImageCell` operations must, of course, be redefined accordingly.

This arrangement avoids within-object dependency tracking at the price of synchronous processing. However, this can be an asset. It opens up a set of design methods based on "data parallel programming" [111], where a group of objects all do one thing, and then all another, and so on. These strategies are well suited to many fine-grained parallel programming environments. They are useful even in asynchronous systems. The framework results in *virtual synchrony* among slaves, thus simplifying controller design.

Many other coordination tasks become simpler when objects are structured into managed groups for the sake of performing particular tasks. For example, most, if not all intragroup communication may be performed via group multicast. Individual members do not need to keep track of others directly. For another example, locking may be performed via *token passing*, in which a single lock token is passed from member to member. Members only execute when they possess the token.

22.2.3 Fault Tolerance

Worker group designs may be employed to improve fault tolerance. For example, rather than distributing helper objects that maintain or solve different parts of tasks, they may all handle the *same* task. In this way, if any of them fail, answers may still be obtained.

Replicated service objects may be arranged in *server groups* in which client service requests are somehow multicast to all replicates. Any of several alternative designs may be employed, including:

Protocol objects: Clients must channel requests through protocol objects that serve as multicast controllers.

Cross-delegation: Each server replicates each request to all others. A coordination protocol ensures that only one member replies (through a callback).

Standby techniques: Each group contains a primary object that receives client requests and multicasts them to all others. Normally, only the primary object executes the service and replies back to the client. If it fails (as detected by a time-out), another standby object is chosen. Individual objects may serve on standby duty for many different tasks. There are several variants of this protocol, including *coordinator-cohort* designs [34].

To achieve fault tolerance, each replicate should be self-contained, and thus share no (or at least few) connections with other downstream service objects. This often requires the replication of additional objects that must also be kept in synchrony to maintain global consistency. For example, in a standby design, all server objects might maintain separate versions of some x: Int. The primary object should multicast all updates to standby objects. However, these updates should be acted upon only when it is known that the primary has successfully completed its task.

Replicated controllers.   Controllers and group managers themselves may be replicated. Further capabilities may be added to controllers in order to manage computation and detect problems. For example, a controller may send occasional probes that track participants, monitor progress, and detect failures. Some architectures and algorithms are described by Andrews [13]. Dealing with failure of a controller is a much more difficult issue. The members of the group must come to agreement about the nature of the failure and responsibility for recovery (see, e.g., [133]).

Tools.   Such protocols can be difficult to devise, implement, and validate. Existing protocols supported by tools such as ISIS may be encapsulated as black-box protocol objects and services at the design level, with the knowledge that corresponding implementations exist.

ISIS [33, 34] is a toolkit of protocols and related mechanisms (implemented in C) that facilitate development of reliable group interaction designs. ISIS includes support for fault-tolerant tracking and control of *process groups*, along with other higher-level protocols useful in common design architectures. ISIS supports a causal multicast protocol that ensures that each of a series of messages to a group are received in issued order by all members, along with coordinator-cohort support, group-based locking protocols, and so on.

22.2.4   Iterative Problem Solving

Further refinements apply to problems that must be solved iteratively by looping across phases that (1) divide the task across slaves, (2) have them compute some results, (3) gather up results, and (4) check if a full solution has finally been reached. Many large-scale scientific and engineering problems are readily, almost mechanically, decomposable in such terms. For example, assuming other appropriate declarations, a special kind of worker group could be designed as follows:

```
class ComputeGroup
  locals
    slaves: SET[Slave];  currentTask: Task; ctl: ProblemSplitter;
    numberReporting: Int; busy: Bool; client: Client;
    op scatter { numberReporting.clear;
        ctl.distributeProblem(slaves, currentTask);
        slaves.applyS(WRAP1(#1.computeAndReport)) }
  end
  op gather(c: Chunk,  s: Slave) {
    currentTask.incorporate(c);
    numberReporting.inc;
    if numberReporting? = slaves.size then
        if ~currentTask.done then scatter
        else client.result(currentTask); busy.f! end
    end }
  op newTask(t: Task, c: Client) when ~busy? then {
    busy.t!; currentTask := t; client := c; scatter } else pend end
end
```

Extensions include designs employing dynamic load balancing in which tasks are reconfigured based on the time it took for slaves to perform previous steps.

Blackboards

An alternative framework for iterative computation is to have the central coordinator serve as a *blackboard*, or work queue for the compute objects. This design is a minor variant of blackboard-based notification structures. In this case, the host initializes a set of worker objects, each of the form:

```
class TaskPerformer ...
  job: Job;  m: TaskManager;
  op mainLoop {
    while true do job := m.take; transform(job); m.put(job) end }
end
```

The `take` operation may be parameterized so that different kinds of `TaskPerformers` perform steps on jobs needing only their special talents. The results may then be fed back to be picked up by different specialists.

This is almost a mirror-image of previous designs. Rather than having the master send messages that may sit in queues until objects are ready to process them, the slaves themselves only take new tasks when they are done with others. Conversion from one form to the other is straightforward.

22.3   Open Systems

Open systems, in the sense coined by Hewitt [110] and Agha [4], are those in which new objects may dynamically join configurations, enter contracts, and generally behave as evolving self-organizing societies of interacting intelligent agents. Many of the specific architectural elements proposed for open systems (e.g., groups of *receptionists* that deal with external events) as well as for related distributed artificial intelligence frameworks (see, e.g., [116, 84]) are very much usable in the design of less experimental applications. However, techniques for reliably supporting the general paradigm do not appear well enough developed to admit routine exploitation.

22.3.1   Metalevel Reasoning

Among the primary hurdles in constructing open systems is supporting full-scale metalevel reasoning. Since new objects belonging to new classes may be introduced at any point, some or all objects must "understand" the underlying meaning of the base language so they can dynamically decode and create new attributes and operations, construct and instantiate new classes, and so on. In a sense, the objects themselves must be able to act as *designers*. Support requires more extensive forms of metaclasses and the like than are presented in Chapters 8 and 18. It also requires further exploitation of reflection than we have so far described. Objects and groups of objects may need to reconfigure themselves dynamically to deal with new situations, as described in [153].

While perhaps exotic, many metalevel facilities are currently supported in languages including CLOS [128] and have been used to good effect. For example, Paepcke [174, 175, 176, 177] discusses the extension of CLOS into PCLOS through the use of metalevel features in which objects behave as local, persistent, and/or cached entities depending on context. Similarly, Rao [187] describes a windowing system supporting programmer-accessible protocol specialization. For example, objects do not need to perform expensive screen updates when they find themselves embedded in nonoverlapping cells in a spreadsheet. Both of these applications are made simpler through the use of CLOS mechanisms enabling state and protocol descriptions to be dynamically modified rather than hard-wired.

22.3.2 Large-Scale Object Systems

Massively distributed object systems may soon pervade the planet. These open object systems do not require the use of fine-grained metalevel reasoning facilities. In fact, because of their scale and intended range of applicability, they require only the most minimal assumptions and information about participating coarse-grained distributed objects. This information generally consists only of a listing of those *services* that each object is willing to provide to others, especially those residing in foreign systems. Service specifications must be expressed in a common interface description language (e.g., CORBA IDL[169] – see Chapter 23).

The specification, design, and implementation of global open object systems is a very different enterprise than that of the application systems discussed in this book. In Chapter 23, we briefly discuss strategies for dealing with foreign systems. However, these methods can break down in the development of such systems themselves. Service interface descriptions are quite a bit weaker than specifications possible in self-contained systems. For example, one may no longer rely on object identity as an analysis, design, or implementation construct. Essentially all communication must use transparent service-based routing mechanisms resting on these weaker assumptions. Available coordination protocols, security measures, and testing techniques are similarly limited.

22.4 Summary

Transitions *interfere* when two or more sequences of actions may be interleaved in undesirable ways. Pragmatically, it is impossible to guarantee that no interference will occur in a system. However, safeguards, design policies, and control protocols may be used as needed to ensure atomicity and consistency. The translation of guarded transitions into concrete form must take potential interference into account.

Delegation provides a basis for scaling up control architectures. A number of ready-made design architectures exist and may be plugged into design efforts.

22.5   Further Reading

There are currently no general accounts or catalogs of OO design architectures. However, beyond the references cited in the text, many articles and papers describe case studies and overviews of particular examples. These may be found in proceedings of the *OOPSLA, ECOOP, Usenix C++*, and *TOOLS* conferences, as well as the *Journal of Object-Oriented Programming* and other magazines and journals.

Synchronization and interference control are central concerns in systems of all sorts. Chandy and Misra [54] describe design issues from a non-OO perspective. Andrews [12] is an excellent technical reference for many control and protocol issues. Apt and Olderog [15] discuss verification. Burns et al [47] describe joint action control in **Ada**. Aksit [7], Detlefs et al [79], and Guerraoui et al [102] describe particular OO transaction architectures.

Further discussions of aliasing in OO contexts may be found in Hogg et al [113]. Language-based interference analysis methods are discussed by Reynolds [189], America and de Boer [10], Jones [127] and Wills [229].

22.6   Exercises

1. Some OO designers and programmers with extensive experience claim never to have encountered an aliasing-related error, despite never having paid explicit attention to the issue. Why might this be so?

2. Explain why unchecked aliasing makes it very difficult to actually *verify* that concrete operations obey certain ==> effects.

3. Can locking be used to deal with self-interference?

4. Design a concrete queue class supporting put2(x, y) that places x and y on adjacent slots in the queue. Do this by controlling a simple queue.

5. Describe the locking protocols of a database system you are familiar with in ODL.

6. Revise and extend the transfer manager class and related classes to meet the full specifications of the automatic overdraft protection service described in Chapter 10.

7. Instead of using state-change notifications, why can't we just build "derivative sensing" in ODL as a primitive capability?

8. Design collection classes that could be used as slaves in the scatter/gather example.

9. Under which conditions would the synchronous `ImageCell` design be better than the asynchronous one?

10. "True" delegation is sometimes described as "self-substitution". Rework our characterization in these terms.

11. Describe in detail how a time daemon like that described in this chapter could be used to implement the automated payment service of Chapter 10.

12. Design a time daemon that accepts particular sequences of `Dates` to trigger actions rather than a set period.

Chapter 23

Clustering Objects

Most OO systems are implemented using a relatively small number of coarse-grained machine processes, or *clusters*, each containing a usually large number of "smaller" objects. Unless you are operating in an ideal automated OO systems development environment, the clustering of objects into processes is one of the main tasks of OO system design.

Clustering is a "packing" problem. A large number of "logical" objects must be embedded into a smaller number of "physical" objects. Each of these physical objects has the form of a standard system *process*, as supported by contemporary operating systems. Each process also serves as an interpreter in the sense of Chapter 15, simulating the actions of its "passivized" components.

In this chapter, we discuss strategies for clustering objects and basic properties of the system infrastructure needed to support them. In the next chapter, we focus on techniques for transforming the resulting embedded objects into passive form.

23.1 Clustering

It is possible to place strict *optimality* criteria on clustering strategies. On pure efficiency grounds, objects should be clustered to achieve the highest possible performance. However, this is a thoroughly useless guideline. Even if you did know the exact CPU and storage requirements of each object in a system, all object lifetimes, the exact communication times for all messages, and the exact resource capacities of all clusters, assigning them optimally is still an *NP-complete* "bin-packing" problem (see [96]). This means that all known algorithms for solving the problem are infeasibly time consuming.

Thus, clustering *must* be performed using heuristic approaches that provide acceptable solutions. For example, the *exact* number of objects generated during the lifetime of a system is usually unknowable. But the number of "big" or "important" objects is almost always at least approximately known, and suffices for clustering. Also, even if efficiency-based clustering could be made algorithmic, performance should not be the only criterion. Performance must be balanced against other design factors, such as maintainability, that argue for the use of functional and structural criteria in addition to resource concerns.

As is true for most decomposition problems, the most natural approach to clustering is top-down. First of all, the entire system may be considered as one big cluster, operating in the manner described by the kernel in Chapter 15. From there, major objects and groups of objects may be partitioned off using any agreed-on criteria. The process may then be repeated on these clusters until all resources are accounted for. These steps must also be applied to top-level `System` operations. However, rather than providing an explicit central or subdivided `System` object, these services may be replicated in each process requiring them. Only those top-level operations actually invoked in each cluster need be supported.

Generally, system designs are most understandable, maintainable, and extensible when cluster groupings correspond to structural and/or functional groupings. From the opposite point of view, attempts to cluster objects based purely via resource criteria sometimes reveal opportunities to refactor classes in conceptually meaningful ways. It is worth attempting to rationalize clusters retrospectively in this way, just to improve human factors and reduce complexity. Several idioms described in previous chapters (e.g., master-slave) may apply.

Most machines and operating systems allow for multiple processes. In these cases, several clusters may be assigned to the same machine. This may (or may not) slightly degrade performance, but allows conceptually meaningful partitioning criteria to be applied in a much larger number of cases. Reasonable choices about the number and size of cluster processes per machine depend on the underlying efficiency of operating system scheduling and interprocess communication mechanisms.

Because clustering remains something of a black art, it is very convenient to use a prototyping tool to assist in the evaluation of clusterings. The interpreter outlined in Chapter 15 may be extended to become a classic simulator by adding simulated communication delays for messages across tentative clusters.

23.1.1 Criteria

Many possible overlapping and/or incompatible criteria may be established. We list some here just to demonstrate the range of options.

Forced: Identify processes with objects as mandated in non-functional requirements documents.

Functional: Identify processes with coarse-grained objects identified in analysis, especially ensembles.

Structural: Identify processes with objects that are easy to isolate. For example, transaction loggers and other "message sinks" consume events generated by a large number of other objects without communicating back to them.

Compute-Based: Place any two objects that ever require substantial amounts of computation time simultaneously in different clusters.

Service-based: Isolate objects that perform well-known, generic services in their own processes.

Visibility-based: When systems constraints preclude full object communication, some objects (e.g., relays) should be housed in distinct processes to facilitate communication.

Task-based: Combine all of those objects involved in particular single-threaded tasks in a cluster.

Class-based: Allocate all objects of particular concrete classes to the same cluster.

Collection-based: Allocate all objects that may be members of the same collection object to the same cluster.

Link-based: Partition clusters so that as many as possible object links point to objects residing in the same cluster. This avoids *fragmentation*, in which objects include some components situated in one cluster and some in another.

Communication-based: Allocate heavily interacting objects to the same cluster.

Performance-based: Allocate slow objects to processes residing on fast computers.

Machine-based: Allocate objects that could exploit special machine characteristics to processes on those machines.

One-Per-Machine: Machines and systems that do not easily support multiprocessing should be assigned only one cluster process.

Device-based: Allocate objects that directly communicate with special devices to processes on the corresponding computers.

Recovery-based: Isolate failure-prone objects (e.g., those interacting with unreliable hardware) in their own processes to facilitate restarts, etc.

Maintenance-based: Isolate objects of classes that are most likely to change in the future.

Splitting Objects

An opposite problem may occur when objects are "too big" to fit into a cluster. In this case, the class needs to be further decomposed. This is not usually an issue in compositionally designed systems.

Cluster Clusters

After a first-level pass at clustering, the individual clusters may themselves be clustered, in a different sense. Groups of heavily intercommunicating clusters may be targeted for placement on one or more machines with fast interprocess communication facilities. For example, if a system resides on several high-speed local area networks (LANs), which are in turn connected by slow modem connections, then clusters should be situated accordingly. Wide-area (long-haul) communication is substantially slower and less reliable than LAN communication, which is in turn slower and less reliable than communication across processes residing on the same machine.

Dynamic Clustering

When resources are not fixed and additional processes may be created dynamically during system execution, clustering may be equally dynamic. Except in special cases, this is hard to achieve. Tractable situations are often limited to those in which the creation of objects of certain classes is always performed by generating a new process.

Migration

Even though clusters are designed around the management of particular sets of objects, in many cases it is sensible and desirable to *migrate* an object from one cluster to another. While conceptually straightforward, this is fraught with implementation difficulties, including synchronization problems and inter-cluster coordination of storage management. It is an option only if system infrastructure services are available to manage this.

Redundancy

A more common and less intimidating variant of migration is object *redundancy*. Clones of objects may reside in multiple clusters. When these objects are stateless, or just immutable for the duration of their duplicate existences, this is easy to arrange. When the objects are mutable, additional support is required to maintain full consistency across copies. This is a very special form of constraint management, in which all changes in one version must transparently trigger changes in the other (see Chapter 22). Redundancy is also a means for achieving greater system reliability. Entire clusters may be redundantly implemented.

Other Mapping Strategies

In some systems, it may be necessary or preferable to avoid the notion of static clusters all together. System-level processes may be able to represent and execute code for different design-level objects at different times. Other mediator objects must route requests to the currently appropriate process. This is an extreme form of dynamic clustering and migration. For example, the states of objects may be centrally held on persistent media, and reconstructed in suitable processes when needed. Systems composed under these assumptions differ in numerous small ways from those adhering to the better-supported models that we will focus on in the remainder of this chapter. Conceptually straightforward but implementation-intensive adaptations are necessary to support an extra level of indirection in the mapping from objects and clusters to processes.

23.1.2   Examples

Clustering is usually much easier than our remarks might suggest. Many of the criteria amount to the application of a bit of common sense.

For example, the system described in Chapter 10 declared `ATM` and `Bank` as highest level subsystems. Assuming there is at least one processor per physical ATM, then device and communications criteria lead to one `ATM` object per ATM station. If there were more than one processor or process available per ATM station, reliability criteria then argue for isolation of individual device-based control systems, `CardControl` and `DispenserControl`. From there, visibility criteria lead to isolation of the communications interface with the `Bank`.

The `Bank` subsystem might be housed on a single powerful computer, or spread out over many computers depending, of course, on the configuration. Even if it were on a single computer it would still be wise to use other criteria to place objects in multiple processes. Structural and service criteria suggest splitting off time based services, perhaps as centralized into a time daemon. If a nonintegrated database is being used for persistent management of `Accounts`, `Clients`, etc., then reliability, maintenance, and communication criteria argue for isolating the database interface veneer objects as processes.

If the `Bank` is physically distributable, then communications performance and visibility criteria lead to separation of processes that communicate with the `ATM` objects. If, instead of a foreign database, extensive use is made of large collections (possibly themselves supporting persistence), these may be split into master-slave configurations. The most important ones (e.g., `ActiveAccounts`) may be supported redundantly through shadowed multiple clusters. Associated `LockMgrs` and the like may also be isolated in processes. Other objects responsible for control logic (e.g., billing) may be split off from there, until all resources are accounted for.

23.2   Cluster Objects

The basic technique for packing objects into clusters is to have each cluster object subsume responsibility for construction, maintenance, dispatching, and execution of held objects and operations. Each of the component objects must ultimately be "passivized", as described in Chapter 24. In principle, cluster objects are just big artificial ensemble objects. Thus, clusters are objects with many, many `own` components that happen to be physically embedded within a common "address space". For much of

Part II, we have downplayed premature commitment to representational embedding, in part to facilitate mappings into clusters.

These designs may be expressed in **ODL** using the attribute qualifier `packed`, that denotes physical embedding requirements of a passive stored component inside another object. Sometimes, this is all that is necessary to define the resulting cluster structure. For a too-simple example, a `LampV1` (Chapter 16) that is isolated in its own cluster may embed its `Bool` switch component via:

```
class LampV1C is LampV1 ...
  packed switch: Bool <>
end
```

In the resulting configuration, each cluster protects components through a well-defined interface. All intercluster communication must pass through cluster interfaces. The system as a whole may be designed and viewed in terms of a relatively small number of possible interactions between very large-grained objects. In practice, clustering usually carries additional constraints, including:

Impermeability: Objects residing within different clusters may not be able to communicate directly, or even know of one another's existence.

Restricted Messages: All intercluster communication is to be directed to the clusters themselves, not inner components. Further, these messages may need to be transformed into different formats and protocols.

Persistence: Because processes are volatile, some or all component objects may be redundantly represented on persistent media.

Resource Management: Clusters may be responsible for keeping track of component objects and their storage and computational requirements.

System Chores: Clusters may need to play roles in keeping track of other clusters, detecting deadlock, restarting processes, and other bookkeeping.

23.2.1 Cluster Interfaces

The interface of each cluster consists of the set of reachable operations on its inner objects. The nicest cases occur when a cluster holds a single reachable object. If this is the case, then the cluster agent interface is the same as that object. Otherwise, the interface must be crafted to support a composite of operations. Cluster interfaces, like all others, need to be meaningful and understandable. This provides an additional reason to perform clustering using structural and functional criteria when possible.

A common technique for representing the interfaces of other clusters inside their clients is through *proxies* (stubs). Proxy classes are among the most trivial kinds of wrappers. They generate cluster-local objects with interfaces identical to those of nonlocal objects (i.e., other clusters). All within-cluster messages consist only of local invocations of operations on these proxies, which in turn forward them to other clusters via interprocess communication facilities.

23.2.2   Interfaces to External Software

Process-level objects may need to communicate with software entities in addition to those represented by other clusters. Most systems interact with other existing software. This software is most commonly non-object-oriented. However, it is still possible to provide object-oriented veneers with respect to desired interactions with the system being designed.

Among the purest applications of abstract class design is interface design for *foreign* software objects that will not even be implemented as part of the target system, but must be used just as they are currently implemented. This may be approached through pure black-box techniques. As far as abstract declarations are concerned, there is little difference between an external component and something that must be implemented. The only problem is that the way in which its functionality is defined and implemented is normally fixed and beyond a designer's control.

Veneers

Interactions between any external component and the system at hand always need to be mediated by a layer of internal processing that *is* controllable, as long as it has the right properties when seen from the external component's point of view. Thus, internal *veneer* classes may be defined via standard constructs, and concrete classes may put together the necessary connections. For example, the application might interact with a native file system in ways described by classes including:

```
class File ...
  op write(c: char) ...;
end
class Directory is File ... end
```

Effects, constraints, and the like can still be described, but the actual composition and computation cannot be determined without committing to a particular programming language, operating system, etc.

These techniques are especially useful for isolating common utility services, which may then be specialized for particular machines, operating systems, and configurations. In particular, a hierarchy of abstract classes can describe particular operating system functions, and a set of concrete classes can be defined to encapsulate system-dependent functionality. For example:

```
class OpSystemInterface ... end

class MC68000UnixSysInterface is OpSystemInterface ... end
```

Atkinson [17] provides a more detailed account of strategies for designing heterogeneous interface classes using the **Ada** OO shell language **DRAGOON**. Most of the ideas may be applied to interface design in general. Similar design steps may be necessary to deal with heterogeneous foreign subsystems with which the system may communicate.

Legacies

The same basic strategies hold for designing-in old non-OO software that may be at least partially *converted* to become a component of the current system. In such cases, the front end of this software may be first encapsulated as a set of class interfaces, along with a bit of internal processing to link internal and external views and conventions. Perhaps over time, internals of the legacy may be "objectified" layer by layer, as far as necessary or desirable.

The most common general form of foreign interface layering is a set of classes that encapsulates arguments, global variables, and other data used in foreign functions as class components, along with relay operations that gather arguments together as necessary to submit to the external components.

For example, if a foreign `fileOpen` procedure required file names, directories, and access modes as arguments, and returned success or failure on completion, the interface `File` class might have `name`, `dirname`, `mode`, `isOpen` attributes, along with an argumentless `open` operation which sends the right arguments (perhaps after some data format conversion) to the `fileOpen` procedure and records the results.

A second layer of conversion might then replace `fileOpen` by directly incorporating its functionality in `open(File)` and/or other components. This strategy could be continued down to the level of operating system file handling primitives, surely using subclassing to manage the different ways of doing things across different operating systems and computers:

```
class UnixFile is File ...
    op write(c: char) ...;
end
```

23.2.3   Clusters and Object Identity

Clustering may lead to *overencapsulated* objects. Embedded objects cannot always communicate in the manner in which they were originally designed. Previously visible objects become hidden within clusters. This is *not* all bad. The inability of foreign objects to exploit internal identities improves security and provides effortless enforcement of local/non-local distinctions. However, when communication is required, it must be supported.

Communication via object identities need not be a problem. In a single-process design, object identity is implemented by ultimately (perhaps through several layers) associating identities with *addresses* of some kind or another. Similarly, operation and class identities are mapped into code and bookkeeping table addresses or surrogates. But any object that is visible *across* clusters (including dedicated persistent data managers, if employed) must have an identity that holds outside of the current process.

Process boundaries do not always correspond to near versus far identities. On systems with *lightweight processes* (LWPs), different processes may share address spaces. This greatly simplifies mappings and transformations. But lightweight processes are only useful for clusters decomposed for functional reasons. Except on shared-memory multiprocessors, LWPs share a CPU, and thus are hardly ever useful for supporting clusters divided for resource reasons. Operating systems and hardware technology may someday solve such problems on a wider scale. For example, computers with 64-bit addresses might hold near or far identities using the same internal representations. Object-oriented operating systems may someday help automate address mappings and translations.

You cannot currently depend on a system to reliably support system-wide identity mappings. However, the representation and management of system-wide identities may be among the services offered by object-oriented databases and other object management systems. There are few reasons for not relying on such services when putting together a system in which object identities may be passed between clusters.

Unless using a system enabling the common representation of both clusters and embedded objects, cluster interfaces should minimize or eliminate operations that somehow refer to the identities of embedded objects. However, this is not always possible. When external objects send messages originally meant to be received by objects that have been embedded in a cluster, they must first discover which cluster to send a message to, and then send some kind of subidentifier as an argument in the cluster-level message. The recipient cluster must then somehow decode this and then emulate the desired processing.

There are many ways to form such internal identities and resulting "fat pointer" tuples of (*clusterID*, *localID*) needed to identify internal objects uniquely. Ready-made formats may be available through tools and services. Other choices range from simple unprotected (*MachineID*, *processID*, *virtualAddress*) tuples to *port* constructs to securely mapped pseudo-IDs for both clusters and objects. In any case, all external messages originally of the form:

```
x.meth
```
must be converted into a form such as:
```
x's-cluster.meth(x's-local-id),
```
which in turn is translated into the format required by the host language and interprocess communication tools. As mentioned, *proxy* mechanisms make this substantially easier by localizing and hiding at least parts of these conversions.

Even in 100% OO system environments, these measures cannot normally solve the problem of dealing with *all* foreign objects that a system may deal with. Different OO services may employ different ID representations and conventions. IDs received from nonconforming foreign systems must be used in a pure black-box fashion. For example, it may be impossible even to perform identity tests among two foreign IDs to see if they refer to the same object. Two IDs that compare as equal may not actually refer to the same object if they were generated by two different foreign systems. Two that compare as different may reflect different encodings of IDs referring to the same object.

23.3 System Tools and Services

The overall physical architecture of a system may depend in part on requirements-level constraints, but more commonly depends on the availability of system-level tools and services. Points on this space include the following.

Traditional.   Assuming that minimal interprocess communication services are available, designs can be mapped to the most common and traditional architectures and services using a fixed number of known processes, using impermeable cluster interfaces, only admitting interprocess messages directed at clusters, using hard-wired point-to-point interprocess message strategies, limiting interprocess message formats, and mapping persistence support to a non-OO database service.

Brokered.   If a centralized interprocess message handling service is available, then some of these restrictions may be lifted. Process interfaces may take a standard form, guided by tools that provide protocols for dealing with the service. Processes may be dynamically constructed and register their interfaces. All or some interprocess messages may be mediated by the broker service. At least some transmission of object identities may be supported.

OODB-based.   If an object-oriented database is employed (perhaps in addition to, or in cooperation with brokering), then full OO communication is likely to be supportable without significant design transformations. OODBs also typically provide support for locking, caching, versioning, long-term checkin/checkout, crash recovery, security, heterogeneous data formats, transaction control, and other necessary and useful features of persistent storage management.

Ideal.   An ideal OO support system would make most of this chapter irrelevant. Systems that provide infrastructure to automatically and transparently cluster, dispatch, maintain, and manage distributed objects appear to be within the realm of technical feasibility. But they do not exist outside of experimental projects as of this writing.

In the remainder of this section, we survey some basic considerations governing the ways in which processes may be constructed and managed. Even at coarse design levels, strategies are often bound to the use of particular tools and support systems that will be used in subsequent implementation. We will restrict ourselves to general issues.

23.3.1 Process Shells

A layer of care-taking capabilities must underly clusters in order to deal with issues that escape the bounds of the virtual system constructed during class design. One way to address these matters is to assume that clusters have an associated *shell*. This shell is an interface of sorts between the virtual system and the operating system (or bare hardware) on which it resides. As far as the virtual system is concerned, there might be one shell overseeing all clusters, one per cluster, or anything in between. Shells are merely abstractions of low-level services. There may not be any one software component that is identifiable as a `shell` object. Instead, the required capabilities are most likely obtained through collections of language based run-time systems, operating system services and even hardware support.

Unless you are building an operating system, you cannot actually design a shell, but instead must learn to live with the peculiarities of existing capabilities. The nature of common hardware and operating systems demands that shells be considered intrinsically interruptible. But they must deal with interruptions in a magical way, somehow saving and restoring state as necessary. Shells are also privileged with the ability to interrupt, probe, stop, suspend, resume, and/or restart cluster objects, perhaps even if they are otherwise conceptually uninterruptible. Given this, we might define some of the capabilities of a generic shell:

```
class Shell ...
   own proc: Any;        % the cluster object
   op start;             % (re)initialize proc
   op shutdown;          % gracefully shutdown proc
   op halt;              % immediately halt proc
   op suspend;           % stop proc and save state
   op resume;            % resume proc from last suspended state
   op ping: Packet;      % tell sender whether proc is alive
   op rcv(p: Packet);    % decode message packet and send to proc
end
```

This is a pure black-box description. All of these capabilities must be implemented through *magic*. Again, there will probably not be any single software object or service that implements this interface.

23.3.2   Process Control

System-wide process control software resides one level below cluster shells. A wide range of services may be available, spanning from none to all of the following:

- · process construction
- · process deletion
- · moving processes across processors
- · replicating processes across machines
- · shutting down processes while persistently saving their states
- · restarting apparently dead processes
- · authentication and access control facilities
- · system-level fault tolerance support through redundant processes
- · logging facilities for recording interprocess message traffic
- · registries reporting the identities of system processes
- · centralized catastrophic system error handlers
- · determining the best machines on which to create new processes
- · highly reliable messaging facilities
- · probes for discovering whether processes are still alive
- · probes for discovering how busy (loaded) particular machines are
- · probes for determining routing information across processes
- · probes for detecting deadlock and initiating recovery
- · time-out and retry facilities for failed interprocess messages
- · information sharing for coordinated intercluster storage management
- · services to broadcast and/or synchronize `time` across processes

Design and implementation of a complete set of such services is tantamount to the construction of a distributed operating system. However, tools and services handling most tasks exist for most systems. Small-scale process management can be performed by directly invoking relevant system services when necessary. This may be approached by building classes and special-purpose tools that isolate the interfaces to such services.

23.3.3   Interprocess Communication Support

Interprocess communications services minimally support pass-by-description style messages routed to their immediate recipients. On heterogeneous systems, state values may be passed among processes using intermediaries that interconvert basic value type representation formats across machines. This is normally accomplished with the help of tools and conventions that convert concrete value representations into canonical forms, *marshall* them into interprocess message packets, and decode them at the other end.

OO designs require services that support one-way point-to-point messages and/or synchronous bidirectional interprocess protocols. Other protocols may be layered on top of these, but only with substantial design effort and/or tool support. Of course, the more protocols supported, the easier the implementation. Standard remote procedure call (RPC), as well as RPC-with-time-out mechanisms are widely available. These may or may not be integrated with special facilities for interacting with timers and I/O devices.

Proxies

Proxies are within-process objects that serve as local stand-ins for remote clusters. Proxy classes are best generated by tools that accept descriptions of cluster interfaces, and simultaneously construct entities representing both the internal and external views. The internal version is embedded only in the single process implementing the interface; all others get external versions. If proxy *classes* cannot be generated automatically, non-OO tools that generate proxy *procedures* are usable after making some minor compromises and/or building corresponding veneers.

Lightweight Processes

For clusters that are isolated for non-performance-based reasons, lightweight processes are a simpler alternative. Because LWPs share address spaces, there may be no need to use proxies for interprocess communication. In the best case messages may be sent directly to the principal object(s) in other clusters. However, for uniformity, lightweight process communication may still go through proxies that are specially implemented to take advantage of LWP communication optimizations.

Topologies and Dispatching

The basic rules by which cluster processes know of each other's existences and capabilities must be selected. Interprocess communication topologies corresponding to the routing structures described in Chapter 21 are supported to varying extents by contemporary software services, utilities, and management facilities.

23.3.4   CORBA

The **OMG** Common Object Request Broker Architecture [169] is an example of a system-level framework assisting in some of the design and implementation tasks described in this chapter. As of this writing, CORBA implementations are not widely available, but it is predicted to be among the most commonly employed services for OO systems in the near future. Also, because it is new, we have no significant first-hand experience with details. We will restrict ourselves to describing a few features that illustrate how **CORBA** supports distributed OO system design and corresponding programming tasks.

The Object Request Broker (ORB) is a semicentralized brokering (dispatching) service that is generally structured as a *relay*. It is "semicentralized" in that accommodations are made for coordinating multiple brokers, but it may be treated as a central service by applications.

Process-level objects register their class interfaces with the ORB in order to receive messages from other objects. Messages from clients are then relayed through the ORB to their recipients. Clients normally communicate with the ORB through proxies (or "adaptors") generated by **CORBA** tools geared to particular languages (including C++). These in turn ordinarily invoke native interprocess communication services. However, the **CORBA** specification includes provisions that make it possible to support efficient lightweight process communication and even within-process messaging.

Class interfaces are specified using the Interface Definition Language (IDL). **IDL** is similar in structure to the declarative aspects of C++. Interfaces may be described as subclasses of others. The rules generally follow the same abstract subclassing conventions as **ODL**. IDL supports approximately the same primitive types as **ODL**, but with the usual provisions for specific word sizes, different character sets, etc. It also includes C-like unions, enumerations, and structures. A process-level object reference (ID) type is defined and used to support OO messaging conventions of point-to-point messages with copy-in/copy-out or process-object-reference arguments and results. Object references have pure black-box semantics. Reference identity tests are not explicitly supported. They may be hand-crafted for the ID representations used in any given system.

Two kinds of operations may be declared. Operations marked as `oneway` correspond to **ODL** one-way ops. Others are defined as RPC-style blocking ops that may be declared to raise any number of named, structured, exceptions. Simple `set/get` procedures are automatically generated for IDL `attribute` declarations. Only `gets` are generated for `readonly` attributes. These map well to stored **ODL** fns. For example, a process that maintains a simple buffer of integers may be defined in IDL as:

```
interface Buffer
{
  readonly attribute int empty;
  readonly attribute int full;
  oneway    put(int item);
  int       take();
};
```

IDL is, by design, "weaker" than notations such as ODL. It is not computationally complete. It is used to generate proxies and related structures that are then bound to code written in other languages. At the declarative level, it does not contain detailed semantic annotations such as invariants, effects, and triggering conditions. It does not allow declaration of internal (`local`) structure, the existence of links to other objects, or constraints among such objects. When translating ODL, classes that share the same interface but differ across such dimensions may be treated as variant instances of the same interface class. Conversely, one process-level ODL object may be defined to support multiple interfaces in IDL.

23.4   Persistence

Rather than individually listing `packed` components, clusters may be described as containing one or more *repositories* that in turn hold all passive within-cluster objects. Recall from Chapter 18 that repositories are objects that both generate and track objects. Repositories form natural venues for managing the storage requirements of component objects in a cluster. In the next chapter, we describe *internal* storage management techniques in which a repository or other agent tracks lifetimes of embedded cluster objects. Here we discuss situations where managed objects must live on even when a cluster and its repository (or repositories) are killed, suspended, and/or restarted. In these cases, objects must be maintained persistently.

Our *design* attitude about persistence is a little backward from some others. We consider the "real" objects to be active. Persistent media merely hold snapshots of state information needed to reinitialize or reconstruct functionally identical objects in case the current ones somehow fail or must be made dormant. This is in opposition to the database-centric view that the "real data" live in a database, and are transiently operated on by a database manager and other programs.

The interaction between any given object and its persistent representation is a form of constraint dependence. State changes must be mirrored on persistent media. This can be simplified by standardizing on a simple get/set protocol for interacting with the persistent representation. This meshes well with most database update facilities.

There are several options. Objects may send update messages to persistence managers themselves whenever they change state, or only at selected intervals. Alternatively, repositories or other agents may intercept messages and forward them both to the internal objects as well as to caretakers that perform the associated updates on the shadow database representations. These may be further combined with locking mechanisms, replication, failure detection, and related control strategies. For example, updates need not be directly shadowed if it is OK to employ a locking check-out/check-in protocol in which objects are constructed from their persistent representations, exclusively operated on, and then later checked back in by transferring their states back to the database.

23.4.1 Saving and Restoring Objects

The simplest form of persistence is a save/restore mechanism. A repository may support save(f:File) and restore(f:File) operations to read and write all held objects to a file. These may be triggered automatically by timers or other events (for saving) and re-initialization or error recovery routines (for restoring). They may be buttressed with history log files that keep track of changes to objects between saves. Because of their complexity and limitations, *ad hoc* save/restore strategies are limited to occasional, small-scale use.

Dealing with links. Persistent storage formats may be based on the description records discussed in Chapter 17. Saving and restoring objects that are fully describable through attribute description records is relatively straightforward. However, relational and composite objects are visibly dependent on links to other objects that must be maintained across saves and restores.

The mechanics of saving and restoring such objects interact in the usual ways with object identity. The only thing that can be saved to a file is a *description* of an object, not an active object itself. Upon restoration, the description may be converted to a *new* object with the same state but possibly a different identity. The repository must shield the rest of the system from such philosophical dilemmas, perhaps using variants of pseudo-identities and smart links discussed in Chapters 18 and 22. A TABLE may be constructed to provide an integer (or whatever) pseudo-ID for each saved object. Links may then be output using pseudo-ID equivalents. During restoration, the table may be dynamically reconstructed, but with pseudo-IDs mapped (or "swizzled") to the new internal equivalents.

Persistent object stores. Tools exist to simplify and extend basic persistence support. As noted in Chapter 22, Kala provides persistence mechanisms specifically geared to OO systems. Conceptually, it uses a *write once* strategy in which each desired state (or version) of each object may be persistently stored and recovered. Inaccessible versions are garbage collected. Related access, locking, and transaction control services are also provided.

Reifying classes. Persistence support requires that *class* descriptions be represented persistently. A hunk of bits representing an object on disk does you no good unless you know its class type in a form that allows interpretation and reconstruction of the object. Thus, representational conventions must be established for describing attributes, operations, messages, and so on, as briefly described in Chapter 18. However, these must be extended to deal with concrete code bodies if they are not already part of the executable image. Binary executable code implementations may differ across hardware architectures. The support mechanics are not only target language dependent but also machine dependent.

Evolution and versioning. Among the most difficult issues in persistent object management of any form is *schema evolution*: What do you do when someone changes the definition of a class? The basic OO paradigm nicely supports restructurings, refinements and other improvements to classes throughout the software development, maintenance, and evolution process. However, when classes describing persistently managed objects are modified, it can be difficult to cope with all of the resulting system problems. These are not limited to the need to redesign and/or reimplement persistent support structures. For example, some clients may only work with previous definitions of classes. Outdated classes and objects may be kept around in order to minimize impact. However, this requires a *versioning* facility, in which version indicators are attached to each class and object, perhaps along with mechanisms to upgrade versions in-place.

Introducing classes.   Both of the previous concerns apply, even more so, when a running system must be able to accommodate instances of classes that were not even defined when the system started running. If the system cannot be restarted, it is necessary to introduce infrastructure to interpret, represent, allocate, and execute new descriptions of classes and objects.

Security.   Persistent representations may require qualitatively different access control and authentication mechanisms than active objects. Because they typically reside in file structures and/or other media accessible outside of the running application, general-purpose system or database policies and mechanisms must be relied on.

23.4.2   Relational Databases

Relational databases (RDBs) operate solely on values, not objects. In order to use an RDB for persistence support, identities *must* be mapped to pseudo-ID values. When an RDB is used extensively for such purposes, it is a good idea to build these into objects themselves, as `unique` key values. These pseudo-IDs may then simultaneously serve as database indexing keys, as well as key arguments that may be sent to relays and name servers to determine internal identities.

   Although many snags may be encountered, the design of database relations underlying a set of objects is conceptually straightforward. Several alternative approaches and increasingly many tools are available for designing RDBs to support OO applications.

   When persistence is supported using a stand-alone database service, implementation is usually based on a structured interface to the database's native data definition and manipulation facilities. For example, in the case of relational databases, an interface class may be defined to mediate `SQL` commands.

   The simplest situations occur for concrete entities that behave as "data records" (e.g., our `MailingLabel` classes). Any class with an interface that sets and gets values from `owned` internal components transparently translates into an RDB table with updatable "value fields" corresponding to the components.

   Classes with essential or visible links must represent these links through pseudo-IDs. When these links are fixed and refer to other `concrete` objects, these may then key into the appropriate tables. But in the much more typical cases where they are rebindable and/or refer only to abstract classes, secondary tags and tables must be employed that "dispatch" an ID to the appropriate concrete table. For example, a link listed with type `Any` might actually be bound to some `MailingLabelV1` object.

This may be handled via a layer of processing in the database interface that maintains a table of IDs along with concrete type-tags, and re-issues RDB requests based on tag retrievals. Without tools, the normalization problems stemming from such schemes are difficult to resolve.

23.4.3 Object-Oriented Databases

OODBs normally provide the most natural mechanisms for persistently maintaining objects. OODB design and OO design amount to nearly the same activities. OODBs use the same kinds of constructs as the other parts of OO systems. While models and their details vary widely across different OODBs, all of them support basic constructs including classes, attributes, objects, and collections. Certain OO-like "extended relational" database systems provide similar constructs. All are designed to maximize performance for typical OO operations.

OODBs vary significantly in how they are accessed and used. Many OODBs are designed as supersets of particular OO programming languages. Additional persistence constructs are supported on top of the base language, enabling more transparent programming and usage. Others are stand-alone services, accessed via "object-oriented SQL" (OSQL) and corresponding language-based interfaces.

OSQL

We will illustrate using OSQL. Several variants exist. The examples here are based on one supported by at least early versions of Iris/OpenODB [93]. They are phrased in the user-oriented OSQL language rather than the language-based interfaces that would actually be employed within a system.

Like ODL, OSQL separates value (LITERAL) types from object types (links). Unlike ODL classes (TYPEs) and subclasses (SUBTYPEs) are always defined independently from attributes. Attributes (and most everything else) are defined as FUNCTIONS. Stored attributes are so annotated. Computed attributes may be coded as other OSQL statements.

Queries are class-based. The most common general form of a query is:

```
SELECT x, y                         (vars to be returned)
FOR EACH X x, Y y, Z z              (all participants)
WHERE R(x, y, z) AND S(x, y) AND T(x)   (predicates)
```

Any query may result in a *bag* of objects. The individual elements are sequentially traversable using a cursor mechanism. Indices may be requested for particular attributes in order to speed up access for otherwise slow attribute-based queries. Other constructs are illustrated in the following examples:

```
CREATE TYPE Counter;
CREATE FUNCTION val(Counter) -> INTEGER AS STORED;

CREATE TYPE Person;
CREATE FUNCTION name(Person) -> CHAR(20) AS STORED
CREATE FUNCTION gender(Person) -> CHAR AS STORED
CREATE FUNCTION nicknames(Person) -> SET(CHAR(20)) AS STORED;
CREATE FUNCTION parent(Person) -> Person AS STORED;

CREATE FUNCTION parentName(Person p) -> Person AS OSQL
  BEGIN RETURN name(parent(p)); END;

CREATE FUNCTION mother(Person child) -> Person AS OSQL
  SELECT m
  FOR EACH Person m
  WHERE parent(child) = m AND gender(m) = "f";

CREATE TYPE Employee SUBTYPE OF Person;
CREATE FUNCTION salary(Employee) -> INTEGER AS STORED;
```

Instances are constructed by binding initial values to all stored attributes (in a CREATE INSTANCE statement). Types, functions, and instances may all be deleted. All stored OSQL attribute changes are performed through set/put mechanics. For example:

```
CREATE FUNCTION ChangeName(Person p, CHAR(20) newname) AS
  UPDATE name(p) := newname;
```

Updates to set-valued attributes and functions are performed using the operations ADD and REMOVE. These are analogous to ODL collection operations. A few simple arithmetic functions are also provided. All other computational operations are performed through bindings to user-supplied external operations.

All updates implicitly generate locks. Sets of updates are committed only when explicitly requested (through COMMIT). ROLLBACK commands abort uncommitted updates. Intermediate SAVE-POINTS may be requested and rolled back to.

23.5 Summary

Clustering objects into processes is an ill-defined problem. Heuristic criteria may be employed to good effect. While clustering has no impact on the general forms of designs, it does not usually have beneficial effects on concrete details.

Clusters must be connected to the underlying computational substrate through a range of system services that may be abstracted as *shells*. Numerous services may be required to realize clusters. They range from those requiring low-level "magical" powers, to those in which interface classes to foreign services provide the necessary coupling and functionality, to those that are in full control of the constructed system itself.

Reliability is enhanced through persistence. Although OODB services provide the best vehicles for managing persistence, most other schemes can be accommodated. Subclassing and the need to preserve object identity separate OO persistence, storage management, and related support services from those of most non-OO systems.

23.6 Further Reading

Distributed object management services and object-oriented operating systems are surveyed by Chin and Chanson [56]. Comparable non-OO system design strategies are described, for example, by Shatz [199]. Atkinson [17] discusses OO physical system design in Ada. Fault tolerant system support is discussed in more depth by Cristian [65]. System-specific manuals remain the best guides for most process management issues. Schmidt [195] presents examples of class veneers on system services. Cattell [52] (among others) provides a much fuller introduction to OO and extended relational database systems. As of this writing, *automated* object clustering is just beginning to be studied as a research topic; see, e.g., [55].

23.7 Exercises

1. Most non-OO accounts of distributed processing concentrate on *splitting*, not *clustering*. Why?

2. How would you cluster the ATM system if there were 100 ATM stations, each with an associated IBM PC, and 1000 other IBM PCs (but nothing else) available? Why would you want more details of the class designs before answering?

3. List some advantages and disadvantages of clusters having any knowledge of between-cluster dispatching matters.

4. Describe how to build proxy classes using only RPC stub generator tools.

5. A cluster residing on a small non-multitasking machine *is*, in a sense, the machine itself. Explain how to deal with this.

6. The described version of **OSQL** contains no access control features. Is this an asset or a liability?

7. Write the **OSQL** declarations necessary to provide persistent support for the Account class.

Chapter 24

Designing Passive Objects

Clustering objects into processes yields a two-tiered architecture. The system as a whole appears as a relatively small number of interacting process-level active objects. Within each cluster lie all the passive objects that have been packed inside it. Internal cluster design activities perform necessary and desirable transformations applicable to those unfortunate objects that find themselves operating in a nonautonomous computational environment.

24.1 Transformations

Each process-level cluster serves as an *agent*, conceptually including:

- mechanisms to receive messages from other clusters
- mechanisms to send messages to other clusters
- a repository of embedded passive objects
- a message queue
- an interpreter (CPU).

This is just a small variation of our basic object model. Each of these properties *could* be ascribed to any object at all. In fact, each cluster serves as an OO simulation kernel as described in Chapter 15. But there are now two additional considerations reflecting the fact that clusters communicate with others. The queue must be able to receive messages from other clusters. Incoming messages that conform to those listed in the cluster's external interface are placed on the queue via system level magic. Also, the

457

agent must be able to send external messages to other clusters, normally as isolated via proxies or related mechanisms.

The addition of intercluster messaging transforms each cluster into a special kind of joint action coordinator (Chapter 22). Not only are the states of all external objects beyond its control, but all internal objects are purely passive and unprotected. However, from a suitably abstract perspective, cluster agents still perform basic interpretation in the manner described in Chapter 15:

- Take from the queue any action that has all of its triggering constraints satisfied and process it:

    o If it is an object construction event, create a new (passive) object with the required initial states and attributes.

    o Else if it is an elementary state change operation on a primitive object, then directly compute it.

    o Else place all component events listed in the body of the transition on an appropriate queue (perhaps that of a remote cluster).

The nature and form of internal passive objects still meet our definition of objecthood in Chapter 1. Any object and its class may be cast in a form that enables passive simulation by a cluster agent. We do not need new **ODL** constructs to distinguish passive zero-threaded objects from active ones. In fact, we adopt the best pragmatic notation later in this chapter, where we transform such classes into common OO programming language constructs that *only* support definition of passive objects.

24.1.1   Single-Threaded Clusters

Clusters may be classified into two basic categories, *single-threaded* and *multithreaded*. Single-threaded clusters are pure *servers*, containing nothing but guardless blocking service operations and/or functional attributes. All others are multithreaded.

Actions within single-threaded clusters can be fully *serialized*. Each event can be made to lead to a single unique next-event within the cluster. For this reason, single-threaded clusters are substantially easier to design and implement than others. With only a few minor snags, most classes retain their forms when moving from active to passive status.

Single-threaded clusters are essentially identical to standard sequential programs. Only one thread of control is ever active within the cluster. When a cluster agent receives a request, it may invoke an operation on the appropriate embedded object using a sequential procedure call, ultimately receiving the result in the same fashion.

Single-threaded clusters may be constructed by transforming all internal operations and messages into `local` procedures and procedure calls. There may still be outbound one-way messages in single-threaded clusters, most typically to "sinks" including loggers, I/O devices, and notification relays.

Internal one-way `ops` may be proceduralized. Since only one thread may execute at any given time, it is harmless for the client to simply wait out an invoked one-way operation. External one-way calls should be handled (usually through proxy mechanisms) so that they return immediately to the internal senders. All other interaction constructs (e.g., early replies) may need to be translated into these more primitive forms before applying the transformations.

Our analysis and design level atomicity guarantees have no consequences at this level. Since no operation will ever be interrupted, there is no need to implement any kind of protection mechanism. Of course, the cluster itself must be protected via *shell*-level mechanics.

Protocols

While the cluster itself may contain a queue to hold requests received while it services others, passive objects residing within single-threaded clusters cannot possibly contain any `pends` associated with tests for internal conditions. (Guards that reference external objects should be converted into other forms described in Chapter 22.) In purely sequential environments, if a guard referencing internal state is not true when a message is invoked, it will not *ever* become true if the sender is blocked waiting for it. For example, if a sender invokes `s.top` for some `s:Stack` when it is empty, it is senseless to wait. The process will simply lock up. Thus, this situation ought to be transformed into an error condition. This is, of course, standard practice in the design of sequential stacks, where attempts to read from an empty stack are treated as exception conditions.

Thus, error protocols in objects designed to operate in pure sequential environments are sometimes defined differently than for those that may operate concurrently. However, this has little to do with passivation in general. The reason that an empty sequential stack `top` access should lead to an error is that we *know* it is pointless to wait, and (implicitly) we *believe* that it is better to enter an error protocol than face certain infinite postponement. If we discovered that nothing could unblock a `top` request in a concurrent design, we might make the same choice.

However, different screening protocols are more widely useful in sequential designs. In a single-threaded cluster, a client of a stack may itself test whether the stack is empty before calling `top`. The client may be confident that if the stack was not empty when tested, the request cannot fail. In a concurrent setting, other messages may intervene between the test and the `top` request unless locking protocols are employed.

24.1.2 Multithreaded Clusters

Multithreaded clusters contain only passive objects, However, at any given time, the component objects may be in states reflecting participation in several partially completed timethreads. Multithreading is possible by virtue of the first-class active status of the cluster agent itself. The continuum of possibilities ranging from one-process-per-object to one-process-per-system rests on the idea that one active object can "swallow up" and service any number of others:

- Per-object message queues may be combined.

- Guard evaluation may be centralized.

- Any (so privileged) computational agent may execute operation code on behalf of any other.

The most general passivation strategy is extremely simple to describe, but extremely painful to perform. All possible "microstates" of all objects must be converted into a canonical form executable by means of the interpretation mechanism described at the beginning of this chapter. This entails converting conditionals to messages, transforming blocking calls and sequences of operations to wait-state guarded callback protocols, adding attributes for each object indicating whether it is logically `ready` (not engaged in a public operation), and so on. These are the same transforms needed in order to implement the simulator described in Chapter 15, as extended to allow multiple concurrent interpreters. Without tools, canonical conversion is impossibly difficult and error-prone.

Moreover, even if these conversions could be performed automatically, the resulting system would not be very useful. Without extensive manual optimization, the overhead required for interpreting objects in this fashion is too high to take seriously for production software. Instead, these mechanisms must be resorted to only when strictly necessary.

24.1.3 Task Scheduling

Objects and sequences of computation in multithreaded clusters may be converted into procedural form using the strategies listed for single-threaded clusters. The scheduling capabilities of the cluster agent need be invoked only when linear proceduralization fails.

This style of processing is sometimes termed "thread" or "task" programming. Effective design relies on a service-centered rather than object-centered approach. The basic idea is to map out all possibly concurrent timethreads, or sequences of operations that may come into play in the servicing of cluster-level messages. All objects that may be involved in multiple threads must be protected using locks, queues, and scheduling mechanisms to avoid interference and lockup.

The "directionality" of this approach makes it more tractable and familiar, but also somewhat more dangerous than canonical conversion. Instead of starting with an assumption of full protection and then loosening mechanisms as optimizations, these methods attempt to determine the minimum set of protection mechanisms necessary for correct functioning. In the worst case, a full conversion to canonical interpretive form may be necessary. However, this never happens in practice.

Thus, even here, most classes retain their original design structure when converted from active to passive forms. However, faithfulness of converted classes to their original active designs can be difficult to assess. Success relies on finding all situations in which objects could possibly interfere, block, or loop. Testing is imperative.

Many tools, support packages, and even programming language constructs (e.g., **Ada tasks**) exist to aid implementation. Details vary widely, and many special techniques apply to only certain tools. We describe only some common capabilities.

Locks

Standard semaphore-based locking mechanisms may be used to indicate whether objects are logically **ready**, and thus to enforce atomicity requirements. These may employ the same locking techniques described in Chapter 22. In fact, semaphore locks may be used to implement those arranged in earlier design steps. Otherwise, only those objects that may participate in multiple tasks need be lockable.

For lockable objects, operations may be converted to invoke LOCK(self) on entry and RELEASE(self) on exit. A less disruptive strategy is to wrap the original inside a view class (see Chapter 17):

```
class X ...    op a: () { ... } end
```

```
class ManagedX
  own x: X;
  op a: () { LOCK(x); x.a; RELEASE(x) }
end
```

Queues

As described in Chapter 19, one or more delay queues may be used to hold waiting operations. Boolean conditions may be associated with each queue. If queues are associated with the above **ready** locks, then locking and queuing may be combined. Queue maintenance is most often performed using *monitor* and/or *port* constructions. These queues are not boundless. Queue overflow may lead to either process-level blocking or failure, requiring associated error protocols.

Queue checking in task packages is normally entirely event-driven. Operations that affect conditions must call the appropriate queue management facilities. Any operation that changes a condition must (perhaps conditionally) trigger processing. For example:

```
class X
  stat: Bool;
  local op doB;
  op b: () { if stat? then doB else pend end }
  op c: () { stat.t! }
end
```

This might be converted to use a delay queue:

```
op b: () { if stat? then doB else DELAY(XStatQ, doB) end }
op c: () { stat.t!; SIGNAL(XStatQ) }
```

Again, we have used these constructions before. These are the same self-notification and queuing strategies described in Chapter 19. Alternatives may be based on several of the designs discussed in Chapter 22; for example, versions of blackboard schemes in which each passive object uses a polling loop to obtain stored operation requests.

Scheduling

An operation may request itself to be suspended in a special queue. This frees the CPU to check other delay queues and/or execute other suspended tasks. Associated timers and predefined policies are typically available to aid in scheduling details. All polling loops and other potentially infinitely looping operations must be broken up with occasional suspension requests to prevent process lockup. Finding all of these situations can be difficult. This is a disguised version of the classic problem of infinite loop detection, which can be unsolvable in theory, but usually conquered through hard work in practice.

24.2 Storage Management

As described in Chapter 23, clusters may be viewed as containing one or more *repositories* holding passive within-cluster objects. In this section, we outline some basic internal storage management techniques based on repositories. However, storage management services are sufficiently complex and sufficiently dependent on quality-of-implementation factors that it is almost always best to *adopt* services rather than design them yourself unless you really need to.

So far, we have been tacitly assuming the standard OO lifetime policy that objects somehow live "as long as they are useful". We need to further dissect this statement to focus in on management strategies. We start with the easiest case. Consider a repository that:

- · always outlives its components;
- · logically serves as a SET or similar collection possessing both logical insertion and logical removal;
- · internally constructs the objects it inserts (never imports them); and
- · never exports component identities or internally references them except via the collection structure.

In this case, logical management may be equated with physical management. In other words, under these conditions, the repository can be sure that a logical `remove` operation may be accompanied by a storage deallocation. In ODL, the storage deletion operation `delete(link)` irrevocably recovers the resources occupied by the object referred to by the link. Here, a `remove` operation may in turn invoke `delete` on the removed object. Similarly, under such circumstances, deletion of the repository itself may trigger deletion of all held objects.

24.2.1   Garbage Collection

While this framework can be extended in various ways, when object identities are imported and/or exported from a repository, useful-lifetime tracking becomes a *nonlocal* issue. A single repository cannot itself determine whether any of the held objects may be safely deleted. Similar remarks hold even when identities are not exported, but internally managed objects contain cross-links (e.g., accounts and clients with links to each other).

The analysis of storage management requirements is a special form of dependency tracking. The useful lifetime of each object is dependent on those of all others that may ever try to communicate with it. A dependency graph could be constructed showing the lifetime dependencies of all objects in a system. At any point during system execution, all of those objects that are not ultimately reachable from one or more "main" system objects may be deallocated.

Establishing storage management methods based on such a graph would be a good idea, except that it is impossible. The dependencies are defined on dynamically constructed objects. Normally, information about exactly which objects will be created in a system cannot be determined without executing or simulating it. In those cases where upper bounds may be determined in advance, the storage for each object may be preallocated before execution time. This is a realistic option in real-time systems and other designs in which resources are fully laid out before execution.

It is conceivable to create run-time mechanisms that implicitly maintain dependency graphs and perform the associated management. For example, if a repository were notified each time one of its held objects were (1) needed and (2) no longer needed by each other client in the system, then it may record clients in a set, and delete the object when the set becomes empty. It must also deal with cases in which, say, each of a pair of objects needs the other, but neither is needed by any other live client. But this kind of tracking is usually completely impractical. The notifications and corresponding bookkeeping operations would swamp a system.

The only alternative is automatic storage management, or garbage collection (GC). GC is an "infrastructure" task that normally needs to be implemented with the help of some system magic. The basic idea is to track lifetimes without requiring explicit notifications. This is performed using methods that track *reachability* by secretly inspecting and traversing links during execution.

There are two basic approaches to GC. Most older methods use variations of *mark and sweep* algorithms. They start with one or more main objects and then mark all objects transitively reachable from them as live. After this pass, all unmarked objects are deallocated. Most newer methods are based on *copying collection*. Memory is divided into two or more regions. At any given time, only one is used for allocation. When space runs out, only the still-live objects are copied from one region to another. Among the advantages of this strategy is that it may be implemented in smaller steps, avoiding situations in which the system appears to be "shut down" for noticeable periods while performing collection.

24.2.2 Manual Storage Management

If garbage collection facilities are not available and cannot be constructed, then manual storage management strategies must be applied. The two most common cases occur when (1) dealing with programming languages that do not provide within-cluster garbage collection, and (2) performing process-level management (i.e., deleting no-longer-needed clusters), for which few tools are currently available.

Manual storage deallocation is highly error prone, and errors are terribly dangerous. A call to delete(ob) may kill off an object that is still potentially useful. Any further invocation of any operation on ob will result in system failures requiring recovery mechanisms that are best avoided.

Despite this, there are many cases in which one object *can* easily tell that another is no longer needed. For example, one object may kill off a component when it is known to be exclusively held but no longer used. Nonexported links qualified by own have this property. This may include the case where the outer object itself is deleted. All components with necessarily coexistent lifetimes may also be killed. It is convenient to wrap these cascades inside "destructor" operations, that are then invokable in one fell swoop.

Primary reliance on this strategy amounts to standardization on particular lock-style acquire/release protocols in which a constructor acquires the resources necessary to generate an object, but the object itself releases them when it is about to die. Similar reasoning applies to many "functional" objects; e.g., most objects constructed via WRAP. These are deletable after being used (invoked) once. Doing so manually simulates standard programming language level run-time mechanisms that delete storage for procedure activations after they return.

While such schemes typically cover many deletion cases, they do not hit all of them. Objects cannot delete others that remain accessible through other means. No single object knows whether there are still other shared links. In such situations, backup strategies are necessary.

24.2.3 Controlling Shared Resources

The notion of manual lifetime tracking may be generalized a bit to apply to other aspects of resource control. Sharable, volatile resources are those that must be created on first access, maintained while being accessed by possibly many other objects, and destroyed when they are no longer being accessed. This is just a small narrowing of basic automatic storage management rules. The main difference is that destruction is triggered as soon as the resource is no longer being used.

Reference Counting

The standard approach is based on an acquire/release protocol. Client objects must cooperate by explicitly requesting access to a resource, and explicitly releasing it when they are done. An agent merely keeps track of how many objects have requested the resource, and maintains things accordingly. For example:

```
class CountedResource
  local r: opt Resource;
  own refCount: Counter <> init refCount? = 0
  op acquire: Resource {
      if refCount.isZero then r := new Resource... end;
      refCount.inc; reply r }
  op release: () {
      refCount.dec; if refCount.isZero then delete(r) end }
end
```

This is a simplification of the general scheme described earlier. Instead of keeping track of users in a SET, the agent only maintains a count. A zero count corresponds to an empty set.

Reference counting is a somewhat fragile protocol. Any such design should include additional provisions to enhance safety. All access to resources must, of course go through CountedResources, normally managed through a repository. This may in turn be made more robust by defining a secondary interface in which all operation requests are mediated through pseudo-IDs.

Reference counting has a more serious limitation. If two objects each maintain a reference to each other, but both are otherwise unreachable, then neither will be killed even though they are both useless.

Copy-On-Write

An extension of reference counting is copy-on-write *sharing*, in which clients share objects as long as they do not change them. However, before they attempt to send a transition request, they must obtain their own local version of an object. This protocol is fragile enough to *demand* intervention from a repository agent that intercepts mutative requests and performs the required actions.

Fixed Resources

A repository may provide access to fixed numbers of functionally identical objects and provide access to *any* one of them on request. For example:

```
class FixedResourceMgr
  own pool: ARRAY[Resource];
  own inuse: ARRAY[Bool];
  allInUse: bool;
  op acquire: Resource when ~allInUse then
              % mark and return an unused resource % end
  op release(x: Resource); % record as free
end
```

24.3   Passive Objects in C++

Most class designs survive embedding and passivization relatively intact. To demonstrate the effects of this, we sketch the syntactic conversion of sequential, passive ODL classes into corresponding C++ constructs that enable clusters of passive ODL objects to be implemented.

We will not describe C++ or how to program in it. In fact, we will assume you know the basics or will find them out before applying the mechanics described here. There are several good "standard" accounts of C++. These include introductory [143], intermediate [212, 158], and advanced [63] texts, as well as a reference manual [88].

We use here only a subset of C++ and stress mechanics over cosmetics. We concentrate on translating *computational* information. We include declarative constructs only when they are available in the language. For example, C++ does not support declarative inv constraints, "==>" effects or anything mappable to them. We also ignore the possible need to employ locks, queues, and scheduling.

24.3.1   Basic Types

ODL value types map into C++ with a few obvious, easily-addressable snags. For example, ODL uses only int for integer values. This must be translated into any of short, int, long, or even special multiprecision representations, on a case-by-case basis. Similar rules apply for real versus float, double, long double. Booleans are conventionally defined as typedef bool int. The type time maps into whatever types are required to represent times on a system. Fixed vectors are easiest to translate as little structs (for example, struct string50 {char s[50];}). This forces copy based calling conventions when they are passed as values. The blob type may be represented as arrays of bytes (char). ODL records may be translated as const structs.

Like most procedurally-based languages (but unlike ODL), C++ does not distinguish between built-in value types and built-in object types at the declaration level. Thus, ODL INTs also map to C++ int. However, there is no C++ analog of the representation-independent Int type. There are only the concrete, nonsubclassable versions. For the moment, we will assume that Int also translates to C++ int. Unlike most other procedural languages, C++ contains mutator operations on built-in object types. For example, ODL c.inc may be mapped to C++ c++.

24.3.2   Classes

Abstract classes may be translated into C++ "abstract base classes" declaring pure virtual features. Generally, fns in ODL translate into "const methods" in C++ abstract classes, and ops into class-based methods. For example:

```
class Counter {
public:
   virtual int  count() const = 0;
   virtual bool isZero const { return count() == 0; };
   virtual void inc() = 0;
   virtual void dec() = 0;
   virtual void clear = 0;
   virtual bool InvCheck()   { return count() >= 0; }
};
```

The invCheck operation is a simple example of a self-test, as described in Chapter 16.

The computed attribute isZero, which was given a constant abstract definition in Chapter 16, is provided here with a concrete definition. Since there are no abstract constraint constructs in C++, this is the best we can do. It is partly a matter of taste whether to declare it `virtual`. If `nonvirtual`, then it is known to compute the right value, but it may not compute it in the best way. For example, if a concrete subclass were based on a list of some sort, it might be easy to tell if it were empty, but harder to find out the exact count.

Links

Internal links correspond to C++ pointer types, and `fixed` links to `const` pointers. Generally, `local` access conventions correspond to C++ `private`. In fully concrete classes, stored links may be represented as member variables. The `Lamp` example might look like this:

```
class Lamp {
public:
   virtual bool on() const = 0;
   virtual void flip() = 0;
};

class LampV1 : public Lamp {
private:
   bool* switch;
public:
   bool on() const { return *switch; }
   void flip() { invertSet(switch, *switch); }
};

void invertSet(bool* dest, bool v) { *dest = !v; }
```

As an extremely common application of the optimizations to be described in Chapter 25, any component of a built-in type that is qualified as `packed` may be directly embedded in its host object. This applies to `own` attributes manufactured by ODL "<>" conventions. For example:

```
class LampV2 : public Lamp {
private:
  bool switch;
public:
  bool on() const { return switch; }
  void flip() { switch = !switch; }
};
```

Standard export policies include never taking the address of such objects.

Value-holding classes generally transform to a special set of idioms in C++. These classes may employ overloaded operators, value-based assignment, copy-constructors, etc., in order to make the resulting objects look as close to built-in values as desirable. Strategies for doing so are described in the standard accounts. These techniques may be used to obtain object status for built-in types, using a variant of the strategy described in Chapter 17:

```
class RealVal {  virtual const float val() const = 0; };

class RealValV1 : public RealVal {
private:
  float _val;
public:
  const float val() const { return _val; };
  RealValV1(float s) : _val(s) {}
};
```

These kinds of classes may be used to simulate raw value types when the assumed characteristics of built-in types do not hold (e.g., for multiple precision integers).

Inheritance

Abstract ODL subclass constructions translate into C++ "public" derivation, with all features (even links) declared as virtual methods. Rather than using property inheritance rules, C++ requires strict signature matching for redeclared versions of operations within subclasses, which may lose information about return types. However, C++ provides a way for *clients* of "mistyped" procedures to recover lost information. Pointers may be "downcast" to more specific types. There is no run-time check to determine that the cast type conforms to the actual type, so correctness depends on the programmer. (This situation may change in the upcoming C++ standard.)

There is no Any root to the C++ type system. However, void* is normally used for analogous purposes. All usages must be downcast into specific class pointer types on dereference.

24.3.3 Construction

In C++, constructors are listed within the class declarations of the objects they construct. It is not hard to recast this ODL-style if desired. A single constructor may be defined that binds all pointers to supplied objects and/or initializes embedded objects to initial values:

```
class LampV1 : public Lamp { ...
public:
  LampV1(bool* init_sw) switch(init_sw) {};
};

class LampV2 : public Lamp { ...
  LampV2(bool initstate) switch(initstate) {};
};
...
Lamp* l1 = new LampV1(new bool(0));
Lamp* l2 = new LampV2(0);
```

Construction may be assigned to a generator by making the constructor private, but declaring its manager as a friend:

```
class LampV1 : public Lamp { ...
  friend class LampV1Gen;
private:
  LampV1(bool* init_sw) switch(init_sw) {};
};

class LampV1Gen { ...
  Lamp* dflt() { return new LampV1(new bool(0)); }
};
...
Lamp* l3 = aLampGen->dflt();
```

24.3.4   Other Constructs

Multiple inheritance.   C++ multiple *abstract* inheritance works in the expected fashion, but only if all superclasses are declared as public virtual, rather than just public. We downplayed the idea of multiple concrete inheritance at the design level. Several authors (e.g., [48, 193]) argue for avoidance of the corresponding C++ constructs.

Generics.   Parameterized classes and operations may be implemented using macros, templates, and/or simple preprocessor tools.

Open reuse.   C++ private subclassing is roughly similar to ODL opens. The main difference is that pure private subclassing does not fully "open" the reused declaration. The private parts of the class remain inaccessible. Also, the reused parts are not reinterpreted in the new context.

Partitioning.   C++ does not support a oneOf subclassing constraint. Regular subclassing may be used instead. Because the set of oneOf classes cannot change, each class may carry an "type tag" enum referenced in switch statements. Recall that oneOf is only useful when the partitions are based on logical necessity, not convenience. Only in these cases are nonextensible tags and switches always OK.

Type tests.   In ODL we use type membership predicates x in X mainly as *specification* devices, rather than as run-time type tests. But some constructs are easier to express using dynamic type testing. As of this writing, it is unclear whether C++ will "officially" support run-time type tests. Many work-around strategies are known and described in the standard accounts.

Dispatching.   Of the three senses of dispatching described in Chapter 21, C++ directly supports only the first, selection, through virtual methods. The second, resolution, may be simulated using type tests and/or double dispatching transformations, as described in Chapter 21. For the third, static class methods may be used in the special but most common case where object dispatching always dispatches to the exact same ODL-level object. In these cases, ODL "$" translates to C++ "::". All other cases must be implemented using explicit name servers and relays. (Similar reasoning leads to the use of static class methods to translate ODL common attributes.)

Wrappers. While not quite equivalent, C++ pointers to member functions may be used to approximate wrappers. A tedious alternative is to predefine all `Wrapper` subclasses that will be used in a program. We defined the `ODL WRAP` macro just to eliminate such tedium. This is difficult to simulate using C++ macros since a new class *name* may need to be generated for each wrapper. A very simple preprocessor tool could handle this and related macros.

Exceptions. Although implementations are not yet widely available as of this writing, the C++ standard incorporates a form of exceptions (see [88]). If they are available, the corresponding `ODL` constructs may be transparently mapped to them. Exceptions may also be used to implement named replies and related constructs discussed in Chapter 20.

Collections. Libraries of collection classes similar to those described in Chapter 18 are commonly available in C++. They may be based on `templates`, macros, or simple tools. Implementation strategies may be found in the standard accounts. Many C++ collections are actually structured as repositories. This is often a better fit to storage allocation schemes.

24.3.5 Storage Management

C++ does not provide automatic storage management. Because of C-based pointer insecurities, it is difficult to design your own program-wide garbage collector. Good ones exist, but they are either *conservative but leaky* (e.g., [37]), meaning that they may fail to deallocate some storage[1], or they are *tight but restricted* (e.g., [85]), meaning that they may only be used if certain programming conventions are flawlessly held to. Failing adoption of such a collector, a multi-tiered approach is taken to implement storage management.

As discussed earlier, destructor methods may be defined that kill off all `own` and `unique` components held by a host object. (No special destructor code is needed for `own` components that have been directly embedded in their hosts.) This helps manage deallocation by distributing responsibility for it. A call to `delete` ob kills off ob and all of the other objects that it knows it can safely destroy. Destructors may also be called for `unique` objects in the course of rebinding. For example:

---

[1]Widespread anecdotal experience suggests that leaks are so rare as to not be an issue.

```
class X { // ...
  Y* y;    // ODL unique
  void rebindY(Y* newY) { if (y != newY) { delete y; y = newY; } }
}
```

Any object that must only be used in the enclosing procedure scope may be declared as a "local" by invoking a constructor rather than new, so that its destructor will be automatically invoked at procedure exit. Supporting this requires changes in construction conventions. "Direct" construction calls should go directly to the class constructor operations, not through generator objects.

Additional infrastructure is needed for handling the many cases where objects cannot tell whether or when to issue destructor calls. Any of the methods described earlier in this chapter may be adapted for use. One implementation strategy is to use *counted pointers* via classes that behave as pointers for others, while also maintaining reference counts whenever the pointer is used. Such classes are variants of *smart links* described in Chapter 22. They may be generated through templates, macros and tools. Details are described by Coplien [63], which we thoroughly recommend.

24.4   Summary

Passive, embedded objects residing in clusters may be constructed using classic within process constructs including semaphores, queues, scheduling, and interprocess messaging. Typically, the vast majority of objects in a cluster need little explicit transformation from their active forms. Unfortunately, successful conversion is not at all mechanical. Effective exploitation of special cases remains crucial for arranging efficient execution.

Translations of ODL constructions describing passive sequential objects are available in C++. Similar translation schemes may be devised to convert this subset of ODL into other OO languages. Translations lose some, but by no means all abstract declarative information. The listed translation techniques provide only a start to full implementation efforts.

24.5   Further Reading

User guides for specific thread and task packages (e.g., under Mach, SunOS) remain among the best references for both design and mechanics. Buhr and Ditchfield [43] and Bershad [29] describe C++ extensions and tools containing requisite features. An alternative to thread packages is to use self-contained systems such as Linda [51] or ISIS [34]. A number of other C++-specific tools and techniques have been described in *Usenix C++* conference proceedings. Garbage collection algorithms are described in more detail in Lee [136].

24.6 Exercises

1. Estimate how much slower a simple fully queue-based cluster interpreter would be compared to (a) interpreted OOPL code (e.g., Smalltalk), (b) compiled OOPL code (e.g., C++), (c) assembly code, and (d) specially designed massively parallel MIMD hardware.

2. If a Stack object is (indirectly) accessible from an external object, is it (a) always (b) ever justifiable to convert pends to errors?

3. Sketch out the structure of a cluster containing the ATM device-control objects (e.g., CardEater).

4. Describe the transformations required to convert an externally directed message originally phrased using an op with a callback Wrapper.

5. If ODL so easily translates to C++, then why didn't we use C++ throughout Part II?

6. Explain the different senses of const in C++ and their relations to ODL constructs.

7. Measure the difference in performance between applications using classes such as RealVal versus simple floats.

8. Show the C++ version of the Balance class described in Chapter 17.

9. Exactly what are the C pointer insecurities that preclude simple garbage collection?

10. Stored attributes may not be redefined in subclasses in C++. Explain why this is not a major impediment in converting most ODL designs.

11. Compare the kinds of C++ constructs generated by our translation techniques with those most commonly employed in a large C++ application program or framework you have available (e.g., InterViews [142]).

12. List three C++ constructs that cannot be described in ODL.

Chapter 25

Performance Optimization

In this chapter, we describe some techniques for improving the performance of object-oriented systems. While most of the ideas are fairly general, making good on them can be environment, language, compiler, and tool dependent. However, for most of this chapter, we maintain the illusion of implementation independence. As a prelude, Table 25.1 lists without comment a set of trade-offs that may be applied in performance optimization.

25.1 Optimization and Evolution

Optimization techniques discover special cases and make associated trade-offs in order to improve performance. Some methods trade off other software quality criteria (especially coupling) for the sake of efficiency. Since performance requirements are usually "hard" and quality requirements "soft", such trade-offs must sometimes be made.

But one would like to optimize systems without *completely* removing the possibility for them to evolve, be repaired, and be reused. As OO systems become larger and run longer, these concerns become increasingly important, especially considering that one of the reasons that OO systems are replacing non-OO ones is because the old ones could not be made to adapt.

General OO design methods usually ensure that performance tuning measures are at least *feasible*. They leave room for as wide a variation in lower-level design and implementation decisions as logically possible. Any concrete implementation class that obeys the required interface of its abstract superclass can be plugged in at any

Usually Faster	Usually Slower	Usually Faster	Usually Slower
Internal	External	Hardware	Software
Storage	Computation	Direct	Indirect
Unmediated	Mediated	Fixed	Variable
Implicit	Explicit	Special Purpose	General Purpose
One Layer	Two Layers	One Message	Two Messages
Unguarded	Guarded	Immediate	Queued
Unconditional	Conditional	Computed	Symbolic
Approximate	Exact	Compile-Time	Run-Time
Optimistic	Pessimistic	Transient	Persistent
Control	Coordination	Event-Driven	Polled
Cooperation	Coordination	Point-to-Point	Routed
Dispatching	Forwarding	Local Call	Remote Call
Inline expansion	Call	Reply	Exception
Signaling	Blocking	Update	Construction
Invocation	Construction	Recycling	Construction
Chunked	One-at-a-time	Binding	Evaluation
Indexing	Searching	Lazy	Eager
Reference	Copy	Better Algorithm	Better Code

Table 25.1: Some Performance Trade-Offs

time in development. The best optimization techniques are those that continue to allow for at least some kinds of evolutionary changes without completely sacrificing performance. But if everything can change, then you cannot optimize anything. While there is a fine line here, some good compromises are available.

The stance most compatible with OO design methods is to support explicitly only those changes representing *extension by addition*. This preserves the ability to adapt to changes resulting from the addition of new objects, operations, and classes, but not destructive modifications of existing ones. Thus, some modifications may break optimized designs, but extensions and improvements will not. Generally, this implies avoidance of optimizations that take advantage of constraints that just so happen to hold, without being declaratively guaranteed to hold. These incidental constraints are the ones that may change. Thus, the declarative constraints, conditions, and effects listed for abstract classes are at least as useful for guiding optimization as are concrete-level considerations. In this sense, optimization is simply "more design".

Except where noted, the techniques described in the remainder of this chapter maintain at least limited opportunities for extensibility. However, even though these tactics are locally safe and permit extension, they are not without cost to overall design integrity. They may accentuate the extent to which future destructive changes propagate throughout a system.

25.2 Algorithmic Optimization

OOA descriptions may contain information useful for helping to locate plausible spots where clever algorithms and data structures might make a big difference. Probabilistic descriptions of ranges, use cases, and other qualitative information can direct attention to expected execution profiles. These may be used in a qualitative way during optimization efforts, directing attention to concrete components that may need redesign before being committed to. Analytic models and execution profiles of prototypes serve similar roles.

The usual route to algorithmic optimization in OO designs is subclassing. Any concrete implementation class that obeys the interface of its abstract superclass can be plugged in at any time in development. Thus, slow list-based concrete collection classes can be replaced with ones based on fast balanced trees, classes with naively constructed numerical operations may be replaced by ones based on more serious algorithms, and so on.

This strategy must be used with care for components geared toward reuse across many applications or subsystems. Different applications will have different invocation profiles. Fast processing times in one operation cannot always be traded for slow execution in another. However, subclassing may be employed to create different concrete classes that make different trade-offs. Each application may then select the one that is best suited to its profile.

Sometimes more efficient representations and algorithms may be employed only after defining *super*classes that define fewer and/or weaker operations. For example, very efficient algorithms exist for implementing UnionFindSETs defining only has(elem) and destructivelyUnion(otherSet) operations [5]. This is not a pure superclass of our SET class, but is a subclass of a superclass containing just has. There are many similar twists and variations, especially for data structure and numerical classes. These kinds of structural modifications enable exploitation of the many known efficient representations and algorithms developed for such purposes.

25.3   Performance Transformations

25.3.1   Caching

In designs full of relays, name servers, and other mediators that perform multistage routing, the identities of ultimate recipients of routed messages may be reported to and cached by senders to streamline future communication. For example, in a model-view design that is mediated by a relay, the viewer can send back an identity-revealing message to the model on receiving its first change notice. From that point onward, the model may send notices directly to the viewer, without mediation.

Caching is used to construct *proxy* objects. Proxies are designed as relays that transform local requests into interprocess messages. However, they may be implemented in a way that locally holds at least some state information, allowing them to reply quickly to internal `fns` probing simple attributes.

Caching always requires backup strategies to recover and adapt when properties of external entities change. This normally requires notification protocols so that cached entities may inform their cachers when they change. Some OODBs provide a great deal of infrastructure supporting local caching of persistently held objects. When available, this infrastructure may be used to exploit other caching opportunities.

25.3.2   Embedding

An extreme version of these tactics is to force an otherwise nonlocal passive object to become local by embedding it in another. For example, in ODL, concrete passive helper objects are accessed through links from their hosts. In some cases, these objects can be directly embedded within their enclosures, in a manner similar to "records" in procedural programming languages. Passive components declared as `own` are always safe for embedding, thus may be relabeled as `packed`. This saves a level of indirection on access and sometimes simplifies storage management.

Most design methods actually preclude thoughtless application of this measure. Since links always refer to *abstract* types, the storage space needed to embed corresponding concrete objects is not knowable, so embedding is impossible. However special subclasses may be designed in order to enable embedding. Any class declaring `fixed` links to other abstract components may be subclassed with versions specifying *concrete* links for each kind of concrete class actually used. These may then be `packed` safely. While the new subclasses are not very extensible, their parents remain so.

Replication. Transient embedding or caching may be obtained through *replication* of immutable objects across processes or even across objects. As is the case for proxies of any sort, no client processing may visibly depend on the *identities* of replicas, just their states and behaviors.

Homogeneous collections. Embedding strategies may be extended to collections, in which case they are normally labeled as *homogeneous*. The particular case of homogeneous ARRAYs of built-in types (e.g., ARRAY[REAL]) is generally well worth special attention. These not only improve performance, but are also useful in constructing interfaces to numerical routines implemented in non-OO languages. However, except in the special case of primitives, homogeneous structures cannot be made to operate in safe ways. They run against standard policies stating that every class may be subclassed. The reason they work for primitives is that we happen to secretly know that built-ins such as REAL are not subclassable.

25.3.3 Protocol Strength Reduction

Communication constructs come in many "strengths". For example, *futures* are more expensive than bidirectional operations, which are in turn more expensive than one-way sends.[1] Splitting bidirectional interactions into further-optimizable callback and continuation protocols has been found to provide substantial speed improvements [83].

Similarly, exceptions are usually more expensive than sentinels. Messages that require resolution, dispatching, and/or multicast are more expensive than fixed point-to-point messages. The cheapest workable protocol should always be employed. The cheapest communication is no communication at all.

Locking

Locks and similar interference control measures inhibit concurrency, generate overhead, and sometimes lead to deadlock. These problems may be minimized through static analysis. For example, if an object is used in only two joint operations that cannot ever interfere with each other (i.e., if all possible interleavings are known to be either safe or impossible), then locking is unnecessary. More generally, operations

---

[1]This is not always true. In some systems, one-way sends are actually built out of wrappers around bidirectional ones.

may be divided into *conflict sets* that describe those pairs or sets of operations that
may interfere. Locking schemes may be adjusted accordingly. The literature on such
techniques is extensive; see, for example [53].

Specialization

Program implementations are at the mercy of native dispatchers and dispatching
rules for most execution support. Different languages even have different rules (as
well as different subclassing rules, argument formats, and so on). They do not always
map precisely to design constructs. However, languages supporting dispatching are
amenable to optimizations based on relatively high-level design information. These
optimizations eliminate run-time uncertainty about the particular operations that
need to be performed given some message. At least some messages can be resolved
at design-time. These cases may be determined through static analysis of the information sitting in a given design.

This is something that a clever compiler or static analysis tool might be able to do.
In fact, most of these techniques were originally reported by researchers implementing
experimental compilers for the OO language **SELF** [222]. Except for such experimental systems, contemporary design and implementation tools do not undertake such
analysis, so it is useful to know how to do this manually.

In an **ODL** framework, the required analyses may be seen as sets of logical in-
ferences based on declarative class information. To illustrate, suppose there is an
abstract class that is implemented by only one concrete class. In this situation, any
client of the abstract class must actually be using the concrete version:

```
class AbstractA
  v: int;
end

class ConcreteA is AbstractA
  v: int { ... }
  inv v = 1
end

op useA(a: AbstractA) { if a.v = 1 then something else otherthing end }
```

It is clear that in useA, something will *always* be invoked. This fact can be hard-wired
at design time. Surprisingly, this can be done in a relatively nondisruptive manner,
by overloading another *customized* version of useA:

```
op useA(a: ConcreteA) { something }
```

Resolution-based dispatching is still required to route a call of `useA` to the concrete version. (This may require further conversions to selection-based dispatching; see Chapter 21.) But once it is invoked, the internals are streamlined away. This applies even if there is another concrete class. For example:

```
class AnotherConcreteA is AbstractA
  v: int { ... }
  inv v = 0
end
```

```
op useA(a: AnotherConcreteA) { otherthing; }
```

These optimizations have no other execution cost except storage of additional customized versions of operations. Some kind of dispatch is needed anyway to invoke the right version of an operation with multiple specializations. The heart of the trick is to replace conditionals with class membership tests and dispatches. Another way of viewing this is that customization synthesizes finer-granularity operations and classes than are otherwise present in a design, and adjusts dispatching requirements accordingly.

These improvements require far less global analysis than do other optimization techniques. You do not have to be sure that only one path is taken; you just have to notice that if it is taken, further simplifications are possible since they are all conditional on the same properties that lead to it being taken in the first place.

These forms of specialization *only* work when there are no subclassing errors. For example, if there were a class `SubConcreteA` that redefined v to return 3, the strategy would fail. But this subclass would also break the v=1 invariant. Of course, it would have been much better to create an intervening abstract class, say, `AbstractAWithVEQ3`. This would reflect and advertise the subclass constraints rather than adding them directly to a concrete class, or worse (but temptingly) leaving the constraints entirely implicit. However, this is the right stance only when the subclass constraints *must* hold, and not when they "just happen" to be true, and are thus overridable in subclasses.

There are several further variations on the basic idea. For example, consider the collection operation `applyC`, which takes an operation and applies it to all elements. This can be customized by defining individual operations that directly apply the operation to all members. Rather than calling `aSet.applyC(WRAP(print))`, a `printAll` operation can be added to a concrete `SET` subclass, and invoked from clients.

25.3.4   Encapsulation

At least at the within-process programming level, caching, embedding, strength reduction, and customization techniques are (only) sometimes more effective when the "insides" of target objects can be opened up to their clients. When operations are made more complex and inefficient than they would be if internal components were not hidden (e.g., due to extra forwarding and dispatching), encapsulation may be broken for the sake of performance. However, blind, random removal of encapsulation barriers may cause irreparable harm to designs. Less disruptive mechanisms exist.

Open subclassing.   As discussed in Chapter 17, constructs such as `opens` can be effective in removing certain encapsulation barriers in a structured fashion. These mechanisms embed (or share) concrete helper class features in ways that allow direct access by hosts, thus avoiding forwarding and indirection. Most OO programming languages support some variant of this construct. For example, in C++, `private` subclassing (sometimes in conjunction with `friend` constructs) may be used to this effect.

Inlining.   *Inlining* is among the most extreme forms of structured encapsulation breakdown. Inside passive components, it is sometimes possible to obtain desired effects without the overhead of a message send.

Inspection of the basic structure of an OO kernel (e.g., in Chapter 15) shows that most of the real execution of internal actions occurs only when operating on primitives. All composite operations just coordinate and relay further requests, usually ultimately reducing to primitive operations. While the notion of "primitive" is somewhat arbitrary, it may be safely assumed that primitive operations are executed relatively quickly.

Any program should run faster when paths to primitives are shorter. In the best case, these primitives can be directly computed by their clients through inlining. This avoids all resolution and procedure call overhead, and causes the code to run at "machine speed", modulo language-specific factors. In fact, inlining often results in OO programs running faster than predicted on the basis of reduced indirection overhead, since it creates code patterns that are further optimizable through standard compilation techniques. Inlining may be available in the native language or may be manually encoded.

Of course, full inlining is only possible and/or desirable in limited contexts. However, inlining opportunities often occur inside the bottlenecks representing the bulk of the "90-10" rule of thumb for efficiency: 90% of the time is spent in 10% of the code in most programs. (Or maybe it's 80-20 or 70-30, but still ...) Selective application of inlining techniques has been found to provide order-of-magnitude speed improvements in some programs and none at all in others. The best means of detecting inlinable calls is customization analysis.

25.3.5   Other Measures

Hiding Computation.   It is almost always possible to obtain better user-visible interactive response times by arranging for slower processing to occur at less visible times. Time-outs and other related mechanisms may be used to control this.

Rebinding.   It is usually faster to change logical state by rebinding a link than by mutating a set of components. Isolating sets of related values in state-classes can clear up bottlenecks filled with excessive modification of value attributes.

Rolling and unrolling operations.   Transformations from top-level operations to relational classes may be run either backward or forward, depending on the relative speeds of object construction versus invocation of multiparameter operations. The backward transformation forces all participants to be listed as arguments. Care is needed to ensure that these sets of participants are always sent in the right way.

Precondition screening.   Overhead for argument error protocols may be bypassed via transformations that provide screening functions that *must* be invoked before calling the operation of interest. This often opens up further opportunities for simplification and optimization on the client side.

Component factoring.   Components that are redundantly held in many objects may be coalesced. For example, collections and repositories may hold single copies of components accessed by all elements.

Recycling objects.   A constructor may re-initialize and recycle an otherwise unused object rather than creating a fresh one via **new**. When objects are maintained in a repository, this is both natural and effective. The repository may place **removed** objects on a special recycling list for use in later constructors. This works well even in a garbage-collection environment. Classes must be fitted with special `reInit` methods to support this.

Sharing stateless objects.   Sometimes it suffices to use only one instance of truly stateless immutable classes. A generator class may simply keep passing out the same object as a constructor result rather than making fresh ones. However, this technique is *only* safe when clients do not test links for object identity. If two clients hold two conceptually distinct objects, but they are actually the same and the clients are able to determine this fact through identity tests, then the technique cannot be used.

Sharing stateful objects.   *Copy-on-write* and related techniques may be used to share objects while they are in the same state. The same concerns about identity apply.

Finite structures.   Most collection classes are designed to be boundless. (This means, of course, that insertions only fail when the system fails, not that they have truly infinite capacity.) Many applications only require predeterminable finite capacities. Implementations of finite capacity structures are usually faster than those for unbounded ones.

Storage management.   Replacing the storage management infrastructure (GC, system memory allocators, etc.) with faster algorithms and implementations speeds up the construction of *all* objects.

Preconstruction.   Many object-oriented programs spend significant time initializing objects before getting around to using them. Examples include programs making extensive use of collection classes that build up complex data structures at system initialization time. This can be avoided by writing a version of the program that initializes these objects and persistently stores their states. The normal, usable version of the program may then more quickly initialize objects by directly reconstructing them from the saved state information.

Reclustering.   As discussed in Chapter 23, repacking objects into different clusters on the basis of monitoring and experience is very likely to improve performance. Intercluster messages are normally orders of magnitude slower than within-cluster messages, so there is a lot of room for improvement. *Dynamic reclustering* strategies that move heavily communicating objects "nearer" to each other for the duration of an interaction sequence may have dramatic effect.

25.4 Optimization in C++

Of course, individual programming languages may offer special optimization opportunities. We illustrate a few such techniques for C++. C++ is a highly tunable language. Most of the optimization strategies described earlier in this chapter may be applied.

Many bottlenecks in C++ programs occur in operations on simple "lightweight" objects. Lightweightness is in the eye of the beholder, and differs across applications. However, generally, classes that may be transformed to possess the following properties may be segregated for special treatment:

- only embedded components
- mostly inlinable methods
- mostly transient, local client usage
- no need for representation independence.
- no need for subclassability (either upwards or downwards).

Common examples include complex numbers, graphics primitives, and fixed-length strings. (Variable-length strings almost fall in this category, but cannot have their representations completely embedded.)

Here, several good design criteria are traded off for the sake of performance. Killing off representation independence and subclassability means that no methods need be declared as `virtual`, at the likely expense of padding class interfaces with operations normally introduced in subclasses. This then enables compile-time message resolution and inlining. The emphasis on embedded components and mostly local use allows the optimization of copy construction. Local copy-construction is usually already optimized by C++ compilers, so need not be specifically coded.

25.5 Summary

Some object-oriented systems are reputed to be slow. They need not be. A number of purely technical manipulations are available to improve performance. However, it is good practice to limit optimizations to those that maintain other software quality criteria. Most OO optimization techniques are *specialization*-driven. They first discover predeterminable message resolutions, representation strategies, and usage patterns. They then hard-wire these special cases before execution.

25.6   Further Reading

Bentley [25], Sedgewick [197], and related texts should be consulted for more thorough treatments of the basic techniques available for writing efficient algorithms and programs. The performance enhancements attempted by some compilers have analogs at coarser design and programming levels. See, for example, Aho et al [6], Lee [136], and Appel [14]. The SELF papers [222] present several OO program optimization techniques beyond those described here.

25.7   Exercises

1. Many "intrinsically efficient" designs are also good when measured by other criteria. Why?

2. Give an example demonstrating the application of each entry in the table of trade-offs.

3. One way to categorize optimization measures is whether they trade more space for less time, or vice versa. Categorize the measures described in this chapter.

4. There is a slogan among some compiler writers that a compiler should never postpone to run-time anything that may be done at compile time. Explain how this slogan has more consequences and requires a great deal more effort in OOPL compilers than those for procedural programming languages.

5. One reason that some OO languages limit representation options for built-in types is to guarantee that corresponding attributes may be embedded in their hosts. Use a language supporting both embedding and nonembedding options to see what difference this really makes.

6. Conversion of abstract links to embeddable concrete form replaces instance generation with subclassing. Why should this form of subclassing be postponed as long as possible?

7. Why would optimization be more difficult if objects were allowed to dynamically rebind concrete code associated with operations?

8. Would optimization be easier if classes could be specifically denoted as *nonsubclassable*?

Chapter 26

From Design to Implementation

The goal of the implementation phase is to implement a system correctly, efficiently, and quickly on a particular set or range of computers, using particular tools and programming languages. This phase is a set of activities with:

Input: Design, environmental, and performance requirements.

Output: A working system.

Techniques: Reconciliation, transformation, conversion, monitoring, testing.

Designers see objects as software abstractions. Implementors see them as software realities. However, as with the transition from analysis to design, structural continuity of concepts and constructs means that design and even analysis notions should flow smoothly and traceably.

The chief inputs from design to implementation may be categorized in a manner similar to those of previous phases. Again, while the headings are the same, the details differ.

Functionality: A computational design of the system.

Resource: The machines, languages, tools, services, and systems available to build the system.

Performance: The expected response times of the system.

Miscellaneous: Quality, scheduling, compatibility with other systems, etc.

Implementation activities are primarily *environmental*. They deal with the realities of particular machines, systems, languages compilers, tools, developers, and clients necessary to translate a design into working code.

Just as the design phase may include some "analysis" efforts approached from a computational standpoint, the implementation phase essentially always includes "design" efforts. Implementation-level design is a *reconciliation* activity, where in-principle executable models, implementation languages and tools, performance requirements, and delivery schedules must finally be combined, while maintaining correctness, reliability, extensibility, maintainability and related criteria.

While OO methods allow and even encourage design iteration, such activities must be tempered during the implementation phase. In analogy with our remarks in Chapter 25, if everything can change, then nothing can be implemented reliably. Implementation phase changes should ideally be restricted to occasional additions rather than destructive modifications.

Implementation activities may be broken across several dimensions, including the construction of intracluster software, intercluster software, infrastructure, tools, and documentation, as well as testing, performance monitoring, configuration management and release management. Most of these were touched on briefly in Chapter 15.

Many excellent texts, articles, manuals, etc., are available on OO programming in various languages, on using various tools and systems, and on managing the implementation process. In keeping with the goals and limitations of this book, we restrict further discussion of the implementation phase to a few comments about testing and assessment that follow from considerations raised in Parts I and II.

26.1   Testing

A design must be *testable*. An implementation must be *tested*. Tests include the following:

Code Inspections. Reviews and walk-throughs.

Self tests. The tests created during the design phase can almost always be built into implemented classes and invoked during test runs and/or during actual system execution.

White-box tests. Tests that force most or all computation paths to be visited, and especially those that place components near the edges of their operating conditions form classic test strategies.

Portability tests. Tests should be applied across the range of systems on which the software may execute. Tests may employ suspected nonportable constructions at the compiler, language, tool, operating system, or machine level.

Integration tests. Tests of interobject and interprocess coordination should be built at several granularity levels. For example, tests of two or three interacting objects, dozens of objects, and thousands of them are all needed.

Use cases. Use cases laid out in the analysis phase should actually be run as tests.

Liveness tests. Tests may be designed to operate for hours, days, or months to determine the presence of deadlock, lockup, or nontermination.

Fault tolerance tests. Hardware and software errors may be infused into systems before or during testing in order to test response to faults.

Human factors tests. While we do not concentrate much in this book on user interface design, *any* system, even one without an interactive interface, must meet basic human factors requirements. Tests and observations with potential users form parts of any test strategy.

Beta tests. Use by outsiders rather than developers often makes up for lack of imagination about possible error paths by testers.

Regression tests. Tests should never be thrown out (unless the tests are wrong). Any changes in classes, etc., should be accompanied by a rerun of tests. Most regression tests begin their lives as bug reports.

When tests fail, the reasons must be diagnosed. People are notoriously poor at identifying the problems actually causing failures. Effective system-level debugging requires instrumentation and tools that may need to be hand-crafted for the application at hand. Classes and tasks may be armed with tracers, graphical event animators, and other tools to help localize errors.

26.2   Performance Assessment

Analysis-level performance requirements may lead to design-phase activities to insert time-outs and related alertness measures in cases where performance may be a problem. However, often, designers cannot be certain whether some of these measures help or hurt.

Thus, while designers provide plans for building software that ought to pass the kinds of performance requirements described in Chapter 11, their effects can usually only be evaluated using live implementations. Poorer alternatives include analytic models, simulations, and stripped-down prototypes. These can sometimes check for gross, ball-park conformance, but are rarely accurate enough to assess detailed performance requirements.

Performance tests may be constructed using analogs of any of the *correctness* tests listed in the previous section. In practice, many of these are the very same tests. However, rather than assessing correctness, these check whether steps were performed within acceptable timing constraints.

The most critical tests are those in which the workings of the system itself are based on timing assumptions about its own operations. In these cases performance tests and correctness tests completely overlap. For example, any processing based on the timed transition declarations described in Chapters 11 and 19 will fail unless the associated code performs within stated requirements.

As with correctness tests, the reasons for performance test failures must be diagnosed. Again, people are notoriously poor at identifying the components actually causing performance problems. Serious tuning requires the use of performance monitors, event replayers, experimentation during live execution, and other feedback-driven techniques to locate message traffic and diagnose where the bulk of processing time is spent and its nature.

Performance tuning strategies described in Chapter 25 may be undertaken to repair problems. Alternatively, or in addition, slower objects may be recoded more carefully, coded in lower level languages, moved to faster processors, and/or moved to clusters with faster interprocess interconnections.

If all other routes fail, then the implementors have discovered an infeasible requirement. After much frustration, many conferences, and too much delay, the requirements must be changed.

26.3 Summary

Ideally, object-oriented implementation methods and practices seamlessly mesh with those of design. Implementation activities transform relatively environment independent design plans into executable systems by wrestling with environment dependent issues surrounding machines, systems, services, tools, and languages.

26.4 Further Reading

As mentioned, many good accounts of implementation processes and activities are available. For example, Berlack [27] describes configuration management. McCall et al [154] provide a step-by-step approach to tracking reliability. OO-specific testing strategies are described more fully by Berard [26]. System performance analysis is discussed in depth by Jain [122]. Shatz [199] describes monitoring techniques for distributed systems.

26.5 Exercises

1. The borders between analysis, design, and implementation are easy to specify in a general way but "leak" a bit here and there. Does this mean the distinctions are meaningless?
2. How do OO programming language constructs ensuring secure access protection make testing (a) easier (b) harder?
3. Describe how to arm classes with `trace` operations.
4. Which of the following is the path to OO utopia?
   (a) better hardware
   (b) better OO development methods
   (c) better OO development tools
   (d) better OO programming languages
   (e) better OO system software support
   (f) better OO software process management
   (g) better economic conditions
   (h) none of the above.

Appendix A

Notation

A.1 OAN

Instance

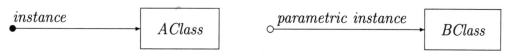

Class

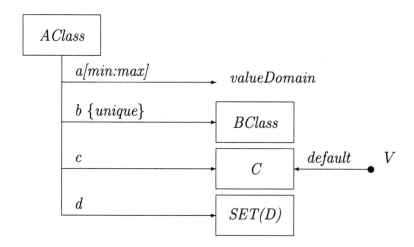

Generic class

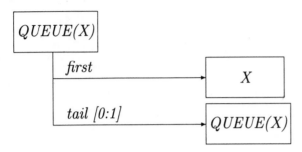

Ensemble

Relation

Relation instance

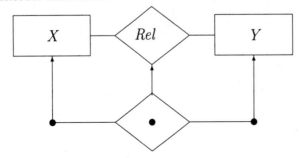

Inheritance

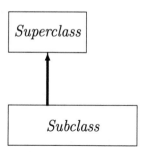

Multiple inheritance

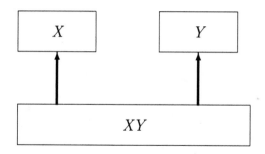

Exclusion, covering, partitioning ($* = E$, C, or P)

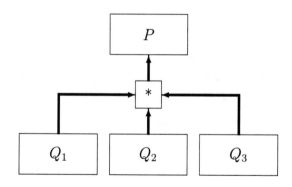

Transition

	transition name		
	guard	action	{event}
condition		pre- and postconditions and/or pseudocode and/or . . .	{v_{out}}
{event(v_{in})}			

S1 → [table] → S2

Service transition

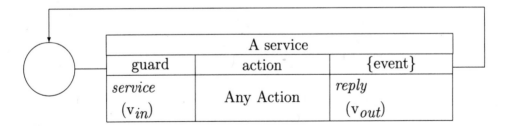

A service		
guard	action	{event}
service (v_{in})	Any Action	*reply* (v_{out})

Exception

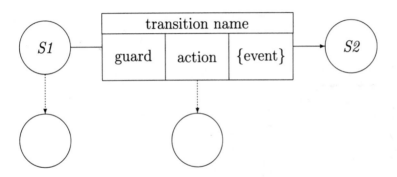

transition name		
guard	action	{event}

S1 → [table] → *S2*

Time-out

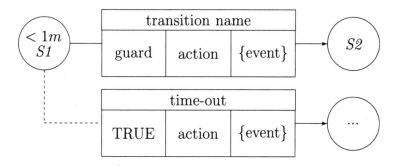

Transition time constraint

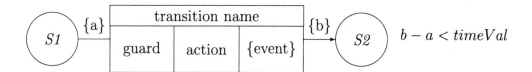

Multiple disjoint transitions

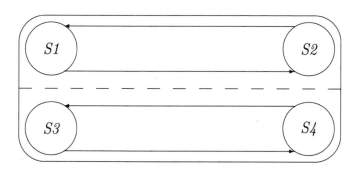

One-way communication

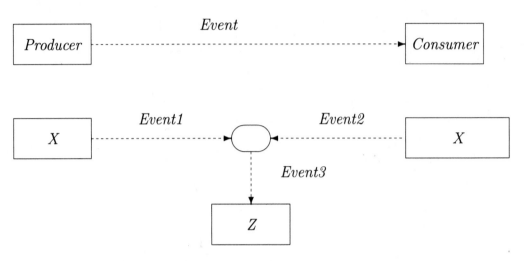

Bidirectional communication

A.2   ODL

The following meaningless declarations illustrate principal **ODL** constructs.

```
class X                        % class declaration
  is SuperX, SuperX2           % all superclasses
  generator XGen;              % All X constructions go through XGens

  fn i: int;                   % value attribute
  b: fixed bool;               % shorten fn, qualify as constant
  c: common char;              % c is same for all X's
  r: unique real;              % r is different for all X's

  inv i > 0;                   % invariant constraint
  j: int = 3;                  % short form

  init i = 2;                  % initial state constraint
  d: int init= 3;              % short form

  local fn l: Y;               % private link attribute
  local m: opt Y;              % short form; qualify as optional
  own q: X;                    % fixed, unique, local

  locals                       % qualify all enclosed decls as local
    p : Int <>                 % bind link to int obj at construction
    k: int { i + j }           % computed attribute
    fn gti(x: int) : bool      % local fn with argument
      = (x > i)                % abstract definition
      { x > i }                % concrete definition
  end                          % end of locals section

  op op1(x: int) : ()          % procedural operation
    ==> i' = x end             % effect/postcondition

  op op2(x: int)               % one-way operation
    ==> p''? = x               % eventual value held in p is x
    { p.set(x) } end           % concrete action
```

```
    op op3                          % argumentless one-way
      when i > 3 then               % guard
        m' = 1                      % effect; prime for post-value
      elsewhen null(m) then         % alternate guard; see if bound
        op2(d)'                     % referenced effect
      elsewhen l in SubY then       % true if l has features of SubY
        pend                        % delay processing (queue request)
      else end                      % empty effect

    when i = 7 then                 % guarded set of concrete ops
      op op4: int {                 % return integer value
        reply 12;                   % reply to sender and continue
        q.op2 }                     % invoke op2 on q
    elsewhen i = 219 then           % accept op5 only when i = 219
      op op5: ok(),bad(i:int)       % alternate terminations
        { if b then ok              % conditional reply
          else bad(2) end }         % reply on second return channel
    else                            % i.e., when i ~= 7 /\ i ~= 219
      op op6 y: Y {                 % y is local name for result
        local a: int := 1;          % local value
        y := YGen$mk;               % ask any YGen to make a Y
        while a > 0 do              % loop
         catch q.op4                % catch q.op4's reply by name
           op ok { a: = 0 }         % value update
           op bad(i:int) {}         % no action
         end;
          a := a - 1;               % value update
        end }
  end


end

inv X = oneOf(X1, X2);             % X1 and X2 fully partition X
record desc(a: A, b: B)            % value-structuring record for messages
fn geti(x: X):int { x.i }          % top-level operation
class List[T] ... end              % generic class with type argument T
op clear[T](l: List[T]);           % operation on any List class
```

A.2.1 ODL Syntax

The following EBNF syntax (with "*[...]*" for "optional" and "*[...]**" for "zero or more") does not reflect static semantic restrictions discussed in the text.

System:	*[Decl]**
Decl:	*Class*	*Fn*	*Op*	*Inv*	*Init*	*Open*	*Gen*	*Locals*	*Accept*	*Rec*	*;*
Class:	class *GID* *[* is *GIDs] [Decl]** end
Fn:	*[* local	own	packed *] [* fn *] GID Params* : *QualType FnDef*
Op:	*[* local *]* op *GID Params ReturnSpec OpDef*
Inv:	inv *Exps*
Init:	init *Exps*
Open:	opens *GID*
Gen:	generator *GID*
Rec:	record *GID Params*
Locals:	locals *[Decl]** end
Accept:	when *Exp* then *[Op]* ElseAccepts* end
ElseAccepts:	*[* elsewhen *Exp* then *[Op]*]** else *[Op]**
Params:	*[(ParamList)]*
ParamList:	*GID* : *QualType [* , *GID* : *QualType]**
QualType:	*[* fixed	unique	common	opt *]* GID*
ReturnSpec:	*[[ID]* : *QualType*	: *Synch [* , *Synch]*]*
Synch:	*[ID]* (*[ParamList]*)
FnDef:	*[[* init *]* = *Exp] FnBind*
FnBind:	<>	*Block*	*;*
OpDef:	*Block*	*Effect*	*;*
Effect:	==> *OpSpec* end	*When*
When:	when *Exp* then *OpSpec ElseWhens* end
ElseWhens:	*[* elsewhen *Exp* then *OpSpec]** else *OpSpec*
OpSpec:	*[When*	*Exps [Block]*	*Block]*
Block:	*{ Statements }*
Statements:	*Statement [* ; *Statement]**
Statement:	*[Exp*	*Assign*	*Loc*	*Catch*	*While*	*If*	*Reply]*
Reply:	reply *[Exp]*
While:	while *Exp* do *Statements* end
If:	if *Exp* then *Statements ElsIfs* end
ElsIfs:	*[* elsif *Exp* then *Statements]* [* else *Statements]*

Catch:	catch *Exp [Op]** end
Assigns:	*Assign [, Assign]**
Assign:	*GID* := *Exp*
Loc:	local *GID* : *QualType [:= Exp]*
Exps:	*Exp* | *Exp* , *Exps*
Exp:	*[@] Exp2*
Exp2:	*[Exp2 OrOp] Exp3*
OrOp:	\/ | =>
Exp3:	*[Exp3 /\ ] Exp4*
Exp4:	*[Exp5 RelOp] Exp5*
RelOp:	= | < | > | ~ | >= | <=
Exp5:	*[Exp5 AddOp] Exp6*
AddOp:	+ | -
Exp6:	*[Exp6 MulOp] Exp7*
MulOp:	* | / | div | mod
Exp7:	*[Unop]** Exp8*
Unop:	- | ~
Exp8:	*PredefFn* | *PredefExp* | *Msg* | (*Exp*)
PredefFn:	*Msg* in *GID* | null (*Msg*) | oneOf (*GIDs*)
PredefExp:	true | false | null | pend | literal
Msg:	*Rcvr [. Send]** [' | '' | ?]*
Rcvr:	self | *[GID $] Send* | new *GID [([Assigns|Exp])]*
Send:	*GID [([Exps])]*
GID:	*ID* | *GID* [*Exps*] | *PredefType*
PredefType:	bool | int | char | real | time | blob | Any | System
GIDs:	*GID [, GID]**
ID:	*[ID ::]** name

Bibliography

[1] Abelson, H. & G. Sussman, *Structure and Interpretation of Computer Programs*, MIT Press, 1985.

[2] Abiteboul, S. & A. Bonner, "Objects and Views", *Proceedings, ACM SIGMOD Conference*, 1991.

[3] Advanced Networked Systems Architecture Project, *The ANSA Programmers' Manual*, Architecture Projects Management Limited, 1991.

[4] Agha, G., *ACTORS: A Model of Concurrent Computation in Distributed Systems*, MIT Press, 1986.

[5] Aho, A., J. Hopcroft, & J. Ullman, *The Design and Analysis of Computer Algorithms*, Addison-Wesley, 1974.

[6] Aho, A., R. Sethi, & J. Ullman, *Compilers: Principles, Techniques, and Tools*, Addison-Wesley, 1986.

[7] Aksit, M., J. Dijkstra, & A. Tripathi, "Atomic Delegation: Object Oriented Transactions", *IEEE Software*, March 1991.

[8] Alford, M.W., "A Requirements Engineering Methodology for Real-Time Processing Requirements", *IEEE Transactions on Software Engineering* SE-3, 1, January 1977.

[9] America, P., "A Parallel Object-Oriented Language with Inheritance and Subtyping", *Proceedings, OOPSLA '90*, ACM, 1990.

[10] America, P. & F. de Boer, *A Sound and Complete Proof System for SPOOL*, Technical Report 505, Philips Research Laboratories, May 1990.

[11] Ananda, A., B. Tay, & E. Koh, "A Survey of Asynchronous Remote Procedure Calls", *Operating Systems Review*, April 1992.

[12] Andrews, G., *Concurrent Programming: Principles and Practice*, Benjamin Cummings, 1991.

[13] Andrews, G., "Paradigms for Interaction in Distributed Programs", *Computing Surveys*, March 1991.

[14] Appel, A., *Compiling with Continuations*, Cambridge University Press, 1992.

[15] Apt, K. & E. Olderog, *Verification of Sequential and Concurrent Programs*, Springer-Verlag, 1991.

[16] Arango, G. & R. Prieto-Diaz, "Domain Analysis: Concepts and Research Directions", in R. Prieto-Diaz & G. Arango (eds.), *Domain Analysis: Acquisition of Reusable Information for Software Construction*, Computer Society Press Tutorial, May 1989.

[17] Atkinson, C. *Object-Oriented Reuse, Concurrency, and Distribution*, Addison-Wesley, 1991.

[18] Atkinson, M., F. Bancilhon, D. DeWitt, K. Dittrich, D. Maier, & S. Zdonick, "The Object-Oriented Database System Manifesto", *Proceedings, Deductive and Object-Oriented Databases*, Springer-Verlag, 1989.

[19] Attardi, G., C. Bonini, M.R. Boscotrecase, T. Flagella, & M. Gaspari, "Metalevel programming in CLOS", *Proceedings, ECOOP '89*, 1989.

[20] Bailin, S.C., "An Object-Oriented Requirements Specification Method", *Communications of the ACM* 32, 5, May 1989.

[21] Bear, S., P. Allen, D. Coleman, & F. Hayes, "Graphical Specification of Object-Oriented Systems", *Proceedings, OOPSLA '90*, ACM, 1990.

[22] Beck, K. & W. Cunningham, "A Laboratory for Teaching Object-Oriented Thinking", *Proceedings, OOPSLA '89*, ACM, 1989.

[23] Bell, T.E. & D.C. Bixler, "A Flow-Oriented Requirements Statement Language", *Symposium on Computer Software Engineering*, Polytechnic Press, NY, 1976.

[24] Belzer, B., *Software Testing Techniques*, Van Nostrand, 1983.

[25] Bentley, J., *Writing Efficient Programs*, Prentice Hall, 1982.

[26] Berard, E., *Essays in Object-Oriented Software Engineering*, Prentice Hall, 1992.

[27] Berlack, H., *Software Configuration Management*, Wiley, 1991.

[28] Bernard, C., *RMT: A Tool for Object-Oriented Analysis*, Technical Report, Cap Gemini Innovation, 7 Chemin du Vieux Chene, Zirst, 38240 Meylan, France, 1990.

[29] Bershad, B., *The PRESTO User's Manual*, University of Washington Department of Computer Science Technical Report 88-01-04, 1988.

[30] Berry, G. & G. Boudol, "The Chemical Abstract Machine", *Proceedings, ACM Conference on Principles of Programming Languages*, ACM, 1990.

[31] Bertsekas, D. & R. Gallager, *Data Networks*, Prentice Hall, 1987.

[32] Biggerstaff, T. & A. Perlis (eds.), *Software Reuse*, ACM Press, 1989.

[33] Birman, K. & K. Marzullo, "ISIS and the META Project", *Sun Technology*, Summer 1989.

[34] Birman, K., et al *ISIS User Guide and Reference Manual*, Isis Distributed Systems, Inc, 111 South Cayuga St., Ithaca NY, 1992.

[35] Bobrow, D., L. DeMichel, R. Gabriel, S. Keene, G. Kiczales, & D. Moon, "Common Lisp Object System Specification", *SIGPLAN Notices*, September 1988.

[36] Boehm, B., "Quantitative Evaluation of Software Quality", *Second IEEE International Conference on Software Engineering*, Washington DC, CS Press of the IEEE, 1976.

[37] Boehm, H.-J. & M. Weiser, "Garbage Collection in an Uncooperative Environment", *Software – Practice and Experience*, 1988.

[38] Booch, G., *Software Components with ADA*, Benjamin/Cummings, 1987.

[39] Booch, G., *Object Oriented Design with Applications*, Benjamin/Cummings, 1990.

[40] Brachman, R.J., *A Structural Paradigm for Representing Knowledge*, Technical Report 3605, BBN, May 1978.

[41] Brachman, R.J. et al, "Living with Classic: When and How to Use a KL-ONE-Like Language", in John F. Sowa (ed.), *Principles of Semantic Networks*, Morgan Kaufmann, 1991.

[42] Brown, F.M. (ed.), *Proceedings, 1987 Workshop on the Frame Problem*, April 1987.

[43] Buhr, P. & G. Ditchfield, "Adding Concurrency to a Programming Language", *Proceedings, Usenix C++ Conference*, 1992.

[44] Buhr, R., *Machine Charts for Visual Prototyping in System Design*, SCE Report 88-2, Dept. of Sys. & Comp. Eng., Carlton University, Ottawa, Ontario Canada, August 1988.

[45] Buhr, R. & R. Casselman, "Architecture with Pictures", *Proceedings, OOPSLA '92*, ACM, 1992.

[46] Burns, A., *Concurrent Programming in Ada*, Cambridge University Press, 1985.

[47] Burns, A., A. Lister, & A. Wellings, *A Review of Ada Tasking*, Springer Verlag, 1987.

[48] Cargill, T., *Elements of C++ Programming Style*, Addison-Wesley, 1992.

[49] Carnap, R., *Meaning and Necessity*, The University of Chicago Press, 1947.

[50] Caromel, D., "Concurrency: An Object-Oriented Approach", *Proceedings, 1991 TOOLS Conference*, 1991.

[51] Carriero, N. & D. Galerntner, *How to Write Parallel Programs*, MIT Press, 1990.

[52] Cattell, R., *Object Data Management*, Addison-Wesley, 1991.

[53] Cellary, W., E. Gelenbe, & T. Morzy, *Concurrency Control in Distributed Database Systems*, North-Holland, 1988.

[54] Chandy, K. & J. Misra, *Parallel Program Design: A Foundation*, Addison-Wesley, 1988.

[55] Chatterjee, A., "The Class as an Abstract Behavior Type for Resource Allocation of Distributed Object-Oriented Programs", *OOPSLA Workshop on Object-Oriented Large Distributed Applications*, 1992.

[56] Chin, R. & S. Chanson, "Distributed Object Based Programming Systems", *Computing Surveys*, March 1991.

[57] Coad, P. & E. Yourdon, *Object-Oriented Analysis*, Yourdon Press, Prentice-Hall, 1990.

[58] Colbert, E., "The Object-Oriented Software Development Method: A Practical Approach to Object-Oriented Development", *Proceedings, TRI-Ada 89*, October 1989.

[59] Cole, R. "A Model for Security in Distributed Systems", *Computers and Security*, 9, 4, 1990.

[60] Conklin, J., & M. Begeman, "gIBIS: a Hypertext Tool for Exploratory Policy Discussions", *ACM Transactions on Office Information Systems*, 6, October 1988.

[61] Constantine, L., Panel on Structured Analysis versus OO Analysis, *Proceedings, OOPSLA '90*, ACM, 1990.

[62] Cook, W., "Object-Oriented Programming versus Abstract Data Types", in J. deBakker, W. deRoever, & G. Rozenberg (eds.), *Foundations of Object-Oriented Languages*, Springer Verlag, 1991.

[63] Coplien, J., *Advanced C++: Programming Styles and Idioms*, Addison-Wesley, 1991.

[64] Cox, B., *Object-Oriented Programming: An Evolutionary Approach*, Addison-Wesley, 1986.

[65] Cristian, F., "Understanding Fault-Tolerant Distributed Systems", *Communications of the ACM*, February 1991.

[66] Dahl, O. & K. Nygaard, "Simula: An Algol-based Simulation Language", in *Communications of the ACM*, 9, 1966.

[67] Dasgupta, S., *Design Theory and Computer Science*, Cambridge University Press, 1991.

[68] Davis, A.M. & W. Rataj, "Requirements Language Processing for the Effective Testing of Real-Time Software", *ACM Software Engineering Notes*, 3, 5, November 1978.

[69] Davis, A.M., "RLP: An Automated Tool for the Processing of Requirements", *IEEE COMPSAC '79*, Washington, DC, CS Press of the IEEE, 1979.

[70] Davis, A.M., *Software Requirements, Analysis and Specification*, Prentice-Hall, 1990.

[71] Davis, C. & C. Vick, "The Software Development System", *IEEE Transactions on Software Engineering* SE-3, 1, January 1977.

[72] de Bakker, J., C. Huizing, W. de Roever, & G. Rozenberg (eds.), *Real-Time: Theory in Practice*, Lecture Notes in Computer Science, 600, Springer Verlag, 1992.

[73] de Champeaux, D., Verification of Some Parallel Algorithms, *Proceedings, 7th Annual Pacific Northwest Software Quality Conference*, Portland, OR, 1989.

[74] de Champeaux, D. & W. Olthoff, "Toward an Object-Oriented Analysis Method", *Proceedings, 7th Annual Pacific Northwest Software Quality Conference*, Portland, OR, 1989.

[75] de Champeaux, D., "Object-Oriented Analysis and Top-Down Software Development", Pierre America (ed), *Proceedings, ECOOP '91*, Lecture Notes in Computer Science, 512, Springer Verlag, July 1991.

[76] de Champeaux, D. & P. Faure, "A Comparative Study of Object-Oriented Analysis Methods", *Journal of Object-Oriented Programming*, 5, 1, March/April 1992.

[77] de Champeaux, D., A. Anderson, M. Dalla Gasperina, E. Feldhousen, F. Fulton, M. Glei, C. Groh, D. Houston, D. Lerman, C. Monroe, R. Raj, & D. Shultheis, "Case Study of Object-Oriented Software Development", *Proceedings, OOPSLA '92*, ACM, 1992.

[78] Delcambre, L., B. Lim, & S. Urban, "Object-Centered Constraints", *Proceedings, IEEE International Data Engineering Conference*, IEEE, 1991.

[79] Detlefs, D., P. Herlihy, & J. Wing, "Inheritance of Synchronization and Recovery Properties in Avalon/C++", *Proceedings, International Conference on System Sciences*, 1988.

[80] Dijkstra, E., *A Discipline of Programming*, Prentice Hall, 1976.

[81] Ditchfield, G., *Contextual Polymorphism*, Thesis, University of Waterloo, Ontario, 1992.

[82] Dony, C., J. Malenfant, & P. Cointe, "Prototype-Based Languages: From a New Taxonomy to Constructive Proposals and their Validation", *Proceedings OOPSLA '92*, ACM, 1992.

[83] Draves, R., B. Bershad, R. Rashid, & R. Dean, "Using Continuation Structures to Implement Thread Management and Communication in Operating Systems", *Proceedings, 13th ACM Symposium on Operating Systems Principles*, ACM, 1991.

[84] Durfee, E., *Coordination of Distributed Problem Solvers*, Kluwer, 1988.

[85] Edelson, D. & I. Pohl, "Copying Garbage Collection in C++", *Proceedings, Usenix C++ Conference*, 1991.

[86] Edwards, J., *Basic Ptech Skills*, Course Notes, Associative Design Technology, Westborough, MA 01581, June 1989.

[87] Edwards, J., *Schemas to Code*, Technical Report, Associative Design Technology, Westborough, MA 01581, June 1990.

[88] Ellis, M. & B. Stroustrup, *The Annotated C++ Reference Manual*, Addison-Wesley, 1990.

[89] Embley, D.W., B. Kurtz, & S.N. Woodfield, *Object-Oriented Systems Analysis*, Yourdon Press/Prentice Hall, 1992.

[90] Fagin, R., J.Y. Halpern, & M.Y. Vardi, "What Can Machines Know? On the Properties of Knowledge in Distributed Systems", *JACM*, 39, 2, April 1992.

[91] Feller, P.H. & W.S. Humphrey, *Software Process Development and Enactment: Concepts and Definitions*, Technical Report, SEI, Pittsburg, PA 15213-3890, January 1992.

[92] Firesmith, D.G., "Identification and Classification Guidelines for Objects, Classes and Subassemblies", paper delivered to the Identification Working Group at OOPSLA '91, Advanced Software Technology Specialists, 17124 Lutz Rd, Ossian, IN 46777; October 1991.

[93] Fishman, D., J. Annevelink, E. Chow, T. Connors, J. Davis, W. Hasan, C. Hoch, W. Kent, S. Leichner, P. Lyngbaek, B. Mahbod, M. Neimat, T. Risch, M. Shan, & W. Wilkinson, "Overview of the Iris DBMS", in W. Kim & F. Lochovsky (eds.), *Object-Oriented Concepts, Databases, and Applications*, ACM Press, 1989.

[94] Frolund, S., "Inheritance of Synchronization Constraints in Concurrent Object-Oriented Programming Languages", *Proceedings, ECOOP '92*, Lecture Notes in Computer Science, 615, Springer-Verlag, 1992.

[95] Gahagan, C. & T. Remple, *Migration to C++*, Report, Hewlett-Packard Colorado Networks Division, November 1990.

[96] Garey, M. & D. Johnson, *Computers and Intractability*, Freeman, 1979.

[97] Gibson, E., "Objects - Born and Bred", *BYTE*, October 1990.

[98] Goguen, J. & J. Meseguer, "Unifying Functional, Object-Oriented, and Relational Programming with Logical Semantics", in B. Shriver and P. Wegner (eds.), *Research Directions in Object-Oriented Programming*, MIT Press, 1987.

[99] Goldberg, A., *Smalltalk 80: The Interactive Programming Environment*, Addison-Wesley, 1984.

[100] Grady, B., *An Investment Model for Software Process Improvement*, Report, Hewlett-Packard Corporate Engineering, February 1992.

[101] Gries, D., *The Science of Programming*, Springer-Verlag, 1981.

[102] Guerraoui, R., R. Capobianchi, A. Lanusse, & P. Roux, "Nesting Actions through Asynchronous Message Passing: the ACS Protocol", *Proceedings, ECOOP '92*, Lecture Notes in Computer Science, 615, Springer Verlag, 1992.

[103] Hailpern, B. & H. Ossher, "Extending Objects to Support Multiple Interfaces and Access Control", *IEEE Transactions in Software Engineering*, November 1990.

[104] Harel, D., "StateCharts: A Visual Formalism for Complex Systems", *Science of Computer Programming*, 8, 1987.

[105] Harel, D., "On Visual Formalisms", *Communications of the ACM* 31, 5, May 1988.

[106] Hazeltine, N., Panel on "Managing the Transition to Object-Oriented Technology" *OOPSLA '91*, *OOPS Messenger*, 3, 4, October 1992.

[107] Helm, R., I. Holland, & D. Gangopadhyay, "Contracts: Specifying Behavioral Compositions in Object-Oriented Systems", *Proceedings, OOPSLA '90*, ACM, 1990.

[108] Helm, R., T. Huynh, K. Marriott, & J. Vlissides, "An Object-Oriented Architecture for Constraint-Based Graphical Editing", *Proceedings, Third Eurographics Workshop on Object-oriented Graphics*, 1992.

[109] Herlihy, M., "A Methodology for Implementing Highly Concurrent Data Structures", *Symposium on Principles and Practices of Parallel Programming*, ACM, 1990.

[110] Hewitt, C., P. Bishop, & R. Steiger, "A Universal Modular ACTOR Formalism for AI", *Third International Joint Conference on Artificial Intelligence*, Stanford University, August 1973.

[111] Hillis, W. & G. Steele, "Data Parallel Algorithms", *Communications of the ACM*, December 1986.

[112] Hogg, J., "Islands: Aliasing Protection In Object-Oriented Languages", *Proceedings, OOPSLA '91*, ACM, 1991.

[113] Hogg, J., D. Lea, R. Holt, A. Wills, & D. de Champeaux, "The Geneva Convention on the Treatment of Object Aliasing", *OOPS Messenger*, April 1992.

[114] HOOD Working Group, *HOOD Reference Manual 3.0*, Report WME/89-173/JB, European Space Agency, PO 299 AG Noordwijk Netherlands, September 1989.

[115] Hoogeboom, B., & W.A. Halang, "The Concept of Time in Software Engineering for Real Time Systems", *Third International Conference on Software Engineering for Real Time Systems*, 1991.

[116] Huhns, M., *Distributed Artificial Intelligence*, Morgan Kaufmann, 1987.

[117] Humphrey, W.S., *Managing the Software Process*, Addison-Wesley, 1990.

[118] Ingalls, D., "A Simple Technique for Handling Multiple Dispatch", *Proceedings, OOPSLA '86*, ACM, 1986.

[119] Jackson, M., *Systems Development*, Prentice Hall, 1982.

[120] Jacobson, I., "Object-Oriented Development in an Industrial Environment", *Proceedings, OOPSLA '87*, ACM, 1987.

[121] Jacobson, I., M. Christerson, P. Jonsson, & G. Overgaard, *Object-Oriented Software Engineering*, Addison-Wesley, 1992.

[122] Jain, R., *The Art of Computer Systems Performance Analysis*, Wiley 1991.

[123] Jaja, J., *An Introduction to Parallel Algorithms*, Addison-Wesley, 1992.

[124] Jarvinen, H., R. Kurki-Suonio, M. Sakkinen, & K. Systa, "Object-Oriented Specification of Reactive Systems". *Proceedings, International Conference on Software Engineering*, IEEE, 1990.

[125] Johnson, R. & V. Russo, *Reusing Object-Oriented Designs*, University of Illinois Technical Report UIUCDCS 91-1696, 1991.

[126] Jones, C., *Systematic Software Development Using VDM*, Prentice Hall, 1986.

[127] Jones, C., *An Object-Based Design Method for Concurrent Programs*, University of Manchester Department of Computer Science Technical Report UMCS-92-12-1, 1992.

[128] Kiczales, G., J. des Rivieres, & D.G. Bobrow, *The Art of the Metaobject Protocol*, MIT Press, 1991.

[129] Knuth, D. E., *The Art of Computer Programming, Volume 1*, Addison-Wesley, 1973.

[130] Korson, T.D. & V.K. Vaishnavi, "Managing Emerging Software Technologies: A Technology Transfer Framework", *Communications of the ACM*, 35, 9, September 1992.

[131] Krasner, G. & S. Pope, "A Cookbook for Using the Model View Controller User Interface Paradigm in Smalltalk-80", *Journal of Object-Oriented Programming*, August/September 1988.

[132] Kristensen, B., O. Madsen, B. Moller-Pedersen, & K. Nygaard, "The BETA Programming Language", in B. Shriver and P. Wegner (eds.), *Research Directions in Object-Oriented Programming*, MIT Press, 1987.

[133] Lamport, L. & N. Lynch, "Distributed Computing Models and Methods", in J. van Leeuwen (ed.), *Handbook of Theoretical Computer Science*, MIT Press, 1990.

[134] Lano, K. & H. Haughton, "Reasoning and Refinement in OO Specification Languages", *Proceedings, ECOOP '92*, Lecture Notes in Computer Science, 615, Springer Verlag, 1992.

[135] Leavens, G. & Y. Cheon, "Preliminary Design of Larch/C++", *Proceedings, Larch Workshop*, 1992.

[136] Lee, P. (ed.), *Advanced Language Implementation*, MIT Press, 1991.

[137] Lee, S. & D.L. Carver, "Object-Oriented Analysis and Specification, a Knowledge Based Approach", *Journal of Object-Oriented Programming*, 3, 5, January 1991.

[138] Lenat, D.B. & R.V. Guha, *Building Large Knowledge-Based Systems*, Addison-Wesley, 1989.

[139] Lenzerini, M., D. Nardi, & M. Simi, *Inheritance Hierarchies in Knowledge Representation and Programming Languages*, Wiley, 1991.

[140] Levi, S. & A. Agrawala, *Real Time System Design*, McGraw-Hill, 1990.

[141] Lieberherr, K. & I. Holland, "Assuring Good Style for Object-Oriented Programs", *IEEE Software*, September 1989.

[142] Linton, M., et al, *InterViews* (Software currently available via anonymous ftp from `interviews.stanford.edu` and elsewhere).

[143] Lippman, S., *C++ Primer*, Addison-Wesley, 1991.

[144] Lipsett, R., C. Schaefer, & C. Ussery, *VHDL: Hardware Description and Design*, Kluwer Academic Press, 1991.

[145] Liskov, B., "Data Abstraction and Hierarchy", *Proceedings, OOPSLA '87*, ACM, 1987.

[146] Lubars, M.D., "Wide-Spectrum Support for Software Reusability", *Proceedings, Workshop on Software Reusability and Maintainability*, National Institute of Software Quality and Productivity, Washington, DC, October 1987.

[147] Lubars, M.D., *Domain Analysis and Domain Engineering in IDeA*, Tech Report STP-295-88, MCC, Austin, TX, September 1988.

[148] Lucassen, H. & D. Gifford, "Polymorphic Effect Systems", *Proceedings, ACM Conference on Principles of Programming Languages*, ACM, 1988.

[149] Madsen, O., "Block-structure and Object-Oriented Languages", in B. Shriver and P. Wegner (eds.), *Research Directions in Object-Oriented Programming*, MIT Press, 1987.

[150] Maier, D., *The Theory of Relational Databases*, Computer Science Press, 1983.

[151] Manna, Z. & R. Waldinger. *The Logical Basis for Computer Programming*, Addison-Wesley, 1985.

[152] Martin, J. & C. McClure, *Diagramming Techniques for Analysts and Programmers*, Prentice Hall, 1985.

[153] Matsuoka, S., T. Watanabe, & A. Yonezawa, "Hybrid Group Reflective Architecture for Object-Oriented Concurrent Reflective Programming", in *Proceedings, ECOOP '91*, Lecture Notes in Computer Science, no 512, Springer Verlag, 1991.

[154] McCall, J., W. Randell, J. Dunham, & L. Lauterbach, *Software Reliability Measurement and Testing Guidebook*, Rome Laboratory USAF Technical Report RL-TR-92-52, 1992.

[155] McCarthy, J. & P.J. Hayes, "Some Philosophical Problems from the Standpoint of Artificial Intelligence", in D. Michie and B. Meltzer (eds.), *Machine Intelligence 4*, Edinburgh University Press, 1969.

[156] McGregor, J.D., personal communication, February 1992.

[157] Meyer, B., *Object-Oriented Software Construction*, Prentice Hall International, 1988.

[158] Meyers, S., *Effective C++*, Addison-Wesley, 1992.

[159] Milner, R., *Communication and Concurrency*, Prentice Hall International, 1989.

[160] Milner, R., J. Parrow, & D. Walker, "A Calculus of Mobile Processes", *Information and Computation*, 100, 1992.

[161] Minsky, M., "A framework for representing Knowledge" in P. Winston (ed.), *The Psychology of Computer Vision*, McGraw-Hill, 1975.

[162] Monarchi, D. & G. Puhr, "A Research Typology for Object-Oriented Analysis and Design", *Communications of the ACM*, September 1992.

[163] Myers, B., D. Giuse, & B. Zanden, "Declarative Programming in a Prototype-Instance System", *Proceedings, OOPSLA '92*, ACM, 1992.

[164] Neighbors, J.M., *Software Construction Using Components*, Tech Report 160, Department of Information and Computer Sciences, University of California, Irvine, 1980.

[165] Neighbors, J.M., "The DRACO Approach to Constructing Software from Reusable Components", *IEEE Transactions of Software Engineering*, SE-10, 5, September 1984.

[166] Nierstrasz, O., "Active Objects in Hybrid", *Proceedings, OOPSLA '87*, ACM, 1987.

[167] Nierstrasz, O., "The next 700 Concurrent Object-Oriented Languages", in D. Tsichritzis (ed.), *Object Composition*, University of Geneva, 1991.

[168] Nierstrasz, O., S. Gibbs, & D. Tsichritzis, "Component-Oriented Software Development", *Communications of the ACM*, September 1992.

[169] OMG, *Common Object Request Broker Architecture and Specification*, Document 91.12.1, Object Management Group, 1991.

[170] Odell, J. & J. Martin, *Object-Oriented Analysis and Design*, Prentice Hall, 1992.

[171] Opdyke, W., *Refactoring Object-Oriented Frameworks*, Thesis, University of Illinois at Urbana-Champain, 1992.

[172] Open Systems Interconnection Standard. *OSI: ASN.1 Encoding Rules*, OSI Standard 8824/5, 1985.

[173] Ossher, H. & W. Harrison, "Combination of Inheritance Hierarchies", *Proceedings, OOPSLA '92*, ACM, 1992.

[174] Paepcke, A., "PCLOS: A Flexible Implementation of CLOS Persistence", *Proceedings, ECOOP '88*, Lecture Notes in Computer Science, Springer Verlag, 1988.

[175] Paepcke, A., "PCLOS: A Critical Review", *Proceedings, OOPSLA '89*, ACM, 1989.

[176] Paepcke, A., "PCLOS: Stress Testing CLOS - Experiencing the Metaobject Protocol", *Proceedings, OOPSLA '90*, ACM, 1990.

[177] Paepcke, A., "User-Level Language Crafting: Introducing the CLOS Metaobject Protocol", Report HPL-91-169, October 1991.

[178] Page-Jones, M. & S. Weiss, *Synthesis: An Object-Oriented Analysis and Design Method*, Technical Report, Wayland Systems, 6920 Roosevelt Way NE, Suite 349, Seattle, WA 98115.

[179] Page-Jones, M. & S. Weiss, *Object-Oriented Methodologies*, Course Notes NTU 1990 November 15, Wayland Systems, 6920 Roosevelt Way N.E., Suite 349, Seattle, WA 98115.

[180] Palsberg, J. & M. Schwartzbach, "Object-Oriented Type Inference", *Proceedings, OOPSLA '91*, ACM, 1991.

[181] Parnas, D. & P. Clements, "A Rational Design Process: How and Why to Fake It", *IEEE Transactions on Software Engineering*, February 1986.

[182] Potts, C., "A Generic Model for Representing Design Methods", *Proceedings, 11th International Conference on Software Engineering*, IEEE, 1989.

[183] Prieto-Diaz, R., "Implementing Faceted Classification of Software Reuse", *Communications of the ACM* 34, 5, May 1991.

[184] Raj, R. & H. Levy, "A Compositional Model for Software Reuse", *Proceedings, ECOOP '89* Cambridge University Press, 1989.

[185] Raj, R., E. Tempero, H. Levy, A. Black, N. Hutchinson, & E. Jul, "Emerald: A General Purpose Programming Language", *Software – Practice and Experience*, 1991.

[186] *The Random House College Dictionary*, Random House, 1975.

[187] Rao, R., "Implementational Reflection", *Proceedings, ECOOP '91*, Lecture Notes in Computer Science, 512, Springer Verlag, 1991.

[188] *Reference Model for Frameworks of Software Engineering Environments*, National Institute of Standards and Technology, United States Department of Commerce publication 500-201, and European Computer Manufacturers Association, technical report ECMA TR/55 2nd ed., December 1991.

[189] Reynolds, J., *Syntactic Control of Interference*, Carnegie-Mellon University Technical Report CMU-CS-89-130, 1989.

[190] Richardson, J., P. Schwarz, & L. Cabrera, "CACL: Efficient Fine-Grained Protection for Objects", *Proceedings, OOPSLA '92*, ACM, 1992.

[191] Rockstrom, A. & R. Saracco, "SDL-CCITT Specification and Description Language", *IEEE Transactions on Communications* 30, 6, June 1982.

[192] Rumbaugh, J., M. Blaha, W. Premerlani, F. Eddy, & W. Lorensen, *Object-Oriented Modeling and Design*, Prentice Hall, 1991.

[193] Sakkinen, M., "A Critique of the Inheritance Principles of C++", *Computing Systems*, Winter 1992.

[194] Saraswat, V., "Concurrent Constraint Programming", *Proceedings, ACM conference on Principles of Programming Languages*, ACM, 1990.

[195] Schmidt, D., "An Objected-Oriented Interface to IPC Services", *The C++ Report*, November/December 1992.

[196] Scholl, M., C. Laasch, & M. Tresch, "Updatable Views in Object Oriented Databases", in C. Delobel, M. Kifer & Y. Masunaga (eds.) *Deductive and Object-Oriented Databases*, Springer-Verlag, 1991.

[197] Sedgewick, R., *Algorithms*, Addison-Wesley, 1990.

[198] Seventh International Software Process Workshop, Yountville, California, Rocky Mountain Institute of Software Engineering. October 15-18, 1991.

[199] Shatz, S., *Development of Distributed Software*, Macmillan, 1993.

[200] Shlaer, S. & S.J. Mellor, *Object-Oriented Systems Analysis*, Yourdon Press, 1988.

[201] Shlaer, S., S.J. Mellor, D. Ohlsen, & W. Hywari, "The Object-Oriented Method for Analysis", *Proceedings of the 10th Structured Development Forum (SDF-X)*, San Francisco, August 1988.

[202] Shlaer, S. & S.J. Mellor, "An Object-Oriented Approach to Domain Analysis", *ACM SIGSOFT Software Engineering Notes*, 14, 5, July 1989.

[203] Shlaer, S. & S.J. Mellor, *Object Life Cycles: Modeling the World in States*, Yourdon Press, 1991.

[204] Shrefl, J. & G. Keppel, "Cooperation Contracts", *Proceedings, 10th International Conference on the Entity-Relational Approach*, Springer-Verlag, 1991.

[205] Shriver, B. & P. Wegner (eds.), *Research Directions in Object-Oriented Programming*, MIT Press, 1987.

[206] Simmel, S., "The Kala Basket: A Semantic Primitive Unifying Object Transactions, Access Control, Versions, and Configurations", *Proceedings, OOPSLA '91*, ACM, 1991.

[207] Smith, H., *Data Structures: Form and Function*, Harcourt, Brace, and Jovanovich, 1987.

[208] Snyder, A., "Modeling the C++ Object Model: An Application of the Abstract Object Model", *Proceedings, ECOOP '91*, Lecture Notes in Computer Science, 512, Springer-Verlag, 1991.

[209] Standish, T.A., *Data Structures Techniques*, Addison-Wesley, 1980.

[210] Stepney, S., R. Barden, & D. Cooper (eds.), *Object Orientation in Z*, Springer Verlag, 1992.

[211] Strom, R., D. Bacon, A. Goldberg, A. Lowry, D. Yellin, & S. Yemeni, *Hermes: A Language for Distributed Computing*, Prentice Hall, 1991.

[212] Stroustrup, B., *The C++ Programming Language*, 2nd ed., Addison-Wesley, 1991.

[213] Sullivan, K.J. & D. Notkin, *Behavioral Relationships in Object-Oriented Analysis*, Technical Report 91-09-03, Department of Computer Science and Engineering, University of Washington, Seattle, WA 98195, September 1991.

[214] Takashio, K. & M. Tokoro, "DROL: An Object-Oriented Programming Language for Distributed Real-Time Systems", *Proceedings, OOPSLA '92*, ACM, 1992.

[215] Thuraisingham, B., "Multilevel Secure Object-Oriented Data Model", *Journal of Object-Oriented Programming*, November 1991.

[216] Tidwell, B.K., "Object-Oriented Analysis State Controlled Implementation", *Proceedings, OOPSLA Workshop on Object-Oriented (Domain) Analysis*, October 1991.

[217] Tracz, W., "Domain Analysis Working Group Report", *First International Workshop on Software Reusability*, Dortmund, Germany, July 3-5, 1991.

[218] Tsichritzis, D. (ed.), *Object Management*, University of Geneva, 1990.

[219] Tsichritzis, D. (ed.), *Object Composition*, University of Geneva, 1991.

[220] Tsichritzis, D. (ed.), *Object Frameworks*, University of Geneva, 1992.

[221] Ullman, J.D., *Principles of Database Systems*, Computer Science Press, 1982.

[222] Ungar, D. (ed.), "The Self Papers", *Lisp and Symbolic Computation*, 1991.

[223] Ward, P.T. & S. Mellor, *Structured Development for Real-Time Systems*, Prentice Hall, 1985.

[224] Ward, P.T., "How to integrate Object Orientation with Structured Analysis and Design", *IEEE Software*, March 1989.

[225] Ward, P.T. & J.W. Brackett, *Object-Oriented Requirements Definition and Software*, Lecture Notes, NTU Satellite Network Broadcast, November 1991.

[226] Wiederhold, G., P. Wegner, & S. Ceri, *Towards Megaprogramming*, Report STAN-CS-90-1341, Dept. of CS, Stanford University, October 1990.

[227] Wieringa, G., "A Formalization of Objects using Equational Dynamic Logic", C. Delobel, M. Kifer, & Y. Masunaga (eds.), *Deductive and Object-Oriented Databases*, Springer-Verlag, 1991.

[228] Wikstrom, A., *Functional Programming Using Standard ML*, Prentice Hall International, 1987.

[229] Wills, A., *Formal Methods Applied to Object Oriented Programming*, Thesis, University of Manchester, 1992.

[230] Wirfs-Brock, R., B. Wilkerson, & L. Wiener, *Designing Object-Oriented Software*, Prentice Hall, 1990.

[231] Wirfs-Brock, R.J., *Responsibility Driven Design*, Lecture Notes, NTU Satellite Network Broadcast, November 1990.

[232] Wolczko, M., "Encapsulation, Delegation, and Inheritance in Object-Oriented Languages", *Software Engineering Journal*, March 1992.

[233] Yonezawa, A. & M. Tokoro (eds.), *Object-Oriented Concurrent Programming*, The MIT Press, 1988.

[234] Yourdon, E., *Modern Structured Analysis*, Yourdon Press, 1989.

[235] Yourdon, E., "OOPSLA '89: Where 2,000 people missed the boat", *American Programmer*, 2, 11, November 1989.

[236] Zave, P. & R.T. Yeh, "Executable Requirements for Embedded Systems", in *Proceedings, Fifth IEEE International Conference on Software Engineering*, Washington DC, Computer Society Press, 1981.

[237] Zave, P., "An Operational Approach to Requirements Specification for Embedded Systems", *IEEE Transactions on Software Engineering*, 8, 3, May 1982.

Index